329.9 BEN

Wiebelms
£6.95

TONY BENN
A POLITICAL BIOGRAPHY

A Political Biography   Robert Jenkins

TONY
BENN

Writers and Readers

First published by
Writers and Readers Publishing Cooperative
9-19 Rupert Street, London W1V 7FS, England, 1980.

Consulting Editor: Peter Melchett
Editor: Lisa Appignanesi
Design: Malcolm Smythe
Typeset in Baskerville by Shanta Thawani, 25 Natal Road, London N11 2HU
Make-up: Julia Osorno
People who have worked on this book include
Richard Appignanesi, Arne Austrheim, Laila Jaatten,
Katarina Kvaavik, Glenn Thompson and Sian Williams.

Printed by Whitstable Litho Ltd., Whitstable, Kent.

ISBN 0 906495 35 0

To
Catherine and Paul

CONTENTS

ACKNOWLEDGEMENTS

I would like to thank the following for their help in the preparation of this book: Tony Benn and his family without whose generous cooperation this book would not have been possible; Peter Melchett, minister in the 1974–79 Labour Government, who acted as consultant editor; Lisa Appignanesi, my editor at Writers and Readers, Richard Appignanesi, and the members of the cooperative; those who managed to decipher my handwriting and type the manuscript in its several versions; my father and mother for their love and assistance; many friends and acquaintances, including Stephen Bohane, Timothy Radcliffe and Rudi Weisweiller whose advice and encouragement were indispensable.

AUTHOR'S PREFACE

The relationship between a biographer and his or her subject is invariably complex and personal. In my own case few people would seem on the surface to be less suited than I to write a biography of Tony Benn. He — a socialist, born into the Labour movement from a radical and dissenting background; I — a life-long Conservative, brought up with a vision of a stable, ordered society; a Roman Catholic by religion, chartered accountant and merchant banker by profession.

I have always been interested in politics; but it was during 1974–75, when Britain was experiencing its most serious economic crisis since 1945, that I began to question the efficacy and justice of the policies by which Britain was governed. Throughout this period Tony Benn was identified with everything that was going wrong with Britain. My interest in him as a political figure surfaced at the time of the Common Market referendum in 1975 when press attacks on Benn reached a near hysterical pitch. He struck me then as being different from conventional, career-minded politicians in three crucial respects. First, he did not share their defeatism and pessimism about Britain's future, but rather offered a coherent analysis of and solution to its problems. Second, he was a politician who had openly changed his views and had become more left-wing with age. The contradictions in his development from internationalist to technocrat to socialist intrigued me. Finally, his emergence as a national figure seemed to parallel Britain's national decline, helping explain why a person advocating fundamental reforms should have achieved such prominence — and received such abuse. As a minister and in Opposition, Benn had been closely involved with the central problem of reversing Britain's industrial decline, and his decisions while in Government changed the course of British industry. The press had also helped to turn him into a national figure by often making him a

9

scapegoat for the country's ills and projecting the collective fears of a disturbed and divided society onto a single individual.

I wanted to distinguish fact from fiction and to discover what Benn was really saying and why. He seemed to me one of the most misunderstood and misrepresented political figures in recent British history. This fact alone was an indictment of the state of British politics and pinpointed the failure of people of differing opinions to hold an open and intelligent debate about the nature of the country's difficulties and its future. For all these reasons I decided to write a biography of Tony Benn. I set out to trace his political development in the context of British history since 1945. My central theme is the breakdown of the post-war consensus and the search for a new one. This provides the framework for understanding the polarisation of British politics since the 1960s, Benn's development as a socialist and his emergence as a figure of national importance.

I have tried to write a balanced, factual, and as much as this is possible, an objective account of Benn's life. I have also tried to be 'sympathetic' to my subject: to see events through his eyes in order to make his views intelligible. When passing judgement — a difficult task when dealing with recent history — I have attempted to make my own preconceptions clear and always preferred the fullest possible presentation of fact to any easy attributing of praise or blame. On the basis of facts set in their proper contexts I hope readers will be able to come to their own conclusions. My own view, simply stated, is that the democratic reforms Benn is proposing in all aspects of public life — in industry, the media and government — are challenging and not necessarily unworkable. They enjoy wide public support and must therefore be taken seriously. Though I do believe that industrial democracy and directed, public investment are essential components in any government programme for the restoration of full employment and prosperity in Britain, I am somewhat sceptical about the potential of the alternative strategy in its present form to achieve this aim.

This biography is a political one: thus I have not undertaken any crude psychoanalysis of Benn's character or drawn conclusions about his motives. Rather I have confined myself to an assessment of his effectiveness in Government and Opposition and a discussion of his political objectives. My main research sources have been Hansard, Government papers from the Departments of Energy, Industry and the former Ministry of Technology, the Research Department of the Labour Party, the minutes of its National Executive Committee and Annual Conference Reports. The many other sources used are detailed in the notes to the text. Finally Tony Benn, himself, has provided virtually open access to his own papers, including articles, broadcasts and speeches. (These carefully indexed and very complete papers will, incidentally, constitute an historical goldmine for future generations.) He has also been very generous with his time and given me numerous interviews.

I have deliberately refrained from discussing Benn's politics with his contemporaries, in part because the circle would have been so wide as to make any sifting of views virtually impossible; in part because bias would be inevitable, given the interested parties; but mainly because of the danger of falling into the trap of gossip. I have also been wary of Benn's judgements on other politicians for the same reasons.

The problems of writing a biography about a living person are considerable. A sense of perspective is difficult to achieve so close to recent events; certain important documents have not been accessible; the story is a continuing one — by definition unfinished — and any interpretations in danger of being overtaken by events. There is also the danger of creating — by the sheer accumulation of material about a single person — a mistaken impression of the isolation of one's subject. Because I have concentrated on Benn, it may occasionally seem from these pages that he is a lone rebel, isolated in his challenge to the Establishment. But, of course, this is not the case. I have tried to convey the fact that Benn has always been part of a wider Labour movement, has never, indeed, been a lone crusader. His own views have been greatly influenced by policies and ideas deliberated from constituency level to Annual Conference. His biography is part of the collective history of this movement.

Since this is a political and not a personal biography, the following pages may sometimes give an impression of a two-dimensional, perhaps somewhat inhuman figure — one subject only to political emotions. This is, of course, not the case. When I first met Tony Benn, I found that he was neither the wild-eyed, fanatical puritan nor the cynical opportunist I had imagined from press and television reports. Rather, he was helpful, open-minded and straightforward. Trusting too, as I now look back on it, since he had no particular reason to believe in my good intentions. The background of Victorian nonconformity was apparent from the relative austerity of his way of life. He seemed almost wholly unmaterialistic; highly disciplined and responsible in his work habits which leave little time for worldly pleasures. Far from being an intense, demoniacal figure, he struck me as a person who delights in verbal gymnastics; an individual with a fine sense of the ironic and indeed, the ridiculous. (On renouncing the peerage, he had once produced a phial of his own blood to prove it was red and not blue.) Benn's intelligence is acute. He likes to explore the possibilities of ideas and theories thoroughly, though he is not an intellectual in the sense of being an abstract thinker. His intelligence seems to be soundly rooted in an understanding of reality.

Family life is very important to him and the Benn family is a closely-knit one. His wife, Caroline, who appears only briefly in this book, is a highly active and talented writer, as committed to social change as her husband. She has written a novel, *A Lion in a Den of Daniels,* published in 1965, which humorously and perceptively analyses the frustrations of an American living in Britain. She is also an educationalist, teacher, a moving spirit in the Comprehensive School movement and joint author of *Half Way There,* as well as numerous articles.

The Benn's home is a middle class one. Tony Benn inherited a private income from his father's share in the publishing firm, Benn Brothers; while Caroline comes from a well-to-do family of lawyers in Cincinnati, Ohio, and is not heiress to Proctor and Gamble millions or the Central Bank Trust. As for the Benn children, the eldest, Stephen, is completing a PhD thesis on the White House presidential advisers and is Secretary of the Kensington Labour Party. The second son, Hilary, whose wife Rosalind died tragically of cancer in 1979, works in the research department of the trade union, ASTMS, and is a local Labour councillor. Their third child, Melissa, left the London School of Economics in 1979 with a first class degree in History and now works in the women's movement; while the youngest, Joshua, is a musician and a music journalist.

Perhaps nothing has done more to unite the Benn family than the numerous press attacks and harassment they have endured over the years. The tricks played to shed a suspicious light on the family, the near slanderous accusations made to discredit Benn, especially during the EEC referendum campaign — including such tactics as calls insisting that a child had suffered an accident and was in a private ward of a hospital — have only succeeded in bringing the family closer together and given the children what Caroline calls a political education. Press misrepresentation has also given Benn, himself, an insight into the way the Establishment treats its dissenters and a taste of the experience of the politically impotent. If he, as a minister, has been subject to this kind of treatment, what chance for people with no public position or influence?

Above all, of course, Tony Benn is a political animal, deeply interested in his work, dedicated to his constituency and devoted to the Labour movement. He is undoubtedly a highly ambitious politician — something not unknown in political circles — a person of exceptional strength and tenacity of purpose, who is prepared to campaign for a decade, if need be, to change public attitudes on any particular issue. Yet the moral passion he brings to politics is singular. It springs from a belief in the absolute equality and freedom of all people and a detestation of all privilege, injustice and oppression, based in turn on a theory of human rights and on Christian teaching.

12

Over the past four years while working on this book, I have come increasingly to see that an understanding of Benn's politics is essential to understanding Britain's problems. I have gradually become convinced that it is a prerequisite for a constructive dialogue between Right and Left without which no solution can be found. I hope readers will approach the following pages in the same spirit of openness.

Marsh Green
Edenbridge, Kent
May 1980

I

1925-1950

THE INHERITANCE OF DISSENT

*It is hard for anyone to be an honest politician, who is not born and bred a
dissenter. . . . No patriotism, no public spirit, not reared in that inclement sky
and harsh soil, in "the hortus siccus of dissent", will generally last: it will
either bend in the storm or droop in the sunshine.*
WILLIAM HAZLITT

Anthony Neil Wedgwood Benn was by birth a dissenter, not an
aristocrat. His father, William Wedgwood Benn, was a life-long radical
in politics, rooted in the tradition of dissenting nonconformity and one of
the most colourful parliamentary figures of his era. In turn Liberal and
Labour MP, he went on to become a Labour Cabinet Minister, and in
1941 Churchill made him first Viscount Stansgate in order to
strengthen the Labour Party in the House of Lords. His mother, born
Margaret Eadie Holmes, is Scottish of Presbyterian descent. Deeply
involved in religious circles, she is in her own way an emancipationist.

Anthony as he was called at home, or Tony as he has always been
called by friends, was born on 3 April 1925 at 40 Grosvenor Road,
the street since renamed Millbank, which lies along the North bank of
the River Thames at Westminster. The Benn's home stood in a row of
Victorian town houses just in front of the present Millbank Tower.
Their library extended into the house next door where Sidney and
Beatrice Webb had lived and written many of their books.

Tony was the second of four sons. His eldest brother, Michael,
deeply religious, had intended to join the ministry, but was killed while
serving as an RAF fighter pilot in 1944. His younger brother, David,
went on to become a barrister and later worked in the BBC external
service; while the youngest brother, Jeremy, died stillborn in 1935.

Like many families, the Benn's knew private grief, but unlike many
during the inter-war years, they enjoyed material security and
modest wealth. Although surrounded by middle class respectability,
they moved in a world of radical politics. The contrast between these
two worlds, the conflict between principle and privilege, would have a
profound effect on the course of Tony Wedgwood Benn's life,
exerting a creative tension that would make him a socialist. Politically,
this contrast would also provide for Benn's opponents an opportunity
to criticise the gulf between his left-wing opinions and his privileged

social position.

The inheritance of dissent was many-sided: the Benns had been independent thinkers, political and religious dissenters for many a generation. The values for which they had lived — a belief in conscience, justice, liberty and reform — were also the foundation of Tony Wedgwood Benn's politics.

Tony's great-grandfather, the Reverend Julius Benn, born in 1823, was the son of a master quiltmaker from Manchester. He was a sensitive child, who had run away from home at the age of thirteen in protest against his father's second marriage. After walking forty miles, Julius collapsed in despair at the quayside in Liverpool where he was befriended by a passing Quaker who apprenticed him to a linen draper in Liverpool. There he used to go and hear the Rev. John de Kewer Williams preach, one of the foremost Congregationalist ministers of the nineteenth century who founded the Eclectic Society, part of the educational and social reform movement that sprang up in the "Hungry Forties" and in effect the seminary for a generation of Congregationalist preachers.

It was in character that Julius Benn should have met and fallen in love with his future wife, Ann Taylor, daughter of a shuttlemaker at Hyde in Cheshire, in church. The hold of evangelical religion over the Victorians was potent, and Congregationalism kindled within Julius an unquenchable thirst for mankind's spiritual and social salvation. Greatly influenced by the writings of Dickens, Shaftesbury and Elizabeth Barrett who expressed the Victorians' concern for child welfare, he felt called to child-rescue work. In 1850 the Benns moved from Hyde to Stepney where Julius took over The Star in the East, a home for destitute boys, a converted old rope and sail warehouse beneath the railway arches at Stepney Causeway. In 1854 they moved to Tithfield, Northamptonshire, where Julius established one of the first government reformatories. Dissenters were very unpopular in Anglican, rural Northamptonshire, and the bitter criticism of the way he taught the catechism there made him conscious how "the poor, despised and ostracised dissenter" suffered for his convictions. On one occasion he marched his pupils out of the Anglican church in protest against a sermon by the vicar attacking the teachings of Martin Luther, and forced the vicar to cease making such remarks. Bankruptcy, however, not unpopularity, compelled the Benns to leave Tithfield in 1858 after Julius had invested all his resources in an unsuccessful agricultural patent.

The family returned to Stepney in cheerless circumstances, living off boiled rice, till Julius had saved enough to take over a toy and newspaper shop on Commercial Road, which he made serve as a depot for the publications of the British and Foreign Bible Society. He resumed his missionary activities and after his work during the severe cholera outbreak of 1864 — carrying cholera patients in his arms to the hospitals — was invited to become City Missionary at Cable Street, St. George's-in-the-East, where he became extremely active in the Sunday School movement. He was best known, however, as a controversial minister and preacher at the Gravel Pit Chapel, Hackney, an independent Puritan meeting place since the seventeenth century. Here he was noted for the extremity of his views as a Cromwellian in favour of parliamentary and social reform.

Julius Benn died tragically in 1883 in Matlock where he had taken his son, William Rutherford Benn, to recuperate after a mental illness. While they were there the young man struck his father and accidentally killed him and then tried to kill himself. William was confined to an institution for some years. Upon his release, calling himself William Rutherford, he was married. He and his wife later had one daughter, Margaret Rutherford, the well-known actress who died in 1972 without ever learning the circumstances of her grandfather's death or her father's part in it.

Tony's grandfather, John Williams Benn, was born at Hyde, in Cheshire in 1850 and grew up in "unreformed" London. He helped his father with missionary work in St. George's and Wapping which Dickens had so vividly described as "a wilderness of dirt, rags and hunger". The experience of rescue work in the brothels and gambling dens along the notorious Ratcliff highway helped turn John Benn into a passionate social reformer: "It was thus that I became able to study on the spot the odds against which some of the poor have to fight and to see for myself the sweating den, the rotten dwellings reeking with filth in every corner, the oftimes brutal parent and worst of all the blighted offspring."[1]

It impressed upon him the relationship between mankind's moral condition and social, physical environment and eventually led him into politics. In a sense, John Benn launched a political dynasty by becoming chairman of the London County Council and a Liberal MP. His biographer, A.G. Gardiner, emphasised the religious source of his political convictions: "The amelioration of the material condition of the life of the people was always to him profoundly associated with the moral and spiritual motive." John Benn himself went to work at the age of eleven, wearing his mother's Sunday boots. An office boy to begin with, he soon developed a talent with the pen and trained himself as a draughtsman. Self-education was the aim of the Stepney mutual improvement society where, as a young man, he learned his politics and the art of debating by discussing the issues of the day: the powers of the House of Lords; whether education would decrease crime; and temperance at "this parliament in miniature".

"The pen," John Benn wrote, "was my lever in life." After becoming an illustrator of furniture design, he returned to Hyde where he married Elizabeth Pickstone, a woman from a Puritan background with immense strength of purpose and self-control. She was distantly connected on her mother's side with the Wedgwoods. John Benn earned his living at first by delivering lectures throughout the country where he used his gifts as a story-teller, mimic and cartoonist. By temperament he was in fact an artist and his first ambition in life was to match the greatness of Bonnington and Constable as a landscape painter. He did indeed develop into a talented water-colourist. He also loved the theatre and produced plays at home for family entertainment, writing two himself, *Theseus and Ariadne* and· *The Last of the Trojans*.

In 1880, John Benn founded a furniture design trades journal called, *The Cabinetmaker*. Its success was to be the foundation of his political career. In 1889, the Borough of Finsbury elected him and the Earl of Rosebery as their representatives for the Progressive Party on the first London County Council under the Conservative Government's Local Government Act of 1888. The split in the Liberal Party in 1886 over Gladstone's Irish Home Rule Bill had brought to a head the debate about the future of Liberalism and John Benn sided with those who sought to make the Liberal Party meet the challenge and demand social reform. If he was principally concerned with the condition of London, it was because he belonged to the great civic awakening of the late nineteenth century. The roots of this civic sense lay in the moral outrage of the Victorians against the squalor caused by unplanned industrialisation and their unshakeable optimism in the possibility of harnessing its technology and wealth to create an orderly, just and civilised society.

The Progressive Party was made up of pioneering individuals who reflected the entire gamut of London politics from the Fabian socialism of John Burns to the Whig aristocracy of Rosebery, but were united by a common civic ideal. Their rule proved to be "the most remarkable experiment in Civic Government which during the eighteen years in which it held power transformed the spirit and machine of London administration".[2] Their electoral achievement was to sustain the Liberal working-class vote where the bond of non-conformity did not exist. John Benn helped lay the foundations of electoral success as an energetic chief whip from 1889–92 and, understanding the challenge of the New Unionism, cooperated throughout with trade unionists such as Tom Mann and Ben Tillett of the Dockers. With John Burns and the socialists, he secured a ten-hour day for the tram drivers. This was a great victory in that the state acknowledged the justice of the cause for which Oastler and others had so long fought, and established the Council's right to employ direct labour and "to pay the trade union rate of wages and observe hours and conditions of labour generally accepted as fair in the trade". In March 1892, the *Pall Mall Gazette* described how Benn "conferred with the London Trades Council and the representatives of the Labour Party and as a result, the Liberal and

Radical Associations cordially joined hands with the Labour Candidates".[3]

In 1892 a meeting at Cable Street invited John Benn to stand as the Liberal candidate in the General Election of that year against the Conservative C.T. Ritchie who was the MP and Chairman of the Local Government Board in Lord Salisbury's Cabinet. Benn campaigned as "MP for the back streets" on a radical programme of temperance, municipal housing and the reform of the electoral registration laws. One of his major campaign themes was Home Rule for Ireland. He toured St. George's with his family in a horse-drawn brake, carrying a banner which urged:

Friends of Labour, Working Men,
Stick to Gladstone, Vote for Benn.

The strategy triumphed, John Benn won and was the only Liberal candidate to defeat a Conservative Cabinet Minister. Rosebery held a luncheon in Benn's honour at Mentmore where he met Gladstone whom he so greatly admired. Gladstone hailed the victory with "Bravo Benn".

John Benn's parliamentary career, however, was chequered and stormy, interrupted in 1895 when his Conservative opponent, Harry Marks, the proprietor of the *Financial News* — who had made his fortune out of the South African gold mines — brought charges of electoral corruption. Marks alleged that Benn had falsified votes in 1892 and had subsequently misapplied electoral funds. The court dismissed the charges, but on a technical point, temporarily disqualified him as a candidate. Benn's misapplication of funds lay in having allowed use of Liberal Party Headquarters for concerts and as a public lending library. He was not returned until later for Devonport where he campaigned on a radical programme of Anglican disestablishment, non-sectarian education and the municipalisation of the London docks.

Though John Benn was Liberal MP for Devonport until 1910, his real achievement lay in his work for the London County Council. Here he was in turn responsible for slum clearance and rehousing programmes, municipalisation of the electricity and water supply, as well as the telephone service and construction of the London tram system. Finally as Chairman of the Council in 1904–05, the now knighted Sir John Benn, together with Sidney Webb and others, implemented the Conservative Government Education Act of 1902 which made local authorities responsible for the administration and finance of schools. The 1902 Education Act was the chief cause of the Progressives' downfall in 1907. The burden the Act placed on ratepayers led to a reaction against public expenditure, and involved John Benn in a bitter dispute over the construction and cost of the London tram system. Nevertheless, he continued to lead the Progressives in defeat until 1918, unshaken in his belief that history would prove the

19

need for active and purposeful local government.

On his death in 1922, Asquith paid tribute to his personal qualities. "There was no finer exemplification of the Christian concept of citizenship," he declared, describing Benn as "the incarnation of perpetual youth" who possessed "a splendid and rare gift to live and fight and work and die with undiminished faith in great ideas".[4] John Benn had left his mark on London as one of the principal architects of "gas and water socialism", but philosophically, he was never a socialist. He was a radical who stood for equality of opportunity and the freedom of the individual. Yet the public ownership of public monopolies was an indispensable part of his creed.

Elizabeth and John Benn had four sons the two elder of whom they christened Ernest John Pickstone and William Wedgwood. Both brothers were born in Hackney, in 1875 and 1877 respectively, and both were educated at the Central Foundation School, City Road, and then at the Lycée Condorcet in Paris under an "au pair" exchange when two French children came to London to live with the Benns. Yet, in public life they became the two faces of Janus, each representing opposing interpretations of Liberalism. Sir Ernest Benn, who was well-known as a publisher and individualist, became second baronet on his father's death. He typified the old Liberalism of Samuel Smiles and self-help, of individual liberty, free trade and the minimum of government. As a publisher, Ernest Benn was forward-looking and imaginative. He developed *The Cabinetmaker* into the successful publishing firm of Benn Brothers by taking over a number of trade journals, and in the late 1920s by launching Benn's sixpenny novels, a precursor of the paperback era. The Benn list included such authors as Arnold Bennett and H.G. Wells.

Politically, Ernest Benn's importance lay in the views he so strongly expressed rather than in any tangible achievement. In 1923, he was asked to be Liberal candidate by four constituency parties in the Free Trade General Election of that year; and in 1937, to be Conservative candidate for East Surrey. But on each occasion, he declined. He was a zealous Cobdenite freetrader who drew his political philosophy from J.S. Mill. He believed that "the worth of the state in the long run, is the worth of the individuals composing it". He agreed with Montesquieu that a paternalist state only encourages people to assume its advantages, while eschewing its burdens, and argued that "the business of Government is to promote a condition of things in which the individual can function to the best advantage".

Individualism made Ernest Benn a national figure and between 1921 and his death in 1954, he wrote over thirty books and pamphlets proclaiming its cause. In 1925, he published *Confessions of a Capitalist* which told the story of the Benn trade periodical empire and boldly asserted the centrality of inequality and profits. The book called for a high wage, high productivity, high profit-earning economy:

> I am an unrepentant believer in free enterprise. I have failed to discover, in a long and diligent search, any material benefit which has ever reached mankind except through the agony of individual enterprise. I therefore regard the whole movement for creating wealth through political agencies as a snare and a delusion.

Confessions of a Capitalist was one of the outstanding pieces of economic literature of the 1920s, and led indirectly to the foundation of the Individualist Bookshop with Sir Hugh Bell in 1926, which set the model for Foyles' literary luncheons.

The individualist movement developed a wide following among the middle classes, because it reflected the fears of many, whose lives and outlook, based on individual struggle, were threatened. It gave Ernest Benn both an audience and a platform and involved him in a life-long campaign. In 1929 he broke with the Liberal Party over Lloyd George's Yellow Book Programme, and as leader of the Friends of Economy attacked the swollen state of public expenditure in 1931, when he led a demonstration through the City and addressed public meetings throughout the country. Benn declared: "The essence of economy is that the individual must decide for himself. We the citizens have erected this colossus of waste and extravagance and we alone can remove it." For one moment the campaign caught the public imagination and played some part in forcing Snowden to cut unemployment benefit, but the wider attempts to influence public opinion failed, as the collapse of Benn's weekly newspaper *The Independent* in 1933 showed.

During the Second World War, Ernest Benn was deeply suspicious that Churchill's wartime coalition would lead to socialism, and in 1942 he established the Society of Individualists with Sir Carlton Allen, which later became the National League for Freedom. Benn used this group — which aimed to influence the intellectual climate on the issue of post-war reconstruction — to publicise the "Pamphlets for Liberty", and contributed three pamphlets himself: *Manifesto on British Liberty, The Profit Motive* and *The State, The Enemy*. It was the most powerfully sustained campaign of his life, a crusade in defence of individual liberty, the rule of law and free enterprise, combined with resistance to bureaucratic controls and to every project for a state-planned economy.

Ernest Benn died an unrepentant Victorian laissez-faire Liberal. In 1951 he had been fined five pounds for failing to complete a national census form. He had refused to do so on the grounds that, "In view of the critical state of the national economy, I must refuse to take any part in this unnecessary waste of manpower, money, paper and print." On his death, *The Times* wrote: "It was easy to mock his views for he knew no middle way and was often exaggerated in the emphasis of his warnings. . . . He was the spokesman of no interest, but of an idea — of one aspect of Liberalism, which not even a collectivist society if it wishes to remain free dare ignore."[5] Ernest Benn too was in his own way a dissenter, and the conflict between his views and those of his brother were the prototype of the intellectual framework within which Tony Benn would, fifty years later, argue the choice between Conservative and Socialist concepts of freedom. The clarity and strength of Ernest's convictions gave Tony Benn a more thorough grounding in the laissez-faire policies of his opponents than many members of the Conservative Party. However, the enduring influence on his politics came from his father, William Wedgwood Benn. Both brothers lived through the decline of the Liberal Party and the rise of Labour. This was the central domestic political development of the world into which Tony Benn was born.

William Wedgwood Benn exemplified the new Liberalism that welcomed social reform and state intervention as an enlargement of liberty for the ordinary citizen. Like many Liberals, he transferred his philosophy and faith in the future to the Labour Party. He shared the Radical view of British history and of Parliament as the place where the people had won their liberties. As he put it:

> Parliament is more than an assembly. It is a workshop or, I should prefer to say, a battlefield. I have often tried to think why it is that when political issues arise I find myself instinctively holding opinions of a particular mould. I have had so far to be content with the explanation that we do not choose our convictions but they choose us and force us to fight for them to the death.[6]

This emotional insistence on the existence of principles in politics was part of the heritage of dissenting nonconformity, with its emphasis on the interplay of faith and action. Though a non-practising Congregationalist, William Wedgwood Benn "could never take episcopacy into his system", and used to quote the preacher Charles Spurgeon who once declared: "I do not defend the Bible — I let it loose." As Tony Benn described his father's politics: "His inherited distrust of established authority and the conventional wisdom of the powerful, his passion for freedom of conscience and his belief in liberty explain all the causes he took up during his life."

These began with a forthright opposition to the Boer War as a student at University College, London. For this stand, he was on one occasion thrown out of the ground floor window by his "patriotic" contemporaries. As a Gladstonian anti-imperialist, sympathetic to nationalism, he profoundly disagreed with the military intervention in Southern Africa. After leaving university in 1898 with a first class honours degree in French, Benn lived in Bermondsey and worked in the family business as a journalist on *The Cabinetmaker*. But by the turn of the century, he was already active in Liberal politics, helping raise funds for the cigar workers locked out in industrial dispute and speaking for Municipal Employees. He believed that workers had a right to form trade unions and exercise their full collective power. In 1903, he won the unanimous support of the Stepney Labour Council when he was adopted as the Liberal parliamentary candidate for St. Georges-in-the-East. In his 1906 election address, William Wedgwood Benn described himself as a "radical non-conformist" and criticised the Conservative Government for "having made laws for their privileged friends and entirely neglected the claims of the workers", pledging himself to support legislation "to protect the funds of trade unions", to work for Irish Home Rule and a national home for the Jews.

At the age of twenty-eight, William Wedgwood Benn was Parliament's youngest MP. He immediately established his reputation as a radical with a maiden speech in favour of the municipalisation of the Port of London in which he drew attention to the rising unemployment among dockers. In the Commons, he always supported women's rights, was a committed freetrader and campaigned vigorously against the Lords' veto. For most of the 1906–10 Liberal Government, he served as Parliamentary Private Secretary to Reginald McKenna. In 1910 Asquith made him a junior whip. The outbreak of the first World War in 1914 cut short what many believed would prove to be a dazzling ministerial career. After raising over two million pounds in two months for the wartime National Relief Fund, Benn resigned from the Government, though remaining an MP, and joined the army. His duty, he believed, was to serve his country at the front. His war record was outstanding. Twice mentioned in despatches, he was decorated with the DSO and DFC, by the French with the Croix de Guerre and as Chevalier de la Legion d'Honneur, and by the Italians with their War Cross and Bronze Medal for Valour. After taking part in fierce fighting on the heights above Suvla bay in the Gallipoli campaign, he remained in the Middle East as an observer with the Royal Naval Air Service and took part in the pinpoint bombing of the Baghdad railway. He was shot down in the Mediterranean and was rescued from the sinking aircraft by his mother ship, the *Ben-my-chree*, a French passenger ship converted to carry seaplanes, from which he commanded a small Anglo-French force, holding out at Castelorizo until it was sunk by Turkish shore batteries. In 1916 Wedgwood Benn returned to Britain to train as an air pilot, and though Lloyd George offered him posts as parliamentary secretary at the Ministry of Munitions and then as joint chief whip in the wartime coalition, he refused. Instead, he served on the Italian front where he helped to plan and flew in the night mission with Tandura, the first spy ever dropped by parachute behind enemy lines in Austria.

The experience of World War brought an international dimension to Wedgwood Benn's radicalism: "I have seen too much of war to believe in it," he told a conference in Toronto in 1933. War deepened his interest in Britain's imperial problems and convinced him that only national self-determination within a framework of parliamentary democracy could create a new stable world order. His book, *In the Side Shows,* about those years in the services, explains how war had radicalised him. Here he describes the professional army officer as someone incapable of "appreciating the diversites of human character and capacity"; someone who discourages "initiative and energy" and is through class prejudice determined to entrench his own class. "There are no regulations to say that none but the privileged class is permitted to enter; the existence of class barriers is denied; but those who have been on the inside know perfectly well that the gate is strictly kept." Benn further notes the "inevitable ignorance" of officers "who live in narrow grooves and are forbidden by the rules of the game to receive any education from those who alone can educate them, namely their subordinates." He argues:

> Wars are people in arms. Leaders are needed, military as well as political, who see the difference between a just and an unjust cause: who understand how much ideals count as a practical force, even in the behaviour of individual soldiers, who know that Right is the steam that drives the engine Might.[7]

On his return home with the Armistice in 1918, William Wedgwood Benn found that his old constituency had been redistributed and a new Liberal candidate was in place. Instead, he was adopted as independent Liberal candidate for Leith and won it against Lloyd George's coalition coupon which had been given to his Conservative opponent. The years of political flux and turmoil between 1918–26 were ones of intense parliamentary activity for him. It was during this time that he made his reputation as a parliamentarian. As one of the leaders of the radical group, he continuously harassed the Government, especially over its Irish policy and use of the Black and Tans against the Nationalists. In 1920 he moved an amendment to the King's Speech, condemning the coalition for having handed over "to the military authorities an unrestricted discretion in the definition and punishment of offences", and "having frustrated the prospects of an agreed settlement to the problems of Irish self-government".

Unlike most politicians who start on the Left and drift steadily to the Right as age and experience combine to disillusion them, William Wedgwood Benn moved to the Left as he grew older. He found himself voting with the Labour Party on many issues, and in 1926 on Lloyd George's election to the leadership, he resigned from the Liberal Party. He distrusted Lloyd George as a man and still more, his coalition with the Conservatives.

He joined the Labour Party and having changed his political allegiance thought it right to resign his seat immediately. This was an act of considerable political courage for a man who had never embraced socialist economic analysis and who had no established following in the constituencies or trade unions. Within the Labour Party, Wedgwood Benn remained a lone crusader. Until the end of his life, his sympathies lay instinctively with the nonconformists, especially when attempts were made to impose party discipline on them. Nevertheless he greatly valued the fellowship of the Labour movement, its moral and practical seriousness of purpose, and he was soon accepted. After attending his first Labour Conference in 1927, he wrote in the *Daily Herald* : "A great sense of responsibility seemed to overshadow the gathering. They were making decisions that in the near future would pass from being the resolutions of a party to becoming the policy of the British Government."

In September 1928, William Wedgwood Benn re-entered Parliament as the Labour MP for Aberdeen North in a by-election, after the local constituency party had adopted him as its candidate. A year later, he was returned in the General Election and Ramsay MacDonald appointed him Secretary of State for India. The radicals brought with them a deep understanding of Britain's imperial problems which Labour lacked and could not afford to ignore. But Benn's appointment was unusual, as Philip Snowden, then Labour Chancellor of the Exchequer, explained: "Although disliking to give office to new recruits, we felt that Benn's was an exceptional case and that if he were included in the Cabinet he would be a considerable augmentation to the debating strength of the front bench."[8] Benn's period as Secretary of State for India was as controversial as his appointment. In particular, he was criticised for pursuing a policy of conciliation and reform at a time when India was enmeshed in turmoil. As a believer in the brotherhood of man, he expected conflicting national claims and interests to be resolved by discussion and was convinced that the British and those over whom they ruled shared the same final goal of democratic self-government. Despite criticism from both Left and Right at home, Benn persisted with his policy of conciliation which ultimately helped to pave the way to India's independence. These years proved to be the climax of his political career.

The 1931 General Election saw Benn — together with a large number of Labour MPs — defeated. Out of Parliament for the next five years, he travelled widely with his wife. Their book, *Beckoning Horizons*, which deals with the politics, religious beliefs and industrial system of America, Japan, China and the Soviet Union, grew out of these travels. At Dearborn in the United States, they met Henry Ford and saw modern industrial capitalism. "With one lens", they wrote, one had "a peep at the 100% efficiency of machine production and waste elimination", but through "the other lens a glimpse of the suppression of individuality of the workman, sensitive and even philosophical, who felt he was a diamond being used to cut glass." At the Molotov works in the USSR they found that the "two mainsprings of human effort (in the West) fear (of unemployment) and hope (of financial reward) had been removed". They were told that "the belief in Bolshevism and all that it means for the uplifting of humanity had replaced both the carrot and the stick," but they asked themselves whether 'the alleged justification for what is called the Dictatorship of the Proletariat. . . is not in fact the Dictatorship of the Communist Party".

Neither Ford nor Stalin had offered Wedgwood Benn a way he wanted to follow. In his 1935 General Election address to the constituents of Dudley, he expressed his horror of unemployment, then at two million: "There is no hope in this patching. A more rational approach must be made to our problems and it is to be found in the principle of socialism. Many repudiate the word, yet approve the thing itself when they see it working. The forces of production need to be liberated and revitalised."[9] In 1937 Wedgwood Benn returned to Parliament, having been adopted Labour candidate for Gorton in a by-election. He threw himself into the battle against Chamberlain and appeasement; on the Privileges Committee, he supported Duncan Sandys' successful appeal against the Government's attempted use of the Official Secrets Act to quash a critical parliamentary question, which Sandys had tabled about gaps in the air defence of London. His speech on the report was a clear assertion of Parliament's importance in wartime as the protector of civil liberties. Though elected top of Labour's Shadow Cabinet in 1939, Benn was determined once more to rejoin the RAF. After serving in the Air Ministry and with the Allied Military Government in Italy, he returned home and, as an Air Commodore, managed to fly on a number of operational missions before this was discovered and stopped. At the age of sixty-seven, he had earned another mention in despatches.

In 1945, Attlee made Viscount Stansgate — as William Wedgwood Benn then was — Secretary of State for Air, responsible for the complex problem of demobilisation. He was sent to renegotiate the Anglo-Egyptian Treaty — a task Ernest Bevin, the Foreign Secretary, had entrusted to him. This foundered on the sensitive issues of British military presence in Suez and its protectortate over the Sudan.

In 1946, Attlee asked Stansgate, then sixty-nine, to retire to make room for younger men. However, this did not spell the end of his political career. The following year he was elected World President of the Inter-Parliamentary Union and over the next twelve years, he travelled widely, developing this association of parliamentarians into a real forum for international cooperation. Abroad, he fought hard against the division of the world, especially of Europe, into two warring camps. He advocated peaceful co-existence and detente twenty years before it was politically respectable to do so. At home, he warned against McCarthyite witchhunts and defended civil liberties, backing Paul Robeson's fight for his passport. He also took up the case of Paul Garland, the Communist boy scout from Bristol, who for that reason had been expelled from the Scouts. Stansgate forced a debate on the issue in the House of Lords, where Lord Rowallan, the chief scout, and almost every peer who spoke, supported Garland's expulsion.

On 16 November 1960, Stansgate suffered a heart attack whilst waiting in the House of Lords to speak against the Central African Federation which, he believed, had been devised to perpetuate White rule in Rhodesia. Only three days earlier he had closed the debate on India with an appeal "to preserve what is a very precious thing, namely friendship with the Indian republic". He died the following day after serving forty-seven years in all in Parliament. Attlee paid a warm tribute: "He was a great character and a man of profound ethical conviction with a great love of his fellow men."

The dissenting tradition was also strong on the maternal side of Tony Benn's family. William Wedgwood Benn had met Margaret Eadie Holmes in 1912 and again in 1920 in Edinburgh where her father was fighting a by-election.

The couple married later that year when he was forty-three years old and she twenty-three. Margaret Benn's grandfather, James Holmes, was a tyler from Ayrshire who belonged to the Irvine Brethren. A God-fearing man who baptised his children in the river Irvine he forbade all secular literature in his home. His eldest son and Tony Benn's maternal grandfather, Daniel Turner Holmes, rebelled against the fundamentalism of the Brethren, became an agnostic, a schoolmaster, and obtained a first class degree in Classics and English Literature. A highly cultured man, he served from 1910–18 as Liberal MP for Goven, and it was during this time that he came to know William Wedgwood Benn in Parliament.

His wife, Margaret Eadie was the daughter of an artisan engineer from Perthshire who had invented the "ring traveller", a device used in the textile industry. Beginning as an apprentice to a firm of shipbuilders on the Clyde, Peter Eadie had travelled round the world, installed the gas systems in Marseilles and Sicily, and founded the firm of Eadie Brothers, still in existence. In later life, he was Provost of Paisley.

Though brought up in an atmosphere of honest doubt, religion would play a dominant role in Margaret Benn's life. She questioned the post-Darwinian attack on the Bible and determined, as she put it, "to make a tour of the devastated areas of the spirit". At the age of twenty, she became an Anglican and later studied for a diploma in theology as a part-time student at King's College, London, where she gained some knowledge of the Old Testament in Hebrew and the New

Testament in Greek. Then, at the age of fifty-one, she became a Congregationalist. She had attended the first conference of the World Conference of Churches in Amsterdam as a member of the study commission and this had convinced her of the pitfalls of conformity as well as of the richness and diversity of Christian experience.

Congregationalism meant more to her than the question of church organisation. It embodied the principles of dissent which were to lie at the heart of her son, Tony's, politics: the rejection of ecclesiastical authority in favour of a communion of free and independent believers. Margaret Benn was active on the Council of Christians and Jews and on the Society for the Ordination of Women. In 1972, she became the first president of the Congregational Federation, and later, emeritus life-president elect, after some congregations had decided to unite with the Presbyterians to form the United Reform Church.

The dissenting tradition into which Tony Benn was born would play a large part in shaping his values and political beliefs. As a child, his interests were ordinary ones: drawing, stamp collecting, making model-aircraft which he flew with his elder brother Michael in Victoria Tower Gardens. In character, young Tony, like so many children, was self-willed and quick to anger if he failed to get his way. The Benn heritage showed itself most, perhaps, in his temperament. Quick-witted, an enthusiast and an optimist, he possessed a super-abundance of energy.

The house in which Tony grew up was a conventional middle-class one. The Benns were comfortably well-off and Margaret Benn employed a daily cook and cleaner. There was also a children's nurse from the Norland Institute, Olive Winch, who came to look after the family in 1928, and in time became a close friend of four generations of Benns. But by today's middle-class standards, the Benn home was more austere than luxurious. There was one gramophone and up until 1938, only one wireless. The influence of noncomformity was evident in an emphasis on simplicity, but even more in the way the Benns led their daily lives. Entertaining was on a modest scale. Tony Benn's father believed that every hour of the day not spent in work or sleep was valuable time wasted. He himself, kept daily time sheets of how he spent every hour. He modelled his life on Arnold Bennett's philosophy of "how to live twenty-four hours a day".

Tony was brought up strictly. At the age of ten, his pocket money was 3d a week, and he had to submit accounts of his expenditure. Bed-time was 8:30 even when he was fifteen, with one late night a week during term time and two in school holidays. There were walks to St. James Park to hear the band play and outings to the cinema followed by tea at Lyons Corner House as a special treat.

Most of all, Tony Benn remembers the holidays spent at Stansgate in Essex where in 1899, his grandfather, John Benn, had built a house in a field facing the river Blackwater, next to a farm in which the ruins of the old Cluniac Priory of Stansgate stood. His father had spent four happy summers there as a young man and in 1926, had rented the house from the owner, Captain Gray, from whose widow he bought it for £1500 in 1933. It was a holiday home, not a country house, and its attraction lay in its simplicity. The Benns never owned the farm, nor Abbey House next door. The water system was powered by windmill; and oil lamps were used after the domestic electricity generator had broken down. The children always teased their father for having installed a coin-operated telephone, which he insisted on partly to control family use and partly because of his own childhood memories of financial insecurity. Tony's memories of Stansgate consist of impressions of farm life interspersed by dinghy-sailing on the river and visits to the fair at Maldon.

Apart from holidays at Stansgate and Christmas-time when the family stayed with his Uncle Ernest at Oxted in Surrey, life for Tony was London-orientated. His one trip abroad before the War was a day-trip to Boulogne. Yet it was only superficially a narrow existence. Growing up in the heart of London was itself exciting and Tony never rebelled against his upbringing – even if he found it intensely annoying and rejected his parents' concern with tidiness and punctuality at meals, which were announced by the ringing of a bell.

As liberally-minded people, his parents taught him that the purpose of discipline was not social conformity, but self-control and personal freedom. Literature and the arts may have been neglected, but the Benns undoubtedly communicated to their children a zest for life and a strong sense of public service. Politics and religion were daily topics of conversation. Tony grew up on tales of London politics, and through discussions at home acquired a long political memory. His earliest is of being taken to tea at the age of three with Oswald Mosley, then Labour Member for Smethwick. He recalls being taken in 1930 to see the Trooping of the Colour and meeting Ramsay MacDonald at No.10 Downing Street; and in 1931 being taken to see Mahatma Gandhi who was in London for the Round Table Conference. Politics thus came naturally to Tony and were "one continuous development of interest". He admired his father greatly, and all he remembers ever wanting to be was a Member of Parliament: "not a very good reason for wanting to be one, but there you are". As a child, he used to help his father with filing, and it was thus he acquired his life-long habit of recording events and keeping a diary. At the age of ten, he helped in the 1935 General Election Campaign and its memory remains among his most vivid. He still has all the Party literature and was furious, in 1937, when school prevented him from taking part in the Gorton by-election.

On his seventeenth birthday in 1942, he walked from home to Transport House in Smith Square where he joined the Labour Party. This was in accordance with the plan he had written the previous year.

It set out the things he wanted to achieve by the age of thirty-one, including service in the RAF and marriage, culminating in election as a Member of Parliament.

The chief intellectual influence on the young Tony's politics was his father. From him he learned the radical view of British history as a progressive growth of liberty through Parliament. 1832, 1885 and 1918 figured as landmarks on the road to democratic self-government. The central theme of British history, he learned, was the conflict between those who had power and those without who challenged it. The struggle between King and Parliament had culminated in the Civil War, laying down the subsequent battle-lines: people were either Parliamentarians (and to that extent Cromwellians) or Royalists. "I was brought up as a child," he later wrote, "to believe that the banging of the door in the face of Black Rod was a really important reminder of the House of Commons' independence of the executive."[10]

Next to radicalism, religion was the most important influence on Tony Benn's life and politics. Yet the connection with dissent was not immediately apparent, for Margaret Benn brought up her children in the Church of England. On Sundays they went to Canon Woodward's children's service at St. John's, Smith Square, and later they were confirmed in Westminster Abbey. There were family prayers, and though Tony was not particularly religious, he grew to love the Old Testament, the voice of the prophets and their passion for a social justice. As he later acknowledged: "The Old Testament teaching of Monotheism and of brotherly love under one God, which flowed from it, was absolutely revolutionary when uttered in a world which still accepted slavery."[11]

Margaret Benn added a spiritual dimension to her son's politics, making religious freedom and its meaning one of his life-long preoccupations. The theologian, Reinhold Niebuhr, was a close friend and certainly had a great influence on the family. In clarifying the relationship between political freedom and religious dissent, and examining the nature of power, Niebuhr incorporated the principle of resistance to government within government itself. Tony's own religious convictions were rooted in the dissenters' belief in the supremacy of conscience. This helps explain why he tended towards a unitarian and voluntarist position in matters of theology. Rejecting the idea of a divine trinity in favour of monotheism, he believed in the self-determination, natural equality and freedom of all men and women. Yet only later, in the 1970s, would Benn go back to religious origins. It was then he discovered that in the Diggers and Levellers demands for political and religious freedom, social justice and greater democracy, lay the basis of his own socialism and indeed that of the British labour movement.

The inheritance of dissent meant that Tony was more conscious of his ancestry than would otherwise have been the case, and it helps to explain why formal education would have so little influence on his political development. Although at the time the middle and upper classes would automatically send their children to private schools the fact that he was sent to private school reflected more the lack of any adequate system of public education in Britain than any deliberate act of privilege. After attending the Francis Holland Infants and Gladstone preparatory schools, Tony went to Westminster in 1938. This famous school was, like most public schools, representative of only a small section of British society, but it differed from many in that it was a day rather than a boarding school and situated in the centre of London. Westminster was traditional, but more liberal than other public schools. Academic standards were high and excellence, healthy competition, individuality and tolerance were encouraged. Academically, Tony never ranked among the scholars. The only award he ever won was the Toplady Prize for Divinity. In sports, he preferred fencing and rowing to traditional team games, though he joined the boy scouts and went to their summer camp.

Throughout his time at Westminster, Tony never felt quite at home. As the son of a Labour MP in the school, he was something of an outsider. The only lasting friendships he made here were with Michael Flanders and Donald Swann. His father, at the beginning of Tony's Westminster days, had told him to "show the Tories". Once there, he felt he should keep his end up and never be frightened of speaking up for his beliefs. Politically, the school was divided between the appeasers, supported by Von Ribbentrop's son who was in the School, and the United Front of Progressive Forces, the Westminster version of the popular front, known as UFPUF. Issues, however, tended to cut across party lines and the first test of principle Tony faced took place on the outbreak of war when he resigned from the Scouts, who were led by a humanitarian and pacifist called Godfrey Barber. Tony believed he should contribute in some way to the struggle against fascism, and so he joined the Air Cadet Corps. Even that proved an uneasy alliance, because of his continued opposition to conscription and the increasing strength of militaristic and right-wing opinion within the school. The level of political awareness at Westminster was by any standards high, and the years of international tension leading up to the Second World War had helped to make it so. The Japanese invasion of Manchuria, the Abyssinian and Spanish Civil Wars, made a deep impression on Tony. But even more so the ranting voice of Hitler at a Nuremburg Rally, heard over the BBC. He remembered the Blackshirts trying to break up an East End Labour meeting when he and his father were on the platform.

The Westminster Debating Society was the focus for all political controversy in the school, and it was here that Tony made his mark. The minutes of the Debating Society reflect the atmosphere of ideological struggle and World War against which Tony and his

generation grew up. The debates were predominantly about international affairs with motions on appeasement, the Spanish Civil War
and a United States of Europe to prevent another World War. The
school magazine, *The Elizabethan,* records a debate in the aftermath of
Munich on the motion: "This House supports the Government's
attitude towards the present international situation." The article
comments: "The Government's condemnation by eleven votes to nine
being largely the result of an excellent speech by a new member,
Wedgwood Benn" — then aged thirteen. On one occasion when
debating the motion "that a policy of friendship with Italy and
Germany would be of more practical use than a renegotiation of the
League of Covenant", Tony is reported to have interrupted the
speaker who was arguing that "if Hitler were left to himself he would
improve conditions in Germany", with the comment, "better
conditions in concentration camps". Tony's early moral fervour and
radicalism were also apparent over domestic issues. He once proposed
the motion that "the Public Schools of England are the breeding
ground of snobbery", condemning the way in which a pupil learns
that he is better than others and to command his equals. On another
occasion, when he opposed a motion on Conservative domestic policy
between the Wars, the minutes recorded that: "Mr. Wedgwood Benn
countered with a speech defining socialist policies and criticised post-
war governments. He argued against many odds and was heckled by
all."

During the war Westminster was evacuated four times. After
Munich, the school moved to Lancing College in Sussex returning to
London at the beginning of the Blitz, when the Benns spent every
night in an air raid shelter in Millbank. After that, the school moved to
Exeter, and finally to Worcestershire. Conditions were often
primitive, food rationed, and there were no sports or outdoor activities
other than "digging for victory", euphemistically called farming. But
it was during this period that Tony became seriously interested in
politics and began thinking about the domestic implications of the
wartime coalition.

On leaving school in July 1942, Tony very much wanted to join the
RAF as his elder brother, Michael, had done; but he was too young
and instead went up to New College, Oxford at the age of seventeen as
a short course cadet to read Politics, Philosophy and Economics. The
War and the challenge of post-war reconstruction were in the
forefront of his mind and he became involved immediately in the
Oxford Union Society where these issues were widely debated. In
March 1943, Benn proposed the motion: "That in the opinion of this
House reconstruction in Europe and in Britain is impossible unless all
the major productive resources entirely ceased to be owned by private
individuals." Both the motion and Benn's speech captured something

of the idealism and radicalism of the War years and revealed the early influence of socialist ideas on his politics. He told his audience why capitalism would not work:

The task which confronts the allies today is that of building a better world. . . The whole essence of monopolistic competition is to restrict output, cultivate demand and restrict price. . . . (Every worker) knows that if he goes slow, he is creating the need for more workers and so is helping his unemployed brothers. . . That isn't the spirit we need. Yet the fault lies not in him but in the system. . . . (It is the capitalists who) are in fact the most calculating and selfish men in the community. How can a sense of service and common responsibility be inculcated into the minds of the many if the people at the top are essentially selfish? . . .Our attitude mustn't be "where can we find work for these men?" but "we need thousands of workers for the task of reconstruction — where can we find them?" Such a policy could never be put into operation with the major productive resources in private hands — and this is why: there is an inseparable divergence of interest between the needs of a crusading nation and the desires of a King-capitalist.[12]

This speech revealed an awareness of the international dimension and scale of the problem, if also a youthful naïvety. After the debate, *The Oxford Magazine* commented: "This was the evening's best undergraduate speech, and excellently delivered."

After a year at university Benn joined the RAF as an Aircraftsman Second Class on 24 July 1943, for pilot training and was posted to Stratford on Avon, then to the Elementary Flying School at Elmdon in Birmingham, and from there to the transit camp at Heaton Park in Manchester. On 11 January 1944, he set sail on the troopship Cameronia from Glasgow to South Africa with the RAF and arrived in Rhodesia in March where he was first stationed in Bulawayo, then at the Flying Training School at Guineafowl, near Gwelo. His experiences in Africa led him to the anti-colonial cause, with which he naturally sympathised. At Bulawayo, he met a long-serving Christian missionary called Percy Ibbotson who took him to see African settlements. He was horrified by their poverty. In Salisbury he met a pioneering trade unionist, called Auld, who worked with building-trade labourers and whose daughter took him to see an African hospital. He was deeply stirred by the appalling conditions. Commissioned as an RAF pilot on 10 March 1945, Benn flew north to Egypt where he wrote to the Jewish agency asking to visit a kibbutz. He thus spent VE day at the kibbutz, *Shaar Hagolan*. Benn returned home from Egypt in June 1945, in time for the General Election. He was on the threshold of public life, having addressed the troopship on the way out to South Africa about War Aims and on the way home about reconstruction. In June he had received a letter from John Parker, the Labour member for Dagenham, asking him to stand as a candidate, but he was too young at the time.

In 1946 Benn went back to university, having been transferred to the Fleet Air Arm in the Navy and stationed around the country before being demobilised. He went on to university matured by the experience of war and very much aware of the opportunities for discussion and encounter which university life offered. Academically he was not a serious student, though he did his regular work. He was interested in Gandhian ideas of non-violence and influenced by theories of socialist planning. However, he was untouched by Marx, whose theories he studied but whom he never actually read until much later, in the 1960s.

The prevailing political climate at Oxford during the later 1940s was militantly social democratic. Like many, Benn was inspired by the socialist promise of the Attlee government and its 1945 manifesto *Let Us Face the Future*. This set out: "a great programme of modernisation and re-equipment of . . . homes, factories and machinery . . . schools (and) social services. . . by drastic policies of replanning and by keeping a firm constructive hand on our whole productive machinery."

Benn joined the Labour Club which had split into the Democratic Socialists and the Socialist factions; the latter being a "popular front" type grouping of Marxists and Christian Socialists of Dick Acland's Commonwealth Party. Though Benn joined the former, he never belonged to the group around Anthony Crosland, then lecturer in politics at Trinity College and one of Benn's tutors. It was in Crosland's rooms that he first met Roy Jenkins. Benn became immersed in the activities of the Oxford Union of which he was secretary, treasurer and eventually president in 1947. The Union's famous, if exclusive, debating was then at the height of its influence. Benn used it as a forum for serious political discussion. He was a consistent advocate of the Labour Government which had just nationalised the basic industries – coal, rail and road transport – and established a National Health Service. During the fuel crisis of the winter of '47, he proposed the motion "That this House has confidence in the domestic policies of Mr Attlee's Government", defending the necessity of Labour's controls over investment location, allocation of building materials, prices and food, at a time of austerity. Describing Anthony Crosland as "the last surviving pupil of Adam Smith", he argued for nationalisation on grounds of efficiency, investment and planning, while acknowledging the dangers of no competition.

> (The) rough equation of supply and demand (is a) rationing according to wealth and not according to need. . . . The fluctuations in trade which caused such industrial and social horror in this country between the wars was . . . a natural result of laissez-faire. . . . Inequality, inefficiency, insecurity, unemployment — these are the gifts of free enterprise in this country.[13]

In September 1947 Benn sailed to the United States with Edward Boyle (later Conservative Minister of Education) and Kenneth Harris (to become a journalist) for a highly successful Oxford Union debating tour. It was a fine time to travel to the United States, since American influence and power were at their height, the American idea and ideal ascendent. In his book about the tour, *Travelling Tongues,* Kenneth Harris described the sense of wonder they felt at this new rugged civilisation, the sixty universities and forty-three states they visited and the lasting friendships they made. In Chicago, he noted, people believed that Labour had turned Britain virtually into a communist country:

> Wedgwood Benn walked up to a book store and bought a newspaper. "You British?" asked the woman behind the counter. "That's right." "Over here on a trip?" "Debating tour." The woman looked kindly at him. "Gosh", she said. "It must be nice for you boys to come to a country where the papers can say what they like." . . . Anthony talked to her about the programme of the socialist government. "And they ain't all reds?" "I am happy to say, no." "And they ain't gonna abolish the king?" "That is not on the programme."[14]

Everywhere they encountered a "passionate faith in private enter-prise" expressed "with an almost religious degree of feeling, dogmatic, glad, reverent". As the socialist, it fell to Benn to propose the motions on full employment and public ownership: "That if full employment is to become an international reality, America must radically alter her tradition of economic policy", and: "that the social and economic arguments for the nationalisation of the basic industries are over-whelming". The debates show the radical state of American opinion in the late 1940s and Benn emphasised the United States' responsibility for sustaining world demand, arguing that only public ownership could grapple with the problems of inefficiency and monopoly, inequality and poverty. It would create a new public spirit and disprove the theory that the absence of competition would lead to inefficiency and irresponsibility: "The nationalisation of the basic industries is the first serious attempt to make ourselves the masters of the economic situation and not its slaves."

After spending Christmas with Reinhold Niebuhr, Benn returned to Britain in Febraury 1948 to prepare for his BA final exams, and the following December received a second class degree in PPE. Life seemed full of opportunities, but his future was unclear and uncertain. At the beginning of August he returned to Oxford where he knew a party of American students would be arriving; and there on the second of August he met a young woman from Cincinnati, Ohio. A week later Tony became engaged to Caroline Middleton De Camp.

Caroline's family were descended from three French Huguenot brothers who fled to America in the seventeenth century. The family genealogy tells how Moses De Camp of Westfield, New Jersey, fought in Washington's army and roused the troops with his oratory. At the age of seventy-seven, Moses and his son Ezekiel crossed the mountains and forded the rivers from New Jersey to Ohio, settling on the rolling plateau and timberland near Indian Creek, Reily Township, in Butler County. There they built a log cabin and, surrounded by Indians, wolves and uncultivated nature, conquered the austerities and privations of frontier life. The De Camps possessed all the Protestant virtues and were "noted for the reliableness of their word and work, for self-reliance, industry, frugality and an energetic force of character beyond the ordinary". They taught their children (who went on to become successful farmers and builders) "the value of work, of industry, of fidelity and temperance". Caroline's father was a lawyer, as were both her grandfathers. Her mother's family had come from Ireland and Scotland in the 19th century; and a maternal great-grandfather, also a lawyer, was a US Solicitor-General.

In the Autumn of 1948 Caroline returned to the United States to complete her masters degree in 17th century English literature. At the beginning of 1949 Tony sailed for America to meet her family in Cincinnati. While Caroline was finishing her studies he set off as a door-to-door magazine salesman with Benn Brothers, selling trade journals in Indianapolis, Chicago and Philadelphia. The American winter was cold, wet and windy and it seemed to underscore the dispiriting life of a salesman — a complete contrast to the glamour of the debating tour. This winter taught him a great deal about a side of the United States he had not seen before.

On 17 June 1949 Caroline and Tony were married at the Church of the Advent in Cincinnati, spending their honeymoon at Leland on Lake Michigan. They also attended a political Summer School at Wellesley College before sailing for Britain on 30 July to start a new life and set up home at Stamford Court, Chiswick, London W.6. Tony had been taken on as a talks producer on the BBC North American Service and Caroline had enrolled for a post-graduate degree in English literature at University College. She obtained her degree in 1951 with a dissertation on the masque-partnership between Ben Jonson and Inigo Jones.

The influence of aspects of American life on Tony Benn remains significant. Since the 1930s when his father had written about his travels in the United States, Tony had been interested in the US; and he occasionally felt more at home there than in Europe. Caroline, with her acute analytical powers, her background in Milton and English 17th century studies, gave Tony not only a fresh perspective on English politics, but also made him highly aware of the democratic legacy of the 17th century — a legacy of English dissent which the American founding fathers had drawn upon in framing their constitution. Benn admired the vigour of American democracy and he found in the US constitution, with its separation of powers, a significant attempt to control power which seemed to be lacking in

Britain.

At the age of twenty-five, Tony Benn was perhaps politically perspicacious but still naive and inexperienced. Fortune had been kind to him and he was full of youthful expectation. He deeply believed in the right of all people to control their own destinies, in social justice and self-government, values which formed part of his inheritance of dissent. He had yet to attempt to put principles into practice.

II
1950–1960
BENN AND THE RADICAL
TRADITION

In short it is Parliament as the sounding board, not Parliament as the law factory that makes public opinion.
JOSIAH WEDGWOOD

The 1950s would prove a productive decade for Tony and Caroline Benn, fulfilling, if in unexpected ways, some of the hopes of their youth. Tony Benn continued to work as a broadcaster and journalist. On radio, he appeared regularly in BBC's *Any Questions* and began his own television series, *Personal Column*. He also wrote regularly for the Bristol and occasionally for the national newspapers. Between 1951 and 1958, the Benns had four children, Stephen, Hilary, Melissa and Joshua. In 1952 the Benns bought a house for £4500 in Holland Park Avenue, where they have lived ever since. It is a large late Georgian house, painted white, with four storeys, a basement, a back and front garden. The interior gives an impression of almost deliberate bohemian neglect. It is cluttered with musical instruments, books and papers that constantly threaten to overwhelm it.

The collapse of Sir Stafford Cripps' health and his resignation in October 1950 as Chancellor of the Exchequer and Member of Parliament for Bristol South East would be the occasion for Tony Benn's entry into national politics. In 1948, Benn had been put on the Labour list of potential parliamentary candidates; he had spoken at the Worcester May Day in 1948 and a number of other meetings around the country. In 1950, he was short-listed for Raymond Blackburn's Birmingham constituency of Northfield, but before the selection conference took place, he received an invitation to go to Bristol South East where a candidate had to be chosen for the by-election to replace Sir Stafford Cripps.

Stafford Cripps had exemplified Bristol's fine and long tradition of political independence that dated back to Edmund Burke's defiant stand over the American War of Independence in the 18th century. The Bristol South East Labour Party had grown out of an Independent Labour Party branch formed in 1908. In the 1910 General Election,

Alderman Frank Shepherd, a boot and shoe operative, who was later Lord Mayor, polled 2000 votes. The Constituency Labour Party was founded in 1918 by Walter Ayles and others, though Ayles was not able to stand as he had served a prison sentence as a pacifist. Nevertheless Luke Bateman of the National Union of Railwaymen almost won the seat. The first Labour MP of the Constituency was Walter Baker of the Post Office Workers, and when he died, Stafford Cripps was chosen to succeed him, winning the by-election of January 1931 by a majority of 11,000 votes. Cripps' campaigns in the 1930s were only possible because of the loyalty of his own local party which stood by him even after his expulsion from the Labour Party.

After Cripps resigned, Mervyn Stockwood, the Vicar of St. Matthews, Bristol, later the Bishop of Southwark, asked Anthony Crosland, MP for South Gloucestershire, whether there was anybody he could recommend. "Tony Benn," he replied. But neither this recommendation, the accolade of presidency of the Oxford Union, nor the goodwill of his father, were worth much in Bristol South East. The General Management Committee had been inundated with applications, particularly from those who had lost their seats in the 1950 General Election; but it refused to consider any carpetbaggers or time-servers. Instead a short-list was made up: Arthur Creech-Jones, the former Secretary of State for the Colonies in Attlee's Cabinet, who had been born in the constituency; Muriel Walhead Nicholl, also a former MP; and Tony Benn. The first two had lost their seats at the General Election, and the National Agent, Dick Windle went down to Bristol to support Creech-Jones as the Transport House official choice.

Bristol South East was a safe Labour seat with nearly a 17,000 majority in 1950 and according to all the rules, Benn stood little chance of selection. Yet having made it onto the short list, he prepared his speech very carefully and travelled to Bristol for the first time in his life, on 1 November 1950. It was a city still visibly scarred by war, lacking in housing and overcrowded; a city of small businesses and dependent upon old industries. Benn made his way to local Party Headquarters where each prospective candidate was asked to speak for ten minutes and answer questions for five. Benn assured them:

I never *became* a socialist. I always was one. The case for continued controls, more nationalisation, more socialism has never been stronger (but . . .) the spirit of the pioneering crusaders for socialism can and must be recaptured. . . . Don't let us ever forget that socialism is not just a question of material progress. It isn't only concerned with wages and taxation nor is a socialist policy a sort of Christmas stocking of a policy with a little bit for everyone. It is a faith and a way of life and a way of thinking that can find its expression in every city and every community and every home. We are trying to build the sort of society where everybody "counts for something" and no one is neglected or left out: where "love your neighbour as yourself" finds practical expression. We must never get so bogged down by detail that we lose sight of that wider vision. We cannot, as a movement, live forever on the black memories of the thirties or on the wisdom of the socialist pioneers. We must inspire people afresh and especially young people with faith. That is our job. Make, teach and keep socialists.[1]

According to Alderman Harry Hennessy, who was in the Chair, Benn's speech made a considerable impression. Benn, himself, recalls that the practical-minded General Management Committee then tested him with their questions.

Two I remember very vividly. One was, "If elected will you live in the constituency?" "No I won't. London is very near; I'm just married and I would not be ready to be away from my wife for so much time in the year." And secondly, "If we select you, how much money will you give to the constituency?" And I said, "None at all, but even if I were going to, I wouldn't tell you before you select me. This is not a Tory selection conference." Those two answers, as a matter of fact, helped a bit.[2]

The selection committee then voted and much to his surprise, Benn found himself the parliamentary candidate, with an overall majority on the first ballot, receiving forty votes to Creech-Jones's eleven and Muriel Nicholl's four.

The by-election, however, was far from easy, with the Labour Government increasingly unpopular over rationing, the balance of payments deficit and inflation caused by the £3600 million Korean war rearmament programme which had been announced in September. Nevertheless, Benn campaigned on a socialist platform of planning, public ownership and the redistribution of wealth, and to his enormous delight was elected MP for Bristol South East on 30 November, though the Labour majority had fallen by almost 10,000.

At the age of twenty-five, he was the youngest Member of Parliament. The dream of his youth had come true, but the general political outlook was a depressing one for Labour. Labour's majority had fallen in the February 1950 General Election and Benn's election restored its majority of five in the House of Commons. Benn now joined the ranks of back-benchers supporting an embattled Labour Government which had run out of steam and was retreating from its commitments on nationalisation. Whereas the 1949 policy statement had promised to "nationalise industrial life assurance, sugar, cement, meat wholesaling and slaughtering, water and 'all suitable minerals' ", the 1950 manifesto made no such claims. Together with the Conservative Party, industry waged a full-scale anti-nationalisation campaign, and in the House of Lords succeeded in postponing the vesting day for the iron and steel industries until January 1951.

Benn's view was that Labour must persevere. On 7 February 1951, he broke with precedent by making his maiden speech on a controversial subject and countered the Opposition's motion condemning the nationalisation of the steel industry. As far as Benn was concerned, the subject of nationalising steel should not have been either controversial, or a matter of party political debate. It seemed to him a practical business matter. He noted that there was a basis for consent between the two parties in what both saw as a need for the re-equipment and public supervision of the steel industry in order to regulate prices and production. The Conservatives, he said, had admitted as much in calling for high production to meet the country's manufacturing and rearmament requirements and this reasoning led him to argue for complete nationalisation on strictly practical and non-ideological grounds.

However, a Conservative Government was soon to denationalise the steel industry. In the General Election of 25 October 1951, Labour was defeated, though Benn nearly doubled his majority. The Government had been weakened by Gaitskell's massive and inflationary £4700 million Korean War rearmament budget in April, as well as by Bevan, Wilson and Freeman's resignations over this and the imposition of health prescription charges. It had also been caught out by the nationalisation of Britain's oil interests in Iran. Benn considered the scale of rearmament misjudged, and as an opponent of conscription voted against the Government's Bill to recall Z reservists. However, he felt the three leading Labourites' resignations to be damaging and futile. This loyalty or insistence on unity would remain a central characteristic of his political career.

Throughout Labour's years of opposition in the 1950s, Benn's preoccupations were with foreign rather than domestic affairs and with issues of civil liberty. The reasons for this shift in focus from his speech to the selection committee in Bristol are complex. First, management of the economy ceased to be a pressing issue: capitalism seemed to be working; living standards were rising. The emergence of a post-war consensus between the two main political parties meant that Labour and Tory politicians were essentially agreed on the mixed economy and the welfare state, as well as committed to full-employment and Keynesian demand management. Simultaneously, the tensions of the Cold War and Britain's position as a great power brought international issues to the forefront. Benn supported the post-war consensus which was largely of Labour's making. However, the Tory foreign policy was another matter, as were civil liberty issues. Indeed, Benn's politics at this time could be described as radical, more than specifically socialist. This radicalism — part of the family tradition — was in essence a perspective, rather than a systematically deliberated political philosophy. Traditionally radicalism had stood for the extension of the franchise and civil liberties; for free trade and opposition to imperialism and military alliances. Perhaps more significantly, to be a radical had always meant — and continued to mean in Benn's case — a persistent questioning of established authority, and a championing of all issues which could lead to greater social justice.

Though his maiden speech on the steel industry was Benn's only contribution of note on economic policy during this period, a look at some of his other parliamentary interventions provides a valuable introduction to the nature of his radicalism and later socialism. In the early 'fifties, he opposed the abolition of wartime controls over scarce materials and equated socialism with this form of planning. He also supported Harold Macmillan's Towns Development Bill, which aimed to attract industry to the new towns, and saw it as a piece of constructive planning. Apart from the Post Office Bill in June 1952, when he argued that lack of capital hindered the expansion of telephone installation, his economics were confined to a belief in the importance of government regulations and a dislike of public expenditure. At most he was a reformist seeking to make capitalism more efficient and to remove its abuses, for example speaking against any exclusion clauses in the Merchant Shipping Bill which sought to improve living conditions at sea. On the other hand, in February 1952, he criticised the provision of £250 million in export credits as excessive. In June of that year he warned that the Marine and Aviation Insurance Bill, which made provision for losses in the Korean War, gave too much power to the Treasury and committed too much public money.

If Tony Benn's radicalism did not extend to the sphere of economics, he still felt himself to be, as indeed he was considered to be, on the left wing of the Labour Party. During the 1950s he was identified with certain radical causes through which he made his reputation as a parliamentarian. Whether these were domestic or international issues, the defence of civil liberties and human rights was their central theme. At home, he supported Victor Gollancz's and Arthur Koestler's National Campaign for the Abolition of Capital Punishment, and was one of six to sponsor Sydney Silverman's Private Member's Bill in '55 to abolish it. He also called for the reform of the divorce laws which he felt discriminated against women and working people. On these issues, he was merely reflecting the current state of liberal and progressive opinion, but he identified the problem of race relations earlier than most. In 1953 he spoke out against racial discrimination, arguing that the class structure was responsible for all oppression. "Colour is the big issue of this century", he told the Labour Party Annual Conference in 1956; and later, in 1958 and 1960, he enthusiastically supported bills to set up advisory bodies on community relations and human rights.

The issue of immigration was a closely related one and Benn pressed for a positive approach, urging the adoption of the American queue and annual quota system as well as the automatic admission of relatives and friends without work permits. In 1951 he called for the clarification and liberalisation of the laws relating to the admission and exclusion of aliens. In 1955 he sponsored the Aliens Employment Bill which would have allowed foreign citizens to work for the British Government without loss of their original citizenship and abolished the petty preliminary regulations to which they were subjected.

During the 1950s immigration was an issue tightly bound up with cold war fears of communist subversion. Benn considered this cold war anti-communism a major threat to liberty and saw the free movement of people as a test of how free the West really was. In 1952 he opposed the renewal of the Aliens Restriction Act. While his much-publicised defences of left-wing dissidents provoked wounding and false charges of pro-communist sympathies, he nevertheless insisted that the suppression of the Communist Party in Britain would be a violation of human rights likely to encourage undemocratic and eventually totalitarian attitudes.

The arrival of a delegation of American senators in 1953 to investigate communist activity helped to create a climate for witch hunts in Britain. Benn was furious, and in February 1954 took up the case of Paul Garland, the communist boy scout leader from Bristol, who became a *cause célèbre* of the Left. This led indirectly to Benn's much-reported defence of Dr. Joseph Cort, an American citizen living in Britain who was called up for military service in the US as a pretext for victimisation on grounds of his pro-communist views. Cort's plight vividly illustrated the conflict between the freedom of the individual and the security of the state. Like many of his generation, he had been a member of the Communist Party at university during and after the war; but he was in no sense a fugitive or "draft dodger", having failed the military medical test and fully registered his British residence with the UK and US authorities. He had come to Britain to study medicine as a research fellow of Cambridge and was now a lecturer at Birmingham University.

The American authorities persuaded the Home Secretary not to review Cort's residence permit, against normal practice. When Benn received a letter from Cort in April 1954 explaining his predicament, he was outraged. He lobbied the Home Secretary, ministers and officials, drew public attention to the scandal in the *Reynolds News* and moved an adjournment motion in the House of Commons. After failing to persuade the Government to take the exceptional "political factors" into account, he commented bitterly: "The irony of it is that Dr. Cort's father is a Russian by birth and had left the Soviet Union as a result of the revolution. He went to America for freedom and his child is now being pushed back again by the hamhandedness, lack of imagination and meanness of the people of the western world."[3]

The dangers to freedom implicit in cold-warriorism struck at the governmental machine itself when the Conservatives introduced a Bill in March '56 to tighten the security vetting of civil servants. It was a denial of intellectual freedom which Benn felt compelled to oppose, partly because it "would be likely to encourage such great caution on the part of those civil servants that their capacity for free thought and independent inquiry would be seriously harmed. To take an exaggerated example, far from dismissing any member of the Foreign Office who had read Karl Marx, my inclination would be to dismiss anyone who had not read Karl Marx." Ministerial answers to his questions about the number of civil servants dismissed between 1951–55 for communist views showed the measure to be unwarranted. Nevertheless, it had exposed "the dilemma of a free society which tries to protect itself from subversion", Benn commented, concluding: "The real security of a free society lies in its freedom."[4]

Benn recognised that personal freedom was a cause which Labour could and should champion to greater effect than the Tories, and the NEC policy statement about this issue in 1956 was the acknowledgement of his and others' campaign for civil liberties. At the Party Conference of that year, he urged that Labour prove itself as the party of individual liberty and not of Stalinism. "The Tory jungle is not a jungle of personal freedom but a jungle of fear — fear of unemployment at home and fear of war abroad."

Tony Benn was principally known in the 1950s for his committed internationalism and anti-imperialism. Together with like-minded MPs — Geoffrey Bing, Fenner Brockway, Leslie Hale, Ian Mikardo and Reginald Paget — a loose grouping of "radicals" was formed which met daily to discuss how the parliamentary timetable could be used to raise issues of primarily international importance. It was on the colonial issue that Benn made his reputation as a parliamentarian.

London in the 'fifties was a mecca for imperial grievances and nationalist leaders, and the Benns' home in Notting Hill Gate became a centre of anti-colonial activity. During these years, Benn kept in close contact with the leaders of the African and Arab nationalist movements and much of his time was taken up by meetings held for them and in making Parliament aware of their situation. Hastings Banda — then Dr. Banda of Brixton, later President of Malawi — would turn up at the House of Commons after his surgery with his Gladstone bag and his black Homburg. Kenneth Kaunda, Joshua Nkomo, Kwame Nkrumah, Julius Nyerere, Harry Nkumbulah, Forbes Burham and Cheddi Jagan, who were all in London at the time, used to attend these meetings.

In Parliament, Benn was one of the Honourable Members for Africa, his constituency stretching from the Cape to Cairo with adjacent territories in the Indian Ocean. The notion of a special "representative" duty inspired MPs like Benn. He explained his

opposition to colonialism in democratic terms: "I am an anti-
colonialist. I believe in national independence as the first stage of
responsible self-government." He considered colonialism immoral
because it suppressed the desire for freedom common to all people.
Benn's involvement in colonial issues reflected the turbulence in the
colonies themselves and in their relationship with Britain as the
imperial power. The 'fifties were a decade of conflict, reform and
repression in the "emerging" colonies, in contrast to the relative peace
of the 'forties.

Colonial policy was characterised by a bi-partisan consensus on the
need for economic and social development as well as peaceful progress
towards self-government. The policy which Oliver Stanley and Arthur
Creech-Jones had forged at the Colonial Office in the 'forties survived
through the 'fifties. It involved the establishment of federations in East
and Central Africa, Malaya and the West Indies. In many respects,
imperialism intensified after 1945, because the case for empire had
become one of principle, of the righteousness of sound administration
and the deliberate development of the colonies. However, the strength
and stability of bi-partisan colonial policy was itself a major obstacle to
change and a cause of disorder.

Oliver Lyttleton, Colonial Secretary between 1951–54, who
pursued a policy of peace and order as a basis for economic and
political advance, found that his reformist initiatives only fuelled
African demands and led to unrest. From the start, Benn was active in
drawing public attention to African grievances and in criticising
Parliament's failure to understand African aspirations. Two issues, in
particular, involved Benn early on in the anti-colonial cause: the
proposal to form a Central African Federation out of Northern and
Southern Rhodesia and Nyasaland; and the exile of Seretse Khama
from Bechuanaland in 1951. In Parliament he called for the
democratic self-government of Bechuanaland and the separate
representation of Nyasaland and Rhodesia. Outside, he served on the
Central Africa Committee and on the Seretse Khama Defence Council
of which Fenner Brockway was the moving spirit. The Council's aim
was to influence opinion and policy, particularly that of the Labour
leadership and Benn helped petition 622 leading public figures against
the Central African Federation as well as raise 10,838 signatures for the
Seretse Khama petition.

The crisis of imperialism only became generally apparent however,
with the Mau Mau rebellion in Kenya, where the death toll rose from
270 in 1952 to 5000 in 1954. Yet its causes were not understood and the
British authorities saw it as "an unholy union of dark and ancient
superstitions with the apparatus of modern gangsterism". In the
Commons, Benn called for information about the trials and the
security situation, and was critical of the Government's repression.
Outside, he addressed meetings, declaring that "refusal to

acknowledge the human rights of the African population had led to Mau Mau", and helped gather 16,434 British signatures while Fenner Brockway organised the collection of 158,643 Kenyan African signatures and thumbprints, some in blood, to signify that "land is life". They were trying to draw attention to the fact that Mau Mau was a revolt of the desperate rural poor, hungry for land and victims of capitalist development. Fenner Brockway's motion which obtained the support of 199 back bench MPs aimed to "seek agreement in Kenya for a policy which will permit Africans, and in particular African cooperatives, to own lands in the highlands and which will enable the Government of Kenya to acquire, as part of a general policy of agricultural development, unused land in that area for African use".

If the Labour Party was privately sceptical about the direction of the Government's plans for colonial political development, it was openly hostile to the suspension of the new constitution in British Guyana in October 1953, after Cheddi Jagan and five ministers of the People's Progressive Party had been dismissed for negligence and arrested for subversion. Benn was outraged, and in the Commons debate strongly condemned the dismissal of men like Burham and Jagan who were patriots and socialists, not communists, struggling to establish democracy under adverse conditions. If Parliament had not been suspended after the Gunpowder plot, why should a similar arson plot in Guyana be an adequate pretext for suspension, he asked.

The wave of protest which swept the colonies during 1953 had a radicalising effect on British politics and led to an upsurge of interest in colonial affairs. It is hard now to convey the passion that the deportations and emergencies raised, and which lay at the source of much activity. The parties were polarised over the Federation issue, and Labour brought a motion of censure on the Government's handling of African policy. Their policy document, *Challenge to Britain*, welcomed the "world uprising of colonial peoples against the old imperialism", and the 1953 conference endorsed the resolution that "in Kenya the repression of the Mau Mau is necessary but the economic and social causes of this reversion to barbarism demand radical treatment". But the real pressure came from the back-benchers like Benn. Lyttleton testified that "the Colonial Office ship rarely faced anything but the roughest weather at question time", and complained of being interrogated "about such things as the dismissal of a clerk in a post office in some colony".

The colonial unrest of the early 'fifties led to a proliferation of liberal and radical pressure groups. The federation issue resulted in the formation of the Africa Bureau by John Hatch and Rev. Michael Scott to "strengthen and further the best traditions of Britain's policy in relation to Africa"; while the British Guyana Association and the Seretse Khama Defence Council were merged into the Movement for Colonial Freedom of which Benn was a founder member. Unlike the liberal and radical pressure groups, such as the Fabian Colonial Bureau, which were concerned chiefly with research, publishing, and education, the Labour Left wanted a popular crusade that would have immediate impact on political decisions. In 1947, Fenner Brockway had formed the Congress of Peoples against Imperialism "to retrieve the honour of British Socialism in the eyes of the colonial peoples", but disbanded it in 1954 because of sectarian Trotskyite influence. On 8 March Benn announced that "a new organisation to rally public opinion in favour of a change in colonial policy will be launched at a special delegate conference on Sunday 11 April 1954 at the Waldorf Hotel". The inaugural conference which elected Fenner Brockway as Chairman and Benn as Treasurer endorsed a declaration of objectives supporting the right of colonial peoples to self-government, economic justice, civil and racial equality, as well as economic assistance and international support.

The inauguration received wide publicity in the press and was attended by representatives of thirty-eight constituency Labour parties, twenty-two trades unions and twenty-one cooperative societies. The MCF soon challenged the Fabian Colonial Bureau's ideological ascendency and monopoly of specialist sympathy. It claimed the support of over one hundred MPs, its membership including Jennie Lee and Leslie Hale; and outside Parliament, Sir Richard Acland, Canon Collins, and Rev. Donald Soper. As Fenner Brockway wrote: It was "a splendid organisation which could bring 20,000 people to Trafalgar Square on any urgent issue", and its emotional appeal lay in the fusion of radical and socialist ideals:

> The Movement's general philosophy embodied attitudes inherited more or less unchanged from earlier generations of Labour radicals. The internationalist ideal, the moral detestation of "exploitation" in any form, the view of colonialism as an extension of domestic capitalism, the conception of colonial policy in terms of a series of liberation struggles.[5]

The MCF was Benn's apprenticeship in extra-parliamentary populist politics, and it taught him how to connect the aspirations of the unrepresented with the political system. His contribution to the MCF took the form of a sustained, unrelenting barrage of parliamentary questions with frequent adjournment motions. In the Commons, he constantly re-emphasised that endemic violence would continue until political oppression had ended either by bloody revolution or by peaceful change; and where cases of injustice could not be brought before the law, he brought them before Parliament. Penal statistics were central to the debate on law and order, and Benn concentrated upon the futility of repressive measures to which colonial governments everywhere resorted to maintain their authority and order. The banishment of political and tribal leaders, such as Odede from Uganda, would, he argued, embitter relations and create political chaos and confusion. He predicted that the retrial of Kenyatta would make him a martyr-figure and that the refusal to recognise the Zulu chief Mpamba would provoke tribal hostility. The suppression of Mau Mau involved the detention of hundreds of thousands of the Kikuyu tribe and its barbarity appalled Benn. He condemned the payments to Africans to murder Mau Mau suspects, the summary beatings in the detention camps for petty offences in connection with malingering, the misuse of prison property and refusal to do prison work. The numerous instances of government injustice drove Benn to campaign for the introduction of courts of appeal in East Africa, the reform of the existing machinery of justice and the definition of offences and punishments.

The suppression of human rights was often so total that he felt compelled to draw public attention to the unnecessary petty violations and punitive restrictions which extended over almost every aspect of African life. In Bechuanaland for example, stray village cattle were confiscated, while books and films were often burned as subversive throughout East Africa. Such measures could only antagonise the African population and Benn denounced this Conservative version of justice as a sham. The Government, after all, had been slow to sign the anti-slavery convention and was reluctant to draw up a convention on human rights for Africa.

In the final analysis Benn saw no distinction between human and political oppression, and like other members of the MCF, he put the campaign for political reform above all others. As the Secretary of the MCF wrote: "As I see it our job . . . is to bring home to the Labour Party the fact that even they are offering too little too late. . . . I feel that it is a race between the Labour Party . . . promising . . . a more progressive policy . . . and a complete loss of confidence by the colonial people in *all* British Government."[6] In theory the Conservative Government was committed to self-government, and in justification of their gradualism claimed that the Labour Party did not understand the primitive nature of tribal society. In fact Benn fully recognised the importance of tribal life as a basis for native councils and as the source for a developing democracy in Africa. He campaigned for the transformation of district councils in Basutoland and Bechuanaland into national assemblies with real power. The crucial test was the Government's commitment to the abolition of educational and landholding qualifications about which he was very sceptical. He saw a dangerous political vacuum which had to be filled, and a lack of trust between Africans and Europeans which had somehow to be overcome. Legislative institutions were crucial, he argued, in colonies like Kenya, Nyasaland and Rhodesia where there were European settlers; while in the case of Tanganyika, he demanded a timetable for independence in view of the strength of Nyerere's African National Union.

Because of the MCF and Benn's work, the colonial issue became an essential ingredient of Labour's Opposition in the 1950s. The MCF exploited the uncertainty over the constitutional rights of the unrepresented colonies; and, on the select committee for procedure, Benn campaigned between 1957–60 for a standing committee on the colonies with inquisitorial powers. Though he got the NEC to accept the idea in 1960, the Government and Parliament rejected the select committee's report. Within the Labour Party, the MCF engendered a creative tension between the internationalist libertarian and radical wing and the humanitarian liberal wing. The NEC appointed John Hatch as colonial officer, separating the international and commonwealth sub-committees; and the flow of policy documents, *From Colonies to Commonwealth*, 1954, *Economic Aid* and *The Smaller Territories*, 1956, culminated in *The Plural Society* which committed Labour to rapid decolonisation and the designation of 1960 as Africa year.

The MCF's relationship with the Labour Party was close, but it remained unaffiliated. Often it embarrassed Labour by its critical approach. In 1959 the NEC reported that "discussions have been held with the officers of the Movement for Colonial Freedom in order to ensure that there is no misunderstanding of the Party's colonial policy, particularly in overseas territories", but nevertheless saw fit to consult it about its policy over Malaya. As Chairman of the MCF's Goan and Mediterranean committees, Benn developed numerous contacts amongst the Arab nationalists. After condemning the Government's support for France's policy on Algeria, he went to Tunis in 1959 to confer with Ferhat Abbas, leader of the Algerian movement in exile. In 1960, he returned as official delegate of the Labour Party at the All Africa Peoples' Conference to proclaim solidarity with Algeria, "a free Africa within five years" and "a major reorientation of our foreign policy". Here he also had talks with Joshua Nkomo with whom he walked around the ruins of ancient Carthage.

It is interesting to speculate about, but difficult to prove, any influence the MCF may have had over the course of colonial policy itself. The repatriation of Seretse Khama in 1956 and the Government's policy towards the two communities in Cyprus, over which Benn was greatly active, were in part due to the direct pressure of the MCF; but its indirect influence was more pervasive and far-reaching. Where Labour was united in opposition to Conservative policy, as over Kenya, the Government accommodated the demands for change in order to preserve the increasingly fragile consensus on colonial affairs. The second factor was the MCF's hold over colonial opinion and the British Government's awareness of their dependence upon internal support for any reform. Reflecting on the Opposition's part in colonial policy, John Hatch concluded: "During these vital years in the history of the British Empire, the Opposition played a unique and significant role in forming colonial policy. . . . Without Labour's constant and not always popular campaign on this issue, it is doubtful if the Tories would ever have scented the post-1959 wind of change."[7] Benn too had played his part in bringing about the transition from gradualism to radicalism in Labour's policy and in the Government's adoption of reformist policies in Africa.

Throughout the 1950s Benn's ideas on foreign policy were far removed from those of the Conservative Government, or indeed from the official line of the Labour Party, both of which were committed to the Atlantic Alliance, Commonwealth or Empire and in the end to the nuclear deterrent. Benn's radicalism was evident in his belief that Britain must be independent from the superpowers; as well as in his belief in the liberation of oppressed peoples from colonial rule. In matters of defence, he was not a pacifist but an advocate of armed neutrality, and he was opposed to the spread of the cold war which threatened to divide the world into two ideological armed camps. The system of military alliances that went along with cold war ideology did more, he felt, to provoke than prevent the spread of communism. He argued that security depended upon disarmament and the cooperation of free peoples in organisations like the United Nations. These, he thought, enabled the strong countries to wield their power for just ends in order to maintain security in disturbed regions.

Such a vision would have been no more than unworldly idealism had it not been tempered by hard-headedness. Benn recognised that the world was still on the brink of war and that disarmament was pointless until peace had been established. At the same time, he was optimistic on a global level, because he saw the ideological, geopolitical struggle between the free world and the proletarian dictatorships breaking down in the face of the aspirations of the emerging nations. The real issues of the age, as he saw them, were the rise of nationalisms and the fall of empire, with the threats this posed to international security; the imminence of a world population explosion and a shortage of food supply; the challenge this presented for technological cooperation, especially the peaceful and constructive use of nuclear power to solve the massive problems the world faced. Benn was convinced that the old world had an historic mission to fulfil in giving birth to new nations and in preventing world war.

What this meant in terms of practical politics was that Benn, at this time, stood for detente and peaceful coexistence rather than cold war. This could be achieved, he believed, through the reunification of Germany as an independent neutral state; the negotiation of peace treaties between Germany and the other European states, and the establishment of a demilitarised zone in Central Europe. Such moves, he argued, could lead to multilateral nuclear disarmament. He fiercely opposed the European Defence Community and German rearmament in the early 'fifties, and later, the creation of the EEC, because they would re-enforce the division of Europe. Similarly, in a global context, he argued that the Baghdad pact between Britain, Iraq and Turkey and SEATO would promote war rather than peace; and he was convinced that only the admission of China to the United Nations, her membership on the Security Council, would bring stability to South East Asia.

It was Suez more than any other single event that led to Labour's adoption of a radical foreign policy by 1960. For Benn, Suez was the nemesis of an imperialism he detested. Throughout the crisis, he was active in Parliament, opposing the Anglo-French invasion of Egypt. He had long been critical of Conservative policy in the Middle East. In 1951-52, he had condemned the military intervention at Ismailia and when British military headquarters were evacuated from Cairo to Cyprus in '54, he condemned the handling of disturbances on the island the following year which taught "the unfailing lesson of history that people denied the prospect of freedom will turn to violence". After Nasser had nationalised the Suez Canal in July 1956, Benn, as vice-chairman of the PLP Committee on Foreign Affairs, led a delegation to express concern over Gaitskell's initial speech which had not championed Egypt's cause sufficiently.

Later, Benn helped Gaitskell prepare for a November television broadcast, in which the Labour leader offered to serve in any Government that would put an end to the war. Acutely aware of the dangers of a Suez war, Benn, on 16 September, addressed a rally of some 7,000 in Trafalgar Square and urged an international intiative to settle the dispute. The question as to whether the canal was inter-nationally or privately-owned could only be resolved, he said, by an international guarantee which safeguarded the rights of its users.

On 29 October Israel attacked Egypt, bombing Alexandria and Port Said, and the following day Britain and France announced their intervention. The invasion and Britain's announcement provoked one of the stormiest debates in the history of Parliament, with the speaker suspending the Commons in uncontrollable uproar on 1 November. The source of the passionate scenes and violent emotions was a belief in the justice of Egypt's actions, and a suspicion about the Government's motives in supporting Israel. Benn shared this sense of outrage, and he accused the Government of not understanding Arab nationalism, "the problem of ex-dependent peoples becoming independent", and of tacitly approving France's collusion with Israel. Though, like his father, Benn had sympathy for Israel in her struggle for survival and quest for security, he saw Eden's claim that Britain had acted to defend Israel, as hypocrisy.

Benn thought it sinister that the Prime Minister did not mention Israel's right to use the canal and saw the defence of Israel as a cynical tactic justifying Anglo-French invasion. He disputed the legality of the invasion, since it contravened article 51 of the UN charter, as well as Egypt's responsibility for the canal under the convention of 1888. But he was more concerned with Britain's conduct during the ensuing weeks. Having with great difficulty obtained the transcripts of the Cyprus broadcasts to Egypt, he launched an attack on the use of propaganda to intimidate the population into surrender: "Radio itself can never defeat an enemy; all it can do is win a friend," he observed, declaring that "it is very important that the true voice of Britain should be heard abroad".

The invasion generated an upsurge in radical opinion and a volume of public protest that the Government had never anticipated. The National Council of Labour unanimously condemned Government policy and organised public meetings on the theme "Law not War" and the largest rally, since the demonstrations of the 'thirties, in Trafalgar Square. Public opinion, pressure from the US government, the United Nations and the Commonwealth, together with the fear of Russian retaliation made the war's end as dramatic and sudden as its beginning.

Britain's loss of the Suez Canal following so quickly upon her loss of India, removed the historical and strategic underpinnings of the Empire. It marked a turning point in British history and led to a redefinition of Britain's defence strategy. Because of his criticism of the Government, Benn had earned the reputation of being a formidable opponent and he was appointed as Labour's second front-bench spokesman on the RAF. When the Government intervened militarily in Muscat and Oman, only six months after Suez, Benn was appalled and demanded a parliamentary debate on a matter of such urgent public importance. When the Speaker refused, Benn responded by tabling a motion of censure on the Speaker. Speaking in the debate, he set out his views on the party system and emphasised that the voice of Parliament was the protector of freedom.

> The party system is well embedded in our form of parliamentary government. . . . I think I am a good party man. . . . For the modern party system, even at its most oppressive does not in any way limit our right to speak. It may limit how we vote at the end of the day, although in my own Party and in the Party opposite we have the right of abstention on grounds of principle. That is a comfort which I draw from the restriction of the party system. "It is not what a man does that matters; it is what he says." It is not the vote at the end of the day that limits our right. It is the right of free thought and free speech that is left unfettered by the party system. If . . . an individual back-bencher cannot raise a point . . . without the support of his Party . . . then you give to the Party a power over the members which I believe would be an imposition on the rights of the House. . . . I am not forming an anti-party faction at all. . . . I am one of the thousand flowers asking permission to be allowed to bloom.[8]

Benn's speech expressed sentiments which would later bring him into conflict with Party leadership. It compelled critics, such as Bernard Levin in *The Spectator,* to enthusiastic praise:

It was eloquent beyond the farthest reach of all but a hand-count of his fellow-members; it was witty, graceful, modest, learned, pointed, and in some strange way deeply moving. More: it was magnificently constructed to make, by easy stages and gentle persuasion his point — that the rights of back-benchers had diminished, were diminishing, and ought to be increased. Mr. Benn, in his oration, struck a great blow for his view and for himself. But he did more: he struck a blow for Parliament.[9]

After Suez, it was recognised that the Middle East Air Command was vulnerable and had to be restructured, and the whole future of Britain's military bases around the world was under review. The Government looked to nuclear weapons. After Macmillan's summit talks with Eisenhower in Bermuda in 1957, Duncan Sandys, the Defence Minister, announced that Britain would abandon a defence policy combining the use of nuclear and conventional arms in favour of a strategy of massive nuclear retaliation. Benn had always been, partly for family reasons, pro-RAF, and when the Commons debated the air estimates, he was in the front line defending the RAF's role. He urged a balance of conventional forces between East and West, though he hoped that the nuclear stalemate would lead to disarmament and a policy for "open skies".

It was the Government and the Labour Party's policy on the nuclear deterrent that eventually forced Benn to resign, quietly, as Air Force spokesman on 3 March 1958. He was opposed to the development of nuclear weapons from the start and would not support a defence policy based on their use. Nor could he condone a policy that threatened the destruction of the human race. He insisted that Britain must never be the first power to use nuclear weapons. The atom-bomb tests on the Monte Bello Islands in 1952 and on the Bikini Islands in 1953; and still more the explosion of a hydrogen bomb by Russia in August 1953 and the US in February 1954, had impressed upon him an image of terrible human destruction. Attlee expressed the general growing anxiety at "this grave threat to civilisation" in an April 1954 resolution which urged Churchill to bring together the leaders of the superpowers "for the purpose anew of considering the control and reduction of armaments".

Benn was appalled that governments had developed the hydrogen bomb in secret and without parliamentary consent. He was determined to alert people to the political meaning of such secret action. On 11 April 1954, he founded the H-Bomb National Committee with Sir Richard Acland, Fenner Brockway, Anthony Greenwood and Donald Soper, to raise fifteen million signatures in support of Attlee's resolution. Though Attlee intensely disliked association with such unparliamentary activity, Benn and the other members of the Committee held a placard demonstration in Whitehall on 27 April to publicise the position. At the opening rally in the Albert

Hall on 30 April, nearly two thousand people attended, and Benn's father spoke. Tony Benn told them that disarmament was only possible if Britain changed her foreign policy from one of force to one of coexistence and cooperation. "Negotiation is the only|course,"[7] he declared; and with some foresight, he said that the French war in Vietnam threatens the whole peace of the world.

Benn took part in meetings around the country and wrote an article in the pacifist journal *Peace News*. In Bristol, he told a May Day rally: "The whole battle for parliamentary control (over nuclear weapons) has been a battle for the rights of people to govern their own destinies." Aneurin Bevan and Lord Beveridge spoke at the final rally in the Albert Hall on 8 December, and though only eight hundred attended, 357,000 signatures had been collected which Benn, Greenwood, Silverman and George Thomas, later to become Speaker in the House of Commons, presented to No. 10 Downing Street on the 31st.

The H-Bomb Campaign in these years was closely connected with the issue of German rearmament and reunification, and fitted into the Bevanite Left's strategy of disarmament through peace and negotiation. Though the Campaign's impact was limited, it initially strengthened Labour's official opposition to the nuclear tests, making it a major issue with thirty-four resolutions on the agenda of the 1954 Annual Conference on nuclear disarmament, thirty in 1955, and fifteen in 1956. There were back-bench revolts by fifty-seven MPs on rearmament in March 1952, sixty-two on manufacture of the H-Bomb, including Benn, in March 1955; and seven over the Paris Treaties on German Rearmament in November 1954, when Annual Conference only approved it by 3,270,000 to 3,022,000. In April 1954, Bevan resigned from the Shadow Cabinet over SEATO.

It would be misleading to compare the H-Bomb National Committee of 1954 with the unilateralist Campaign for Nuclear Disarmament of 1958–63, for the traumatic events of Suez stood between them, creating an entirely new situation. Suez radicalised the public and made people question Britain's role as a great power. The new policy of massive nuclear retaliation — over which Benn had resigned as Air Force spokesman - accompanied by a return to cold war politics, presented the public with a sense of the imminence of holocaust. Benn felt himself caught up in the terrible contradiction between the realities of international power politics and the potential horrors of thermo-nuclear war. Though the PLP had condemned the proposed Christmas Islands hydrogen-bomb tests in April 1957, Labour was divided on the issue as a whole. At the 1957 Annual Conference in Brighton, there were 127 resolutions on the nuclear deterrent, sixty in favour of unilateral disarmament. The leadership secured the rejection of a motion to pledge that "the next Labour Government will take the lead by itself, refusing to continue to test, manufacture or use nuclear weapons, and that it will appeal to people of other countries to follow their lead", by 5,836,000 votes to 781,000. Benn agreed with the Conference that it was an "agonising decision. I am not a pacifist and I have never been a pacifist. I believe we miss the whole point of this challenge if we think that the answer lies only in the stopping of tests, only in the renunciation of the Bomb. The answer lies in the control of power which nature has given to mankind." In his peroration, he called for the moral leadership of the United Nations and the supremacy of Parliament: "We are drifting towards disaster because we have not yet asserted popular control over the hydrogen bomb." Bevan, in his speech, described unilateralism as an "emotional spasm" which would send a British Foreign Secretary "naked into the conference chamber" powerless to negotiate the disarmament everyone wanted. Benn, too, believed that disarmament was meaningless unless it was done on a world scale and had a system of international inspection to enforce it. The leadership won a victory, but the criticisms from the Left which ensued broke Bevan and reflected the split in the Party.

The disarmament issue became a tensely emotional one and led to the formation in February 1958 of the Campaign for Nuclear Disarmament. The "Ban the Bomb" movement was on its way, and the first of the annual Easter marches from Trafalgar Square to Aldermaston took place. By 1959 the CND seemed to be more of a crusade than an organisation, and a million people took part in that year's march. As *Peace News* put it, "It was the type of movement which career politicians most fear — a largely spontaneous and self-organised wave of protest on a single issue." Its thirty-eight sponsors included Canon Collins, Donald Soper, Sir Julian Huxley, A.J.P. Taylor, J.B. Priestley, Arnold Wesker and Michael Foot, and reflected progressive opinion.

Benn refused to join the CND and was alarmed by the resurgence of unilateralism as an issue in 1960. Though the CND was already past its peak by the time the Labour Party Conference took place in October, the cancellation of the Blue Streak Missile project in April was the pretext for a rebellion by the trade unions, particularly the TGWU and AEU. Despite pressure from the leadership, Conference rejected official policy and came out in favour of unilateral disarmament. Benn's role in the unilateralist controversy was highly ambiguous and widely criticised. He believed that unilateral nuclear disarmament was unrealistic without a negotiated peace in Europe and world-wide control over armaments. He also believed that in terms of the Labour Party itself, the issue was a damaging one and destroyed a necessary unity. He chastised membership at the Conference for not taking up the leadership's line: Though "diversity is Labour's greatest strength . . . there must be leadership that transmits our sense of common purpose." He warned that "if you allow discussion to be dominated by extremists in the Labour Party, then you will find that the fight will be the struggle between condemned men in a cell." At the same time, he threatened resignation from the NEC if Gaitskell and Cousins did not compromise with membership, and did in fact resign over the issue, though he stood again immediately for re-election. From the vantage point of his later development and the issue of nuclear power, it is interesting to note that Benn, at this juncture, had more to say about the proper procedure to be followed in decision-making, than about the merits of the argument on either side.

Benn failed to get re-elected to the NEC, but was eighth and runner-up in the constituency section with 444,000 votes. At Scarborough, he learned what he felt to be an important lesson: that influence was of greater value than isolation, and that resignations, on the whole, achieved nothing. Looking at this period in a wider context the unilateralist issue was in part indicative of the Labour movement's dislike of Gaitskell's obdurate leadership and the social-democratic ideas he was seeking to impose.

The ambiguity of Benn's position over unilateral disarmament was part of the general dilemma of a radical caught in the crossfire of the dispute over socialism that so bitterly divided the Labour Party in the 'fifties. As the decade progressed, so the argument became more bitter. At its source was the controversy about how the economy had developed and the way in which society and the electorate were changing. The fundamentalist-socialists, led by Bevan, who were in the minority, saw the public ownership of the "commanding heights of the economy" as the object of all policy and contended that the prosperity of post-war Britain was a temporary phenomenon. They maintained the conviction that the inherent contradictions of capitalism would soon lead to insoluble crisis. The revisionist social democrats, led by Gaitskell, saw public ownership as only one of many paths to achieving a socialist society which, they argued, was not dependent upon the common ownership of the means of production. They argued, first of all, that the success of capitalism in providing full employment and in raising living standards had disproved Marx's predictions. They equated socialism with the welfare state, educational opportunity, the fair distribution of income and wealth, putting a new emphasis on equality. As Roy Jenkins wrote in *New Fabian Essays:* "Where there is no egalitarianism, there is no socialism." Believing in the autonomy and power of the state, they looked to taxation and social engineering rather than public ownership to construct their socialist society. Finally they drew upon liberal ideology, arguing that political democracy was incompatible with a state-controlled economy, and they endeavoured to present the mixed economy as an ideal. Thus in *Socialism in the New Society*, Douglas Jay wrote that "socialists believe in Liberty, political and personal, as firmly as they believe in Equality."

The circumstances of the 'fifties undoubtedly favoured revisionism. The epoch of growing affluence, opportunity and social mobility coincided with Labour's electoral decline, leading to a desperate search for ways of reversing it. In 1951 Labour won 13.9 million or 48.8% of the votes and in 1955 12.4 million or 46.4%; but in 1959 it only polled 12.2 million or 43.7% of the votes. If the socialist resurgence of the early 'fifties was reflected in the extensive public ownership proposals in *Challenge to Britain* (1953), Labour's General Election manifestos, *Forward with Labour* and *Britain Belongs to You,* contained hardly any references to nationalisation. Meanwhile both defeats strengthened the position of the revisionists. Harold Wilson's report after the 1955 election recommended the modernisation of the Labour Party, and the publication of Anthony Crosland's *The Future of Socialism* in 1956 was seminal. It provided the intellectual basis of the 1957 policy document, *Industry and Society.* Crosland argued that the managerial revolution, separating ownership from control, had eroded the capitalist class structure, making public ownership irrelevant except where industries "were failing the nation" and large amounts of high risk capital were involved.

Labour's defeat in the 1959 General Election brought its crisis of identity to a climax. Morgan Philips' report to the NEC observed that the Conservatives had exploited the fears arising out of the uncertainty of Labour's plans for nationalisation. Furthermore, given the threat of inflation, Labour had failed to state how it would pay for its ambitious social programme: "Too many of the electorate saw us as an exclusively class party and a party of restrictions and controls." Abrams and Rose corroborated this view in their influential study, *Must Labour Lose?,* concluding that: "The image of the Labour Party, held by both its supporters and its non-supporters, is one that is increasingly obsolete in terms of contemporary Britain." In the *New Statesman,* Paul Johnson wrote that nationalisation was an electoral albatross; while Douglas Jay stated that the Labour Party should change its name and break with the trade unions. In 1959, Labour idealism had been conspicuous only by its absence, and Butler and Rose noted that Labour "as in all recent elections . . . played down any claim to stand, as a socialist party, for a radically different form of society. . . . It asked the voters to say that it could administer the mixed economy welfare state better than the Conservatives."

Gaitskell's initiative at the 1959 Labour Party Conference turned the struggle for the definition of the Labour Party into an immediate constitutional crisis. He proposed the replacement of public ownership in Clause IV of the Party's constitution. While the NEC rejected this, his draft was accepted as "a valuable expression . . . in the second half of the twentieth century" of Labour's aims. Benn remained on the fringes of the debate, but in the ensuing battle on the NEC, he sided with those who opposed abandonment of Clause IV and public ownership. He believed that Labour could never win support by dropping its fundamental beliefs. However, he regarded the conduct of Labour's internal ideological conflicts as sterile and backward-looking. His radicalism showed itself in his belief that ideology must not remain a mere party issue, but must emerge from wider popular debate. As early as 1955, he was looking for a populist alternative: "We stand for the participation of ordinary men and women in the work of the community." This emphasis on popular participation has been with him until the present day.

After the 1959 General Election, Benn was convinced that Labour must modernise; and at the ensuing Conference, he urged it to project itself as the party of progress and affluence.

> If this Party is to survive, it must win not just the votes of young people, but the loyalty of young people. . . . Listen to them and think about the world in which they are going to live. . . . I am not a party to those who say that this evidence of rising living standards necessarily means a fall in moral standards (and) I feel we cannot turn the eyes of the British people forward if we do not at the same time modernise the Labour movement.[10]

By 1960, Benn came to fear that the obsolescence of socialist ideology had opened up a generation gap in Labour politics: "The Labour Party must capture the imagination of youth," he declared. "We have to convince young people that the Labour Party is the only instrument of change open to them." At the 1960 Annual Conference, he made it clear during the debate on Labour in the 'sixties that he put "national regeneration" and the "regeneration of this movement" above unilateral disarmament. However, the issues he envisaged — apart from the control of technology — were the old ones of ending the cold war, liberating the colonies and transforming the United Nations from the parliament of men into the government of mankind. But his statement did contain the seeds of his future democratic rebellion:

> We shall release the energy particularly of the young people who are sick and tired of the 'fifties and want to get into the 'sixties. I believe that if we harness that energy there will be no stopping this movement because after all, this is a movement dedicated to the pre-supposition that man can and must take charge of his own destiny.[11]

By the turn of the decade, Benn was considered a rising star of the Labour Party. He had been elected in 1959 to the NEC and had come close to joining the Parliamentary Committee or Shadow Cabinet. This indicated the growing influence of the radicalism for which he stood and the revisionism with which he was associated. Yet Benn's position was partly one of isolation. His support came largely from outside the Party and was based on his popular standing. He never belonged to any faction within the Party. He admired the intensity and passion of Bevan, but when he was asked to join the Bevanite group in 1951, he refused, disliking the idea of an all-purpose pressure group.

And although the MCF was involved in the Left's "Victory for Socialism Campaign" in 1957, Benn during the second half of the 'fifties was closer in many of his ideas to the social-democratic wing of the Party. He worked with Peter Shore on Labour Party Committees, argued with Dick Crossman, saw Roy Jenkins and the Fabians occasionally, and admired the intellectual integrity of Gaitskell — even though Gaitskell thought him lacking in judgement. But despite these relationships, both personal and professional, Benn never actually belonged to any circle.

His popularity was as a "House of Commons man", as someone who was conscious of its traditions and historical importance and believed that the purpose of Parliament in some ways transcended party divisions. Throughout the 'fifties, he assiduously applied himself to learning how Parliament worked. He was considered a future "constitutionalist", and he joined the select committee on procedure in 1956, where he asserted the right of MPs to be consulted and informed, to criticise and examine. On the select committee, he demanded improved facilities for MPs to make the Commons a stronger and more efficient legislature; and in debate he warned: "The Parliamentary system is on trial . . . I do not think that the answer lies in trying to make the House of Commons a legislative body, only an appendage of the Executive, (for) the value of Parliament is the value of debate." Distrusting all power which was unaccountable, he criticised the remoteness and inefficiency of public authorities and he stressed the importance of better public relations.

Benn's practical experience of broadcasting and journalism led him from the first to take an interest in broadcasting policy. Even in the early days, he had a keen appreciation of the power and dangers of the media as an instrument of mass control and opinion formation. This undoubtedly contributed to his election as Chairman of the Labour Party's Advisory Committee on Broadcasting in 1957. During the 1959 General Election campaign, he was closely involved in monitoring daily progress on the campaign committee and masterminding Labour's programmes in the first-ever television election. He sought to project the image of a modern, progressive, youthful Labour Party, and his influence was evident in the style and content of the 1959 Party Political Broadcasts. He acted as linkman between well-known television interviewers and Labour politicians, using gadgets, cartoons and film on location to put over Labour's message. The public verdict on the whole was favourable, though some thought the broadcasts too slick. But if Labour did badly in the election, all agreed that the failure was due to more fundamental reasons than simply that of presentation.

After the election, Gaitskell recognised Benn's talents as a parliamentarian by appointing him front-bench spokesman on transport. He had failed to get elected to the Shadow Cabinet by only five votes. At the age of thirty-four, he was Labour's youngest shadow minister, and he knew that success or failure here would be crucial to his future prospects. Transport was an entirely new departure for Benn and he gradually began to see the area as one where a coherent alternative to Conservative domestic policy could be developed. The keynote for Labour policy, he saw, was planning — for the larger public's interest. Attacking the Conservative Government's lack of any overall transport policy, he called for massive investment in public transport, particularly the railways; and he criticised the Government's snail-like pace in implementing a road-safety programme. He deplored the extent of traffic congestion in urban areas and denounced the obscurantism and obstinacy of the Conservative Transport Minister, Ernest Marples. Before the annual Whitsun carnage, he commented: "Public holidays are established as periods of ritual slaughter . . . while even the Minotaur of Minos called for only seven men and seven maidens every nine years." His campaign helped bring about the Road Traffic and Road Improvements Bill which introduced fines for certain motoring offences and traffic wardens. Labour supported the proposals, though Benn called for more far-reaching measures, such as compulsory safety-belts and periodic testing of all vehicles, stiffer penalties for drunken drivers and better regulations governing the manufacture and maintenance of vehicles. Benn was ahead of his time in his enthusiasm for regulations of all kinds — such as a continuous radio programme on traffic congestion, monitored nationally to control the tidal flow on public holidays. He argued that public transport was superior in principle and campaigned for expanded, subsidised bus and taxi services. To him, the chaos on the roads was symptomatic of the failure to put public before private interest.

The condition of the roads could not be divorced from any other aspect of transport in Benn's mind and for this reason he was concerned that the Government retain the British Transport Commission and define its role as an instrument of planning. In a censure debate on 13 April 1959 he accused the Minister of seeking to break up and decentralise the Commission, of making profitability the criterion for transport policy and ignoring the broader economic, social and environmental factors.

The uncertainty surrounding the future of the railways strengthened the argument for planning and the identification of requirements and resources. The railways had depended upon grants and loans since 1938, and the annual interest payable on these accumulated loans was vast. Loss of profitability was mainly due to these loans and the absence of investment. If Benn urged the Government to write off their inherited, accumulated losses, he also emphasised the importance of a type of investment that increased productivity and traffic.

After visiting Stockholm and Germany in July 1960 to study road developments, Benn returned to condemn the congestion of Britain's roads as a reflection of the "problem of a technological revolution that has outdated our existing transport system". "Everyone wants planning," he asserted, calling for "a twenty year programme based on scientific study" to modernise Britain's transport system. A faith in centralisation and planning informed Benn's entire approach to transport and his conception of public ownership. Thus he opposed legislation for the administrative decentralisation and regional accounting of British railways on the grounds that public monopolies had to plan in order to meet demand and innovate.

If by the end of the 'fifties, Benn's concept of planning was still naïve, he had at least succeeded in developing his views by detailed work on a specific area of public policy. Furthermore, the transport portfolio stimulated his interest in domestic politics — an interest which was to grow in the 'sixties into a deep involvement with industrial policy. But first, there was to be the crisis of his elevation to the peerage.

III

1960-1963

THE PERSISTENT COMMONER

But for this unwanted interruption I should tip him to go to the summit of his party.

SIR WINSTON CHURCHILL

The death of his father William Wedgwood Benn, first Viscount Stansgate, on 17 November 1960 was a turning point in Tony Benn's life. His succession to the peerage meant exclusion from the House of Commons and threatened an abrupt end to a promising political career. It was an eventuality for which he had long prepared, and his father's death sparked the final phase of his ten-year struggle to remain a commoner. The battle, which lasted for three years, was one for political survival but tangentially it served to radicalise Benn and crystallised his attitude to democracy — and it made him a national figure. For many people, Benn's cause represented a wide-spread desire to modernise Britain and free it from antiquated traditions.

The peerage was an accident of history or birth, as Lord Curzon once bitterly said describing his own fate. In Benn's case it was a curse not a privilege. It dated back only to the second World War when, on 2 December 1941, Downing Street announced that Churchill was to create four Labour peerages, including that of his father, William Wedgwood Benn. "These creations are not made as political honours or rewards, but as a special measure of state policy. They are designed to strengthen the Labour Party in the Upper House, where its representation is disproportionate at a time when a coalition Government of three parties is charged with the direction of affairs."[1]

William Wedgwood Benn accepted the Viscountcy of Stansgate after consulting his eldest son, Michael, who consented, because the peerage would not interfere with his intention to take Holy Orders. However, his father recalled that "the second son (Tony Benn) was a schoolboy, rather a chatterbox, and I did not consider it necessary to consult him at all . . . I can remember when the announcement was made in *The Times* he was very angry and abused me." Benn was furious, precisely because he had not been consulted; but the tragic death of his elder brother Michael in 1944, made the existence of the peerage a much more serious problem.

From the moment Benn entered Parliament in 1950 he was determined to rid himself of this incubus. At the beginning of the 'fifties the prospects for a comprehensive reform of the House of Lords seemed reasonably good, but in 1953 the Parliamentary Labour Party rejected Churchill's offer of a bipartisan reform by a narrow majority. Though Benn for personal reasons had supported such an approach, he was, like many Labour MPs, not deeply interested in the issue, and saw an individual initiative as the best way for him to renounce the peerage.

Thus on 11 February 1953, Reginald Paget, QC, the Labour MP for Northampton, introduced the Peers Bill in the Commons on his behalf. It consisted of a short straightforward proposal to allow peers to sit in the House of Commons. The Bill stipulated : "That no persons shall exercise the privilege or suffer the disqualifications of the peerage until such a time as they have taken the oath in the House of Lords." Paget argued that it neither affected the Royal prerogative nor the hereditary principle because "no patent of nobility imposes an obligation to become a peer of Parliament", maintaining that it was a measure of justice which did not confer any additional privilege on peers. After a brief debate in which the Conservative MP, Col. Elliot, criticised the intolerable temerity of introducing constitutional legislation under the ten minute rule, the Bill was defeated by 238 votes to 145.

Having raised the issue under a ten minute Bill, Benn decided that his best hope of success lay through personal renunciation. Throughout 1954 he assiduously studied peerage law and worked on the drafting of a Personal Bill, which, as distinct from a Public Bill that had general application, would affect him alone. In December he presented The Wedgwood Benn (Renunciation) Bill to the Personal Bills Committee, whose members, named the following month, included Lord Drogheda and the Lord Chancellor, Lord Simmonds. It read: "The Bill provides that the title shall be deemed to be in abeyance for the period when the petitioner would otherwise have held it." Clement Attlee, Aneurin Bevan, Julian Amery and Jo Grimond witnessed the Instrument of Renunciation that stipulated: "I, Anthony Neil Wedgwood Benn, do hereby declare my irrevocable desire to cease to be the heir male to the home, state, degree, title and honour of the Viscount Stansgate of Stansgate in Essex."

Benn prepared his own case, having submitted evidence of letters, certificates and the consent of those affected, and presented it to the Committee on 18 February. His case rested on the distinction, which he claimed existed, between peerage cases affecting individuals and constitutional law concerned with the powers, function and composition of the Crown and Parliament. He argued that past judgements on peerage cases were not pronouncements on constitutional law, but rather individual judgements. The view that they were of constitutional interest dated from Lord Shaftesbury's ruling on the Purbeck case in 1678: "The whole kingdom has an interest in the peerage. It is a dangerous doctrine to say that such legislation is only your concern and not the interest and concern of the whole nation." In fact disqualification from the House of Lords had been a punishment for fraud in the Purbeck case, though rulings in the 19th century on the Selborne case had barred peers from the Commons. Nevertheless, Benn maintained that Parliament had thought fit to legislate and deal with peerage cases on their individual merits because of their diversity. He detailed ten categories of peerage cases that encompassed creations, attainders and their reversal, disablement for life, degradation, deprivation, termination and abeyance. The type of case was so varied that no Public Bill of surrender was possible, and consequently a Personal Bill was the only solution.

Finally, Benn made a sincere personal appeal to the Committee, as a citizen rather than as a member of Parliament: "The right of petitioning the Crown through Parliament is one of the most ancient rights open to the subject," he declared, observing that the Sumner Committee of 1927 had recommended that in cases of termination or abeyance "regard should be had to the character, fitness and position of the petitioner". He stressed the unique and unprecedented nature of his own predicament. I seek only to be allowed to continue to serve my constituents as their representative in the House of Commons. I am the first person in history who has ever offered to renounce the peerage for this reason." In support of his cause Benn presented the resolution of the Bristol City Council on 10 February, empowering the Lord Mayor and town clerk "to take all necessary action" to retain him as their MP and produced a letter from Sir Winston Churchill in 1953 expressing sympathy for his position. He protested that "a bankrupt may pay his debts, a lunatic may recover, a clergyman may renounce his holy orders; the only inherited and inescapable disqualification is that which comes to the heir of a peerage."[2]

The Committee withdrew, conferred briefly and then recalled the petitioner: "Mr. Wedgwood Benn, the Committee do not feel able to report that the objects of the Bill are proper to be enacted by a Personal Bill."

Why did his petition fail? He had set out to gain their sympathy: "I could not have brought my plea more respectfully forward than by not taking advantage of the machinery that exists in the House of Lords . . . " Lord Drogheda replied that "the whole Committee are very grateful to you for the very able, and if I may say so attractive way in which you have presented your petition." But he had not convinced them that the law permitted surrender of the peerage. Behind the legal technicalities lay the Committee's fear that Benn's Bill would undermine the hereditary principle. As Viscount Simmonds put it:

"You seek to introduce a wholly new principle by which an heir male to a peerage can surrender his peerage."

In protest, Benn's father Viscount Stansgate reintroduced the measure as a Public Bill on 17 March 1955, which the Lords debated on 26 April. The debate coincided with the delivery of a petition from the Bristol City Council which provoked a storm of criticism from Conservative peers as Viscount Stansgate rose to speak. "It is most improper to receive a political petition from the mayor and corporation of one of our cities," interjected the Earl of Saltoun. Stansgate explained how he had become a peer and the unique position of his son, and urged the acceptance of the Bill as a just, reasonable measure; he denied that it was a challenge to the House of Lords and the constitution. However, conflict with the Lords was implicit in his assertion that disqualification was a breach of parliamentary privilege and the rights of the electors. Thus the Lord Chancellor, Viscount Kilmuir, expressed the fears of the absent, silent majority of the Lords, declaring the constitution to be more important than any individual grievance. As he put it, "Liberty and freedom in our land depend on the functioning of an ordered constitution accepted throughout the land." After an hour and a half of debate the Bill was killed off, defeated by 52 votes to 24. Failure more than disappointed Benn. He felt deeply disillusioned because he had honestly believed that common sense and reason would prevail. Nevertheless, the attempt prepared the ground for the future by publicising his grievance and exposing the obstacles to its resolution. The experience had taught him that it was no good just being polite to the Establishment, and he concluded that only drastic personal action or the reform of the House of Lords could persuade the Conservative Establishment to allow him to remain in the Commons.

Yet the likelihood of a radical reform of the Lords was small, so long as it depended on the cooperation of the Conservative and Labour parties. Historically, Labour was strongly opposed to the powers of the Lords, though it had never really been interested in its reform. Its antecedents were the great campaigns of the Liberal Party in which Gladstone, Rosebery and Asquith had sought to unite the Liberals through this highly emotional cause, as they had tried to do over other issues like Home Rule, free trade and social reform. The climax of this conflict in 1911, when the Liberal Government curbed the House of Lords' powers because it had obstructed their progressive welfare legislation, was well remembered. The House of Lords held a similar position for the Labour Party. It had been a factor in bringing down Ramsay Macdonald's Government of 1929-31. When Labour returned to power in 1945, Herbert Morrison warned the Lords that obstruction of the nationalisation legislation would provoke its abolition. In the end, the Upper House cooperated, even if it opposed legislation that went beyond the manifesto. Power also tempered the radicalism of the Labour Government, which increasingly preferred legislative efficiency and stability to a battle over the House of Lords. From a position of strength, with the Conservative Party fearing a debilitating reform of the Lords, Attlee was able to conclude an historic compromise in May 1948 between the party leaders on the future of the House of Lords. The 1948 white paper, embodying the agreement, stipulated nine criteria as the basis for any reform. These were intended to create an efficient second chamber and included the separation of the principle of heredity from that of service by designating those worthy to serve as "Lords in Parliament". In retrospect the agreement was historic because it effectively ended any prospect of reform. It was an agreement of the highest common political denominator, and a victory for consensus politics, putting stability above ideology. Therefore it was short-lived, because it did not reflect the views of the majority in either political party.

On becoming Prime Minister for the second time in 1951, Churchill was the moving spirit in efforts to establish an all-party committee to work out agreed legislation for the reform of the House of Lords. His initiative was strategically aimed at strengthening the Conservative Party and the constitution by resolving this contentious issue which had threatened the stability of the constitution for almost a century. Yet not even Churchill's vision could inspire the Conservative Party to reform, and it steadfastly resisted all change; nor did it persuade Labour, which eventually rejected the offer in January 1953. Michael Foot pointed out that the 1948 agreement had never committed the Labour Party, which had always been opposed to the hereditary principle as anti-democratic and saw the final goal of the struggle between Lords and Commons as the abolition of the second chamber.

The 1948 agreement served to dampen controversy about the Lords and was in effect inimical to reform. The reality was that the House of Lords was slowly dying on its feet and a crisis brewing as the ranks of the hereditary peers swelled. Macmillan was aware of this and in 1957 took the initiative by promising legislation to introduce life peerages in the 1957-8 parliamentary session. So was Benn, who published his own scheme of reform, *The Privy Council as a Second Chamber*, as a Fabian society pamphlet in January 1957. He went back to first principles, asking whether a second chamber was needed, and if so of what type. He outlined the functions and powers of the Lords; its right to initiate legislation, and limited powers of delay; its role as a forum for debate and private members' Bills and as the supreme court of appeal. However, in practice the right to legislate was confined to non-controversial matters; and he concluded that it successfully fulfilled few of these functions, pointing to the growing pressure for reform from within the House of Lords. Indeed, there had been dozens of attempts at reform, such as that by Lord Simmonds to introduce life peers, as well as moves to admit peeresses and introduce qualifications for voting and attendance, but all of them had been frustrated.

In view of these shortcomings and the fact that "the House of Lords rests upon the creation and maintenance of the peerage," Benn felt that the Labour Party seriously ought to consider its abolition. The inherited right to legislate was intolerable to him in principle, dangerous and absurd in practice. Yet he still believed that a second chamber could be of value as a non-political institution which could help the task of government by revising, scrutinising and digesting its legislation. The Lords' proven ability to bring in worthwhile amendments, its value as a forum for general debate and an opportunity to air grievances ought to be preserved. In this connection, he felt a Labour Government that sought to carry out major social and educational reforms had greater need of one than a Conservative Government.

Benn's scheme, which involved replacing the House of Lords by the Privy Council, reflected this administrative outlook. He was attracted by the Privy Council's historic role as adviser to the Monarch since the times of the Curia Regis following the Norman Conquest, when it had united all executive, judicial and legislative powers. As it stood, the Privy Council comprised 283 members, of which 125 were peers, 77 MPs and 81 other distinguished public figures. He proposed to mobilise this dormant reserve of experience and wisdom by appointing all privy councillors to the House of Lords and excluding all peers who did not already belong to the Privy Council. Any MP who was a privy councillor would have to choose between the two Houses of Parliament so that it would become a resting-place for elder statesmen, and would release seats for younger MPs. The composition of the revamped Privy Council would be along the lines proposed in the 1948 White Paper and Councillors would receive salaries and pensions at the same level as MPs, according to their attendance. Benn argued for a reduction in the powers of delay to three months, as this would allow enough time for debate and reconsideration without obstructing the passage of legislation. However, he proposed that the House of Commons should be able to overrule amendments on the third reading by the innovation of an unopposed fourth reading. Finally, he proposed that the theoretical parity in powers between Lords and Commons over orders in council and statutory instruments should be regulated to prevent any conflict or abuse of power.

How far-reaching were Benn's proposals? They were certainly original and he believed they combined the best of both institutions. The pageant and traditions of the Lords would have remained, and he hoped for a more effective second chamber. "By applying itself constructively to a detailed examination of measures introduced by all governments and by its general debates on public affairs it can greatly enrich our parliamentary system." On reflection, Benn did not make out the pragmatic and technical case for the second chamber as well as he might have done. The Privy Council was probably less suited to the revision and scrutiny of legislation than other bodies such as local authorities, the courts, the trades unions and industrialists' lobbies which were more closely involved in the implementation of the law and were arguably better qualified to suggest improvements or comment on the practicability or desirability of legislation. Finally, such a Privy Council would not give a fresh or alternative view on legislation, being largely comprised of "elder statesmen". In this sense, *The Privy Council as a Second Chamber* was profoundly undemocratic; and it had the added defect of potentially increasing patronage. Nevertheless, Benn was perceptive in analysing the political complexities of the issue, and the theme of administrative efficiency was designed to give the Labour Party a policy for the House of Lords that commanded the support of the centre of British politics.

Labour had always been unclear about its attitude to the Lords, with the militants wanting its abolition, while leading socialist thinkers such as Sydney Webb and Laski had favoured an elected second chamber. Webb's scheme entailed the Commons electing a second chamber that reflected its own political balance. Laski had rejected an appointed second chamber on grounds of patronage, and the Fabian pamphlet, *Reform of the House of Lords*, published in 1954, reproduced this confusion in a compromise between an elected and appointed second chamber. Benn described Labour's attitude as one more of limitation than reform, and recognised that its opposition to change had in fact provoked the Conservative Government into reform. "The plain fact is that the Government's decision to change the composition of the Lords will itself destroy the basis of Labour's existing policy." Furthermore the Conservatives aimed to make the House of Lords more effective, a Conservative majority perpetual, and were ready, if need be, to prevent Labour legislation. In Benn's judgement the bipartisan consensus on the issue was a dangerous mirage: "The differences between the Conservative and Labour approaches to the problem are as wide as ever," though there was reason to believe too, "that the Government plan will recommend itself to a very large body of intelligent opinion in the country". For instance, Labour peers were likely to support a rationalisation of their own house and he feared a sinister plot to make the restoration of two year powers of delay acceptable. "For, like the Duke of Wellington, it (the Conservative Party) believes that the British constitution rests on the acceptance of Conservative principles, and it conceives of the House of Lords as guaranteeing the maintenance of that very desirable state of affairs."[3]

There was some truth in this exaggeration, for Benn correctly predicted that the Lords would be a major obstacle to social and institutional change in Britain, as indeed it proved over the hereditary peerage issue from 1960-63, and during the Labour Government of 1974-79. Benn's *Privy Council* did reveal a political awareness of the need to break fresh ground in this stale, if historic, controversy; to win back the initiative from the Government on the question and to resolve the dispute over whether to "end or mend" the House of Lords. Philosophically, it sheds much light on Benn's understanding of democracy at the time. His proposals were framed within the "universal acceptance" of the supremacy of the elected assembly, specifically rejecting the views which Lord Salisbury had expressed in the debate on the Death Penalty Abolition Bill: "Our function (is) not to oppose the will of the people, but very definitely to give a breathing-space to enable public opinion to crystallise." Benn inferred a claim to represent public opinion:

> Certainly since Edmund Burke, the idea that it was a representative rather than a delegated assembly has inspired the work of the Commons. Indeed it is essential for good government that the House should be prepared to take the long view. To claim that a House based on appointment and heredity should act as a mouthpiece for the opinions of the nation, is not only dangerous because it is untrue, but it would be very undesirable even if it were true.[4]

The effect of Benn's pamphlet on the Labour Party was negligible and if anything it discouraged the Government from seeking comprehensive reform. Fearing internal disagreement, Macmillan introduced a more limited Life Peerages Bill in November 1957; but Benn nevertheless endeavoured to influence the legislation in the Lords, where on 17 December Lord Silkin introduced an amendment to allow hereditary peers to become life peers, thus allowing heirs such as Benn to remain commoners. Not surprisingly the proposal met with hostile reaction. The Lord Chancellor, Viscount Kilmuir, said the peerage was inalienable; the Earl of Macclesfield described the amendment as "detestable" because it was a Bill to strengthen not weaken the Lords, to admit, not release distinguished members. The Silkin amendment was accordingly rejected by 75 votes to 25.

The Life Peerages Bill polarised opinion and further divided the two political parties on the reform of the House of Lords. It enabled Benn to press his own ideas more openly, and on 28 February 1958 he introduced the "Parliament Bill" as a Private Members Bill. Convinced that Labour should now advocate a more radical solution, he proposed the abolition of the hereditary right to belong to the House of Lords and the substitution of writs of attendance. The Bill enabled the House of Commons to reverse any decision taken by the House of Lords, and the Lords' power to reject statutory instruments would be removed.

The Life Peerages Act received royal assent on 30 April 1958, ending for a time controversy about and interest in the reform of the House of Lords. Benn knew that he would now have to prepare actively to fight an open democratic battle in defiance of the law, if he was to have any hope of remaining a commoner and a MP. Thus the sudden death of his father on 17 November 1960 did not find him unprepared, but it did open a new and more dramatic phase in his personal struggle. Immediately he renounced the Viscountcy of Stansgate by returning the letters patent unopened to the Lord Chamberlain, knowing that if he did not do so he would lose credibility and never mobilise support. He met with R.A. Butler, the Leader of the House, and Hugh Gaitskell who was very helpful about the possibility of forming a select committee to consider the legal arguments which would permit him to renounce his title and remain in the Commons. Though many were sympathetic to Benn, some in the Labour movement did not see how his personal case related to the Party's real concerns.

On 23 November Benn held a press conference and announced that he had returned the letters patent symbolically, describing himself as "not a reluctant peer but a persistent commoner". He detailed three new grounds in support of his claim which he hoped a select committee would examine: firstly, he had made an instrument of renunciation which, though it had been common in the past, was the first of its kind since 1678. His renunciation had raised the question of "whether a Lords resolution can decide the membership of the House of Commons"; secondly, under the Disqualification Act, 1957, an MP could refuse to accept any office that would disqualify him from the Commons; thirdly, he questioned the prerogative of the Crown to prevent a member from taking his seat in the Commons, thus overiding the privileges and supremacy of the House of Commons.

Benn argued that the Commons was able to decide upon its composition by a simple resolution as it had done during the Commonwealth period in the 17th Century. Should his case fail, the select committee could recommend legislation enabling peers to stand for the Commons, as Irish peers could. What would happen if the committee did not recommend legislation? Benn replied that he would stand repeatedly for election to the Commons, like Charles Bradlaugh, the militant atheist, who refused to swear the oath and stood for Northampton between 1880–84, and that he would do so with the goodwill of his constituency until Parliament had finally decided to accept the verdict of the electors. Nevertheless, Benn recognised that the outcome of his case was uncertain: he was asking for a precedent to be set in a field where "the spirit of innovation is not at its strongest".

The following day Benn's stand made the headlines in the national newspapers and he was amazed by the response. The boldness of his challenge provoked spontaneous expressions of support from MPs of all political parties. Randolph Churchill, for instance, amusingly suggested that he commit a nominal act of treason, such as impaling the Royal Coat of Arms, in order to be dismissed by act of attainder as a peer. Royal clemency would then allow him to stand again for election to the House of Commons.

But Benn's fate depended above all on the attitude of his local constituency party. On 26 November, he addressed a mass meeting in Bristol: "This fight is really just a small part of the struggle to bring Britain up to date. Tradition should breathe life into things that are dead, it should not breathe death into things that are alive." The General Management Committee of the Bristol South East Labour Party met on 28 November to decide their position and unanimously supported Benn's fight to remain their MP. The people who would play a key role in the success or failure of Benn's struggle were individuals of independence of mind like Herbert Rogers, a founder member of the local party and agent for seventeen years who had fought fifteen parliamentary elections. An old member of the ILP who had been greatly influenced by Marx, he joined the Fabian Society in 1915 and was also a member of the CND. Ted Bishop, a draughtsman with the British Aircraft Corporation, was a JP and a former chairman of the Finance Committee on the City Council. As a Christian Socialist, he had worked closely with the Bishop of Bristol and his industrial chaplain. Desmond Brown, secretary of the Hanham Labour Party and extremely active for his local Methodist chapel, worked at Fry's chocolate factory where he was also secretary of one of the largest branches of the TGWU. Ready to support him were Florence Berry, for years the guiding spirit in the Women's Co-operative Guild in Britain, and Councillor Bert Peglar, who despite ill health was constituency chairman and deputy leader of the Labour Group on the City Council. Finally, there was Alderman Harry Hennessy whom Benn described as "a legendary figure in the city, a real rebel with a saintly concern for his fellow men". In 1932 he had brought a deputation of the unemployed right into the Council Chamber, for which the Conservatives voted him out of his Aldermanic seat; but he was re-elected a Councillor immediately.

After the meeting, the constituency Party issued a statement arguing that two fundamental principles were involved: the right of the electors to choose its MP and the right of the MP whom it had elected to serve it in Parliament.

The following day, on 29 November, Sir Lynn Ungoed-Thomas, the Labour MP and QC, presented Benn's own petition to be read by the Clerk of the House, in which he summarised his case and asked a select committee to "grant him such other relief as it may think fit and proper". The petition outlined arguments put forward in the press conference and added that disqualification by inheritance "has never been laid down by statute, nor has it been judicially determined". However, the Home Secretary, R.A. Butler, proposed to refer it to the Committee of Privileges, agreeing that Benn's exclusion from the Commons would "raise *prima facie* questions of privilege in depriving him of his seat in the House"; but he assured George Brown that "the fact that it is going to that committee does not preclude further action on the matter". Though the House of Commons accepted the proposal without division, in reality neither Party was enthusiastic about Benn's cause and it was a case of advance by delay. The Government simply sought to avoid controversy. It feared discussion of wider reforms and hoped to settle the matter by clarifying the legal position. The Committee of Privileges set up on 17 November, comprised 14 MPs drawn from all parties under Butler's chairmanship. The Conservative members included Sir Reginald Manningham Buller, the Attorney General, while Labour was represented by Hugh Gaitskell, George Brown and Chuter Ede, the former Home Secretary, and the Liberals by Clement Davies.

The Committee summoned Benn to attend on 12 December. His legal case rested on the denial that succession to the peerage meant disqualification from the House of Commons. Though Erskine May had written that "English peers are ineligible for the House of Commons as having a seat in the Upper House", on the basis of Speaker Onslow's ruling of 1760 Benn contended that the validity of this law was very questionable. An examination of the cases in question revealed that the House of Lords had no machinery or criteria for deciding peerage cases, but had dealt with them on an ad hoc basis. However, his case was "not a question of mere law", for it involved parliamentary privilege. The 1895 select committee on the Selborne case, which concluded that a peer could not lay down his title, had avoided this issue. Benn submitted that the constitution had altered radically over the past two hundred years, quoting Gladstone's letter on the reform of the House of Lords: this would "allow any heir apparent or heir presumptive to a peerage, upon being elected to the House of Commons, to declare by option that he could sit for the Parliament and so lose the power to take up the peerage . . . "

He drew encouragement from the 1955 Lords' select committee on procedure and attendance, which ruled that the House was no longer bound by its past resolutions. "It can hardly be argued that a resolution of the House of Lords, unsupported by statute, is strong enough", he concluded, pleading his case as "overwhelming on grounds of equity and commonsense".[5]

The Committee of Privileges was concerned with clarifying the position in law rather than defining and protecting the privileges of the Commons. It exhaustively cross-examined Benn to establish that he had succeeded to the Viscountcy of Stansgate and whether this disqualified him from the Commons. As Clement Davies put it: "It is your case that the House of Commons, under the guise of privilege, can ignore the law of England." The committee went on to consider further evidence, because there existed no authoritative statement on the constitutional position of the peerage. Sir Dingle Foot, who was

Benn's legal adviser, argued that "disqualification from sitting in the House of Commons arises not from the status of a peer but from the summons to sit in the House of Lords". Though he showed that surrenders had occurred before 1642 *sub silentio* and without contest, his argument foundered on the Norfolk case of 1302, which the leading authorities interpreted as a denial of surrender. This stumbling-block largely diminished the force of the supporting evidence given by Dick Taverne, in which he cited fourteen cases of surrender between 1205 and 1426. Taverne observed that the resolution of 1642 against surrender had significantly occurred during Charles the First's Long Parliament, when the law was invoked to strengthen Lords against Commons. Unhappily G.R. Squibb, QC, then disproved twelve of the fourteen cases of surrender, and Sir Edward Fellowes, the Clerk of the House, testified that Benn had succeeded to the peerage on the death of his father and was thereby disqualified from the Commons.

After ten long hearings of abstruse legal argument, the Committee of Privileges came on 14 March 1961 to its crucial meeting to consider the Attorney General's draft report and to decide the fate of Benn's petition. There existed general agreement that the peerage could not be surrendered and that succession to it entailed a disqualification from the House of Commons, and this *was* "settled law". Justice Dodderidge had ruled on the Earl of Oxford's case in 1626 : "It is a personal dignity annexed to the posterity and fixed in the blood." The Labour members of the committee felt compelled to accept this verdict in the light of the combined authority of legal precedent and the opinion of the leading jurists. However, they consistently strove to remedy Benn's grievance by forcing a series of divisions over a number of amendments. The committee accepted an amendment recommending a joint committee with the House of Lords to investigate its reform; but rejected another one to make Benn eligible for election. R.A. Butler used his casting vote as chairman to defeat by 6 votes to 5 an amendment in favour of legislation to redress Benn's grievance.

The committee published its report of 21 March, summarising these conclusions, emphasising that the instrument of renunciation had no legal effect, and concluding that a writ of summons did not raise any question of parliamentary privilege. It recommended no legislation, on the grounds that the terms of the petition did not require an expression of view on its desirability. Benn was furious, but the findings of the committee did not deter him. He commented: "Far from being the end of the matter, it marks the beginning of a campaign of common sense, personal freedom and elementary democracy."[6] In the Commons, the Government came under immediate pressure. On 22 March, Charles Pannell, the Labour MP and Benn's staunchest ally, intervened to assert his right to speak from the bar of the House; but the speaker, Sir Harry Hylton Foster, deferred his decision until 27 March when he ruled that Benn could only be admitted to the distinguished strangers' gallery. Pannell refrained from introducing a motion to enable Benn to address the House; but he had raised an issue which would play a significant role in the Parliamentary battle to come.

On 24 March, Sir Lynn Ungoed-Thomas presented a Bill "to provide machinery whereby certain peerages may be renounced for life" and to enable former Peers to sit in the Commons if elected for a constituency. Barbara Castle, Michael Foot and Roy Jenkins and the two Liberal MP's Arthur Holt and Donald Wade also sponsored the Bill. It drew to Parliament's attention the absurdity of the situation and marked the start of the gathering of "liberal" all-party support for Benn's cause, with Conservative MPs such as Peter Kirk, Lord Lambton, Gilbert Longden and Gerald Nabarro coming out in support of it. Having committed itself to a debate on the committee's conclusions, the Government feared a revolt on what they considered to be an issue of confidence, and announced the imposition of a three line whip for the debate on 13 April. In so doing, they turned Benn's grievance into a Party political issue; and on 29 March the Shadow Cabinet decided to support Benn at a crucial juncture in the entire story. The Government were handling the matter very ineptly. The press were next to seize upon Benn's cause and then champion it unanimously. Even the Conservative *Economist,* and *The Daily Telegraph* in its leader article "Conscript Peer", demanded immediate legislation. Benn himself campaigned to maximise the public significance of the debate of 13 April by delivering to every Conservative MP on the day before a copy of the letter Churchill had sent him in 1955.

My dear Wedgwood Benn,

As I wrote to you confidentially in September 1953, I certainly feel yours is a very hard case, and I am personally strongly in favour of sons having the right to renounce irrevocably the peerage they inherit from their fathers. This would not of course prevent them from accepting another peerage, if they were offered one, later on.

Yours sincerely,

Winston S. Churchill.

On the same day, William Wilkins, the Labour MP for Bristol South and himself one of Benn's constituents, presented a petition to the Commons signed by 10,357 electors of Bristol South East protesting "that they may be unjustly denied their right of free choice in the member they have elected to represent them in the present Parliament".

When the House of Commons met on 13 April, the speaker announced that he had received a letter from Benn asking that he be allowed to address the House on the subject of the Committee of Privileges' report. Hugh Gaitskell, leader of the Opposition, then proposed the motion: "That Mr. Wedgwood Benn be admitted and heard." He added: "There is no single case in the history of the House of Commons where a member whose right to sit is in dispute and who has asked leave to address the House has been refused." Comparing Benn's case to that of Daniel O'Connell, the Irish nationalist and Charles Bradlaugh, the militant atheist, he attacked the Government for denying him the opportunity to comment on the report. Gaitskell praised his "passionate intensity" and appealed to a sense of fair play and common justice. But Butler insisted that the case was fundamentally different: "The truth is that Mr. Wedgwood Benn ceased to be a member of this House on the death of his father on 17 November 1960", and it would be contrary to legal precedent to hear him.

Butler's firm speech failed to silence opposition but instead aroused emotions of hostility and self-righteousness, and the debate soon lost all semblance of rationality. Charles Pannell tiraded against the Government's obstinacy: "Never before has the House of Commons denied a hearing to a member whose seat is in jeopardy . . . When I think of the intolerance I almost sniff and smell fire and think we are in the Reichstag." Jo Grimond, the Liberal leader, said that the issue was not really a legal one and warned that refusal to admit Benn "would do the reputation of the House no good whatever". After a stormy debate full of interruptions, the motion was defeated by 221 votes to 152. Butler was upset because he had lost the reputation of being a liberal, and describing the debate as the most disagreeable in his whole parliamentary career, proposed a Government motion, taking note of the report and recognising Benn's disqualification. He was prepared to consider an amendment to set up a joint committee with the House of Lords to examine the reform of the second chamber, but it was "not in the interests of the body politic at the present moment". Gerald Nabarro interrupted to draw Butler's attention to a "substantial volume of opinion in the Conservative Party" in favour of reforming the House of Lords. Butler replied that he was ever ready to discuss this "in an orderly manner, but would not preside over the dismantling of the constitution". Gaitskell then moved an amendment calling on the Government to introduce legislation immediately allowing the renunciation of titles. Criticising the cavalier manner in which the Home Secretary had ignored the merits of the case, he observed that Benn's request to "grant (him) such other relief as it may think fit and necessary" had been ignored. The Labour amendment was rejected by 207 votes to 143, and after three further hours of impassioned debate, the Government's motion was adopted by 204 votes to 126. The Liberals and fifteen Conservative MPs, among whom were Julian Critchley and Humphrey Berkeley, had voted with Labour.

The Government had only succeeded in alienating public opinion, and the next day the headlines in *The Daily Telegraph* read: "Angry Tory MPs defy Butler over peerages".It was now clear that there would have to be a by-election: and on 18 April, Herbert Bowden, the

Labour Chief Whip, requested a parliamentary writ for a by-election in Bristol South East. The constituency Labour Party had unanimously re-selected Benn as their candidate the previous day, and on 24 April both he and Malcolm St. Clair, the Conservative candidate who had unsuccessfully opposed him at the 1959 General Election, handed in their nomination papers.

Benn's campaign began with his adoption meeting and a press conference held on 26 April at the Transport and General Workers' Union Headquarters in the centre of Bristol. Over 200 people attended. Anthony Greenwood MP, and the Bristol MPs S.S. Awbery and W.A. Wilkins, spoke at the meeting on behalf of the Labour Party, and Peter Bessell for the Liberal Party. Malcolm Muggeridge and Lord Lambton, heir to the Earl of Durham and a Conservative MP also spoke. Lambton was warmly congratulated for appearing on the same platform as a political opponent, and though he could not think of a single issue on which he had ever agreed with Benn, felt this to be a constitutional issue that transcended party loyalties. Benn thanked Lambton for his "enormous courage": "I give him this pledge — on the unhappy day his father dies, I will speak for him in his constituency if he decides to stand again." He began by echoing Lambton's remarks. The Government's action had necessitated a by-election "which in my view is unnecessary".

> Should a man have the choice between going unwillingly to the House of Lords to sit as a hereditary peer, or of continuing to serve as an elected member of the Commons in response to the demands of his constituents? . . . What the Government have done by their action is to turn this issue into one between the House of Lords and the people of Bristol. . . It is given to Bristol in this election to wrench the Parliamentary system away from its feudal origins and pitchfork it kicking and screaming into the twentieth century. . . . I have accepted this invitation because I feel that an MP is the servant of his constituents. To allow this issue to be settled without Bristol being consulted would be a betrayal of those people who have sent me four times to Parliament. I am asking the Party to take a risk, and I am taking a tremendous risk myself.[7]

As in all by-elections, the problem was how to create and sustain public interest and an issue as narrow as the peerage only made it more difficult. Yet it was, in Gaitskell's words "a very unusual by-election".

The two-week Bristol campaign was unconventional, and its theme, "the new generation", symbolised the wider issues that Benn summarised in his declaration of campaign principles:

> To take this personal and constitutional absurdity as a symbol of a deeper malaise in Britain today: namely our failure to adapt ourselves to modern life; our fear of the future and our need to mobilise all our national resources. . . . To encourage public discussion of areas of policy which have been held to be outside the usual range of political controversy and to make the public aware of its responsibilities in these fields . . .[8]

The Bristol petition, the 10,000 copies of Churchill's 1955 letter which Benn circulated in the constituency, and the daily newsheet *The Bristol Campaigner,* all helped create public interest. At Bristol University Union, Benn debated the motion "That hereditary peerages — like so much in Britain — are out of date". Speakers came to Bristol from all over the country to support Benn and explain how they thought Britain must be modernised. Mainly they were Labour politicians, like Michael Foot, who spoke on the reform of Parliament, Harold Wilson on a four-year plan for Britain, Richard Crossman on the future of the Left. The campaign also commanded all-party support, and academics, churchmen, educationalists and scientists came to speak. Benn described the campaign in *Tribune*:

> A number of new campaign techniques were tested out. The meetings were run like a sort of summer school and the speakers who came down were asked to use our platform to get across some of the fundamental things that have got to be done in Britain. Professor Blackett spoke about the scientific revolution, James Cameron about the press and John Horner about the future of the trades unions. We held an architectural exhibition on town planning in our headquarters and took some exhibits around to our meetings. Afterwards we held seminars for young people from all over the city so that they could come and talk into the small hours with the speakers whom they had heard earlier.[9]

The local and national press gave Benn every support, with *The Guardian* declaring on 24 April that it would be a national disaster if he were not re-elected. Messages of encouragement poured in from people of differing persuasions, in response to Benn's appeal. Lady Violet Bonham-Carter, Mervyn Stockwood, Bishop of Southwark, and Frank Cousins were only a few among many. Hugh Gaitskell, leader of the Opposition, gave the full support of the Labour Party:

> ... The fact that you have been obliged to emphasise the constitutional issue in your campaign must not be allowed to obscure the wider political issues which are also involved. As Labour candidate you are fighting against out-of-date, stick-in-the-mud attitudes everywhere. You are attacking a Government which accepts complacently that Britain's economic development must lag behind that of almost every other industrial nation in the world.[10]

There was support also from the academic, artistic and scientific communities. Lindsay Anderson, Professor A.J. Ayer, Cecil Day Lewis, Augustus John, Sir Compton Mackenzie, Wolf Mankowitz, John Osborne, Raymond Williams, Sir Charles Snow, Graham Sutherland, Kenneth Tynan, Vicky, Arnold Wesker and many other public figures sent messages of encouragement. The historian Arnold Toynbee declared: "A compulsory hereditary disqualification is a lingering relic of serfdom and this ought to be abolished as a matter of principle. . . . Our country is a living community not a historical museum."[11]

Perhaps Richard Clements, editor of *Tribune,* grasped the socialist significance of Benn's stand best of all:

Your fight in Bristol is the fight of all true radicals in this country against the mealy-mouthed Establishmentarians who try to turn every issue about which people argue into the trivia of gossip and personalities. I am quite convinced that more and more young people reject the current idea of the popular press which tries to debase the real meaning of political discussion and argument . . .[12]

The Conservative campaign was by contrast highly ambiguous and negative. Malcolm St. Clair stated his own position following his adoption on 18 April. "Should Lord Stansgate be nominated . . . I shall give formal notice to the electorate during the by-election campaign that he is a disqualified person and that any votes for him will be votes thrown away." If nevertheless Lord Stansgate won, "I would then present an election seeking my return as the legitimate member." In his address to the constituents, St. Clair wrote that he was not concerned with "the rights and wrongs of Lord Stansgate's case", but that he intended to fight the election "on the issues of the Government's record of achievement and courage, and the unfitness of the disunited Labour Party to assume control of the country's affairs".[13] In fact the "don't waste your vote" theme was the hallmark of the Conservative campaign. St. Clair issued a petition to the electors published as a notice in the local press, which asserted that his "duty as I conceive it (is) to inform the electors of your disqualification and that votes for you will be votes thrown away". Benn took the advice of counsel and was unperturbed: "It is not for Mr. St. Clair to determine whether I am disqualified or not. If I am elected, and if Mr. St. Clair presents an election petition, it will be for the election court to decide this question."

The Labour campaign overwhelmed and neutralised the Conservative one. Butler received a hostile reception in Bristol and after his visit, Conservative Central Office gave the by-election no publicity and belittled its significance. The Prime Minister, Harold Macmillan, sent Malcolm St. Clair a message of support, and in it dismissed the Bristol South East by-election with disdain. "Since Mr. Wedgwood Benn became Viscount Stansgate last November, he has been disqualified from sitting in the House of Commons; that is the law and this by-election cannot change it." The Labour Party had repeatedly rejected offers to discuss the reform of the House of Lords, thereby throwing away "the chance to make these changes in the law for which they are clamouring in this by-election". Macmillan added: "Our hope is that this time all parties will cooperate in producing proposals which will maintain the efficiency of the House of Lords under modern conditions."[14]

Then, on 26 April, the Government announced that it would set up a joint committee with the House of Lords to review its composition, the law relating to the peerage, including the right of surrender, and the introduction of remuneration for peers. In the Commons, Butler justified the move as a recognition of anomalies and the need for a broad inquiry, which his speech on 13 April had foreshadowed. Gaitskell welcomed the initiative and paid tribute to Benn's single-mindedness: "I believe that, as far as it goes, this step constitutes a victory for Benn," he said, demanding wider inquiry to consider the further limitation of the Lords' powers of delay. Lord Hailsham simultaneously announced the decision in the Lords in more forceful terms. "Though not indifferent to the electors of Bristol, there is no doubt in the Government's mind as to the need to maintain an efficient second chamber."

The timing of this announcement could have been interpreted as an attempt to undermine Benn's campaign. But that was not its effect. On 1 May, *The Daily Telegraph* published the results of a Gallup Poll, showing that 69% of those asked thought that Benn should be allowed to remain an MP. The final evening rally on 3 May took place at an open air meeting in St. Georges Park Bristol, where George Brown also spoke. Then on 4 May Benn was decisively vindicated at the polls, receiving 23,275 votes to 10,231, more than doubling his majority of 5827 at the 1959 general election to 13,044. Commentators estimated that the majority would have been 2000 greater had it not been for incessant rain on polling day, which discouraged electors from voting. Others attributed 3000 of his majority to Conservative votes, and as many again from the Liberals.

The celebrations after the Count in Bristol, where over 2000 people, the press and television cameras were gathered, was an occasion Benn would never forget. The election agent, Herbert Rogers, emphasised the achievement in his report:

The by-election was unique: there has not been one before which has created greater general interest in all parts of the country as the one of South East Bristol. Our candidate has been referred to as a human dynamo; a more apt description would have been a power station. He was always on the ball. His energy and enthusiasm were untiring and became contagious as the campaign progressed. He would address bus queues at 6 am, and attend works canteens at 8 am, press conferences at 11 am, and spend his afternoons with a loudspeaker and canvassing. After the evening meeting he would be found with other evening speakers at the Hotel with groups of 30 to 40 young persons discussing politics. Tony Benn proved to be the type of candidate any constituency should be proud to have.[15]

Yet once again the law was invoked to overturn the popular verdict, and in such a way as to make Benn's future entirely uncertain, by sending the issue back to the courts and the committees of Parliament. Malcolm St. Clair refused to admit defeat, and on 4 May issued a writ of alleged libel against Benn and his election agent for an advertisement in the *Bristol Evening Post* which had questioned the legality of St. Clair's petition to the electors regarding Benn's disqualification. After a bitter exchange and a visit to Conservative Central Office on 5 May, St. Clair came "to the conclusion that it is my clear duty to petition the court of the Queen's Bench to declare that Viscount Stansgate is incapable of sitting in the House of Commons, that he has not been duly elected", and that he, St. Clair, ought to have been returned as Member of Parliament for the constituency.[16]

The prospect of an election tribunal in no way dampened Benn's spirits. On 5 May he told his constituency that he would "go from this city armed with the authority you, the electors, have given me and present myself at the House of Commons to take my seat as your representative". Accompanied by his wife, his eldest son, Herbert Bowden and W.A. Wilkins, Benn made his way to the House of Commons on 8 May in expectation of a triumphant return. Yet on arrival he found his path barred. As Herbert Bowden reported the incident: "I have a certificate here which returns me as the member for Bristol South East", Benn declared. "You cannot enter, Sir", replied Victor Stockley, the principal doorkeeper. "On whose instructions?" "By Mr. Speaker's, Sir." "Are you instructed to prevent me entering by physical force if necessary?" "I am, Sir."[17] Indignant, Benn wrote immediately to the Speaker complaining of his treatment, and went to the Strangers' Gallery from where he heard the House debate the Opposition motion "that he be admitted and heard". Before Gaitskell spoke, the Speaker announced: "I have been informed . . . that Mr. Wedgwood Benn this day desires to take his seat", and read out his letter:

> Dear Mr. Speaker — on Friday last (5 May), in Bristol, the Returning Officer made a statutory declaration that I have been duly elected to represent the constituency of Bristol South East in the present Parliament. Just after prayers this afternoon, on my way to the Bar of the House, I was stopped at the door and informed that you, Mr. Speaker, had given instructions that physical force should if necessary be used to prevent me entering. As a duly elected Member of Parliament I request you to countermand that order, for which I can find no parallel in parliamentary history. I ask to be heard at the Bar as to why I should not be permitted to take the oath, following my election by an overwhelming majority of the people of Bristol South East, whose servant I am.

The Speaker insisted that the decision was not his, but rested with the House.

Gaitskell protested, introducing the motion in a forthright manner. The case for admitting Benn rested on popular verdict and was overwhelming. "The Government know very well that they are in an impossible position on this matter. They are defending the indefensible by arguments which, when not obscure, are obscurantist." In the face of this attack Butler simply reiterated the Government's position, that the law had disqualified Benn, that under a resolution of 1868 he could not even address the House on his right to speak there; but he did not deny the justice of Benn's grievance and promised that he was "ever ready to discuss the reform of the House of Lords". The Liberal leader, Jo Grimond, understood why the Government did not want to admit a peer to speak in the Commons. Yet he believed its attitude seemed nonsensical to the general public. Describing himself as a progressive Conservative, William Yates warned them "they are making a big mistake in this matter with the younger generation . . . The people of this country respect heredity and tradition, but also they expect a man to be able to, plead his case.".

The Opposition motion was defeated by 259 votes to 162 and it was the Home Secretary's turn to defend the Government's motion excluding Benn. Butler insisted that Benn was not being victimised but argued that it was essential to uphold the rule of law and preserve the status quo until the election court had reported. He added that there could be no legislation until the Joint Committee had completed an examination of the peerage, which embraced an almost infinite number of possibilities. George, Brown considered this wholly inadequate, and he scorned the decision to exclude Benn in face of what was the truly historic decision of the Bristol South East constituency. At the same time Brown recognised that the popular verdict was not enough: "The Government will be drawn in this issue and only be brought to the point of making a change in the law by a consistent, deliberate and sustained challenge at every point in the proceedings."

After a long debate in which successive Conservative speakers developed legal arguments for exclusion, and sympathisers of Benn ridiculed the absurdity of the situation, the Government's motion was carried by 259 votes to 162. "How democratic really is the House of Commons?", asked the former Labour Attorney General, Sir Frank Soskice, during the debate. Benn was appalled by this denial of the popular will, and on the same day released to the press the text of the speech which he would have made had he been allowed to address the Commons. It was a passionate speech that marked his total repudiation of parliamentary sovereignty in favour of popular democracy:

I am here to claim my seat as Member of Parliament for Bristol South East. My sole authority for doing so is that the electors of that constituency have decisively chosen me to represent them . . . We, who are members of the House of Commons, do not sit here by the whim of the Crown or by courtesy of the Lords. We do not come here by the discretion of Mr. Speaker, or even by consent of the House — and least of all by virtue of any personal merit. We sit here because we have been elected by our constituents and for no other reason whatsoever . . .

It should therefore be clearly understood that the issue is a simple one: Are the people of Bristol South East to have the right to choose their own member, or is this right to be usurped by the Government of the day using its parliamentary majority under the discipline of the Whips? No other issue arises. In its report the Committee (of Privileges) saw fit to make no reference whatever to the rights of my constituents and contented itself with a microscopic study of medieval customs. I come not as a supplicant for special favours but as the servant of those whose will must be sovereign. What happens to me matters not at all. But their right of free choice is of tremendous constitutional importance and it is my clear duty to defend it whatever the consequences for me may be. My opponent has declared his intention to petition the Election Court to claim the seat. If he succeeds and is seated here it will make a mockery of parliamentary democracy and all it stands for. For my part I would rather be disqualified for life than sit and vote here in flat contradiction to the expressed will of those whom one is intended to represent.

The manifest absurdity of hereditary disqualification is widely recognised and overwhelmingly rejected. To enforce it today against the wishes of the electors will inevitably bring British parliamentary government into disrepute . . .

The only obstacles to action are customs and prejudices which stemmed from circumstances that have long since changed. It is true that to set them aside would be to create a precedent. But the history of Parliament is the history of precedent wisely created to meet new conditions.

The great glory of this House is its record of the defence of freedom against all who have sought to undermine it. In the world of today political freedom is still so rare a thing that it is not to be lightly set aside, but rather should be especially cherished.[18]

The events of 8 May abruptly halted Benn's triumphal return to Parliament as a hero of democracy. The same day, Malcolm St. Clair, together with one of his electors, presented a petition for an election court to establish who was legally the MP for South East Bristol. Benn, who was convinced that he would win, decided to conduct his own defence, not least because of the cost of employing barristers. Together with Michael Zander, later well-known as a law reformer but at the time a friend who was qualifying as a solicitor, he worked resolutely to master the complexities of peerage law. The election hearing took place between 10 and 28 July at the Royal Courts of Justice on the Strand in the presence of Justices Gorman and McNair. Benn arrived with his family who helped him carry in ninety-one volumes of legal documents for what was billed as the case of the century. The public gallery was constantly full and the court's proceedings made the national press headlines immediately.

Benn's presentation, which was 125,000 words long and lasted in total some twenty-three hours, was generally regarded as formidable. Sir Andrew Clark, on behalf of Malcolm St. Clair, went to great lengths to prove that Benn had succeeded to the Viscountcy of Stansgate. Benn did not deny that this was the case, but argued that only a writ of summons, not succession, could disqualify a peer from the House of Commons. He strove to prove that the incompatibility of the two Houses had only arisen as a result of physical impossibility and political undesirability. Previously a writ of summons had been essential to membership of the House of Lords. Quoting Sir Edward Coke's *Institutes,* that "whosoever is not a Lord of Parliament is of the House of Commons either in person or by representation", he cited the authority of Halsbury, who commented on the Bedford Borough case of 1833: "The writ of summons to the House of Lords must be issued before the disqualification attaches." Thus Benn concluded that until he claimed the Viscountcy of Stansgate it lay dormant, like "a sleeping beauty only to be awakened by the Lord Chancellor with a writ of summons". Even today, Irish and Scottish peers could be elected to sit in the House of Commons.

The court praised the "magnificent way" in which Benn had conducted his case but ruled that succession to the peerage was in itself a disqualification from the House of Commons. They explained that their decision was based on the authority of leading jurists and recent precedent, in particular Lord Birkenhead's ruling on the Rhondda case in 1933 that a title "imposed a liability to receive and act upon it" (the writ of summons). Yet they were forced to admit that these judgements were based on the view that "the hereditary principle is still firmly embodied in the constitution".

On 31 July the Speaker declared Malcolm St. Clair duly elected. The announcement was greeted by shouts of "humiliating and intolerable" from George Brown, and "utterly ridiculous and indefensible" from Sydney Silverman. Labour MPs present left the Chamber in protest as Malcolm St. Clair took his seat. The Government held that the case had been settled and a motion to debate and amend the ruling was defeated by 235 votes to 145. Privately Benn felt close to despair at the outcome; yet his belief in the justice of his cause had been reinforced. Understandably bitter, he said that the election court had revealed "the fundamentally un-democratic character of the law", but that its effect would be to precipitate a change in the law. It had shown that the House of Lords was "still more important than the House of Commons", that the democratic right of electors to choose their own member was only legal "so long as it did not endanger the hereditary system", and that the electors of Bristol South East "must be punished for trying to challenge the hereditary system by having a man they rejected". To add injury to insult, the election court had ordered him to pay the costs of the petition, amounting to £8000. Benn's supporters did not desert him in his hour of need, but launched an appeal on 29 July which successfully raised the sum. Attlee, Grimond, the Revd. Mervyn Stockwood, Lady Violet Bonham-Carter, Sir Harold Nicholson, Augustus John and Sir Compton Mackenzie supported the appeal and Churchill contributed. Dr. J. Bronowski wrote a covering letter: "We feel that Mr. Wedgwood Benn's fight raises issues of such importance, and so clearly concerns all those who believe in democracy, that it would be unjust for him to bear personally the great expenses involved."[19]

The continued pressure of public opinion weakened Malcolm St. Clair's resolve, and on 14 August he announced that he was prepared to resign as MP, provided Benn gave an undertaking not to stand again for the constituency unless he became legally qualified to do so. Though aware that he did not represent the majority, he felt it his paramount duty to ensure that the constituency was not disenfranchised by Benn in the future. Defiant and scornful, Benn issued a statement the same day refusing to give the required understanding:

> I can well understand Mr. St. Clair's embarrassment at the position he now finds himself in. Following his defeat at the by-election, he deliberately chose to get into Parliament by means of an election petition. It has now been explained to him that an MP ought to be elected by a majority vote — the very point on which the Bristol election was fought. He now asks me to solve his problems for him by abandoning the whole campaign so that he can withdraw from the difficulties into which the Government have led him. But it is not for Mr. St. Clair or the Conservative Party to decide who the Labour candidate at the next election in Bristol shall be or not be. To ask for that is to add fresh absurdity to the present law. Mr. St. Clair's duty is perfectly clear: he should seek an immediate public pledge from the Government that the law will be changed, and when it has been changed he should resign immediately. This is the honourable course open to him.[20]

The following day Malcolm St. Clair told a press conference that he would not resign. The prospect of any change in the peerage law now seemed very remote and Benn felt pessimistic. The effect of the election court ruling had been to make the Parliamentary Labour Party reject cooperation with the Government in an all-party Joint Committee concerning the reform of the peerage law, and it was now uncertain whether it would be formed. Silence was broken on 30 November 1961 when Iain Macleod told Jeremy Thorpe that the Government still intended to form a Joint Committee even if the Labour Party refused to participate. Discussion soon took place between Macleod, Gaitskell and Grimond, and on 31 January 1962 the PLP reversed its previous decision and agreed to take part. The agreement was a breakthrough in that it separated the reform of the peerage law from the more controversial issue of the Lords, making the former possible.

On 28 March 1962, Iain Macleod proposed a motion empowering the Committee to formulate its own terms of reference. The House welcomed and passed it without division, after a generally harmonious debate. The only dissenting voice was Michael Foot's, who raised the spectre of new forms of corrosive patronage; while a few Labour MPs renewed their call for a further reduction of the House of Lords' powers. The Lords debated the proposal on 10 April. Any fears that they would refuse to cooperate at the last moment evaporated after Lord Hailsham had spoken, and in a magnificent apologia for the House of Lords, succeeded in dominating the debate. "It is only the superficial," he began, "who would mock at the medieval framework of our institutions." The authority, stability and independence of the English monarchy and institutions had given the country a unique balance of freedom and order. When constitutions failed "the fall has been due to the inveterate defect of government by discussion". Echoing Hailsham, Lord Salisbury said that the House of Lords must be independent to be respected and argued that the public image of the House of Lords as reactionary was false. Some Conservative peers feared that reform might precipitate the extinction of the hereditary peerage, but Labour peers welcomed the motion, though calling for wider terms of reference.

The composition of the Joint Committee was soon announced, consisting of twenty-two members drawn equally from both Houses in proportion to the relative strength of the political parties in the Commons. The Conservatives included Edward du Cann, Viscount Kilmuir and Lord Salisbury, and the Labour members Patrick Gordon Walker, Charles Pannell, Lords Hillsborough, Morrison and Silkin. The Joint Committee faced a formidable task in finding agreement over its terms of reference, let alone changes in the peerage law or the reform of the House of Lords. It first considered the possibility of a radical reform making the Lords elective by a college of peers, but rejected the idea. Only on 27 July, when the Joint Committee published its interim report did it define the scope of its work, agreeing in principle to the surrender of peerages. However, it was still deeply divided over the terms of surrender. The controversy over whether the title or the writ of summons caused disqualification was much debated; and in this connection the Committee exhaustively discussed the position of the Irish and Scottish peers who were excluded from the House of Lords by the Acts of Union.. In the Committee, Conservatives defeated the motion to allow the extinguishing of peerages by 12 votes to 6, and they were opposed to surrender for life or in favour of another person because the peerage might then become instantly convertible, and its position in the constitution undermined.

On 5 December 1962 the Joint Committee published its final report, recommending legislation to enable peerages to be surrendered for life and become dormant, on execution of an instrument of renunciation. It proposed strict time limits for surrender and a prohibition on the subsequent use of other courtesy titles after renunciation in order to protect the principle of the hereditary peerage. It also suggested that Scottish peers should become members of the House of Lords in order to strengthen the Upper House.

For Benn these concrete, if narrow, proposals were a turning-point and were widely regarded as a vindication of his long campaign. *The Times* commented that "not only would Lord Stansgate have a chance of re-appearing in the Commons", but so would Lord Sandwich who, as the former Viscount Hinchingbrooke, had been a Conservative MP; as well as Lords Hailsham and Home, either of whom might "be considered as a potential leader of the Conservative Party". Benn understandably felt elated by this development and promised that he would be "queuing up with my thermos the moment the doors are open" and "taking up a camp-bed outside the Lord Chancellor's office". It was "a victory for commonsense" and "an immensely powerful endorsement of the nine-year Bristol campaign", but the recommendations did not command overwhelming support. The Earl of Sandwich, for one wanted to renounce his peerage and retain his courtesy title, and condemned the report as "partial and inadequate", describing it as "unnecessarily republican in character". The fact that Irish peers could retain their titles and stand for the House of Commons proved, he said, that the report had been "tailor-made to the needs of Mr. Wedgwood Benn".

Benn's euphoria soon passed as it became clear that the reform of the peerage law was very low on the Government's legislative priorities. In their desire to appear a progressive administration, the Conservatives had only succeeded in bringing about a parliamentary log-jam, and legislation on the peerage question seemed unlikely until 1964. The Government had still to agree on the provisions of the Bill, which politically would be interpreted as a further retreat in the wake of three major setbacks: De Gaulle's refusal to allow Britain to join the EEC; the Profumo affair; and the rising rate of unemployment throughout the winter of 1962–63, following Selwyn Lloyd's deflationary measures of 1962. At the end of January 1963, the Liberal MP Donald Wade demanded a debate on the Joint Committee's report, which eventually took place on 28 March, when Iain Macleod announced the Government's intention to legislate. He envisaged a short Bill and hoped for the minimum of conflict over the principle of surrender, its terms and the loss of courtesy titles. Michael Foot praised Benn's diligence, energy and imagination. But many Labour MPs, especially George Brown, complained that it was more a Wedgwood Benn "enabling Bill" and that the reform of the House of Lords had been totally avoided. Charles Pannell also criticised the proposals as no more than "a little pruning measure", but argued that it was more than a victory for Benn. In his experience "the narrower the issue, the sharper the weapon, and the earlier one is likely to get reform".

The Lord Chancellor, Lord Dilhorne, put the Government's proposals simultaneously to the Lords, who in general accepted the surrender of peerages as a rationalisation of the law, but denied that there was any need for drastic reform. The obstacles to translating a declaration of intent into law remained great, and tension continued to the last moment. At the nadir of its fortunes, the unity of the Conservative Party was a façade and many feared that the surrender of hereditary peerages was the first step to the abolition of the House of Lords. The situation was further complicated by uncertainty about the future leadership of the Conservative Party and the fact that some candidates for the succession were peers. After a run of Conservative policy failures, it was possible that Labour would refuse to cooperate and exploit the weakness to maximum political advantage. These were the unspoken reasons behind Macleod's statement that legislation was unlikely in the present session, when Harold Wilson asked him on 2 May how soon the Government would introduce a Bill. By 9 May continued pressure had forced Macleod to promise legislation, and on 15 May he announced the parliamentary timetable.

The Peerage Bill was published on 30 May and enacted on 31 July 1963. This sudden climax to Benn's long struggle consisted of a short Bill of seven clauses that almost totally embodied the recommendations of the Joint Committee. Renunciation of the peerage would be termed a "disclaimer" for legal reasons and not to offend the hereditary principle. The Bill received an unopposed second reading in both Houses of Parliament, though with several attempts at amendment. In the Commons, Lady Megan Lloyd-George and Donald Wade failed to alter "surrender" to "extinction", and the Commons rejected Patrick Gordon Walker's move to make the Bill take effect on Royal assent. Macleod denied that any "political considerations came into the drafting of this Bill" which excluded Benn until after the next General Election.

The Lords were concerned with the question of titles, the continued anomaly in the position of Irish peers; they pushed through amendments to standardise the time limits on renunciation and to make the Bill take effect on enactment. Despite newspaper headlines of "peers in revolt", the Lords wisely understood that it was better finally to resolve the issue and rejected the Government's argument that it was a major constitutional change which ought only to be introduced at the following general election. The Government persisted, but the coalition of Salisbury, Silkin and Swinton courageously stuck out, perhaps influenced by the knowledge of an impending Conservative leadership crisis, and forced the Bill's acceptance and immediate enactment.

Over four hundred constituents and supporters of Benn's campaign came to the victory party at the House of Commons on 29 July. "It was wonderful to see them pouring through the entrance that leads to the Commons as if they owned the place — for of course they do", he wrote in *Tribune*, and added "10,000 ordinary men and women living in a very ordinary constituency have defeated Macmillan, the Cabinet and the Courts to change the constitution."

On 31 July the Peerage Bill became law, Malcolm St. Clair resigned his seat and within five minutes Benn was the first person to have renounced his title. As the press described it:

> Immediately the words "La Reyne le veult" were pronounced in the House of Lords, signifying Royal assent, Mr. Benn left the gallery as if a starting-pistol had been fired. Accompanied by his wife and his mother, Lady Stansgate, he hurried downstairs and handed to Sir George Coldstream, Clerk to the Crown in Chancery, an instrument of disclaimer renouncing for himself the Stansgate peerage. A press conference was then held at which he declared himself statutorily immunised — the first man in history to be prevented by Act of Parliament from receiving a hereditary peerage".[21]

The ensuing by-election at Bristol South East was more a celebration of the triumph of popular will than a party contest. A writ for an election was issued on 2 August, and on 20 August, Benn was returned by a majority of 15,479, receiving 20,373 votes against 4,834 for his leading opponent Edward Martell of the National Fellowship. He returned to Parliament a changed and and much politicised man. As he described the experience:

> Like a little test-card going through a computer system, it tested the House of Commons and its Committees, the House of Lords and its Committees, the Crown in so far as it was involved, the press, local government, the Labour Party, the Conference, the Constituency . . . It was a most extraordinary way of learning how the British Constitution worked and where power resided, and I learned a lot of things that shocked me very much, particularly the ideas of those who ran Parliamentary government — I learned that they were not particularly democratic at all.[22]

Before 1960 he had believed in parliamentary democracy as an ideal and a reality. He saw a body of representatives ruling in the interests of the people. By 1963, the bitter experience of the peerage episode had taught him that Parliament did not necessarily reflect the interests or opinions of the people.

The successful outcome of his ten-year campaign to remain a commoner had been in the last resort, due to the consistent, unswerving loyalty and support of his constituency. It was a victory from below and it showed that reform only came about through the public bringing unceasing pressure to bear on Parliament. It drove Benn to the conclusion that parliamentary democracy and the rule of law were empty phrases unless rooted in popular democracy, and that Parliament was either an instrument of the popular will or it was nothing. Success had also reinforced his optimism about and belief in the historic mission of Parliament as the instrument through which the British people would achieve self-government and participatory democracy. Benn had been radicalised by practice.

The Peerage Act was soon to acquire an unexpected relevance following the collapse and resignation of Macmillan in October 1963, in that it enabled both Lords Hailsham and Home to be considered for the leadership of the Conservative Party and for Prime Minister. As Macmillan acknowledged:

> Had the Government's proposal . . . that the new system should only come into force at the dissolution of the present Parliament, been acceptable to the House of Lords . . . all our troubles would have been avoided. Neither Lord Hailsham nor Lord Home could in practice have ever been considered for the premiership. Butler must have succeeded, almost without challenge. Out of such slender threads are woven the fortunes of states and men.[23]

Macmillan's departure coincided with Benn's return, and on 24 October, Parliament reassembled to debate the postponement of the new parliamentary session which the upheaval had caused. For Benn, it was almost the occasion for a second maiden speech, as he paid "tribute to my constituents without whose loyalty I would not be in this House today". The issue of the premiership and its succession was much more than a procedural question. Benn saw "something much more fundamental — the imbalance which has entered the relationship between the Crown and its prerogatives and the other place (the Lords) and this House, not just in this respect, but over a period which stretches much further back".

He brought three charges against the Government: first, "that they have consistently attempted to use the prerogative of the Crown . . . for their own party purposes"; second, "they have always in every one of these issues sought to maintain the hereditary privileges of the House of Lords at all costs"; third, "in the process they have seen this House — and allowed it to be — demeaned and denigrated, so that in consequence we now cannot meet to discuss the urgent affairs of the state". The contempt for the elected chamber appalled him:

> I am afraid that the new Prime Minister has got it exactly the wrong way round. He thinks that Parliament cannot act without a Prime Minister, but our constitution says that a Prime Minister has no authority without the House of Commons. I do not believe that this debate is a dry, procedural wrangle, or merely a Party demonstration. I believe that it bears on the character and purpose of this House. There are people outside the House who look upon us as the instrument of change, who see the only hope of realising their dreams is for this country to have a modern, effective, lively, vital Parliament, . . . an instrument by which they can participate in the future of their own country.[24]

His speech was "not an attack upon tradition, for tradition is not the Beefeaters and Mr. Speaker's wig and silver buckles. The true tradition of this country is the ingenuity of its people, the creativeness, the inventiveness, the innovating skill of the people represented at the best periods in our history by the same sort of leadership given in this House." "Few speakers could have been more controversial than that to which we have listened," commented Sir Spencer Summers, the Conservative MP. The sentiments it expressed were rooted in the traditions of radicalism and dissent, and foreshadowed Benn's future advocacy of popular democracy. The peerage episode had radicalised him, making him identify with the growing demands for modernisation and social change in Britain. In looking back on the struggle to remain a commoner, Benn reflected:

> It taught me more about the British Establishment and how it really works and how to defeat it than any other episode in my life. . . . This battle and the victory we won taught me lessons about the British class system, the role of the courts and the countervailing power of the people if aroused, that I shall never forget. Unusually, it gave me, who had never experienced any hardship in life just enough of a taste of what happens when authority decides to crush a dissident. From that moment on, both as an MP and as a minister, I saw through completely new eyes and understood the experience of all those who really suffered from far more serious abuses directed against them by those enjoying authority deriving from wealth or status or power. It was a very strange way to learn a basic lesson, but everyone learns best from his own experience.[25]

TONY BENN

IV
1963–1966
THE NEW BRITAIN

There will be a great awakening in the forthcoming big push when huge
task forces of rough young new frontiersmen will be moving in to blast a hole
in Britain's cotton wool complacency.
CHRISTOPHER BOOKER.

The peerage episode brought Tony Benn from the radical fringe of
the Labour Party into its mainstream and to the centre of political
affairs. His struggle to remain a commoner had reflected the
aspirations of a new generation, their demands for modernisation
and reform which swept Britain during the early 1960s. Their dream
of a classless, dynamic and scientific society echoed his. Perhaps more
than any other politician, he embodied the spirit of the times, of
progress and rebellion against authority, of a new Britain "forged in
the white heat of a technological revolution".
   The change in Benn's political interests from the 'fifties to the
'sixties is immediately striking. A shift in focus had occurred away
from issues of civil liberty and internationalism towards questions of
economic and industrial policy. On closer examination, however, the
continuities are as apparent as the contradictions. The fascination
with technological progress that was so noticeable a theme of his
politics during the 1960s was a direct result of the peerage battle
which had convinced him that Britain must bring itself up to date.

   The years in the political wilderness between 1960–63 had not been
barren ones for Benn. They had given him an opportunity to read,
think and travel. He had managed to earn a living as a broadcaster
and journalist and in 1963, had lectured nation-wide to various
organisations that booked speakers through Foyle's agency. During
these years he had also made three lecture tours of the United States,
speaking at universities and luncheon clubs and visiting Washington
for political discussions. He attended the Goa Conference in Delhi,
the Anglo-German Conference at Königswinter on polycentrism and
coexistence; and visited Berlin where in April 1962 he met Willy
Brandt. In December 1962 he took part in a symposium on
Arab-Jewish relations in Jerusalem and met the philosopher Martin

Buber, before returning through Poland in January for a conference on Anglo-Polish relations which explored the possibility of an east-west dialogue on European politics.

Benn's thinking on foreign affairs during these years was a direct development of the views he first formulated in the early 1950s. Addressing the Anglo-Israel Association in 1963, he prophetically warned that "the whole conception in the Arab mind of the establishment of a Jewish National Home in Palestine, of the establishment and creation of a State of Israel is to the majority of Arabs wholly repugnant". A passionate believer in Israel's right to existence, he argued that Israel's very survival depended on its determination to resolve the Palestinian question, on the ability of the great powers to guarantee frontiers and create a nuclear-free zone in the Middle East within a context of detente. If he underestimated the severity of the subsequent Israeli-Palestinian conflict, he nevertheless was one of the few to recognise the problem and foresee the dangers it would lead to.

Benn also spoke sense about peaceful co-existence, predicting in Parliament that the nuclear stalemate would lead to "a recognition by both the United States and the Soviet Union of a common interest in certain clear items of policy", such as arms control and the mutual acceptance of frontiers. He believed that the nuclear stalemate had made Britain's independent deterrent totally irrelevant, and urged a policy of friendship towards the developing and non-aligned countries. He advocated the creation of a permanent United Nations peacekeeping-force, a policy of working for international security and understanding through the UN, using "the traditions of this country: those of compromise, improvisation, energy, adventure".

Benn was convinced now more than ever that the beliefs and traditions of radicalism could play a major role in making Britain a more progressive nation. This was evident in the weekly column he wrote for *The Guardian* during 1963–64, and in the collection stemming from this in 1965, *The Regeneration of Britain*. His ideas reflected the influence of some of the more popular, progressive thinkers of the early 'sixties: J.K. Galbraith and his "affluent society"; Marshall McLuhan's concept of the global village, created by the revolution in communications; Bishop John Robinson's definition of a new libertarian morality; and Anthony Sampson's *Anatomy of Britain*, which exposed the structure of power in the nation. Benn saw himself in alliance with those "heroic heretics" who create intellectual ferment, encourage independent thought and give others the courage to think for themselves. *The Regeneration of Britain* shows Benn moving from the idealistic radicalism of his youth towards a passion for democratic and technological advance:

We are on the eve of a period of revolutionary change in Britain. . . The mood of reform goes far beyond a desire for fresh and vigorous political leadership. It reflects a growing dissatisfaction with the accepted institutions and methods in Britain today. . . . The history of the British ruling class is the history of judicial retreats in the face of the inevitable. . . . Reformers have to campaign for a lifetime before their chance comes. When it comes they must seize it and act quickly or it will be too late.[1] Benn's radicalism reflected the sense of optimism which permeated the times. But what type of revolutionary change did he envisage? With his belief in the fundamental value of parliamentary democracy, institutional reform was foremost in his mind — and this revealed the radicalising effect the peerage struggle was having upon him. He used this personal battle as a platform from which to campaign for the reform and eventual abolition of the House of Lords.

The Honours system as it now exists, serves to buttress the class structure in Britain, dividing people into social categories on the basis that they are superior and inferior human beings. . . . The worship of status and the enrichment of privilege behind the camouflage of hereditary pageantry will always kill initiative and frustrate new ideas.[2]

Embedded in this denunciation of privilege and affirmation of equality was a half-articulated argument for the sovereignty of the people over Parliament which would be the seed of Benn's later democratic socialism.

Benn's enthusiam for institutional reform stemmed in part from the observation that technological progress had caused galloping obsolescence, making the modernisation of the civil service, the educational system, the judiciary and local government an urgent priority. At the same time, he was aware that technology posed both challenge and threat to democracy. He had always felt that the advantage of parliamentary democracy was "that it gives ordinary people an effective say over their own destiny". Yet he saw technology giving rise to "new factors which inhibit the sense of belonging which should characterise a self-governing community". The explosion of knowledge and wealth "enriches us materially and simultaneously alienates us the more effectively from the processes of understanding and informed judgement", making it imperative "to assert human authority over the new technical Frankensteins of the present". Benn's book concluded that Britain needed more than modernisation; it needed regeneration, by which he meant a reawakening of the people and "an all-embracing interest in the total affairs of the community".

The distinction between reform and revolution had become blurred in Benn's mind, subsumed in the idea of regeneration itself. He believed that the educational role of protest was immense, but he simultaneously hoped that Labour could turn the apathy and aimless violence of "anti-politics" into direct action through "practical socialism": the planning of housing, transport and the environment. He noted that Harold Wilson had shown the way already by

mobilising the intelligentsia, the middle classes and scientists with his
vision of a new Britain and had made it respectable to be on the Left.
"Even Kennedy, with his huge new frontier task forces, never
commanded such a formidable army of brains as now are at Wilson's
disposal," he commented; and welcomed this intellectual and
political ferment as well as the resulting recrudescence of ideology.
He regarded the New Left, the growth of the radical Right led by
Senator Goldwater in the US and Enoch Powell in Britain, as healthy
developments because they offered the electorate a real choice, in
place of the sterile battle between "the ins and the outs rotating
forever round issues of administrative efficiency, enlivened by
auctions of electoral promises tailored to meet the sophisticated
desires of affluent voters".

Benn's hopes for the regeneration of Britain found their first
expression in Bristol where the widespread support for his peerage
campaign had brought people together in a new civic consciousness.
The 1961 election campaign had stimulated interest in community
politics, as Herbert Rogers noted in his agent's report:

 I would suggest that arising from the election a group should be
 established in Bristol "of the new generation" to discuss socialist
 principles and to apply these to our everyday problems. Our member
 would become its sponsor and the groups should become centres for
 education. The idea could be developed in all the big centres of the country
 where socialist education is so badly needed.[3]

The 1961 by-election convinced Benn of the need to reintegrate the
Left with Labour, if Labour was to meet the challenge of a local revival
and avoid disillusionment amongst its own supporters. As he told a
Nuffield College seminar in Oxford:

 What is really worrying about the present trend in British politics, is the
 isolation of the Labour Party from all these creative forces which should
 be enriching it with their ideas and supporting it in practical terms . . . We
 have a supreme chance and maybe the last one to make the Labour Party
 into an instrument that will carry us through the second and more radical
 stage of our post-war revolution.[4]

In June 1962 he founded the New Bristol Group along with three
other local Labour leaders, Edward Bishop, David Watkins and
William Wilkins. The New Bristol Group set itself three aims:
• To bring together those people in Bristol who care sufficiently
  about the city to secure its future growth and welfare.
• To begin an active study of the problems now facing or likely to
  face the citizens of Bristol and to work out constructive proposals
  designed to meet them.
• To stimulate a wider public discussion of these issues in the city
  so as to mobilise the skill and energy of thoughtful people in the
  task of carrying through the necessary reforms.
It was a non-party group, and though the Labour Bristol City

Council denounced it as factional, public response was positive and well over a hundred people representing a broad cross-section of the community became active members. "They included councillors, magistrates, engineers, doctors, trade unionists, students, teachers, designers, university professors and a farmer, many of whom had never been involved in this work before . . . We have no collective view", Benn commented, stressing that the New Bristol Group was an association of individuals, not a party political organisation.

Between 1962-66, the New Bristol Group published over thirty broadsheets and held seminars on a range of civic issues from race relations to regional development. A belief in planning, an understanding of the complexity of civic government, a faith in the potential for human cooperation and a desire to break down barriers and cross-fertilise specialist knowledge, inspired its work. The Group's proposals were a microcosm of the new Britain, of an ideal planned society, and had a considerable effect on Benn's thinking, clarifying his ideas about the interrelationship of democracy and planning. The Group urged a more positive role for local government in regional policy and the assumption of total responsibility for the region's infrastructure, including the Bristol docks and omnibus company, the co-ordination of public transport and the use of computers to solve the city's chronic traffic problems. At the same time, it believed that a militant, thriving local democracy was essential to good government, and proposed that the people elect the entire City Council simultaneously, instead of the then current rotating basis, in order to give the electorate a real choice and the opportunity to judge the incumbent Council on its results. In addition, the New Bristol Group argued that the establishment of ward councils with single representatives would further strengthen democracy at the grass roots, and bring about genuine popular control of local services.

The view that "the history of Local Government is the history of an extension of services to meet new needs as they arise", lay behind the Group's decision to undertake a comprehensive survey of the city's educational and housing requirements. The Group put forward an imaginative urban renewal scheme, concluding that the municipalisation of all development land was necessary. It was equally progressive about education, strongly in favour of comprehensive schools, and brought a greater degree of public understanding to this controversial issue. A sense of civic identity also inspired its efforts to improve race relations in Bristol. It advocated educational and housing policies to disperse ghettoes, the establishment of a Bristol citizenship council to organise joint cultural activities and the cooperation of state with voluntary services.

In the three years of its existence the New Bristol Group could claim to have had influence over decisions taken on secondary education, fluoridation of the water supplies, health centres, the integration of coloured immigrants and a variety of other topics. The Group's views were taken seriously by those in positions of public responsibility. For his own part, Benn found it "intensely exhilarating" to work from within a group, and he was greatly encouraged by the tangible achievements of "this experiment in responsible citizenship".

The results of these years outside Parliament were apparent soon after Benn's re-election in 1963. He discovered that both he and the Labour Party had altered considerably during the intervening period. The Tony Benn who returned to the House of Commons had been through experiences very different from those of his fellow MPs. He had become more militantly democratic, while the Parliamentary Labour Party had grown increasingly revisionist. It believed capitalism was working, had changed in character and had only to be "civilised". These fundamental differences would be the dominant theme of his relationship with the parliamentary leadership in years ahead. Temporarily, however, they were masked by Benn's popularity among social democrats for his heroic stand over the peerage — a cause supported by a liberal consensus.

In November 1963 Benn failed to be elected to the Shadow Cabinet, coming fifteenth out of twenty-nine with 83 votes; but he was reelected to the NEC in 1962 when he came fourth in the constituency section with 613,000 votes; and the following year third, with 725,000 votes. His election to the chairmanship of the Fabian Society in 1964 reflected his long-standing reputation as an internationalist and his recent contribution in helping project Labour as a progressive radical party.

The most important single factor in transforming the Labour Party's prospects, and those of Benn himself, was the election of Harold Wilson to the leadership following Gaitskell's death in February 1963. Wilson had been elected from the Left, having resigned with Bevan in 1951 and stood against Gaitskell for the leadership in 1960; but he led from the centre. He succeeded in uniting both left and right wings of the Party by offering the vision of a scientific revolution in place of the stale debate over the extent and scope of public ownership. At the 1960 annual Labour Party Conference, he declared:

> Our message for the sixties — a socialist inspired scientific and technological revolution releasing energy on an enormous scale and deployed not for the destruction of mankind but for enriching mankind beyond our wildest dreams. . . . Socialism must be harnessed to science and science to socialism.[5]

At the 1963 Scarborough Conference, Wilson captured the imagination of the Labour Party and the country with the promise of a new Britain: "A comprehensive plan of national development can recreate a dynamic sense of national purpose and restore our place in the world." He explained that technological progress had put the whole argument about industry, economics and socialism into a new perspective: "We are redefining and restating our socialism in terms of the scientific revolution. ... The Britain that is going to be forged in the white heat of this revolution will be no place for restrictive practices or outdated methods."

Underlying this development was the growing public concern over Britain's poor economic performance which, by 1963, was becoming a national obsession. Economists and politicians argued why the balance of payments was deteriorating and the rate of economic growth so low. The conclusions they reached were to be crucial in shaping the approach of the 1964–70 Labour Government, as well as Benn's ideas about the role of government in industrial policy. The general consensus was that only active government intervention in planning the growth of incomes, controlling prices,stimulating labour productivity, restructuring industry and harnessing technology, modernising management and reforming the educational system could restore the health of the British economy.

These issues dominated the 1964 General Election and contributed to Wilson's success in winning and retaining the initiative. Bipartisan agreement was emerging about the need for economic planning; but though the Conservative Government had established the National Economic Development Council (NEDC), the inflationary dangers evident in Maudling's dash for growth during 1963–64 only re-enforced the case for planning in the public mind. Wilson was obsessed with image-making, and his electoral strategy was to project Labour as the party of progress rather than protest. Like many, Benn at first found his leadership invigorating. In return, Wilson was impressed by Benn's political flair, his work as chairman of Labour's Broadcasting Advisory Committee, and soon brought him into his counsels in planning for the General Election.

In December 1963, Wilson asked Benn to be his unofficial speech writer; and on 9 January 1964 Benn went to see him to discuss a winter campaign in preparation for a possible spring election. He worked on Wilson's policy speeches, particularly the Swansea speech on Labour's economic policy in which Wilson acknowledged that Labour's ambitious social programme and reformist dreams entirely depended on the success of its economic planning. On 3 March Benn began a series of meetings with Wilson about the television side of the campaign, and it was a sign of Wilson's confidence that he asked Benn to accompany him to *The Guardian* luncheon in May, for the paper's support throughout 1964 would be vital.

Benn was to a lesser extent involved in the preparation of Labour's manifesto: his influence here was tangential. Policy-making lay largely in the hands of Wilson's circle, while the Home Policy Committee of the National Executive — of which Benn was a member — was not then the assertive institution it has become. Benn submitted a paper in January 1964 demanding the reform of the Honours system but found that Labour remained deeply divided about the whole issue of a second chamber, and he failed to obtain agreement on any specific manifesto commitments. Similarly, on the NEC Overseas Subcommittee there was little opportunity to influence foreign policy. In any case, the broad areas had already been decided along radical lines with which he agreed. At public meetings he campaigned for the integration of immigrants into British society and for educational reform. The experience of the peerage episode had convinced him that private education and the public school system were a form of unacceptable privilege and mainstay of the establishment and class system. He and his wife, Caroline, who from then on would devote much of her life to education, became advocates of the merits of and need for a comprehensive system, and in 1964 decided to remove their children from Westminster Preparatory School and send them to Holland Park comprehensive school, one of the first of its kind in Britain. More important, however, in relation to policy, were his close association with Peter Shore, who wrote most of the manifesto, and his weekly discussions with Dick Crossman who belonged to Wilson's circle. Benn stressed the advantages of Labour projecting the unifying themes of planning and institutional reform, but it was Caroline who actually suggested *The New Britain* as a possible title for the manifesto.

Let's go with Labour for the New Britain caught the mood of the times, promising a "just, dynamic and go-ahead Britain", "fresh and virile leadership", a sense of purpose, an end to the stop-go economic cycle, the modernisation of industry and the social services at home, and a new role for Britain abroad. "Labour is ready", the manifesto declared, "poised to swing its plans into instant operation. Impatient to apply the New Thinking that will end the chaos and sterility." It insisted that these objectives would only be secured by a deliberate and massive effort to modernise the economy; "to change its structure and to develop with all possible speed the advanced technology and the new science-based industries with which our future lies. In short, they will only be achieved by socialist planning."

Though the rhetoric was radical, the content, on closer examination, did not represent a radically different type of society or envisage any redistribution of wealth and power. Proposals for public ownership were confined to the nationalisation of the steel industry and justified on grounds of planning alone, while the theme of planning was itself subordinate to technology and the need to harness it. *The New Britain* had little to do with socialism, but rather represented the high-water mark of revisionism and its claim to be able to make capitalism work by indirect means as "an alternative board of management for the affluent society".

The New Britain won a narrow victory for Labour — a precarious working majority of four — at the General Election of 15 October 1964. Benn himself had almost doubled his majority of 1959 and had played some part in projecting Labour as the party of the new generation. During the election campaign, he had coordinated the Party Political Broadcasts, and on 25 September had interviewed Harold Wilson on television. He realised that Labour had to widen its appeal if it was to win the election. His particular contribution was to launch "Citizens for Labour" as an organisation encouraging a two-way traffic in ideas, through which sympathetic individuals could become affiliated to the Labour Party — like the registered voters in the US — without formal membership. However, the NEC was hostile to this "liberal" accommodation and little happened beyond the television testimonials given by public figures like Sir Compton McKenzie.

The Labour Party felt euphoric, and understandably so after thirteen years in opposition. But if Wilson promised a hundred days of Kennedy-style dynamic government, Benn was in a more radical frame of mind: "I am much more left-wing than I used to be. ... I am becoming more revolutionary as I grow older."

Wilson was adventurous in his appointments, introducing academics and establishing new departments in Whitehall, but most of his ministers had no previous experience of government. George Brown headed the Department of Economic Affairs advised by Michael Shanks; Jim Callaghan became Chancellor of the Exchequer, advised by Thomas Balogh and Nicholas Kaldor; Gerald Gardiner, a radical barrister and founder member of CND, was made Lord Chancellor. The frenetic activity of Labour's first hundred days of Government only exacerbated the economic chaos it inherited. It exposed the total absence of any policy to tackle the fundamental disequilibrium of the balance of payments — in deficit by an estimated £600m over 1964— and in so doing, the element of fantasy inherent in Labour's dream of a New Britain. The crisis of confidence which greeted Labour's victory turned an adverse balance of payments into a run on sterling. The Government lived from day to day, imposing a 15% import surcharge and giving a 2% export rebate; but these measures failed to stem the speculative tide. The only obvious, remaining alternatives were deflation or devaluation, and Callaghan was soon compelled to introduce a mildly deflationary budget. On 11 November he increased the standard rate of income tax and the duty on petrol. On 23 November he raised the bank rate from 5% to 7%; and by the end of the year, the Government had negotiated $3000m in loans from the International Monetary Fund.[6]

Benn felt that Labour must persevere and not be deflected from its expansionist aims by international speculation. Though disappointed not to be in the Cabinet, Benn had been appointed Postmaster-General. When he re-entered Parliament in 1963, he had realised the urgency of mastering a particular area of government, if he was to have any prospect of office. In October 1963, he had written a Post Office Development Plan which he submitted as a paper to Harold Wilson. Before the election he had published an article in *The Guardian* outlining his ideas, which aroused some public interest; and at the Durham Miners' Gala in July, Wilson had intimated that he would appoint Benn Postmaster-General if Labour were to win the election. Benn's article had displayed a positive attitude to public ownership and a fascination with innovation. "The GPO is a science-based industry," he wrote, "but it has not yet utilised the full potentialities of the revolution in communications that has taken place." He saw the potential of the Post Office for strengthening other industries, such as computers and machine tools, by ordering advanced equipment and contributing to regional policy in opening up declining areas for expansion through its employment-location policy. Thus he urged "the use of public enterprise alone, or in partnership, to develop science-based industries as key points of growth in the economy". His approach to public ownership was consistent with Labour's emphasis throughout the 'fifties and 'sixties in proving to the public that nationalised industries could be made efficient and successful. He was anxious that the Post Office should be seen to provide a public service and to be in the vanguard of technological advance. The article suggested that the GPO might develop both a special telephone service for British exporters with interpreters and a local information service, offering facilities to welfare groups like the Samaritans. It could also exploit opportunities for improving efficiency through the standardising of telegrams, envelopes, telephone and postal codes. By speeding up communications, the GPO could encourage trade, and Benn urged both the coordination of the postal with the rail parcel-service, as well as the expansion of the Post Office's banking services.

Benn may have been full of ideas on becoming Postmaster-General; but to move at the age of thirty-nine from being a back-bencher to running a Government Department employing over 400,000 people was not an easy task. He felt a sense of ignorance, dependence and isolation, combined with a determination to do well and an early conviction that there was "far too much secrecy by Government". His period as Postmaster-General between October 1964 and July 1966, proved to be a valuable apprenticeship. As an industrial minister, he was responsible for running a vast organisation and working with the trade unions. The experience was a formative one and would shape his ideas about industry, socialist planning, and relations between management and workers.

The Post Office was an anomalous, non-political department, and generally considered a Government backwater with less able administrators. The challenge Benn faced of transforming the antiquated, bureaucratic and slow-moving organisation at St. Martin's-le-Grand into a modern nationalised industry was formidable: "The basic jobs that we had waiting for us on our desks were these — to get the finances put right, to improve staff relations, to expand the capital investment programme of the telephone service and to deal with the problem of BBC finances."[7]

The role of administrator absorbed much of Benn's energy and imagination. He adopted a progressive model of "scientific management" that was both participative and technocratic, in so far as he made use of the advice of experts. The Post Office Board was revived "to restore some sense of corporate management", and he tried to act "as if I were chairman of one of the huge industrial concerns" bringing in the management consultants, McKinsey and Company, to investigate ways of raising the productivity and profitability of the Postal Services. He visited Japan to study its advanced telecommunications organisation, appointed a director of statistics and business management, developed a recruitment policy and career structure that would attract able engineers and administrators.

Benn was also concerned to strengthen the political impulse at the Post Office. He began by circulating the election manifesto to all the senior officials and to the trade unions most directly involved, marked to show how it might possibly affect the work of the Department. Like Stafford Cripps at the Board of Trade in 1945, he adopted the practice of holding mass-meetings of officials; on one occasion taking the Albert Hall to explain the decision adopted by his predecessor, Reginald Bevins, to transfer the Post Office Savings Bank to Glasgow, as part of the Government's dispersal and regional policy — a move the staff much resented. Every Monday, he and his Junior Minister, Joe Slater, would meet the branch managers and trade union representatives over informal sandwich lunches. They discussed matters such as the future of the Post Office, the impact of technology and the changes concerning the industry and the people who worked in it. He was the first ever Postmaster-General to visit the headquarters of the Post Office trade unions, the UPW and POEU, and these contacts made him "think a lot about these inter-relationships which later got me off on even deeper and more fundamental thinking about the possibilities of industrial democracy".

Benn's iconoclasm, his love of innovation, detestation of petty rules and status, attracted considerable public attention. His habit of lunching at the ministry canteen, his much-noted refusal to use the porcelain tea service in preference to his own pint mug, the memoranda he issued on administrative improvements, at first alarmed and shocked his officials; but he soon won the respect of the conventionally-minded civil servants at St. Martin's-le-Grand who came to see him as an unrivalled champion of their Ministry. In many ways, Benn was the victim of his own outstanding gifts as a publicist, and he succeeded more in drawing attention to himself than to the real progress being made at the Post Office. If he became impressed with the importance to British society of his own job, it was because he had an imagination capable of believing he had "the most exciting job in the Government". "The Post Office is the control mechanism of our society. We are a Ministry of Communications, not a Post Office."[8] Peter Shore commented: "He is not easy to categorise. But he has a unique quality which is that to him the future is as real, if not more real, than the past or the present."[9]

Behind the glamour of the technological revolution, Benn grappled with the pressing practical problems of turning the Post Office into a profitable organisation. He found the organisation in serious financial straits, which his predecessor had admitted to concealing; while the Post Office's own forecasted cumulative deficit totalled £150m. It was a labour-intensive, loss-making service, starved of capital investment by previous governments and faced with an explosion in demand for telephones. Benn accepted the bi-partisan commitment to self-financing nationalised industries and was highly commercial in his approach. His strategy was to invest massively in postal mechanisation, sophisticated telecommunication equipment, and to increase both productivity and turnover in order to reform the Post Office into a dynamic and financially viable service. Determined to carry out this policy, he took several unpopular decisions, including the abolition of the household delivery service and increases in postal and telephone charges. This pitched him into the dangerous political arena of public-sector finance. Against a barrage of Conservative protest, he argued that higher prices were necessary if investment was to be self-financed, insisting that "the first and most important task is . . . to improve the productivity and profitability of the postal service".

If he succeeded in persuading the Cabinet to agree to the increases, the real problem lay in getting the unions to agree to higher productivity at a time when industrial relations were poor, following the first strike in seventy years. Despite acute staff shortages, he managed to persuade the trade unions to accept wage settlements during 1965–66 in line with the Government's prices and incomes policy. However, his real achievement was to involve the trade unions in plans for modernisation of the Post Office and obtain agreement on modernisation and acceptance of the principle that real wage increases depended upon higher productivity. As he recalled, "It was quite a struggle getting things moving and overcoming the difficulties associated with change."

Between October 1964 and July 1966, the Post Office invested two million pounds in advanced electronic sorting equipment designed to save ten million annually in operating costs. The telephone service was in a more precarious state. The waiting list rose from 46,000 to 71,000 during Benn's period of office; and an increasing number of calls failed to connect while the new STD system was being introduced. On becoming Postmaster-General, Benn also discovered that the decision to develop the Strowger instead of the superior Crossbar system had resulted in the irreversible loss of large export markets. Despite pressures to cut public expenditure, Benn secured substantial increases in capital expenditure on automated exchanges and telephone equipment to £212m during 1965–66, and a projected increase to £340m for 1969–70. Benn also tried to expand the Post Office's telephone manufacturing capacity; but found that the previous Government's agreement with the leading companies had given them a virtual cartel limiting the Post Office's output.

Benn's commitment to the Post Office's profitability was not separate from his wider vision of its role as a public service. In certain areas, social obligations conflicted with commercial criteria, and here he defended the value of subsidies totalling approximately £17m p.a. for the maintenance of telephone kiosks in remote areas and the parcel and printed-paper services. The moribund Post Office Advisory Board was replaced by a Post Office Users' Council, strengthening the representation of consumers' interests, and a system of personalised letters to answer complaints was introduced. The issue of commemorative stamps was the most imaginative and popular of Benn's innovations and it extended public patronage of the arts. He established a fellowship of minuscule design, setting criteria for special stamps to mark national and international events and great British achievements, as well as a philatelic bureau to market them. Perhaps the most glittering symbol of the new Britain was London's Post Office Tower — capable of transmitting 150,000 telephone calls simultaneously and receiving forty television stations via the early bird and telstar satellites — which Benn opened while Postmaster-General, though the previous Government had decided to build it.

Above all, Benn was determined to diversify the Post Office's services and make it an advertisement for dynamic public ownership. In February 1966 he introduced legislation to enable the Post Office Savings Bank to increase its deposit account interest rate from 2.5% to 4% p.a. He also encouraged the Post Office to establish its own banking service, a national giro that provided credit transfer and deposit facilities. He envisaged it as a people's bank providing a free service in the absence of one offered by the private sector. Certainly the banking service's rapid growth during the first years after its foundation proved the existence of such a market. If Giro made losses at the start, this was due to the interest payable on its borrowed capital, as well as the fact that legislation restricted it from lending and earning interest like other banks.[10]

Under Benn, the Post Office simultaneously tried to foster the technological revolution by purchasing £2.5m of computers for Giro and its National Data Processing Service. Benn had established this to provide industry with fast and inexpensive access to computers through terminals and its telephone connected Datel service, thus generating income for its highly profitable computer rental service. His final and most significant initiative as Postmaster-General was to turn the Post Office into a nationalised industry, a public corporation fully accountable to Parliament. Having read all the memoirs of his predecessors since Rowland Hill, he found that they had all recommended this reform, and he managed to persuade the Cabinet of its merits before he was moved. "The real difference between the Party opposite and ourselves is our attitude to the public services," Benn declared, during a debate in which he was attacked by the Conservatives who demanded his salary be cut. The Conservatives were seeking to exploit the public clamour over the growing telephone waiting list, and they criticised Benn's record as Postmaster-General. In fact the waiting list was not of Benn's making and his actions would lead to its disappearance.

Throughout his time as Postmaster-General, Benn's attempts at change were hampered and his personal competence and credibility as a Minister questioned. His attempts to improve the Post Office's image were perhaps justifiably criticised as "gimmickery", but unfairly dismissed as purely a public relations exercise. Whether it was his style, or in fact the nature of the measures he undertook, Benn seemed to stir and expose a deep and irrational fear of change in many people. He encountered hostility and suspicion wherever he acted to modernise and streamline the Post Office. Thus, the introduction of postal and all-figure dialling-codes, the standardisation of envelope sizes, were interpreted as an attack upon individual liberty and a prologue to socialist tyranny. The issue of commemorative stamps, in particular, was seen as an instrument of political propaganda, rather than a form of popular art and education. Benn faced a barrage of parliamentary questions criticising every stamp issue. The Rulers of Great Britain series, for example, was never put out, partly because the absence of the monarch's image on the Cromwell stamp was considered to have republican overtones. The Opposition's attitude was contradictory: they criticised reduction in services and simultaneously condemned subsidies. Similarly, they supported the Post Office Savings Bill (which was a consensus measure, in that both parties were in favour of encouraging saving), but criticised the national giro as an attack on free enterprise, an unnecessary intervention in the market economy and a waste of public money. The dispute revealed two totally opposed concepts of the role of the public sector.

Despite these criticisms, Benn did succeed in restoring the Post

Office to profitability, as the figures themselves showed.[11] He was deeply impressed by the spirit of the Post Office which was one of "public service", and he undoubtedly had a galvanising effect upon it. There were tangible achievements, in that the Post Office had greatly improved its capacity to undertake detailed economic and cost-benefit analyses, taking advantage of computers to solve its organisational problems and cope with its growing volume of business. The long-term decisions he took about investment and prices resulted in profits and self-financing expansion of a public corporation; but the scope for stimulating the wider application of technology was limited. Thus, the mechanisation of the postal service, for example, could not in any way stimulate the demand for machine tools, and if the Post Office's computer services may have encouraged the development of the computer industry, it did not have any noticeable effect upon the rate of economic growth.

As Postmaster-General, Benn was also responsible for the media, and the current revolution in communications fuelled irresistible demands for the expansion of broadcasting. Here he faced a number of problems: whether to introduce third and fourth television channels; the choice of a colour television system; the expansion of educational broadcasting; the growing demands for local radio; and the popularity of the illegal pirate radio stations. All of these would aggravate the deterioration of the BBC's financial position, whose accumulated deficit was already expected to rise to £125m by 1968-69. The gap between these far-reaching demands and the resources available presented Benn with the dilemma of choosing between no expansion and an unjustifiable and unpopular increase in radio and television license fees. These problems re-ignited the debate about the Government's policy and responsibility for broadcasting and its relationship to the broadcasting authorities: should the Government set standards for programmes? should it intervene to control advertising, content or style? how should the BBC be financed, and was there a case for commercial broadcasting?

Benn's handling of these important issues created an impression of indecision. On 3 March 1966 the Opposition initiated a debate in which Conservative MPs complained that "this chap really cannot decide anything", observing "how extraordinary it is that although we have the first PMG with a broadcasting background, he appears to have no influence on broadcasting". The problem was that broadcasting policy was decided at Cabinet level where Benn could never get his views accepted because his ideas were unfashionable and unpopular among his colleagues. He wanted to decentralise and diversify the BBC, so that it could develop local and popular radio, financed both by advertising and rates; but he remained strongly opposed to commercial radio and television because of the implications for programme standards. In the event his announcement of an increase in the license fees was only a temporary solution to the BBC's financial difficulties which prevented it from exceeding its borrowing limits.

What emerges from Benn's actions and pronouncements on broadcasting is not so much personal indecision as government inaction, stemming from the contradiction between the Government's acceptance of its public responsibility for broadcasting and its fear of direct intervention. "Broadcasting policy is a jungle of special interests", Benn acknowledged, observing that the Government could not impose decisions, and defending the impartiality and independence of the authorities from demands for popular control. "Programme content is a matter for broadcasting organisations. . . . The establishment by me of a viewer's council would tend to diminish the authority of the two broadcasting authorities and in consequence their capacity to discharge their responsibility."[12]

On the other hand, where the Government had an obligation to intervene, decisions were necessarily slow. Benn knew that he could not afford to make the wrong choice in deciding which system of colour television Britain was to adopt. Therefore, he had to consider *all* the technical arguments, despite the manufacturers' protests about the commercial damage caused by the delay and uncertainty. On 3 March 1966 he announced the choice of the German PAL system after a thorough review of the alternative US NSTC and French SECAM systems, which the failure of the Vienna Conference to adopt a common European network had necessitated. The dangers of government responsibility for broadcasting became apparent in Labour's slowness to suppress the highly popular pirate radio stations, such as Radios Caroline, City, Essex, London, Scotland, 270, 387, which broadcast pop music between 1964–66 from converted forts, ships and lighthouses around Britain. Benn, who was totally opposed to commercial radio, argued that "the disposition of scarce and valuable wavelengths is a matter of high policy", claiming that there was evidence of pirate radios interfering with shipping. But the Cabinet was not ready to act against them even though they had been condemned by the Council of Europe. This apparent indecision really reflected the Cabinet's failure to determine a policy for popular broadcasting and its fear of unpopularity before the March 1966 General Election. When, finally, the macabre shooting of Radio City's owner in July gave the Government a pretext to legislate the outlawing of pirate radios, Benn emphasised that "it was certainly not due to any puritanical prejudice against light music or a bureaucratic hatred of enjoyment". The suppression of the pirate radios was Benn's final act as Postmaster-General before the crisis surrounding the seamen's strike would lead to his appointment as Minister of Technology.

Between October 1964 and July 1966, Labour's strategy was to win time to demonstrate its political will by letting its long-term politics of industrial reconstruction take effect. The Government hoped that the National Plan, setting a target economic growth rate of 3.8%, would create a climate of confidence, and that the joint declaration on productivity, prices and incomes with the TUC would keep wage increases within this limit. Labour believed, in Callaghan's words, that "there is no undue pressure on resources calling for action". The economy continued to expand and the balance of payments improved, with the deficit on the current account falling from £356m in 1964 to £26m in response to import controls which acted as a short-term dam. However, incomes rose faster than anticipated, by 5.5% in 1965, and Labour rode on the crest of the Conservative's consumer boom in preparation for an expected General Election.[13] Like many members of the Government, Benn believed that the voluntary early-warning system on incomes would probably achieve most of what was needed. As the Election approached, he wrote a memo to Harold Wilson on electoral strategy, and argued that Labour should counter the hysteria of Tory propaganda with reasoned argument and project itself as a pragmatic and progressive party. On 6 February 1966, Benn attended the joint Cabinet-NEC meeting at Chequers, and a week later he spent all day there planning the election campaign with Wilson. As in previous elections, Benn was to coordinate broadcasting.

The manifesto, *You Know a Labour Government works*, paradoxically identified Labour as the Party of patriotism and stability. On 31 March 1966, the Party won a convincing victory at the polls with an overall majority of ninety-seven seats. But Labour had won the election on a false prospectus. The truth was that its plans for a New Britain and a technological revolution depended upon an expansionist economic policy which the Government pursued in defiance of the balance of payments and economic reality between 1964-66. The National Plan was an illusion, not a solution; and as successive economists pointed out, it was inflationary because it set a target for economic growth in excess of the underlying potential. There was nothing new in the economic policy of Labour's New Britain, except for an almost pathological preoccupation with respectability and a refusal to face either devaluation or deflation. Herein lay the basic contradiction between Labour's expanionist strategy and the reality of an enfeebled economy whose balance of payments was permanently in deficit; between the dream of a dynamic and the reality, of a disintegrating society. It was a contradiction which Benn would find intolerable. It would lead him off in search of more radical solutions to fulfill Labour's original promise.

V

1966-1970
MINTECH

The Ministry of Technology made me a Socialist.
TONY BENN

Frank Cousins' resignation as Minister of Technology on 3 July 1966, after prolonged disagreement over the Government's proposed prices and incomes legislation, was the occasion for Tony Benn's elevation to the Cabinet. Harold Wilson had asked Benn to become Minister of Works immediately after the election, predicting that Cousins would resign over the prices and incomes issue. Benn was sceptical, however, and remained at the Post Office where there was still much he wanted to achieve. In replacing Cousins with Benn "who had proved a successfully technological Postmaster-General," Harold Wilson noted that Benn "was more than a little overcome by the magnitude of the job. I suggested to him that he should go easy on publicity until he had mastered the intricacies of this large and expanding Ministry."[1]

Benn's appointment as Minister of Technology occurred at a significant moment in the life of the 1964-70 Labour Government. An economic storm had been gathering for some time, and it now broke. On 16 May 1966 the National Union of Seamen began a forty-seven day strike in support of their 17% pay claim. The strike closed the ports, held up exports, thereby adversely affecting the balance of payments in May and June, and culminated in intense international speculation against sterling in July. The seamen had struck at the root of Labour's strategy for strengthening the balance of payments by restraining incomes and consumption. But Wilson turned the strike into an issue of confidence. He accused "a tightly knit group of politically motivated men" of communist subversion. On 14 July Callaghan announced an additional £100m in special deposits and raised the bank rate from 6% to 7%. This, however, failed to stem the speculative tide. When a fraught Cabinet met on 19 July to resolve the crisis, Benn supported George Brown's call for devaluation, while Crosland and Jenkins argued that sterling should be allowed to float. After only cursory consideration of the available options, the Cabinet endorsed the deflationary package which Wilson announced the following day. The package entailed taking an estimated £500m out of the economy with a six-month freeze on all increase in prices and incomes, followed by a similar period of severe restraint.

The July Measures were arguably the turning-point in the history of the 1964–70 Labour Government. They began a parallel process of economic deflation and political disillusionment, climaxed by the Government's defeat at the General Election of 1970. The Measures shattered the illusion of the New Britain, the dreams of the National Plan with its prospects for economic growth. For Benn the contrast between the great expectations of 1964 and the bitter disappointments that followed was deeply felt. Yet, paradoxically, the July crisis would also lead to his emergence as an industrial minister and his pre-eminence as official prophet of the technological revolution. This latter was due not so much to his ability to communicate a vision of progress, as to a major shift from reliance upon macro-economic management to micro-industrial policies. Labour now depended on interventionist measures to stimulate expansion: restructuring industry and fostering the application of technology. Consequently, between 1966 and 1970, Benn increasingly came to occupy a central position in Labour's plans for the growth and modernisation of the economy.

Much of the history of British industry from the mid 'sixties on, is inextricably connected with Benn's actions as Minister of Technology. The decisions he took during this time altered the future course and shape of industry just as this ministerial experience was to have a seminal influence on his own political development.

The Ministry of Technology, or Mintech as it was known, exemplified the spirit of the 1964–70 Labour Government and was a testament to its belief — articulated by Kaldor, Blackett and others — that technology was the mainspring of economic growth. Mintech was a new departure in government: cooperation with industry through intervention. It spoke a new language, was commercial in its decision-making and operated in a highly technocratic manner, introducing a new type of public official, the qualified scientist and engineer with industrial experience. *The New Britain* had envisaged a ministry "to guide and stimulate a major national effort to bring advanced technology and new processes into British industry". Harold Wilson conceived of this ministry as "the National Research and Development Corporation writ large", disseminating technology and fostering its application.

But Mintech had had an inauspicious birth. When Frank Cousins, then General Secretary of the TGWU, had been appointed Minister in October 1964 and Lord Snow, the author and scientist, his junior minister, the press immediately dismissed the Ministry's inception as an example of Wilson's gimmickery. Neither man had experience of government or was an MP, and there remained considerable doubt about the extent of Wilson's own commitment to the Ministry's establishment. He had skilfully exploited the idea to electoral advantage; but once in power, political will appeared lacking. For over a year Mintech stood on the verge of dissolution. There were no defined plans for its future; there existed none but the vaguest of briefs, and certainly no clear idea of how technology would be harnessed to industry. Furthermore, and most ominously, the civil service was strongly opposed to the new Ministry. Frank Cousins was responsible for a large and amorphous department with an annual expenditure of £450m, employing over 22,000 scientists and civil servants. He took his role seriously. Yet, in practice, Mintech exerted little influence over the research establishments which it nominally controlled, nor the four key industrial sectors it sponsored: computers, electronics, machine tools and telecommunications, areas in which the Government saw the introduction of new technology as national priority.

Mintech's birth coincided with a major crisis in the young and struggling British computer industry — brought on by savage competition from the American giants — that tested Labour's interventionist philosophy. Cousins quickly grasped that the industry's problems were more financial than technical, and rising to the challenge, committed the Government to its success. The NRDC agreed to advance £4m between 1965–68 to ICT. Cousins used the purse strings to obtain agreement on the formation of a single British computer firm, large enough to compete at home and abroad. After a shaky start, his successful establishment of this wholly new Ministry led to a further period of expansion: "It was soon evident that the Ministry could not make a wide enough impact or rapid progress with its remit, so long as it operated from such a limited industrial base."[2] Thus, in February 1966, Mintech assumed responsibility for the electrical and mechanical engineering industries, which included motor vehicles; and aviation, shipbuilding and procurement were transferred from the Board of Trade and the Ministry of Aviation to Mintech during February 1967.

Thus Benn became Minister of Technology at a time of rapid growth. Staff had increased to 37,000 and annual expenditure to £750m. He was determined from the start to weld Mintech into a unified Ministry and to make it a catalyst of economic growth. Certainly his commitment and enthusiasm brought a dynamic impulse to the Ministry's work, making an enduring impression on all involved. An 8am arrival at Millbank Tower on Monday 5 July 1966, two hours before Frank Cousins turned up to hand over the Ministry, exemplified this dedication. Benn had arrived in time to answer his own letter as Postmaster-General to the Minister of Technology, recommending a National Data Processing Service, and to welcome the idea.

Benn immediately made it a practice to hold long weekly meetings with junior ministers and his senior advisers who included at various stages Peter Shore, Eric Varley, Harold Lever, and Professor Bruce Williams. They discussed what the Ministry was about, and "it became quite clear, of course, when one thought about it, that the scientific emphasis was an illusion. [The Ministry] was about industry, and when one looked at industry it was about the difference between big industry and small industry."[3] Benn rapidly reached the conclusion that technology was more the consequence than the cause of economic growth, that the scale of industry was the crucial factor determining the rate of growth. He saw a role for government in stimulating industrial expansion and rationalisation of industry — to the extent that both technologically advanced and traditional declining industries operated outside the normal market mechanism and were dependent on state support.

Benn aimed to help industry to help itself by forging a partnership between government and industry, not in the legal sense, but in terms of cooperation and collaboration. Mintech would adopt a firm's eye-view and its role would be "to pick out and fertilise the points of growth in the economy". Benn saw himself as "a national entrepreneur helping to turn the nation's assets into cash", and he proclaimed Britain's new role as "industrial excellence". This interventionist philosophy, while considered left-wing by both Left and Right, was hardly socialist in origin. Benn simply believed, in "revisionist" fashion, that "technology outdates not only our methods of production but also methods of government and management". The challenge posed to both "has in fact created a strong common interest between them". Benn recognised that key areas of disagreement remained: distribution of profits; the extent of government industrial intervention; the accountability of power; the rights of workers. Yet he suspected that "the mixed economy may well turn out to be the system to which the whole world is moving".

Benn's efforts to publicise technology and stimulate its wider application brought allegations of "technomania". He certainly took Mintech's educational role seriously and greatly extended the points of contact with industry. The Advisory Council on Technology, which represented some sixty associations, met quarterly under his chairmanship, and its role was to define policy objectives. Mintech developed regular formal contacts with official bodies like the CBI (Confederation of British Industry) and the NEDC with its 21 EDCs. Together they established working parties, such as that on the process-plant industry, as well as informal contacts with over 500 firms, including forty out of the top 100. In January 1967 Mintech launched a monthly journal, *New Technology*, which by 1970 had reached a circulation of 62,000. Benn's aim was to connect higher education to industry, and a joint committee with the universities was set up "to consider and report upon proposals for the formation and development of Institutes of Advanced Technology". These signposts to the future also served as the base for a network of 75 industrial liaison centres where firms could come for information or assistance in solving technological problems. The view of Associated Industrial Consultants was that these fully justified their cost of less than £100,000 p.a. The results of the Production Engineering Advisory Service were less tangible, though by 1969, 170,000 people form 2400 firms had attended 15,000 sessions demonstrating advanced production techniques. The nineteen low cost Automation Centres and the "Approaching Automation" campaign did stimulate mechanisation, such as the automated BSC rolling mills and the CWS warehouses. Most important of all was the development of a procurement policy, through which the Government could use its influence as customer to encourage innovation and standardisation. The range of Mintech's services was indeed extensive, reflecting Benn's conception of its role. In all these, he saw an opportunity to create the conditions for economic growth.

Contrary to his public image, Benn's own attitude to technology was now highly commercial and critical. He pointed out that although Britain spent proportionately more on research and development than its competitors, "expenditure is no guarantee of industrial success". One of Benn's central objectives was to redirect resources from military to industrial programmes. In 1966 Mintech accounted for nearly 50% of Britain's annual expenditure on research — £325m out of £700m — but the Government spent £240m on defence and only £150m on civil projects. In 1967 Benn published a white paper outlining research and development (R&D) policy which set out for the first time criteria by which such programmes could be determined. The white paper specified seven areas where the Government had an interest in financing research, including defence, national economic advantage and protection of the environment. These criteria might undoubtedly conflict; but they at least attempted to define the limits of government action in a highly politically-sensitive area.

Benn faced formidable opposition in carrying through this policy, not least from the R&D establishments themselves, and his own civil servants who generally took the view that the experts knew best. To counterbalance the weight of technical opinion, he relied upon the Programmes Analysis Unit within the Atomic Energy Authority at Harwell "to assess the effectiveness of resource use on as comprehensive and rigorous a basis as possible". The PAU made a considerable impact on Mintech's research programmes, conducting over 70 input-output, cost benefit analyses between 1966–70. The result of Benn's policy was a proliferation of industrial research from the development of new materials to marine technology. The Government opened up its research establishments to industry, and the AEA was encouraged to undertake non-nuclear work such as desalination and lubrication research. Mintech increasingly subcontracted its growing civil programme to the private sector, chiefly through the NRDC and grants to research associations. It entered into numerous contracts with universities, developing advanced computer techniques and the hydrofoil, for example, at Leeds.

The industrial units at seven universities, for instance, the Centre for Industrial Innovation at Strathclyde, were also focal points for the dissemination of technology. Benn's involvement and personal interest in these projects — such as the hovercraft or the hover-tracked train — earned for him the nickname of "Hover Benn" from those who scorned the science-fiction world they alleged he inhabited. Moreover they accused him of indecision. More often than not, Benn was reluctant to approve projects in case they might not be commercially viable — whether nuclear-powered ships or efficient fuel cells — and he often found himself restraining the very enthusiasm that he had inspired.

Despite Mintech's activities, there were not enough jobs in Britain to accommodate the ever-increasing numbers of science graduates, and a serious brain-drain — blamed by Conservatives on Labour's taxation policies — resulted. In fact, the situation illustrated Benn's fundamental problem as Minister of Technology: how to stimulate innovation and productivity in a depressed economic climate. The July Measures had slowed down the economy, and during 1966–67, he was more preoccupied with the difficulties of Britain's declining and traditional manufacturing industries than with technology as such. As the Government struggled to overcome Britain's balance of payments deficit, Benn became acutely aware that international competition was a double-edged sword, a spur to modernisation yet also potentially lethal. He felt that the Government had a duty to intervene in a harsh economic climate to help industry rationalise and re-equip, reverse the trend towards contraction and take advantage of the explosion in world trade.

Developments in the motor vehicle industry during 1966–67 were particularly dramatic. The manufacturers felt bitter about the increase in hire-purchase down-payments to $33\frac{1}{3}$% in the July Measures, since only three years earlier, the Government had promised to maintain an expanding home market. But after a surge in investment, the optimism of the early 'sixties had now vanished. Labour's use of the regulator — by which it could adjust hire purchase and interest rates — was undoubtedly irresponsible because it depressed sales; while the motor vehicle industry could only operate profitably, and generate the capital to finance its investment programme, if it was working at full capacity. As chairman of NACMMI (National Advisory Council for Motor Manufacturing Industry), Benn had to face the manufacturers' collective wrath. However he did his best to discuss dispassionately the industry's problems and its reorganisation with them. He was strongly in favour of a single merger of the British manufacturers, and he persuaded BMC not to close its commercial vehicle plant at Bathgate in Scotland, arguing that the recession would be short-lived. He was also naturally concerned about the level of unemployment in Scotland.

If the recession would eventually precipitate a merger of the British manufacturers, the catalyst in bringing about negotiations was the imminent collapse of Rootes Motors. Rootes was an old family firm which had expanded with Government assistance, but in 1964 it sold 49% of its equity to US Chrysler with Government approval. However, Rootes still lacked the capital and scale to compete with the giants, and by 1966 the company was in deep financial difficulties. When Rootes came to see Benn in October 1966, threatening to sell out to Chrysler if they received no support, he called in George Harriman of BMC with Donald Stokes of Leyland Motors and asked them "whether they would be happy to see all three (Ford, GM and Chrysler) American manufacturers operating in Britain". He told them that if they were prepared to join together, this could be prevented, and he would claw Rootes back from Chrysler to form a single British company. Unable to agree on a merger between themselves, Harriman and Stokes refused to take on the ailing Rootes even though the Government offered to put up 90% of the cost of acquisition. Reluctantly, Benn was forced to admit that the problems were insuperable, though negotiations continued and it was from his initiative that the merger eventually sprang. (Wilson brought the two sides together in October 1967, after it had become clear there was only room for one British manufacturer in the deteriorating economic climate.)[4]

Neither Benn nor the Government were prepared to let Rootes go under or tolerate 15,000 unemployed in Scotland and 10,000 in Coventry. The Cabinet considered nationalisation but rejected the solution because, as Benn put it: "We did not believe that Rootes by itself was a viable organisation with or without Government support, owned or not by a British company." At the beginning of December, Chrysler offered to acquire the whole of Rootes, and in so doing gave the Government a way of averting disaster. For Labour it was a political embarrassment, having condemned the original decision to accept Chrysler's offer in 1964; but they were not in a position to argue. Benn, for his part, was not then hostile to multinational investment, though he was aware of the dangers of foreign domination, insisting during the negotiations on the protection of essential British interests. On 17 January 1977 he announced that the Government and Chrysler had reached agreement on the acquisition in exchange for several important undertakings, committing Chrysler to expand its UK operations and exports. Chrysler would raise £10m in additional capital as unsecured loan stock, while the Industrial Reorganisation Corporation (IRC) would take a 3% shareholding, investing £1.6m and appoint a director. Benn asserted that no takeover was possible "against the wishes of the British Government of the day", and in private admitted that the tragedy would have been greater had the Government rejected Chrysler's offer.

Yet many were skeptical about this solution. Labour MPs, like Stanley Orme, argued that the Rootes episode demonstrated the failure of capitalism and the inevitability of public ownership; while Conservatives, such as Reginald Maudling, warned that decisions would be taken by the majority of Chrysler's shareholders in Chrysler's worldwide interests, and doubted that British interests were fully protected. Ominously, Benn soon found himself having to justify the closure of Rootes' Maberly and Thrupp components factories, as being consistent with the company's plan for rationalisation and the spirit of the agreement. Both Labour and Conservative critics were proved right in the end. Chrysler's eventual collapse in 1975 seemed to confirm their original misgivings.

Benn was even more directly involved in the reorganisation of the shipbuilding industry, where he carried through a policy based on consensus about the need for larger groupings to take advantage of the boom in world shipping. British shipbuilding output had remained stagnant at around one million tons a year, while world tonnage had grown at 10% a year. Britain's share of world shipbuilding had as a result declined from 50% in 1914 to under 10% in 1964. In February 1965, Douglas Jay, President of the Board of Trade, appointed the Geddes Commission to examine the causes of decline and formulate proposals for restructuring the industry. A year later Geddes reported, documenting a saga of bad management, chronic industrial relations problems, restrictive practices, poor investment and low productivity. The report recommended the grouping of the sixteen yards capable of constructing ships over 5000 tons on an estuarial basis, and urged the Government to make financial assistance dependent upon efficient reorganisation and improved productivity.

The Cabinet approved the Geddes' plan before Benn was a member of it, but he shared Geddes' optimism, believing that a combination of modern management and government support could create a flourishing shipbuilding industry in Britain. The success of the Conservatives' own shipbuilding credit scheme, and in the short term, George Brown's rescue of Fairfields in 1965 — in which the Government invested £1.23m — had convinced him that systematic state intervention to aid private industry was both practicable and beneficial. In February 1967 he introduced the Shipbuilding Industry Bill as the centrepiece of Labour's legislative programme for industry in the 1966-67 Parliamentary session. The Government's reforms were more far-reaching than Geddes', involving over sixty yards — all those which could build ships of a hundred tons or over. The Bill envisaged a new government agency, the Shipbuilding Industry Board (SIB), to supervise reorganisation and to extend credit up to £100m for long-term contracts. Under the scheme, the SIB would have powers to make loans of up to £32.5m and grants of up to £20m, including £5m to cover transitional losses as well as the right to take, by agreement, a shareholding up to the value of the loans given.

Benn commended the establishment of an independent agency as a new development in state intervention: one which preserved parliamentary accountability and yet was free from political interference. He declared: "We are relaunching British shipbuilding with this bill. Nothing would be more fatal for this country than to concentrate only on the science-based industries and exclude from consideration the equally, if not more important question of applying science and technology more rapidly in all industries."[5] He admitted that size did not guarantee economies of scale, but presented reorganisation of buildings, equipment and manpower as a dramatic challenge to management and workers. He claimed that the availability of cheap long-term credit would enable British shipbuilders to compete on equal terms with foreign yards, though he was anxious to preserve the discipline of market forces.

Yet the Bill's proposals were certainly open to criticism: they either discouraged or did not do enough to secure the implementation of the desired reforms. The industry's profits and the assistance available under the Bill could not possibly have financed its re-equipment. In addition, the new groupings faced the burden of interest and loan repayments. *The Financial Times* warned:

> The risk in Mr. Benn's decision is that credit will be made available too easily, that uncompetitive firms will be kept in existence longer than otherwise and that the rationalisation of the industry will be hampered and delayed. It would have been better to wait until reorganisation had gone further before producing this succulent carrot.[6]

While the Opposition supported the Bill, their Shadow Minister of Technology, David Price, warned "Yard modernisation is not of itself any guarantee of commercial efficiency. Therefore the mere provision of more capital is not in itself sufficient." Nicholas Ridley, a leading advocate of free enterprise, condemned the emergence of a grants economy and called for the closure of the inefficient yards. For many Conservatives, state intervention was anathema, and, as a result, Benn became identified with creeping socialism — though the Shipbuilding Industry Act had little to do with socialism. In fact, its chief weakness was its permissive nature. The SIB lacked the powers to implement the policy and its members knew little about the shipbuilding industry. Sir William Swallow, the chairman, came from Vauxhall Motors and his deputy, Anthony Hepper, from Pretty Polly tights.

The unsatisfactory nature of the relationship established by the Act, the intractibility of the industry's problems and the need for more radical remedies were soon sharply illustrated by Benn's personal intervention in April 1967 to rescue the Firth of Clyde's modern dry dock from liquidation. The reorganisation of the shipbuilding industry into groups on the Tyne, Tees, Lower and Upper Clyde, as well as in East Scotland, was only completed with great difficulty. Devaluation and the Regional Employment Premium had reduced construction costs by an estimated 15% and led to an unprecedented increase in orders on the crest of a world boom. Benn raised the ceiling on credit guarantees from £200m to £400m in 1969 and to £600m in 1970 in order to enable Britain to increase its share of the world market. "We never intended the guarantee scheme to be a feather-bedding for the industry," he commented; but the underlying problems of chronic industrial relations, low productivity and re-equipment remained unsolved. Benn was forced to admit that the "effects of the reorganisation and of the productivity agreements have been slower than we may have expected or hoped." The grouping of the yards in practice had not increased efficiency but had made management more remote and further embittered industrial relations. Of the £155m assistance which the SIB provided between 1967–70, only £54m went towards capital investment, and the way in which it was disembursed discouraged reform. Firstly, government assistance before the reorganisation was completed, encouraged management and workers to continue with existing work methods and practices. Secondly, assistance was used to impose a solution from above, which could not work without the wholehearted support of those below — the shipyard owners, management and trade unions. Finally, it failed to stimulate a surge of investment in the industry.

The crisis of Upper Clyde Shipbuilders in 1969 was a direct challenge to Labour's shipbuilding reforms and to its entire interventionist strategy. The Clyde shipyards had from the first been unwilling partners. Yarrow felt it would be dragged down by the ailing yards, Stephens and Connell's. The agreement which the shipyards' chairman, Tony Hepper, had negotiated, stipulated that a major objective was to eliminate the possibility of redundancy; yet the SIB working-party had estimated that the work-force would have to be reduced from 13,000 to 7500 if UCS was to be viable. The workers were thus justified in feeling insecure; and after Dan McGarvey, President of the Boilermakers Union, had failed to secure a workers' charter, Alex McGuiness, the Fairfields convenor and shop steward, expressed their fears: "We are back in the hands of the old shipbuilders. We have no confidence in the new consortium." The scandal surrounding the late delivery and subsequent engine failure of the prestige liner QE 2 at the end of 1968 was a bad omen for UCS — and an indictment of the old management at John Brown in particular. Since £20m of public money had been invested, there was enormous pressure on Benn to intervene; but he resisted demands for a public enquiry and asked Sir Arnold Lindley to make a full technical assessment instead. Benn described it as a disappointment, not a disaster, and condemned the way in which "self-denigration in this country has long overtaken cricket and football as our favourite national pastime". But UCS made a loss of £9.5m in its first year, and he soon recognised that its problems could no longer be dismissed. He felt compelled to intervene, yet was restrained by his very position: while he was responsible for shipbuilding policy, he could not directly interfere with SIB's reorganisation. Nonetheless, on 14 March 1969 he and his Junior Minister, Gerry Fowler, visited all the UCS shipyards to discover what was wrong and explain the Government's concern. (The Cabinet had warned that it was not prepared to put money in one end and see it come out the other at the same rate.) He was shocked by what they found: "No proper records had been kept by the constituent companies and they were not able to estimate the cost of discharging their contracts." In addition, UCS had entered into unprofitable contracts which would bankrupt the company without massive subsidies. By April 1969, the group faced liquidation.

UCS demanded a further £12m, including £7m as working capital, and the Scottish TUC lobbied Benn at the House of Commons on 29 April. On 2 May, Tony Hepper, UCS chairman, came to see Benn and claimed that with assistance UCS would break even by 1971. Benn was skeptical. On 7 May he went to the Central Hotel, Glasgow, with the SIB Chairman, Sir William Swallow, to meet the management and the trade unions. Here he told them that there would be no money without reforms:

> This is a moment of truth . . . It is the profitable . . . discharge of orders alone which will guarantee the security of employment for those working on Upper Clyde . . . The Government is still waiting for evidence that the seriousness of the position is understood on Upper Clyde with all those involved ready to shoulder their full responsibility for stemming the present losses and facing up to the inescapable decisions which will be required.[7]

The next day Hepper issued a statement predicting the end of the road for UCS and Benn, angered, accused him of irresponsibility since the case was still under consideration.

Public confidence had now been completely undermined, and in Parliament Benn was accused of incompetence. As the Conservative MP, Tom Galbraith, remarked: "Responsible for the shotgun marriage which created UCS, he has some responsibility to see that there is a sufficient dowry to make the marriage." Yet Benn remained determined to prove that UCS could solve its own problems. Over the next months he held innumerable meetings on the Clyde with management, TUC, shop stewards, and workers. His objective was "to create viable shipbuilding groups to compete profitably for orders at home and abroad," but he now realised that this "required a new approach by management and a new sense of responsibility by the workers involved". Experience had now taught him that it was not just a matter of *telling* the workers, but of involving all those concerned. Both sides needed to accept responsibility for the solution to their problems. Negotiations reached a climax when Benn told UCS on 6 June that "there is no safety net". A week later the company agreed to the appointment of new management under Ken Douglas, formerly of Austin and Pickersgill, while the trade unions accepted 3500 redundancies and an end to demarcation disputes. In return the SIB would inject £4.5m as capital, taking a 48% shareholding, and provide a further £5m in loans. The Cabinet Economic Policy Committee reluctantly endorsed the agreement on the basis that there could be no further assistance.

No amount of goodwill could conceal the fact that UCS needed more money to cope with its short-term liquidity crisis while the long-term reforms took effect. Within three months the magnitude of the problem once more threatened to engulf Benn, and after several visits from Jack Diamond of the Treasury and Harold Lever from Mintech, he announced a further £7m loan on 11 December 1979. The SIB was opposed to such further assistance on the grounds that UCS was unviable and its difficulties intractable; but the Government, approaching a General Election, was afraid of further unemployment in Scotland. Benn acknowledged that wider economic and social considerations had played a part in the latest stage of the UCS crisis, yet he continued to hope that UCS's new management would cooperate with the unions to make a viable company.

Looking back on the events, Benn admitted that UCS problems would not have been solved even if twice the amount of money asked for had been offered at any point in time. "So I think we were right to insist on certain reforms and changes being carried out at every stage." Both sides had made mistakes: the Government in uncritically regarding modern management techniques as a solution; UCS in their dealing with the unions; and both parties had dramatised the situation to negative effect. "I recognise that in going around saying 'there is no safety net', there was a danger that I would give the impression that the company was about to be dropped by the Government, which was a view we never took."[8]

Whatever the defects of Labour's *indirect* intervention in reorganising the shipbuilding industry, the *direct* dependence of the aircraft industry upon Government support seemed to provide further complications. As Minister of Technology, Benn was responsible for the Government's procurement of military aircraft, amounting to £200m a year, as well as the controversial Concorde project. The industry was vital to Britain's prosperity, with sales reaching £550m in 1967 and exports of £232m making a significant contribution to the balance of payments. However, a gradual shift from military to civil aircraft production had led to a decline in Government assistance, and was exposing the industry to fierce international competition. The new Labour Government was anxious about uncontrollable development costs and before Benn took charge had cancelled several major projects, including the TSR 2, HS 681 and P II54. The doubts about the future of the industry and its viability led the Government to appoint the Plowden Commission in December 1964. Plowden reported a year later recommending a merger of the two airframe-makers, the British Aircraft Corporation and Hawker Siddley, with a minority government shareholding. The Plowden conclusion was that Britain should never again develop a major aircraft alone, but ought instead collaborate in developing a European aircraft-industry capable of competing with the US.

The problems, Benn foresaw, were two fold: governments could easily make wrong decisions about complex and costly projects; yet aircraft manufacturers could not afford to develop these on their own or exploit the international market. Second, there was a danger that firms might abuse the enormous concentration of economic power which they controlled. Nevertheless, in February 1967 Benn began negotiations for the merger of the two airframe-makers to gear up the industry for international collaboration. When agreement was not forthcoming, he pressed for full public ownership, but the Cabinet Committee, chaired by Anthony Crosland, rejected this solution as politically unacceptable.

The continued uncertainty about the future of the aircraft industry and its relations with Government made for many bitter conflicts. The most publicised was Benn's dismissal of Cyril Wrangham, managing director of Shorts Brothers, the Belfast missile manufacturers in which the Government held a 69.5% shareholding. The dispute concerned the discovery of Shorts' £1.5m excess profits on the Seacat missile and its future corporate strategy. The company had been badly affected by the Government's cancellation of the Belfast freighter aircraft; but its objective remained to diversify into the aircraft industry, and hopes rested on the Skyvan light aircraft it was developing. Both Roy Jenkins, who had been Minister of Aviation, and the Treasury were opposed in principle to the expansion of the public sector and to the Skyvan in particular. Benn supported Shorts' strategy and managed to persuade the Cabinet to agree to £1.2m assistance — despite the recent losses — on the strength of Plowden's optimism about the market prospects for light aircraft. However, when Shorts soon returned for a further £3.5m loan to fund Skyvan's development, Benn was forced to refuse and was criticised in Cabinet for having supported the project in the first place. Yet Skyvan turned out to be a huge commercial success and helped safeguard employment of over 7000 people at Shorts in Belfast alone. The price for Government support was the dismissal of Wrangham, to whom Benn's civil servants were hostile, and in protest, the resignation of the entire board of directors.

If the Shorts affair raised important questions about the relationship between the state and the public sector, the sums of money involved were small in comparison with other projects in the private sector where relations were also increasingly strained. The withdrawal of France, in June 1967, from the Anglo-French variable geometry (AF/VG) aircraft-project precipitated its cancellation by Britain, after £18.7m had already been spent on development. It was a blow to the cause of European cooperation, as well as British national prestige, and in Parliament the Opposition castigated Labour as unpatriotic. Benn had disagreed with the abandonment of the project in Cabinet; but in public he concentrated on attacking the hypocrisy of those who opposed support for civil aircraft on commercial grounds, yet were in favour of military and prestige projects. He criticised past Governments for spending £3500m on military aircraft and £1500m on research between 1945–65, while the millions lost in cancellations would have met the cost of the world's airforces for a generation. "Ministers of Aviation ran off with sums of money that made the great train robbers look like schoolboys pinching pennies from a blind man's tin."[9]

Benn's attitude to the launching or cancellation of aircraft projects and to technology in general was, if anything, consistently commercial. It was evident from his contributions in parliamentary debates and public speeches that he considered the commercial exploitation of technology as inseparable from the scale of industry. He thought it

... broadly speaking true that the scale on which they (companies) operate is too small (and consequently) one of the principal objects of Mintech (is) to try to bring about larger units in British engineering industry. . . . Technology imposes an inexorable scale in our economic life . . . We want a climate favourable to large companies if we are to stand up to the . . . competition from across the Atlantic.[10]

However, the costs and risks associated with advanced technology also meant that in practice only the state was able to undertake the required research, and consequently it became closely involved in the affairs of the private sector.

The most complete statement of Benn's conception of government-industry relations was set out in a lecture he delivered at Imperial College, London, on "The Government's Policy for Technology". He described Mintech as

... really a Government commitment to the success and profitability of the private sector and the prosperity of all who work in it. Mintech uses direct methods to help industry improve the quality of its productive effort to secure higher rewards for those who work for them and to provide for the community the resources it requires for its collective purposes. . . . Ministers have tended to think of industries as if they had a corporate existence. But they do not. . . . Realism compels me to recognise that in many instances large-scale operations provide the best opportunity for technological exploitation. . . . Our technological policy is an industrial policy, it is a systematic attempt to strengthen our competitive ability.[11]

Benn's interventionist philosophy was a form of "corporatism", in that it consisted of selective government assistance to and cooperation with big business. Indeed, the Imperial College lecture marked the furthest extent of Benn's assimilation of revisionist economic theory. "There will always be arguments about how profits should be distributed as between customer, employer, worker and the community (but) the profitability of a mixed economy is an essential prerequisite of economic growth and commercial success." He found it distressing that capitalism and communism had inspired passionate belief, yet "our own mixed economy has never been capable of stirring an equal degree of enthusiasm". Nevertheless, he drew encouragement from the increasing acceptance of planning in the USA, and the recognition of the profit motive in the USSR, as evidence that two radically different types of society were converging through economic evolution and the passage of time. He called for a renewed commitment to the mixed economy on these grounds and because he believed "that part of the dynamism of all societies stems from a faith in their own character".

If Benn's undiminished optimism contrasted sharply with the generally low morale of his ministerial colleagues, he nevertheless now shared their belief that the July Measures of 1966 had put Britain on the road to recovery. In particular he supported Wilson's strategy of hidden reflation through expanded public support to industry.

On 18 November 1967, Wilson had announced a 14.3% devaluation of sterling from $2.80 to $2.40, blaming the closure of the Suez canal after the seven day Arab-Israeli war in June; the dock strike of September-October; and the speculation against sterling which these events had caused. However, as Samuel Brittan noted: "The sharp turn around in the sterling market occurred, in fact, in the middle of May — about three weeks before the Arab-Israeli war." The real cause of devaluation remained the disequilibrium of the balance of payments and the "failure to achieve a surplus . . . in 1967 represented for the Government a defeat for its economic strategy."[12] The Government were inhabiting a make-believe world and the measures taken only helped turn a surplus of £104m on the current account in 1966 into a deficit of £303m over 1967. The increase in public expenditure, and the decrease in the bank rate from 7% to 5.5%, were inflationary because Labour's fiscal policies restricted the growth in output to 1% during 1967, and as a result imports rose by 5.75%.

The crisis revealed "a situation of chaotic volume", the absence of any devaluation budget or post-devaluation strategy. The bank-rate was increased to a record 8%, hire-purchase down-payments to 40%, corporation tax from 40% to 42.5%, while the selective employment-tax rebate to manufacturers was cancelled and reductions in public expenditure of £200m brought forward. The letter of intent to the IMF pledged Britain to £200m surplus in 1968 and £500m thereafter in exchange for $3000m in loans. On 29 November Roy Jenkins became Chancellor of the Exchequer in a straight transfer with Callaghan, who took over from him as Home Secretary. He adopted a strategy of massive deflation designed to transfer resources out of imports and into exports. A stringent review of public expenditure began immediately, culminating in the cuts of 16 January 1968 which set out to save £325m during 1968–69, £411m in 1969–70, and end Britain's military presence east of Suez. For a Labour Government these were painful decisions; and during the Cabinet discussions, Benn opposed the postponement of raising the school-leaving age from fifteen to sixteen and the reimposition of prescription charges. At the 1968 Labour Party Conference, he admitted:

> We underestimated the time it would take to create the economic resources to back up our social commitments. The fundamental weakness of our industrial structure required more time to correct than anyone could have foreseen. . . . I assure you that anyone observing . . . what is happening in British industry today would, if he were open-minded at all, be converted to the need for public enterprise and public accountability.[13]

Benn began the practice of holding regular meetings with the largest companies with which Mintech had contact, "to intermesh their corporate strategies with the nation's general economic requirement". This innovation was considered by many to be a breakthrough in government-industry relations and helped create a climate of confidence and trust. In the case of Fords, these meetings led to an embryonic planning agreement. But Benn was also prepared to use Mintech's influence to counteract the power of multinational companies, preventing monopolistic price increases by IBM and unfair transfer pricing by Philips. In addition, there were parallel meetings with trade unions, because "we believe it right that the unions should have as close relations with an industrial Ministry as management have".

Throughout 1968–69 Benn was preoccupied with the maintenance of investment during a period of recession and "the task of strengthening our industrial structure". Yet the limitations of Mintech's sponsorship role had become evident early on. His initiative to reorganise the machine-tool industry, which was generally considered too fragmented to be competitive, came to nothing and was opposed by his Mintech officials as dangerously interventionist. In 1967 he established an Institute of Advanced Machine-Tool and Control Technology at East Kilbride in Scotland to meet the industry's research requirements and to stimulate automation in engineering. In January 1968 he introduced two counter-cyclical measures, the machine-tool stock-building and pre-production order schemes. Under the former, Mintech made available £2.5m until the end of 1968 to underwrite the production of machine-tools, so that when the upturn came there would be enough standard components to meet the demand. The purpose of the pre-production order scheme was, as Benn explained "to reduce the gap between the completion of the development of new and advanced designs and their acceptance in industry on a sufficient scale to justify the laying down of adequate production lines". Yet the experiment was not a success, chiefly because most machine-tools had to be made to order and could not easily be standardised. Between 1966 and 1970 Mintech also invested £8m in advanced machine-tools which it leased to companies in order to stimulate demand. The results were encouraging, though Benn admitted that they were not as far-reaching as he had hoped.

With Harold Wilson's support, Benn worked on legislation during 1967 to expand government assistance to private industry and to put this on a more systematic basis. On 1 February 1968 he introduced the Industrial Expansion Bill which the Queen's speech in 1967 had foreshadowed. The Bill was designed to promote schemes for industrial projects calculated "to improve efficiency, create, expand or sustain productive capacity". The Bill also contained a clause to finance Concorde and the QE 2 liner. It raised the NRDC's borrowing powers to £50m and allocated £150m for schemes of industrial expansion. An independent advisory committee under Lord Kearton would recommend assistance and have the right to take an equity in return, but parliamentary approval would be required for any scheme and prior consent for all assistance over £2m. Benn emphasised the Bill's democratic purpose as being

> ... to reform the ragbag of differing powers which had grown up piecemeal over the years without any obvious logic whatever. ... There is a strong case for an Act of Parliament which formally lays down the ground rules upon which such intervention should take place and provides machinery for authorising specific acts of intervention as when Ministers decide to recommend them to Parliament and Parliament to approve them.[14]

Benn argued the case for increased state intervention on wholly pragmatic and strictly non-ideological grounds, looking for all-party support for the measure. It would enable Mintech

> ... to relate the work that will be done under it to the central economic problems facing Britain. . . The Bill seeks to make effective a partnership with industry designed to see that the country is competitive with its foreign competitors. . . . The Government does not intend to prop up declining industries but rather to build on the success of those growth industries where selective assistance is likely to pay off in terms of the national economic interest. . . . There is little disagreement between the two sides of the House on the need for Government financial support for industry. . . . A doctrinal

objection to all intervention is wholly unpracticable. ... Those who criticise the idea of Government interference have a responsibility to provide an alternative answer to this problem.[15]

Nevertheless, even this mild form of intervention aroused violent hostility. The Industrial Expansion Bill was widely interpreted as a socialist concession to the Left, largely because of a speech attacking it by Callaghan to the "under forty" group of MPs. The Confederation of British Industry was totally opposed to it: "We cannot see the need of British Industry was totally opposed to it: "We cannot see the need for this legislation in any way." Ronald Grierson of the temporary expedient to a major principle of economic administration".[16] In Parliament, the Conservatives attacked the Bill's discriminatory basis and exploited the fears of back-door nationalisation. Sir Keith Joseph complained: "We wish to repeat and repeat again that the public sector is inherently likely to be more inefficient than the private sector because it is not subject to the discipline of the market and because in many cases it is subsidised."

The Industrial Expansion Act was certainly open to criticism, but the fears about nationalisation and criticisms of subsidisation were misplaced. The Act was never intended as an instrument of public ownership; and the Government's right to take shareholding by agreement was designed to protect public money invested, while subsidies in the form of grants only related to Concorde and shipbuilding. However, it remained to be seen whether the Act could stimulate capital expenditure, since the relatively small sums involved, £150m, and the selective basis of assistance made it unlikely that a broad wave of investment across the economy would result. Moreover, investment decisions under the Act would involve other factors not directly related to profitability, such as the possibility of exports or import substitution. Similarly, the view that a government loan could turn a marginal investment decision into a profitable one, implied limited potential for a project. In the final analysis, the case for the Act rested on the proposition that the Government could identify the points of growth in the economy which the private sector was unable or had failed to do. But in this aspect the Act was defective. First it was not clear by what criteria the advisory committee or the Government were to recommend investment decision. Secondly, the advisory committee was not a strong independent body with teeth; and thirdly, the disclosure of information between the firms concerned and the Government, as well as between it and Parliament, was inadequate.

While Benn became aware of these shortcomings later on, they were immediately apparent from the time of his intervention in helping Rolls Royce with the Lockheed Tristar contract. In 1967 he had promised launching aid for the project, though he was careful to make clear that it would be limited to 70% of the original development

Read counter-clockwise
Tower Gardens, *1931*. Holiday *1929*, Mother,
Tony, Michael, David, Father. Westminster
School, *1941 (Tony, second left)*. With cousin,
Margaret Rutherford. Holiday *1932*, Michael,
Father, David, Tony. RAF, Pyramids, *1945*.

1

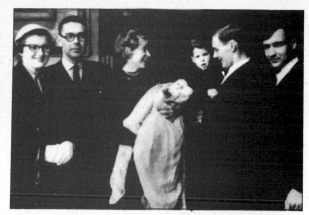

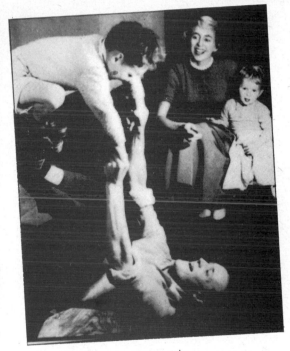

Read top to bottom and left to right
Kenneth Harris, Benn, Edward Boyle, Oxford,
1947. Holiday at Stansgate, 1958. Benns and
children, 1961. Honeymoon, 1949. Children
with grandparents, Lady and Viscount Stansgate.
Caroline and Tony holding Instrument of
Renunciation, Commons, 1963. Melissa's
christening, 1957. At home, 1955.

Family and friends, Stansgate, *1979 (Margaret Stansgate, centre)*. Stephen, Caroline, Melissa, Tony, Joshua, Rosalind *(wife of Hilary who died in 1979)*, Hilary, *1973*. Aunt Rene's 88th birthday, House of Commons, *1970*. Labour Conference, *1978*, Tony, Caroline, Hilary, Stephen.

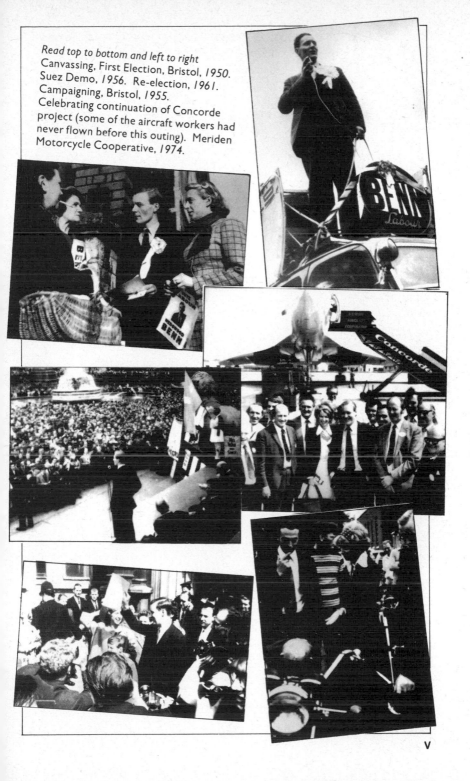

Read top to bottom and left to right
Canvassing, First Election, Bristol, 1950.
Suez Demo, 1956. Re-election, 1961.
Campaigning, Bristol, 1955.
Celebrating continuation of Concorde
project (some of the aircraft workers had
never flown before this outing). Meriden
Motorcycle Cooperative, 1974.

Read top to bottom and left to right
Labour Cabinet, *1974*. President of EEC Council of Ministers,
with Sir Donald Maitland, *1977*. Labour Conference, *1979*.
With Wilson and Vic Feather, *1972*. *June 1975*: first North
Sea oil comes ashore. Wilson's last Cabinet, *1979*.
Yorkshire Area Miner's Banner presentation, DOE, *1976*.

Read top to bottom and left to right
Seretse Khama Defence Council, 1953.
With Alexei Kosygin, Electronics
factory, 1967. With Helmut Schmidt,
Bonn, during lecture tour, 1963. With
Li Xiannian (centre), Peking, 1971.
With Hugh Gaitskell and Bristol MPs,
1955. With LBJ, Washington, 1967.
With U Thant, New York, 1971.

budget and conditional upon "the receipt of an order which in our view will lead to production on an adequate scale". Devaluation transformed Rolls Royce's competitiveness, and in March 1968 the negotiations reached a dramatic climax when it emerged that the Company could win orders against fierce competition from General Electric's CF 6 engine, for perhaps both the Tristar and the Douglas DC10 aircraft. At a critical juncture, Benn offered £9m under the Industrial Expansion Act towards Rolls Royce's working capital requirements, and on 29 March, Rolls Royce's chairman, Sir Denning Pearson, announced that Lockheed had accepted its offer of US $300m for 540 engines. At the press conference, he acknowledged that only "the greatest help and cooperation from the British Government" had made the contract possible.

Benn bathed in the reflected glory of Rolls Royce's triumph and jubilation greeted his statement about the contract on 1 April. Yet when the euphoria had passed, it became clear that both he and Rolls Royce had been seduced by the grandeur of the scheme and that the company's eventual collapse in 1971 in part stemmed from these events. Rolls' agreement to a fixed price contract amounted to commercial suicide: several major technological problems remained unresolved and the size of the engineering task was seriously under-estimated. Benn's spectacular intervention and decision to provide £47.1m launching aid on the basis of inadequate technical budgets and profit forecasts were equally speculative, and, as such, an indictment of his conception of government-industry relations, though later the RB 211 became the basis upon which Rolls Royce could build its future.

The second important aircraft project to be financed under the Industrial Expansion Act was the Anglo-French Concorde which the Conservative Government had begun in 1962. To Conservatives it was a symbol of national prestige, to Benn of a new technological era; and to some, of extravagance and folly. The Labour Government was unsentimental about Concorde, and in October 1964 tried to cancel the project after they had learned that development costs would far exceed the original estimate of £190m, only to discover they were bound to the treaty by international law. By 1967, costs had risen to £450m and were projected to reach £730 by 1970. Concorde was out of control and Benn faced growing demands for its cancellation, though most politicians and powerful vested interests continued to support it. He admitted that the mounting cost was "a matter of serious concern", but warned against "hysteria and panic". Devaluation had put Concorde's future in doubt, and he only persuaded the Cabinet to continue it after successfully renegotiating the original treaty with France. "The Government remains committed to this great project," he declared, though "the commercial equation with which I have to live daily" had made him realise that Concorde must prove itself economically viable. This constant preoccupation helped explain why he was initially so insensitive to popular anxiety about Concorde's sonic boom.

The third major aircraft project Benn supported under the Industrial Expansion Act was the production of the Bulldog and Pup light aircraft by the Beagle Aircraft Company. Pressed Steel Fisher had formed Beagle by merging with Auster and Miles Aircraft Companies in 1960, but decided to liquidate it when it itself merged with British Leyland in 1968. Though Beagle had made losses in 1966–67 because of military aircraft cancellations and development expenditure, Benn was convinced that a market existed for the light aircraft it had designed. Plowden had recommended assistance for this industry and in 1968 Benn managed to persuade the Cabinet to agree to a grant of £2.4m on the strength of the Company's own projections of sales of 3000 aircraft worth £200m and a return to profitability by 1972. However, with the American market nearly 100% dominated by US companies, a failure was likely; and in 1969 the Government had to make a further loan of £3.3m. But by the autumn, it was clear that Beagle could not break even by 1972. On 1 October 1969 Benn visited the company and reluctantly concluded that it was unviable, announcing the appointment of a government receiver on 2 December.

When the receivers reported at the end of February 1970, the outcry against Benn was deafening. They revealed that Beagle was insolvent by £1.2m. Frederick Corfield, the Conservative Aviation spokesman, condemned Benn's "mammoth miscalculation" and mishandling of the affair. It has, he said, been "the most shocking act of callous irresponsibility that the Minister of Technology has been prepared to sacrifice this company on the altar of his own political ambitions. I am sure that the truth will catch up with him. I believe that if he does not resign now, he will be destroyed later."[17]

How fair were these judgements? The wave of inflammatory weekend speeches attacking Benn revealed more about the growing polarisation of the two Parties on industrial policy than about the episode itself. Benn had acted in accordance with strict commercial criteria and arguably with courage, since it was difficult to pull out at a late date. "The temptation for any Government to go on and hope that things will come out right is extremely great."

Years after the event Benn continued to feel that "I ought to have fought for money. We ought to be able to produce light aircraft in this country." However, the central question at the time remained whether Britain could *sell* light aircraft profitably. According to the Ministry's original assessment, this could have been the case. Yet Benn's handling of the matter had meant that Beagle had been undercapitalised from the start, and neither Mintech nor the Company had managed its finances properly. The grants and loans had gone to finance the Company's working capital requirements, rather than capital expenditure, and consequently it never had the means to capture the share of the market it had originally hoped for.

In promoting schemes of industrial expansion, Benn's objective was the profitable exploitation of existing, rather than the development of, new technology: "Half our problems in the past stemmed from the decision to remain in the most advanced fields and hope later to be able to sell equipment instead of gearing our own efforts to what the market really wants."[19] The state had become an entrepreneur and Mintech encouraged the NRDC to use its extended borrowing powers under the Act to lend £5m for the development of carbon fibres, micro-electronic and silicon integrated circuits and other projects. More controversially, Mintech made loans of £63m under the Act for the establishment of a British aluminium smelting industry, saving an estimated £50m a year in imports — but this needed cheap subsidised electricity to make it a profitable venture. The idea of import substitution was further extended to the paper industry where loans of £2.85m would benefit the balance of payments by £2.1m a year.

Benn mainly used the Industrial Expansion Act to bring about economies of scale in British industry. As he put it, "The achievement of a more efficient industrial structure, especially in manufacturing industry has been a major concern of the Ministry of Technology." He was enthusiastic about the spate of mergers of the late 1960s, and supported the IRC £25m investment in the GEC takeover battle, which enabled it to acquire the ailing AEI without reference to the monopolies commission. The IRC was highly active in this area, and both it and Benn were criticised by companies and investors for interfering with the market mechanism. Its wheeling and dealing on the stock-exchange led to a number of mergers that would otherwise never have taken place, such as the takeover of Kent Instruments by Cambridge Instruments and the merger of Delta, GEC and Pirelli's cable manufacturing interests. The most spectacular was the formation of the Ransome, Hoffman, Pollard ball-bearings group. Both Benn and the IRC were perturbed by the Swedish manufacturer, SKF's increasing domination of the UK market, and successfully fought its takeover of Brown Bayley, helping Ransome and Marke to buy out Pollard Ball and Roller Bearing Co. Ltd, then married the two businesses on the ground that a strong British-controlled element was essential to a beneficial rationalisation of the ball-bearing industry.

This growing concentration was arguably the most important long-term development under the 1964–70 Labour Government. Between 1965–70, the leading 100 manufacturing companies' share of output rose from 37% to 45%; but the merger movement of the late 'sixties had little to do with industrial efficiency. None of the mergers led to either increased investment or expansion. The majority were caused by an unfavourable economic climate which inflated asset values and depressed trading profits and share prices. Those who worked in the firms concerned were never consulted: the GEC merger resulted in the closures of marginally less profitable factories in Liverpool, while Tube Investments did the same at Bedford, in the name of rationalisation.

Those mergers which Benn inspired had industrial logic behind them at least, and the formation of International Computers Ltd (ICL), which he announced in March 1968, was the best example of positive restructuring. The Government had provided £13.5m in grants and loans and now proposed to invest a further £3.5m, taking a 10.5% shareholding and appointing a director under the Industrial Expansion Act. Benn defended state participation against charges of backdoor nationalisation and said it was necessary to enable ICL to develop and exploit the next generation of computers which were "so fundamental to our industrial structure and competitive power that we cannot as a nation afford to depend wholly on foreign or foreign-controlled manufacturers. . ." A state holding in ICL was a non-ideological and temporary measure.

The restructuring of the nuclear power industry did not take place under the Industrial Expansion Act. The central problem Benn faced here was not one of nuclear-reactor choice or safety, but failure to obtain orders for the nuclear reactors already developed. A Conservative Government had established the Atomic Energy Authority in 1954, full of optimism; but since then, Britain had only ever sold two magnox reactors to Italy and Japan. In 1965 Labour opted for the Advanced Gas Cooled Reactor (AGR), in preference to the Steam-Generating High-Water Reactor (SGHWR) — though both of these had been developed by the AEA — and the American Boiling Water Reactor (BWR). In addition, Britain had played a major role in the OECD Dragon Project to develop a high temperature reactor (HTR). Though the AGR was less economical than other reactors, its electricity generating capacity was greater and its commercial prospects were considered good. In 1966 the CEGB ordered four AGR power-stations and the three UK consortia set up a British Nuclear Export Executive to market nuclear technology; but no further orders resulted. Benn concluded that the industry's organisational structure, the separation of design from marketing and construction, lay at the root of its commercial problems. He also considered that competition between the UK consortia was wasteful and unreal since the industry was dependent on the Government as its customer and needed a stable ordering programme if it was to survive. In August 1966 he initiated a full review of its institutions, calling in the heads of the three consortia in early 1967 to discuss the formation of a single company to merge with the AEA, but with majority Government participation. The consortia, however, refused to submerge their own interests. A powerful lobby, they attacked Benn's plans as socialist-inspired, because he had insisted on majority public participation, which was reasonable given that the Government had a responsibility to regulate this kind of technology. His chief objective was to bring the AEA closer to the market rather than public ownership, and in 1968 he tried an alternative approach of minority public participation, hiving off the AEA's nuclear research. On 17 July he announced plans for the reorganisation of the nuclear power industry. The AEA would be replaced by an Atomic Energy Board which "would concern itself with R&D programming, expert coordination and major policy matters"; while a new publicly owned company would take over its fuel-processing operations. By the end of the year he had won agreement for the proposals and in early 1969 announced the formation of two new consortia, Atomic Power Construction Limited and British Nuclear Construction and Design Limited.

Benn's reorganisation failed to solve the basic problem of designing a commercially competitive nuclear reactor because research still remained divorced from construction. However, on the nuclear fuel-supply side, and in the sphere of international collaboration, the state had a much more obvious role to play: and Benn, in these areas, enjoyed greater success. British Nuclear Fuels was established and prospered as an independent company. In 1967 Mintech reached agreement with the Italian Government to reprocess spent fuel at Windscale and entered into a contract with Rio Alcan for domestic uranium supplies. The enriched uranium project at Capenhurst culminated in the Gas Centrifuge Treaty with Germany and Holland for the production of 150 tons a year of enriched uranium by 1970, making Britain the world's leading power in this area.

Benn endeavoured to adopt a positive but realistic attitude to international collaboration. When the Cabinet met at Chequers on 30 April 1967 to review the Government's policy towards the EEC, he supported Britain's application. Later commenting in the House of Commons on the factors which led him to that view, he admitted that he had been disappointed by the failure of successive Government policies to solve Britain's economic problems, and this pessimism had played a part in shaping his approach to the Common Market.

Benn was able to achieve much greater success in relations with Eastern Europe, where cooperation rather than competition prevailed. In 1967 he negotiated a technology and trade agreement with the Soviet Union after Kosygin had visited Britain. It was hailed as a breakthrough in East-West relations and set a precedent for similar agreements with Czechoslovakia, Hungary, Rumania and Yugoslavia for the export of computers, chemicals and textiles, in exchange for minerals and agricultural products. In political terms,

Benn saw trade and technological cooperation as an instrument of detente creating common interests; and in Moscow he expounded to a Russian audience his theory of convergence through progress. He spoke of the damage which imperialism and high defence-expenditure had done to the British economy, arguing that incentive and planning were bringing about its modernisation. Yet, political restraint was the price of detente, and he found himself, and the Government, much criticised for not openly protesting about Gerald Brooke's imprisonment — though Benn did appeal in private.

Despite the continuing problematic nature of Government-industry relations, the crises at UCS and elsewhere, Benn's record as Minister of Technology sufficiently impressed Wilson to have him put Benn at the helm of the expanded Mintech, the "super-ministry" he announced in his Governmental reorganisation of 5 October 1969. The new colossus took over the Ministry of Power, the Board of Trade's responsibility for regional policy and the Department of Economic Affairs' role in supervising the work of the IRC.

It employed 39,600 people; its budgeted expenditure for 1970–71 came to £2530m, and it was in effect a Department of Industry. Benn was supported by three ministers, Harold Lever, who was in the Cabinet as Paymaster-General, Eric Varley and Lord Delacourt-Smith. Sir Keith Joseph felt it was "too big for any Minister", denounced Benn as the "biggest takeover bidder of all time" and the interventionism for which he stood. "The objective I have set myself... is that the new department should be run as a united department and not as a conglomerate of its component parts. .... The division of responsibility must not lead to fragmentation of effort," Benn replied.

The new super Mintech retained the essential characteristics of the old, with new delegated responsibility for all programmes and a central ministerial decision for policy initiatives. Benn's permanent secretary, Sir Richard Clarke, wrote: "The Ministry's main task is to be the central point of contact between Government and most of industry . . . and to initiate action where necessary to improve economic performance and technological capability."[18] Later he came to the conclusion that "it never had anything approaching the resources which would have been required for this purpose". Benn faced an enormous challenge and initiated a comprehensive review of industrial policy. But the absence of any serious re-thinking was disturbingly apparent. "A degree of confidence in the stability of Government measures to encourage investment is an essential part of the future growth of investment," he declared, defending the cost-effectiveness of Labour's investment grants and Regional Employment Premium. Yet changes in policy were few. In March 1970 Mintech relaxed the conditions for granting Industrial Development Certificates to encourage the location of more industry in the Midlands and the South. Benn also raised the IRC's funds from £150m to £340m to strengthen its emerging role as a state merchant bank. The Ministry was satisfied that the contribution made by the IRC in helping with industrial expansion and restructuring was a sound investment. The Queen's Speech had foreshadowed legislation to reorganise the gas and electricity supply industries, and Benn claimed that one of the results of this industrial restructuring was a growth in private-sector research expenditure: "We have helped to create units big enough to run and finance more of their own scientific and research capability." His Green Paper on R&D policy of January 1970 was the logical conclusion of this policy, proposing, as it did, to concentrate all Government research in an expanded National Research and Development Corporation as a publicly-owned company and a subcontractor for private industry.

Though Benn still talked of technology bringing about "a third industrial revolultion", he was increasingly pessimistic and critical of its value in isolation: "Industrial stagnation inevitably leads to the curtailment of science spending, just as industrial success allows its growth." The Labour Government seemed generally more complacent than the economic situation justified. During 1968 the balance of payments had continued to deteriorate, the visible deficit widening from £555m in 1967 to £667m. The current account showed an adverse payments balance of £287m and many commentators at the time thought this was chiefly due to the Government's failure to control the money supply. Consumer spending grew unchecked, and after renewed speculation against sterling in November 1968, Roy Jenkins was forced to deflate the economy still further. During the next two years the balance of payments at last came right; but as Jenkins admitted: "We were floated up more by the buoyancy of world trade than by our own efforts."[19] At home, the economy stagnated as a result of Labour's tax measures, while Wilson irresponsibly allowed wages to rise for electoral purposes — thus creating the conditions for a future inflationary and balance of payments crisis. Investment remained firm despite the average 1.8% growth rate experienced between 1966–70, chiefly due to the large scale of Labour's subsidies. The most significant development was the collapse of business profits in the face of intensified international competition and workers' demands. The long-term outlook was frightening as industry entered a spiral of decline with lower profits depressing the rate of investment.

Benn failed to recognise either these disturbing symptoms or the underlying malaise. During the debate on the Queen's Speech, in November 1969, he argued that the best guarantee of economic growth was "the confidence of the business community that the balance of payments will go right and stay right . . . The truth is that the relationship between Government and industry is close because there is a powerful common interest joining them together." He denied that the burden of taxation had wrecked the economy, attacking the myth that Britain was overtaxed: "It has long been accepted that the redistribution function of taxation is part of the normal process of modern government (and) an essential part of economic management."

Events during 1969-70 did much to confirm the limitations of Labour's industrial and economic policies. The low level of demand led to excess capacity in the energy sector, created problems of economic pricing and threatened to disrupt the gradual peaceful contraction of the coal-mining industry. It caused Benn to introduce further protectionist legislation, extending grants for losses incurred through the postponement of pit closures. Investment in the basic nationalised industries was minimal, reflecting the general stagnation of the economy, while the steel industry was particularly affected because nationalisation had failed to solve its structural problems. More concerned with efficiency than expansion here, Benn postponed plans for new steel mills in Lanarkshire and Yorkshire and initiated a further reorganisation of BSC.

The re-emergence of unemployment as a political issue, for the first time since the 1930s, was symptomatic of the seriousness of the deepening recession. The numbers out of work had doubled from 300,000 to 600,000 between 1966-70, and the Conservative Party condemned the Government because of the lengthening dole queues. Roy Jenkins had endorsed a higher underlying rate of unemployment in order to keep the economy in equilibrium in his 1970 budget. Benn saw unemployment as a regional and structural problem, and so was strong in his defence of Labour's policies: "The white heat of the technological revolution is what happens to a man when his job, because of the process by which he earns his living, is replaced by a new process, disappears . . . (Unemployment) in its long-term sense is a problem of trying to enable an industrial structure to be competitive enough to sustain full employment."

By 1970, the politics with which Benn had been so deeply associated during the 1960s had been discredited, and the picture painted by Labour's manifesto, *Now Britain's Strong, Let's Make it Great to Live in*, was a false one. The balance of payments was only temporarily restored, at the price of deflation, and the overall effect of Labour's taxation and public expenditure policies was to accelerate the deindustrialisation of Britain, encouraging the movement out of the market and manufacturing sectors of the economy. The interventionist policies which Benn had stood for as Minister of Technology had failed to raise the underlying level of investment, though they had sustained it. But they were defective in restructuring industry and lacked any notion of government as being part of the economy and operating within it. By 1970, Benn too had come to recognise the shortcomings of relations between Government and industry, and in his plan for

"Mintech 1970–75" predicted:

> Economic planning will consist more and more of the intermeshing of national and corporate strategies . . . We must recognise the division of ownership from control . . . Shareholders no longer perform a monitoring function . . . Government and the trade unions are therefore going to be driven into a position where they assume the function of shareholders.[20]

In particular, he stressed the role that the trade union movement and industrial democracy must play in reshaping economic relations. In so doing, he began to make clear how his experiences as Minister of Technology and Labour's uninspiring legacy would make him into a socialist.

TONY BENN

VI

1968-1970

THE NEW POLITICS

As for the best leaders the people do not notice their existence. The next best the people honour and praise; the next the people fear; and the next the people hate. But when the best leaders' work is done, the people say 'we did it ourselves'.

ATTRIBUTED TO LAO TZI

Between 1968-70 Tony Benn laid the theoretical foundations of his socialism. The contrast between the libertarian politics he was developing and the mechanistic corporatism with which he was closely identified at Mintech was striking. The views he expounded during these years about the meaning of democracy received considerable and adverse publicity. Benn was criticised for the contradiction between his thoughts as a politician and actions as a Minister. This was seen as proof of a calculating opportunism.

On closer examination, Benn's new politics were neither completely new nor contradictory. They were the direct result of his experience as Minister of Technology and as a member of the 1966-70 Labour Government. Labour's industrial policies had both failed to stimulate investment and alienated the working classes. Benn reacted more strongly than many against this failure to fulfil the promise of modernisation and reform. His search for explanations and potential solutions led him back to the democratic roots of his politics in the dissenting and radical traditions.

Benn was one of the first members of the Government to recognise that its deflationary economic policies would have far-reaching political consequences. The limitations of Labour's interventionist policies and the contradictory nature of its objectives now lay exposed. Economic growth, full employment, stable prices, balance of payments and exchange-rate equilibrium were seen to be incompatible. The consensus framework, along with the existing distribution of economic power within which they were conceived, were increasingly being questioned. The July Measures of 1966, the devaluation of sterling in November 1967 and the public expenditure cuts of January 1968 had created a crisis within the Party about its aims and identity. As Peter Jenkins put it: "The Party was rotting at the grass roots." The 1966 annual Party Conference, albeit by small majorities, had demanded stricter control of prices, rents and dividends, as well as condemning the Government's pro-American policy on the Vietnam war. The morale of the PLP was low and several back-bench revolts had occurred: twenty-seven abstained on the prices and incomes legislation in 1966; sixty-three on the defence white paper in February 1967; twenty-five on the 1968 public expenditure cuts in an opposition motion of no confidence.

Benn saw these trends as symptomatic of the breakdown of the post-war consensus. Having identified closely with the ideals of the New Britain, he shared the disillusionment of many Party members. In February 1968 he wrote an open letter to his constituents in which he analysed what had gone wrong with the Labour Party. He distinguished three broad possibilities: either the Labour Government had merely been blown off course by economic difficulties, or the Government had compromised its principles, or most extremely, a Labour Government would inevitably and deliberately seek to betray the Party which had elected it. The central problem, he stated, was that Members of Parliament and the Government were responsible to the electorate as a whole, as well as to the Labour Party, and this conflicted with the conception of the Labour Government as being in a special sense, the agent of the Party. In practice, the Cabinet, or Shadow Cabinet, jointly agreed the manifesto with the NEC. Benn's solution was for the NEC to play a more active role in fostering relations between Government and Party. It should represent the views and anxieties of Party members to the Cabinet, interpret Government policy in the context of Labour's philosophy and itself function as a policy-making body. Finally, he stressed the need to strengthen the Party's organisation and for it to sustain the Government in power during its period of great unpopularity.

Benn's appeal was seen as a firm declaration of the importance of the Party at a time when it was wholly overshadowed by the Government, and this marked the beginning of a campaign for a mid-term manifesto. In May, Benn outlined his ideas about the manifesto's shape to the NEC, arguing that only a dispassionate analysis and assessment of the Labour Government's record, combined with healthy self-criticism and a restatement of objectives could restore Labour's credibility. The mid-term manifesto, he wrote, "should underline the revolutionary character of the changes that have to be made. . . The identification of the Labour Party with the ideals of a participating democracy is a real one."[1]

In Cabinet, Benn was criticised for undermining the Government, as well as for issuing a confidential paper to the national press. Its value, however, was soon recognised and the idea taken up by George Brown who introduced the NEC statement, "Britain: Progress and Change", at the Party Conference in October. The text of the document closely reflected Benn's draft and summing up the debate,

Benn stated:

> The main thing that has emerged . . . was that in a modern democracy
> people want to be invited to participate more fully . . . The fundamental role
> of the Party, the alliance between the trade unions, the cooperative
> movement and the Political Party is of critical importance for this country
> . . . The truth of interdependence is this . . . without the Party, the Cabinet is
> powerless and without the people the Party is powerless and here is the
> message, without the Party the people of this country are powerless to
> control their own destinies.[2]

The campaign for a mid-term manifesto was in fact part of a more
general attempt on Benn's part during 1968 to open up parliamentary
politics to a wider discussion of contemporary issues. The series of
speeches he made reflected the intellectual ferment of the late 'sixties
and stood out against a backcloth of industrial unrest in Britain and
Europe, student protest on an interntional scale and the Vietnam war.
As Minister of Technology, Benn had come to the conclusion that the
malaise of the time was a direct consequence of technological change,
and this led him to a new appreciation of the relevance of Marxist
economic theory. As Marx himself had written in *Das Kapital:*
"Technology discloses man's mode of dealing with nature, the process
of production by which he sustains his life and thereby lays bare the
mode of formation of his social relations and the mental conceptions
that flow from them."[3]

For Benn, technology helped explain how the economy worked and
human consciousness changed; but his analysis remained fundamentally an open-minded rather than a determinist one modelled on
historical materialism or scientific socialism. Benn's vision, as always
was primarily moral and stressed the challenge technology presented
to the human spirit. Technology may have led to the concentration of
power in the hands of big business and government; but it had also led
to greater interdependence of capital and labour and sharpened the
conflict between them. The enormous complexity of modern industrial
society, the effect it had upon popular attitudes, had not only outdated national institutions but had rendered the idea of authority
obsolete. As Benn put it, "Technology . . . releases forces that
simultaneously permit and encourage decentralisation, diversity and
the fuller development of the human personality." Affluence and the
spread of education had caused a revolution of rising expectations: and
in liberating people from poverty, presented them with moral choices
concerning the distribution and use of power and wealth.

At the same time Benn saw that modern technology had brought
alienation and frustration by separating people from the process of
decision-making. Benn argued that the contradiction inherent here
had stimulated demands for greater democracy in all aspects of public
life as the proliferation of pressure groups — such as the Child Poverty
Action Group and Shelter — proved. The thesis he advanced could be

described as a dialectic of democracy, in which the opposing trends towards the centralisation of state power and its decentralisation on behalf of the people would resolve themselves through democratic popular control.

On 25 May 1968, at a meeting of the Welsh Council of Labour in Llandudno, Benn first publicly discussed the challenge these developments posed to the parliamentary system and the issues they raised. The speech, "From Parliamentary to Popular Democracy", analysed the need for democratic reforms and set out the main themes that would characterise his politics during the 1970s and beyond.

Much of the present wave of anxiety, disenchantment and discontent is actually directed at the present parliamentary structure. Many people do not think that it is responding quickly enough to the mounting pressure of events or the individual or collective aspirations of the community . . . People want a much greater say. That certainly explains some of the student protests against the authoritarian hierarchies in some of our universities . . . Much of the industrial unrest — especially in unofficial strikes — stems from worker resentment and their sense of exclusion from the decision making process . . . All these tendencies are indicative of a general and inevitable trend away from authoritarianism and towards personal responsibility . . . We are moving rapidly towards a situation where the pressure for the redistribution of political power will have to be faced as a major political issue. The implications of this for our system of parliamentary democracy and for the Labour Party which works within it are far-reaching . . . I am not dealing here with the demand for the ownership or control of growing sections of the economy. I am thinking of the demand for more political responsibility and power for the individual than the present system of parliamentary democracy provides . . . of a participating democracy under which more and more people will have an opportunity to make their influence felt on decisions that effect them.[4]

Benn proposed major changes in several areas of public life. First, there would have to be parallel moves towards open government and greater disclosure of information to government and society, since "nothing buttresses the established order so effectively as secrecy". Second, the principle of direct sharing in decision-making by the electorate led logically to consultative and affirmative referenda with legislation submitted to popular instead of royal assent. Third, a participating democracy would involve a radical re-examination of mass communications to make these more accessible to the diversity of views held by the public. Fourth, Benn stressed the increasing importance of minority pressure groups to democracy in a highly complex industrial society. These should be consulted on matters of policy and encouraged to develop as self-regulating and representative organisations. Finally, a self-governing community would also devolve much more responsibility to regions and localities. "This does not involve the fragmentation of society into geographic areas. It means identifying those decisions which ought to be taken in and by an area most affected by those decisions."

Benn prophesied that:

The pressures for change along these lines are as inevitable as was the incoming tide that ultimately engulfed King Canute. These are among the main political issues that will be argued about in the 'seventies and beyond. . . . Adjustments will have to be made . . . If they are not, discontent, expressing itself in despairing apathy or violent protest, could engulf us all in bloodshed. It is no good saying it could not happen here. It could . . . The widening gulf between the Labour Party and those who supported it last time could well be an index of the Party's own obsolescence . . . A participating Labour Party will involve . . . many changes . . . The evolution of the Labour Party is very closely bound up with the evolution of parliamentary democracy. In a world where authoritarianism of the left or right is a very real possibility, the question of whether ordinary people can govern themselves by consent is still on trial — as it always has been and always will be. Beyond parliamentary democracy as we know it, we shall have to find a new popular democracy to replace it.[5]

Benn's Llandudno speech made national headlines and caused an uproar in parliamentary circles. Controversy centred on the proposal to introduce referenda, particularly Benn's futuristic and unfortunate reference to push-button electronic referenda which caused the issues he raised to be obscured and trivialised. *The Guardian* leader, "The Risks of Referenda", ignored his comments about the limitations of referenda and was in Benn's view an arrogant assertion that MPs were more intelligent than their electors. Taking the example of capital punishment, he maintained that "I've no reason to believe that ordinary people, after they'd reflected on the question in the full light of their own responsibility, wouldn't reach the same conclusions as those of the House of Commons."

Benn's speech coincided with the May events in Paris and he was accused of inciting violence as well as undermining the Government and parliamentary democracy itself — though in fact he had worked on the speech for over two months. Quintin Hogg dismissed his ideas as "a load of old codswallop" on the television programme, *Panorama;* and on 29 May, Benn was forced to defend his own behaviour at a meeting of the PLP where George Strauss attacked him. As he was later to claim again, Benn here maintained that "Cabinet responsibility relates to what a Cabinet has done, is doing or is seriously thinking of doing. It does not limit the right to think aloud about long-term future policy."

Benn was not deterred by the hostile reaction, and during 1968 went on to make the series of speeches he had planned, examining in greater depth the issues he had raised in Llandudno. Their unifying theme was the need to extend democracy and actively involve people in all spheres from which they had thus far been excluded. His most controversial speech was about "Broadcasting in a Participating Democracy" which he made at a meeting of the Hanham Labour Party in Bristol on 18 October. Yet, in many respects, Benn's recommendations to allow popular access to broadcasting were not new ones but an extension of the proposals he had advocated for the decentralisation and devolution of the BBC during the 1950s and as Postmaster-General. His concern about the political implications of broadcasting and its control over dissemination of information and the formation of opinion arose from the traditional radical view of Parliament's role as a national talking shop.

> The mass media, and especially broadcasting, now play a large part in shaping our attitudes, our outlook, our values and indeed the whole nature of our society . . .
>
> Parliament imperfectly performed this function in the centuries that preceeded the adoption of the universal franchise. Through talk we tamed kings, restrained tyrants, averted revolution and ultimately reflected public needs in such a way as to help to shape public policy. In this the BBC has assumed some of the role of Parliament.[6]

Benn did not denigrate the BBC's achievements and emphasised that he was not "proposing direct or indirect Government control of the mass media to which I would be wholly opposed". However, he criticised the narrowness of the range of opinion represented, the personalisation and over-simplification of current affairs, the emphasis on the sensational and dramatic, and the editorial control over their presentation. "What is wrong is that availability or access is still too restricted . . . We have lived with this publishing gap ever since the BBC was established . . . Broadcasting is really too important to be left to the broadcasters, and somehow we must find some new way of using radio and television to allow us to talk to each other."

Benn's speech and especially his final rhetorical sentence, which was never quoted in full, provoked a barrage of criticism that was only explicable in terms of the vested interests he had challenged. As *The Sunday Times* put it: "Let Mr. Benn imagine the untold suffering that would be inflicted upon innocent people by the endless procession of self-esteeming, flatulent and unedited worthies."[7] *The Times* chose to avoid the issue of popular access altogether and claimed: "He exaggerates the superficiality of the BBC's current affairs programmes."[8] In private, the BBC, whom Benn had informed about the speech, complained of interference to Harold Wilson who rebuked Benn in a memo: "Gurus should remain on the Wolverhampton circuit", he wrote, comparing Benn to Enoch Powell. To this, Benn replied as "the Guru of Millbank Tower" dissenting from this view. Wilson was probably afraid that the Opposition and press would use the speech in a smear campaign to blacken Labour as the Party hostile to freedom of speech. Certainly, Ray Gunter, former Minister of Labour who called for Benn's dismissal, thought at least as much.

Wilson had also hoped to use Crossman's forthcoming Guildhall Granada Lecture to appeal for Labour's fairer treatment in the press; while Crossman himself was angry because his own speech, which merely called for more in-depth and serious broadcasting, had been preempted. Benn's justification lay in the resolution of the 1968 Labour Party Annual Conference demanding the democratisation of the media, and he had undoubtedly helped start the campaign for open broadcasting by supporting the establishment of the Free Communications Group and Labour's own working-party whose influential report, "The People and the Media", would be published in the summer of 1974.

The second theme Benn developed after Llandudno was the need for greater openness to make the parliamentary system effective. As Minister of Technology, responsible for large scale projects such as Concorde and the nuclear programme, he felt that complex decisions could only be properly made with complete disclosure and an assessment of the wider human and social consequences. In formulating criteria for the assessment of new technology, Benn emphasised the central importance of accountability.

> The time scale of technological development is so long and the costs so high that if there is no discussion during the formative stage, people may wake up one day and find that major technological changes are well advanced and it is too late to stop them . . .
>
> To argue for the exclusion of these issues from popular control is not only fundamentally undemocratic but is also completely impracticable. As the implications of scientific and technological decisions become more and more the subject of public interest, people will insist on having a greater say in these decisions . . .
>
> The political leadership that has the most lasting effect exists . . . in the stream of analysis, exploration, interpretation and argument that surely but slowly changes the collective will. What I am saying is not at all new. It is no more than that the method we use to reach our decisions is at least as important, if not more important, as the decisions themselves . . . (This is) what the parliamentary system is all about. It is based upon the belief that how you govern yourself — by argument, election, and accountability . . . — is what really matters.[9]

Benn also recognised the difficulty of political leadership in a scientific age. He believed governments should concentrate more on education, on explaining issues to people, and less on administration. In general, he regarded secrecy as the greatest barrier to leadership, and in particular proposed that ministers be able to use back-bench MPs to strengthen lines of communication between Government, Party and public, as well as the political impulse. In addition, he hoped that the increased participation of the PLP would diminish the sense of frustration engendered by Government policy.

However, Benn was concerned that changes in the political system should not be limited solely to reforms within the Government machine. The emergence of progressively-oriented pressure groups, such as the Comprehensive Schools Committee and the Child Poverty Action Group, were a consequence of technological change that would alter the norms of party politics. Indeed, this was already apparent from intra-party groupings such as the Chartist Socialists, the Monday Club and Liberal Red Guards. In November, he told the Young Fabians:

> To suppose that the vitality of contemporary democratic politics is synonymous with the state of health of the major political parties is to miss the significance of what is happening. . . . The nature of political activity is in the middle of a profound process of change. Greater complexity of issues, greater interdependence of people, the rapid breakdown of authoritarianism and the growing maturity of the people making up the community, are among some of the factors combining to create a completely new situation, calling for a new style in politics. . . . More and more people are banding themselves together to get things done outside the party system. . . . This phenomenon of a myriad of political action groups is not really new. What is new is the realisation that they have now become an integral part of a new style parliamentary democracy, and may, in the process, be undermining the monolithic character of the parties and in part supplanting them.[10]

Benn suggested a number of ways in which the Labour Party could reassert its claim to popular leadership. Firstly, it should broaden the basis of its policy-making by harnessing the expertise of these specialist organisations; but in offering them formal associate status, it should maintain Labour's identity by re-emphasising the importance of ideology. There had been too much pragmatism of late and not enough principle:

> All political parties of the left require both a moral inspiration and a bag of analytical tools to help them diagnose the causes of the current discontent, and to identify the character of the power struggle which lies behind important political controversies. (But) if the Labour Party is to re-emphasise the role of ideology, it has got to do so in an intelligent and liberal way.[11]

In drawing upon its rich and diverse intellectual heritage, Labour could offer coherent and thematic leadership. In addition, it could restore the credibility of Government by acknowledging its limitations, subcontracting some of its work to accountable agencies and so freeing itself to "concentrate on thinking more deeply about the direction and purpose of society and how national aspirations could be realised".

Like many of the ideas Benn now advanced, these could be traced back to the early 'sixties. The proposal to establish contact with pressure groups — which many condemned as a Liberal error — was first expressed in the New Bristol Group and set out in *The Regeneration of Britain.* Indeed none of Benn's proposals to reform the Labour Party or Government were revolutionary in the sense that they involved immediate democratisation; but the democratic principles on which they were based nevertheless did have far-reaching implications.

The same could be said of Benn's new interest in industrial democracy which the Ministry of Technology, particularly the work-in at UCS and the occupation of the GEC factories in Liverpool, had aroused.

> The rush of industrial mergers, many of which Mintech has helped to bring about, is now going on at such a pace that the balance will, unless it is corrected, inevitably tilt against the man at work, in relation to his employer. Indeed one of the problems we have got to face involves a much deeper analysis of the rights of those affected by mergers.[12]

The Labour Party and the trade union movement had only just begun to consider this matter, debating an NEC report at the 1968 annual conference. When Benn addressed the Industrial Society on 27 November, he discussed it in terms of human fulfillment, consultation and participation; but even then he was critical of the limitations of the industrial democracy debate:

> Industrial democracy in the past has tended to rotate around too limited a range of arguments for, or against, nationalisation, workers' control, co-ownership and the planning of worker-directors on the board of management. The role of the trade unions has too often been similarly confined into arguments about wage negotiations, unofficial strikes, and cooling-off periods and prices and incomes legislation.[13]

His future commitment to workers' control or self-management was already present in germ at this period and showed itself in his acknowledgement of the principle that, "if democracy means anything, it means the establishment of institutions through which an individual can influence his own destiny by having some share of control over his material and human environment."

However, Benn's future views on workers' control were not apparent in his initial support for Barabara Castle's White Paper *In Place of Strife,* which proposed powers to impose solutions, strike ballots and conciliation pauses backed by financial penalties. He was in favour of modernising the trade unions and believed that unofficial strikes were damaging the British economy. If he did not understand that the proposals would exacerbate conflict rather than strengthening the unions' democratic organisation, he nevertheless feared the effect the proposals would have on the Labour Party: "Is it right that a Labour Government can under no circumstances seek to modernise because it must accept that it is only the political arm of an established trade union movement?" The deep ambiguity of Benn's plea is evident: "The immediate argument is about industrial relations, but in fact it goes wider than that. It is about the role and function of a Labour Government, and its relationship with the Party that fought to put it into power."[14]

The Government's defeat over *In Place of Strife* on 18 June 1969
— in the face of implacable trade union opposition after the NEC had
rejected the paper, with fifty-three Labour MPs voting against it and
forty more abstaining — was a blow from which it never fully
recovered. Exactly a year later, Labour was defeated in the General
Election of 18 June 1970, despite efforts to restore the Government's
credibility with the public. Although Benn was recognised as the most
outspoken member of the administration, Wilson nevertheless asked
him in August to help coordinate and plan Labour's election
campaign. At the beginning of September, Benn wrote to Wilson
enclosing the memorandum he had circulated to the campaign
committee: "It touches on the role of government as distinct from the
party and may be relevant to your thinking for phase II starting next
January."

The paper described the difficulties of fighting a campaign after five
years in power. In addition, "too few people are yet aware of how
much they stand to lose by the defeat of the Government and the
return to Tory policies. . . . Our approach to the Election must be
designed to overcome each of these difficulties." Benn also drew
attention to new factors inhibiting leadership: the demise of traditional
party loyalties and the rise of a pragmatic problem-solving attitude;
rapid social and technological change combined with the ever-
lengthening period needed for policies to take effect.

> The progressive post-war collapse of national self-confidence is now a major
> problem that has got to be overcome if people are to be persuaded that
> anything can be achieved. Without that, no policy proposals will seem
> credible . . . Without . . . a perspective, a clearer vision of the future, people
> will be more likely to vote according to their apparent, immediate, short-
> term self-interest.

He suggested that Labour emphasise the strength of its team and give
an impression of vigour, as opposed to the Conservative's image as the
party of the past, and revive the message of a "do it yourself" social
revolution to appeal to a wider electorate.

> We should aim to be as candid as possible about our disappointments as well
> as our achievements . . . We should initiate direct talks with the TUC . . . to
> discuss with them the policies that they would like to see implemented in the
> next Parliament . . . Such an approach would be useful to us in formulating
> future policy; and would consolidate the traditional links within the Labour
> movement . . . Above all we should aim to conduct as much of the campaign
> as possible out in the country . . . The grass roots today means going to where
> people meet for their own purposes; being where the problems are.[15]

Few were more zealous in proclaiming the achievements of the
Labour Government or more optimistic than Benn. At the end of
December he gave a Party Political Broadcast reviewing "the most

colossal programme of institutional reform ever undertaken in Britain
. . . I am sure the 'seventies will really see a New Britain emerge." On
6 June 1970, he discussed Labour's aims in the context of
parliamentary democracy in a similar broadcast. Yet it was evident
from his main election speech, "The Test of a Civilised Society", in
Bristol on 15 June, that he feared economic pressures might undermine
the foundations of the "middle ground" in British politics. It was this
fear and the realisation of the extremism this would unleash that drove
him to make a much publicised attack on Enoch Powell. If he over-
reacted, it was because he recognised Powell's election address as the
manifesto of the new right which he had already identified in the early
'sixties.

> Enoch Powell has emerged as the real leader of the Conservative Party in
> this campaign . . . Those who want to know what a Tory Britain could be
> like should read the speeches of Enoch Powell and study them . . . The most
> evil feature of Powell's new conservatism is the hatred it is stirring up,
> playing on fear, fanning suspicion. It has started with an attack on Asians
> and Blacks . . . The flag of racialism hoisted in Wolverhampton is beginning
> to look like the one that fluttered over Dachau and Belsen.[16]

Benn was much criticised for helping to make Powell an election issue
and thus aiding Conservative victory. Indeed, against the background
of the critical speeches he had been making since 1968, Benn's
electioneering, his outward election optimism, rang hollow. By June
1970, it was evident that his inner faith in the Labour Government
policies had been completely undermined. The New Politics, written in
defeat and published in September 1970 as a Fabian pamphlet, was
the culmination of prolonged reflection on the causes of Labour's
failure and the changing nature of politics. It was also a personal
expression of emotions that welled up in defeat. The subtitle, "A
Socialist Reconaissance", was indicative of the new direction of Benn's
thinking. The pamphlet sought to describe "how a Socialist Party,
within the limits of democratic consent, can confront the issues arising
from industrial and technical change in the 1970s". It was concerned
with "the method of politics rather than the content of specific
policies", and underlined that "there are no instant utopias".

Benn had become critical of consensus government because "the
underlying problems of Britain's economic performance have
occupied a central position in all political argument" and its policies
had failed to solve them. Instead, they had frustrated the democratic
aspirations of the New Britain. He had come to the conclusion that
"the alienation of Parliament from the people constituted a genuine
cause for concern. People want to see more real choice in politics and
less personal contest between alternative management teams . . ." He
recognised that the very failure of consensus politics, which had
brought about the election of a radical right wing Government under
Heath, would also give rise to a re-examination of socialist theory and

policies. Conservative policies were based on a disciplinary and managerial view of an ordered society that could not tolerate either democracy or dissent if there were a breakdown in the system. By contrast, Benn held that Labour's commitment to democratic principles and consent meant that, even in crisis, power would be accountable to Parliament and the people. Indeed, his realisation in *The New Politics* that "the campaign (for industrial democracy) is very gradually crystallising into a demand for real workers' control" was evidence of the democratic source of socialism. "It cannot, almost by definition, be imposed from above, having to grow from below in discussion between those concerned, creating a new leadership in the process of discussion, negotiation and conflict which must accompany such a radical change in the relationship between workers and owners of capital". He urged the Labour Party to recognise that the technological revolution it had fostered in the 'sixties had brought about a social revolution "by first creating and then distributing new wealth and the considerable potential power that goes with it". He claimed that the new criteria and the new style of political leadership — committed to a cause rather than the search for elected authority — to which Labour had given birth were Labour's allies.

> Change from below . . . supported by direct action has played a far larger part in the shaping of British democracy than most . . . have ever cared to admit . . . This is not a charter for anarchism, nor a dream of creating a wholly self-regulating economic and political system.
>
> . . . If the Labour Party could see in this rising tide of opinion a new expression of grass roots socialism, then it might renew itself and move nearer to the time when it is seen as the normal government of a more fully self-governing society. . . . To create the conditions which will allow the people to do it themselves is the central task of leadership today.[17]

If Benn's new politics were populist in inspiration, the democratic values he espoused could be traced back to the principles of dissent and a radical view of British history; and looking ahead, to the foundation of his socialist transformation.

VII

1970-1974
CHAIRMAN BENN

Bombard the headquarters.
CHAIRMAN MAO

Tony Benn regarded the Conservatives' electoral victory in 1970 as marking the end of the post-war consensus. The new Conservative Government took office with a coherent programme, determined to reverse Britain's decline and revitalise its economy. Their manifesto, *A Better Tomorrow*, looked forward to the reduction and reform of taxation, less government interference in industry, British membership of the EEC and legislation to control the activities of trade unions. In opposition, Benn soon recognised the nature of the Conservative challenge:

> In a way I admire Heath for confronting at Selsdon and afterwards the reality of the situation which was that you couldn't patch it (the post-war consensus) any more. You had in his view to deal with the root causes of British weakness or decline and you had to do it by rolling back the power of the trade unions and by introducing more competition, and I think that one of his main motives for taking us into Europe was the competition it would bring.[1]

Such were the issues which dominated British politics during the years from 1970 to 1974, polarising and radicalising opinion. As Benn put it, "The Tories went back to Adam Smith, the Labour Party to Clause IV, and the Archbishop of Canterbury to the ten commandments." Throughout this period, Benn was closely associated with deliberating Labour's response to Conservative economic policy, reappraising Labour's own thinking, its attitude towards the EEC, and to a lesser extent, its rapprochment with the trade union movement.

The Conservative commitment to laissez-faire economics meant that Benn, as Shadow Secretary for Trade and Industry, immediately found himself in the front line, having to defend his own ministerial record and to fight against the demolition of Labour's interventionist policies. He pleaded for the retention of the Industrial Liaison Centres, warned against the effects of ending investment grants and of the regional employment premium, and condemned the hiving-off of profitable parts of the nationalised industries. In January 1971, the Secretary of State, John Davies, introduced the Industry Bill to abolish the Industrial Reorganisation Corporation, wind up the Shipbuilding Industry Board and repeal the Industrial Expansion Act. "This Bill is purely destructive," Benn protested, likening the Government to an "old fashioned medieval surgeon who pulls out a hack-saw and cuts off a leg". He observed that the effect of Conservative policies upon employment and incomes had already gravely damaged industrial relations. "In many ways the most serious condemnation of the Government is how they have abandoned the relationship with the trade union movement on everything except industrial disputes . . . The real way ahead (is) to allow the trade unions and their members a growing part in the development of industrial policy."[2]

The logic of laissez-faire Conservatism expressed itself in the Government's decision on 4 February 1971 to allow Britain's most famous company, Rolls Royce, to go into receivership over the Lockheed RB 211 contract. In September 1970, Rolls Royce had approached the Government, submitting a request for £60m additional "launching aid" because the development costs of the RB 211 engine had soared. After the chairman, Lord Cole, had seen the Prime Minister, the Government announced, on 11 November 1970, that they would agree to put up £42m, provided that Rolls Royce obtained a further £18m from private sources and allowed an investigation by independent accountants. Benn was suspicious of the Government's intentions and in Parliament urged the nationalisation of the aircraft industry, regretting "the lack of both consistency and effective accountability in the industrial policy for the private sector pursued by the Government. . . . Competition as it is preached by the Prime Minister and the Secretary of State between firms in a laissez-faire atmosphere has not existed for years."

The truth was that neither Benn nor the Government knew the seriousness of Rolls Royce position until on 21 January 1971 the investigating accountants had reported a probable loss of £100m on the RB 211 contract. The report set out the alternatives and costs of cancellation or postponement, concluding that an increase of £100,000 in the price of each engine would be necessary to make the project viable if contract renegotiations were possible. Rolls Royce otherwise faced the immediate prospect of receivership because of its illiquidity and the extent of its liabilities. On 26 January the Government published the report and its own view as a White Paper. It was not prepared to put up more public money, but would let Rolls Royce go into receivership or liquidation and nationalise those parts where national interest was concerned — such as the production of the Olympus 593 engines for Concorde. Meanwhile, Lord Cole and two other directors urged the Government to reconsider their position.

Lockheed were also in financial difficulties but were willing to renegotiate the RB 211 contract given time. Would not receivership endanger its successful outcome and irreparably damage British industry's international reputation? After minimal consideration, the Cabinet decided on 3 February not to rescue the company, though news that the RB 211 engine had reached the required performance levels came just as the end approached.

The collapse of Britain's most famous company shocked the entire country and was, as Benn put it, "a national tragedy . . . probably the most important industrial decision announced in the House since the war". On 7 February he went to Derby, promising a mass meeting of angry workers that Labour would defend their right to work, and the following day impressed on the Government the danger of 45,000 redundancies. So great was the public anxiety that the Government introduced a one clause Bill on 11 February to nationalise Rolls Royce's entire assets. In search for a scapegoat, the Government found an easy target in Benn. His original decision to support Rolls Royce was undeniably open to criticism as having been speculative and uninformed. At Mintech he had been aware of Rolls Royce's financial and technical problems on the RB 211 and in the Autumn of 1969 had asked the IRC to investigate. The IRC had reported that Rolls Royce's profit forecasts were over-optimistic and that the Company faced future profitability rather than immediate liquidity problems; but it failed to put a financial figure on the known technical difficulties and thereby to point out the dangers of collapse. On the grounds of Rolls Royce's importance, the IRC recommended that it itself make a £10m convertible loan to the Company, that the Government provide a further £10m in launching aid subsequently, and that the IRC appoint a non-executive director. But by the time Lord Beeching was appointed in August 1970, it was already too late.

In encouraging Rolls Royce, Benn had made it clear that there would be no further aid, that the Company would have to absorb any overspending. Should he have known better? He admitted to the Commons in February 1971, "The Government did not have the expertise to check the figures of the most experienced air engineering company in Britain." Later, in evidence to the DTI investigation, he added "I was dealing not only with the most famous engineering company but a company that had blue chip reputation. I am afraid that these factors influenced me." He explained that the Government's attitude had been that Rolls Royce must commit its entire resources to the project and that this would free the Government from having to assess every detail. On reflection, he concluded, "To commit so much to a single project was a very appalling risk."

The Rolls Royce affair made Benn think deeply about the relationship between Government and industry; investment in advanced technology and profits; as well as the importance of disclosure and public accountability. He found it ironical that "If Rolls Royce had been able to build the Lockheed engine on the same basis as they built the Concorde engine, of course they would not have been bankrupt today, and if the Concorde had been built on the same basis as the RB 211 for the Tristar, Rolls Royce would have been bankrupt along with BAC years ago on Concorde."[3] In fact, the collapse of Rolls Royce did affect confidence in Concorde, encouraging its opponents in the US to exploit the environmentalists' anxiety about its noise level. As a Bristol MP with a large number of Concorde workers in his constituency, Benn flew to New York in February to lobby Governor Rockefeller and give evidence to a committee of inquiry in support of the project he had already once helped to save as a Labour minister.

The collapse of the Upper Clyde Shipbuilders in June 1971 thrust Benn into the centre of controversy yet again. As the minister who had been responsible for its creation in 1967, and its rescue in 1969, he was soon to be the most prominent advocate of the UCS workers' cause. The Conservatives had criticised Labour's reorganisation of the ship-building industry as muddled, and were hostile to UCS in particular. Since its formation, the company had made losses of £9.5m in 1967–68, £12.1m in 1968–69, £4.1m in 1969–70, and as Sir Keith Joseph put it, "In a progressive economy, there is no room for loss-makers." After visiting the Clyde in December 1969, Nicholas Ridley had noted that the UCS merger had resulted in little investment or rationalisation, commenting that "firms are being encouraged by unions to go bust so that the state will take over responsibility for paying higher wages". The Ridley plan, as set out in two memoranda, meant the Government giving no more public money to UCS, financing the Yarrow Yard to leave the group and allowing UCS to go into liquidation. "We could put in a Government 'Butcher' to cut up UCS and to sell (cheaply) to Lower Clyde and others, the assets of UCS to minimise upheaval and dislocation. ... After liquidation or reconstruction as above, we should sell the Government holding in UCS even for a pittance."

As the minister responsible for the shipbuilding industry, Ridley applied this plan rigorously, and in November 1970 refused to extend any further guarantees, causing UCS to lose profitable contracts. UCS appealed to John Davies who asked for detailed profit forecasts on each contract which he then insisted should be renegotiated to increase their value by £3m. UCS succeeded in doing this, and on 11 February 1971 Davies announced the renewal of guarantees and a capital reconstruction of the group. Yarrow, which built naval vessels, would leave UCS and receive a £4.5m loan from the Ministry of Defence as working capital "to maintain its programme and regain profitability", while UCS would write off its inherited losses and Government loans. In Benn's view, UCS without Yarrow was "a lame duck proposing to lay a golden egg" and Davies was "presiding over the total shambles of an industrial policy". In early May, UCS informed Davies: "While the trading results show a most encouraging trend the cash position continues to be acutely difficult." Though its letter did not mention the alternatives of liquidation or more public money, the Government should have understood the gravity of the financial position from the first quarterly accounts. On 9 June the UCS chairman, Tony Hepper, told Davies that the company was unable to meet the next week's wages, that its overdraft would exceed its limits and reach £5m by August, and asked for a £6m loan facility as working capital.

The Government rejected the request and events now moved swiftly. On 14 June Davies announced the appointment of Robert Courtney Smith as the official receiver and an advisory group to investigate UCS's affairs. The move deeply shocked Benn as a "massive and wholly characteristic betrayal" of the workers who had since 1969 agreed to reduce the work force by 3500 and had increased productivity by an estimated 87%. While Davies was speaking, mass meetings were taking place in all the five UCS yards, where the workers endorsed the shop stewards' plan to charter a special train for London immediately. The UCS workers refused to be so lightly discarded and Benn was determined that Labour should stand by them. The following day he met the delegation at 6am at Euston Station and listened to their views, putting their case later that day to Parliament. The Government had an obligation to reverse the decline of this important industry, he said. Progress over 1969–71 suggested that UCS could be viable. Losses had been caused by £2m p.a. payable in loan-interest and unprofitable contracts entered into before the company's formation and in the first year of its existence. The reforms undertaken by the management of Ken Douglas since June 1969 had produced profitable orders for bulk cargo ships; and in March 1971, the SIB had felt sufficiently optimistic to report: "With the end of the loss-making orders, more settled industrial relations and improved production, the company should make the long-awaited return to profitability." In Benn's view:

> The greatest gain in the three years work that has been done in Upper Clyde is the transformation of the labour force from people utterly dejected by the failures of private management, the restructuring of the unions; and the resumption of responsibility. Now the Government have awakened a force in Scotland, and I believe in industry generally, that will not easily be put back.[4]

The Government had clearly underestimated the strength of popular feeling about UCS. On 16 June, Heath received the Provost of Clydebank, Robert Fleming, and the UCS shop stewards who left angry after only tea and sympathy. Jim Airlie, the chairman of the shop stewards committee, warned Davies: "We will resist any closure of this key basic industry", and that contraction would "precipitate a struggle not seen in the political life of this century".

The Parliamentary Labour Party unanimously endorsed Benn's resolution for the nationalisation of the shipbuilding industry, and on 22 June he introduced a private member's Bill in the House of Commons to take UCS into public ownership. The Bill was inspired by Clause IV of the Labour Party's constitution:

> Whereas it is desirable for the workers by hand and by brain in UCS Ltd that the assets of the Company should be secured upon the basis of common ownership under the best obtainable system of popular administration and control.

> The management and workers in UCS Ltd shall jointly prepare in consultation, a plan for the development of a new company under public ownership designed to ensure the viability of the undertaking. . . .[5]

Meanwhile the UCS campaign was generating massive support. On 23 June 100,000 Scottish workers struck in sympathy for their UCS brethren, while 30,000 marched through Glasgow led by Benn and the UCS shop stewards. It was an act of considerable political courage, since Wilson was enraged by this unparliamentary behaviour, as was Vic Feather, because Benn had urged the STUC to lobby the Prime Minister. But by reconnecting the parliamentary system with popular feeling, Benn had succeeded in winning over those in authority to the workers' cause. During July, Vic Feather and the CSEU met Ridley, the STUC petitioned Heath and Sir Donald Liddle, while the Lord Provost of Glasgow and a delegations of local government leaders had talks with Davies and Heath. Religious leaders too felt compelled to intervene. The moderator of the General Assembly of the Church of Scotland, the Rev. Andrew Herron in alliance with the Roman Catholic Archbishop, Gordon Gray, appealed by telegram: "The dissolution of the UCS without the existence of alternative industry would be so damaging to the economy of Scotland, and, in an area of severe unemployment, would have such social and economic consequences as to be totally unacceptable in a responsive society."

The Government and the Advisory Group[6] remained impervious to the public clamour and on 29 July Davies made a statement about their report and the future of UCS. "Their principal findings are that UCS Ltd as organised in 1967, was doomed from the start as a result of the faulty concept of structure within which it was organised, the burden of eventual loss with which it was saddled, and the inadequate management with which it was provided." Davies' advisors had not only concluded that "the continuation of UCS in its present form is unjustified" but had even contemplated the total disappearance of shipbuilding on the Clyde. Davies accepted their view that the Govan and Linthouse yards could provide employment for 2500 with good management, if the trade unions cooperated totally with them. A cry of "God Almighty" pierced the silence of the numbed chamber, followed by a furious row unheard in the Commons since the dramatic scenes over Suez. In a heated exchange, Benn predicted 25,000 unemployed — for which, in turn, Davies blamed him: "With characteristic exaggeration the Rt. Hon. Gentleman seeks to cloak his own manifest responsibility for the situation."

The following day, Jimmy Reid announced the start of a work-in at UCS. Since the middle of June the joint shop stewards' committee had been examining the possibility of direct action and resolving the practical problems of accident, sickness insurance and redundancy payments. "This is the first campaign of its kind in trade unionism," Reid declared emotionally. "We are not strikers, we are responsible people and we will conduct ourselves with dignity and discipline." The heroism of the UCS workers did not involve barricades or bloodshed but cooperation and self-sacrifice. The redundant workers took the initiative, starting work on recent contracts that the receiver had sought to abandon; while those employed contributed fifty pence of their wages each week to support the work-in. The entire work force cooperated with the management and the police so that at no stage did violence occur.

Benn alone of Labour's parliamentary leadership gave his immediate support for the work-in and was bitterly criticised for condoning an unlawful act. Undeterred he went to the Clyde to encourage the workers: "We are seeing the birth pang of industrial democracy . . . This is an historic moment. The power of the workers has gone from the negative to the positive. This is something to be recorded when the history of the British Labour movement is written. The power which has been awakened in the yards is not going to be snuffed out." On 2 August in a debate he "clobbered the Government", as a colleague put it. It was the occasion for a detailed defence of his own actions and an attack upon the Government's conduct. He agreed that the original structure was defective, but criticised the Advisory Group's report for ignoring the circumstances in which UCS had been formed or the arguments for maintaining a shipbuilding industry on the Clyde: "Looking back over the years of UCS, and with the benefit of hindsight, I have no doubt in my mind that it would have been better if the previous Government had taken the whole industry into public ownership at the time we launched our programme. We should have re-equipped and rationalised and swept aside the old owners." He was also prepared to admit the mistakes in handling the 1969 crisis, but the harsh conditions he insisted upon were aimed at producing the necessary reforms to make UCS viable. Instead, the Government had deliberately destroyed UCS:

> Over the years I have seen the labour force on Clyde about-turn from a defeated, demoralised and divided group engaged in demarcation disputes and unofficial strikes into a determined and responsible body of men welded into unity, into defending the public assets which have been made available to them by this House. The work-in is for reasons I will give the House, an historic event. The men have rediscovered by what they have done their

self-respect which they never had under private management in the past. They want a future in shipbuilding and they mean to have a say in that future. They have shown the way to responsibility in industry by assuming responsibility in industry.[7]

In a furious tirade he accused the Government of "deliberately sentencing thousands of people to a slow and living-death of long-term unemployment in the wasteland of central Scotland", and finished by writing the Prime Minister's epitaph: "He is the man who forgot the people and the people will never forgive him for it."

The effect of Benn's speech was to consolidate the Labour movement's support for the UCS workers. Wilson felt compelled to visit the Clyde; but when he did so, on 4 August, refused to endorse the work-in because it was illegal. However, he urged the Government to assume responsibility for UCS and place orders for ships as part of a counter-cyclical programme. At a special STUC conference, Vic Feather suggested that a Clydeside development authority be established to tackle the long-term problem of alternative industry. On 6 August, Davies eventually visited the Clyde to discuss a separate run-down of the Clydetown and Scotstown yards with J.H.F. Carmichael of P-E Consultants. However, the UCS workers continued to demand "all four yards and the work force intact". The CSEU and STUC organised appeals, concerts and exhibitions, raising £486,000 for the work-in, including a £500 cheque and a bunch of roses from John Lennon and Yoko Ono addressed "To the workers of UCS with love". This expression of solidarity culminated in a demonstration of 18 August in George Square, Glasgow, which an estimated 70,000 people attended. Benn, Feather, Danny McGarvey, Willie Ross and Hugh Scanlon were present as Jimmy Reid spoke: "The real power of this country has been forged today in Clydeside and will be forged now in the pits, the factories, the shipyards and the offices. Once that force is given proper leadership, is disciplined and determined, there is no force in Britain, or indeed in the world, that can stand against it."

What did the UCS work-in achieve? At its height, it involved a thousand men; but by June 1972 the numbers had dwindled to 161, and it ended on 9 October 1972 after the boilermakers refused to contribute to the work-in levy. Jimmy Reid was bitterly disappointed by this breakdown of solidarity and the re-emergence of self-interest; but the UCS work-in had not been in vain. On 28 February 1972, Davies announced that the Government would contribute £35m to Govan Shipbuilders and later £12m to entice the US company Marathon to take over the Clydebank and Scotstown yards. If the boilermakers' negotiations had held the Marathon bid in the balance until 18 September 1972, then this too was further proof of the workers' new self-confidence.

John Davies always maintained that the UCS work-in was a figment of the imagination, but for Benn it was a real breakthrough in terms of industrial democracy. In *Tribune* he insisted it was not a "Trotskyite dream but a necessary practical policy", and in October he told the Labour Party Conference: "The workers in UCS have done more in ten weeks to advance the cause of industrial democracy than all the blue prints we have worked on over the last ten years."

The stagnation and industrial collapse which characterised the early 'seventies was the result of the Government's deflationary economic strategy and its philosophy of inequality, much more than its policy of disengagement from industry or Benn's interventions as Minister of Technology. The "N minus 1" incomes policy which aimed to gradually reduce wage settlements in the public sector; Anthony Barber's budgets in November 1970 and April 1971 cutting direct taxation and public expenditure, failed to dampen either inflation or unemployment. Retail prices rose by 9.4% in 1971, while unemployment nearly doubled and investment stagnated.

Benn attacked "the political judgement" of the April budget and its philosophy of inequality, arguing that incentives would have no magic effect on the economy, while unemployment would fail to curb inflation.

> The dreams of Selsdon Park have become the nation's nightmares. . . . The fact is that the Government are deliberately gearing the economy down to a lower level of production. Unemployment is now seen by the Cabinet as a main instrument of economic policy. High wages do not explain unemployment in declining industries where wages tend to be lower. High wages do not cause unemployment where there is a high capital investment and low labour content. . . . High wages do not explain redundancies where there is a market, nor do they explain changes in the structure of unemployment and its longer duration. . . . The Cabinet has deliberately set out to destroy the whole post-war consensus based on the maintenance of a high and stable level of employment and the social fabric that went with it. The Government will have to rethink their attitude to the trade union movement.[8]

During the debate on the Queen's Speech in November 1971, Benn had argued that market forces could not restore full employment, and predicted that the climate of hostility towards state intervention would alter. The role of public enterprise in stimulating investment and employment soon became the subject of general discussion with the idea of a state holding company being canvassed by Edmund Dell, Roy Jenkins and others. Conservatives too acknowledged the obligation of the state to protect the economy. But for Benn the whole question of public ownership was inseparable from that of industrial democracy.

> I hope that we will have in mind that we are discussing not only economic and financial matters but essentially the ways and means by which we can best mobilise the ability of the people, and in doing so allow the economy to

grow in a way that really meets our deepest human needs. One day, I do not know when, society will realise that the power of working people in a modern industrial society has a great positive potential for producing wealth.[9]

The miners' victory in February 1972 was a turning point. A major reversal for the Government led to a reversal of policy in favour of a reflation of the economy and re-engagement in industry. Barber's March 1972 budget, arguably the most expansionary of all time, injected an estimated £2000m into the economy and fuelled an inflationary consumer boom, causing public expenditure to rise from £27,806m in 1971 to £41,930m in 1974, and the Government's deficit public sector borrowing requirement to increase from £671m to £4276m over the same period. In addition, the 1972 Industry Act made £550m available for selective assistance and regional investment grants. To Benn, these measures proved that "debate and argument do shift opinion, and it is very important that people should know (this) . . . By his own second Industry Bill (he has) signed the death warrant of market forces and competition as a solution to all our problems."

The Conservatives were determined not to allow balance of payments and exchange-rate consideration to override the pursuit of economic growth. As a result of its measures, a surplus of £1058m on the current account in 1971 became a deficit of £922m in 1973, while sterling depreciated in value by 20% following its free-float between June 1972 and September 1973. The Government realised that an expansionist strategy would be inflationary and could not possibly succeed without an incomes policy. They therefore offered the TUC a commitment to a 5% economic growth rate over the next two years to obtain their agreement to wage restraint. The miners' strike had also convinced Heath of the need for "a more sensible way to settle our differences", and he spent more time than any of his predecessors in seeking to bring the trade unions into the process of government, offering them "nothing less than a share in managing the economy". Benn remained sceptical about the motives and wisdom of the Conservatives' conversion to incomes policy. He felt that events were unfolding as he had predicted. Prices and incomes policy was unworkable because the Government's underlying economic strategy was inflationary; and now they were utterly dependent on the support of the working people. On 31 October 1972 he prepared a paper for the Shadow Cabinet on law and order, connecting this traditional Conservative theme with incomes policy and the attack upon the unions. His central argument was that the Conservative Party's overriding objective remained to shackle the unions.

Since 1970 the trade unions have been in the front line. They have had to bear the brunt of government policy, whether it was in killing off "lame ducks", reversing regional policies with its consequence in redundancy and higher unemployment. The Industrial Relations Act was aimed directly at them, and they are now being drawn into what looks more and more like a political trap set by Mr. Heath. . . . The Chequers talks were much more than a new initiative on inflation. By deliberately raising public expectations and appearing to be so reasonable, the Cabinet was making a crude bid for public support and simultaneously preparing the ground for a further assault on the unions. . . . It is widely believed that if a voluntary policy for controlling wages is not acceptable the Government will quickly move to a statutory policy. Then if industrial dispute takes place they will switch at once to a "Who Governs Britain?" campaign directed against the trade union movement holding them responsible for unemployment, inflation and for undermining law and order.[10]

After a long summer of negotiations, unions and Government failed to reach agreement, and on 6 November 1972 Heath announced a ninety-day standstill on increases in prices and incomes, along with immediate emergency legislation. The Govenment's aim was to break the inflationary spiral, 7.5% in 1972, and to control wages and prices over the next two years. Though the decision was greeted with widespread relief, Benn was highly critical of the ineffectiveness of the proposed price controls. He warned that working people would not accept wage restraint unless they were protected against a depreciating pound and increases in the price of food. This is "a fraud perpetrated upon the country to get a wages freeze carried through".

The question of prices and incomes policy inevitably dominated the parliamentary session of 1972-73, as the Conservatives strove to reoccupy the middle ground of British politics and drive Labour onto the defensive. Labour's leadership was highly concerned to appear consistent and responsible, as the 1973 Report to Annual Conference noted: "We opposed every stage of the Government's counter-inflation measures on a 'reasoned amendment' basis — that is to say, we recognised the need for strong Government action, but were unable to support policies which were both unfair and ineffective."

During this period, Benn's many contributions in the House earned him the reputation of a formidable adversary. The tradition of dissenting oratory he exemplified had no place in his opponents' general dislike of ideas. As Sir John Hall commented: "He generally builds up an absolutely brilliant argument which seems to be unanswerable — except that it is generally based on an entirely false premise." Amazed by his "gift of attaching all sorts of dimensions to questions which are unrelated to them", Sir Geoffrey Howe found his speeches "always a fascinating journey of exploration. One commences listening . . . in the belief that one will get an insight into his attitude, if not that of his Party, towards the question before the House. One ends by getting an insight into the thought processes that make up his own mind, which sometimes frighten the House a great deal."[11]

The argument Benn developed throughout 1973 was that Conservative-style intervention was bureaucratic and undermined the role of Parliament, as well as the sovereignty of the people, and would destroy the basis of popular consent. State intervention reminded people about the meaning of Parliament, that "who governs Britain is what this place is all about." Conservative policies were making people ask "in whose interest is the economy to be managed?" Benn prophesised that the need for popular consent would give rise to demands for democratic and socialist reforms.

The long-term shape of the Government's prices and incomes policy emerged on 17 January 1973, when Heath unveiled Stage II, appealing over the heads of Parliament to the public in a presidential-style press-conference in Lancaster House. Under Stage II, incomes could rise by £1 and 4% over the year with an upper limit of £250, while dividend increases would be limited to 10%. Companies would be classified by size into three categories to simplify the administration of price controls, based on certain allowable costs and profit-margin controls. There would be legislation to establish a Pay Board and Prices Commission as independent agencies, supported by a pay and prices code. The standstill on prices would continue a further sixty days until 29 April and the new pay policy would come into force at the beginning of April.

Stage II was undoubtedly bureaucratic and likely to produce disastrous tensions within the economy. Benn considered it a constitutional outrage and an embodiment of the corporate state in its naked undisguised form. In the Shadow Cabinet he advocated a militant course of action in support of a one-day national strike, but the proposal was rejected. In Parliament he predicted that the undemocratic nature of the policy would generate revolutionary demands: "This is a permanent Bill, entirely isolated from parliamentary control. It will operate arbitrarily under the cloak of artificial legality. It abdicates ministerial responsibility and it derogates from our parliamentary code." Prophesying militancy and unrest, he warned that the preliminary discussions on Stage III had already

> . . . alienated the TUC which genuinely wanted and was ready to talk to the Government about these problems . . . The problem which this Government must face is much more fundamental. It is how to achieve consent for any policy they put forward. If we are to recreate a social contract in this country, upon which agreed economic policies can rest, there has got to be a marked shift of power and wealth to the working people.[12]

By the spring of 1973 the focus of debate had already shifted to Stage III of the counter-inflation programme. Benn increasingly believed in the inevitability of democratic socialism: wage-controls were radicalising working people by making them conscious of being imprisoned in an industrial dungeon from which there was no visible escape. During the budget resolutions debate in March, he identified an emerging choice between reform and repression, warning that the Government might choose "to intensify the campaign against the trade unions". Throughout successive debates attacking the ineffectiveness of existing price-controls, Benn's thesis was that the increasing concentration of economic power had made public accountability and planning both necessary and possible. He called for a "great extension of public ownership" and the implementation of the joint Labour Party-TUC statement on "Economic Policy and the Cost of Living". "It reflects the deepest needs of the people represented in their work by the trade union movement and politically by the Labour Party." But like Aneurin Bevan before him, he remained staggered by "the modesty of the claims made by British working people against a society which treated them so unjustly". The Government's intransigence over price-controls in formulating Stage III soon made Benn conclude that they had "abdicated their responsibility in the way in which they have sought to tackle these problems. They have used the deepening economic crisis to weaken the democratic control of the economy." He pointed out that the world inflationary crisis had made it a "virtual certainty that Phase III will not be acceptable".

> Therefore I do not believe that the present Cabinet have the reserves of political support, even among their own people, to which they can appeal in the event of a crisis of this kind developing. I very much hope that the Cabinet do not think that they can appeal to the sense of responsibility of the British people at a time when they have systematically stripped the people of this country of the institutions of democracy and self-discipline upon which our society has rested . . . The more serious the situation becomes, the more it will be necessary to win the support of ordinary working people for the remedies that will be necessary and that can duly be done by policies that redistribute wealth and power in favour of working people. . . . They have misunderstood the temper of the people.[13]

Benn regarded the Government's counter-inflation policy as part of a wider trend towards state intervention. He saw a corporate state emerging in which Government collaborated with big business outside the discipline of parliamentary accountability or of market forces. This process explained the apparent contradiction between *ad hoc* intervention in some areas and disengagement from others. Conservative state intervention was quite unlike what Benn was in favour of. For him state intervention served the purpose of facilitating the democratising of industry and the decentralisation of economic power.

He saw that a purely administrative measure, the Statutory Corporations (Financial Provisions) Bill which subsidised price restraint by the nationalised industries, was historically significant: it was the culmination "of a long line of Government measures which are taking this country away from market forces towards a tightly controlled, centrally directed economy (demonstrating) the need for a large public sector to re-enforce Government objectives".

Like many in the early 'seventies, Benn was highly critical of the abuse of corporate power, exemplified by the boardroom scandals of Lonrho and the excess profits earned by Hoffman la Roche on the sale of drugs. In particular, he expressed concern about the growing power of the multinational companies, like Ford which repatriated UK profits for investment in Spain, and the pace and consequences of takeovers. He opposed the mergers of Hill Samuel with Slater Walker, of BAT with Trafalgar House and of Boots with House of Fraser, criticising the prevalence of asset-stripping and the absence of any "legal requirements on firms to pay regard to the interests of their workers who rightly regard themselves as the real assets of a company". The Conservative response to these problems, as set out in the Companies and Insurance Companies Bills, was in Benn's view an admission of the need to protect public interest. Though Labour supported these Bills, Benn emphasised that it looked to a more complete and radical solution of the historic conflict between capital and labour: "We are seeking a new framework for industry and not just a public relations facelift for capitalism."

Developments in Conservative policy drove Benn to the conclusion that the Conservative Government was preparing the way for a democratic socialist one. "Heath's Spadework for Socialism", the title of an article he wrote for *The Sunday Times* on 25 March, detailed the extensive powers the Conservatives had taken, including the power to appoint a Government director or commissioner, to control profit margins and monitor investment plans. He also described how Labour should use these to strengthen British industry and its public accountability. Benn argued that the Conservatives had created the tools of a managed economy because capitalism had failed and the post-war consensus broken down in the face of mounting pressure from working people for a better deal. In the democratic dialectic he postulated, the contradiction between working people's aspirations and the emerging corporate state would only be resolved through democratic socialism. As he put it: "Heath has performed a very important historical role, in preparing for the fundamental and irreversible shift in the balance of power and wealth."

Benn's advocacy of socialist policies was criticised by many as opportunism — of exploiting the leftward direction of the Labour movement for personal advantage. More relevant though was the comment that as an ambitious politician he could only damage his future leadership prospects by encouraging those outside the Parliamentary Labour Party to campaign for a socialist programme. He had everything to lose by straying from the conventional path to power and prestige, outside of which he knew there could be no certain future. Moreover, closely identified with the revisionist policies of the

Wilson Government, he realised that if conventional power were in question, he had most to fear from the Left who were naturally suspicious of his overtures. Thus there is good reason to assume that Benn's position, his call for socialism, was and continues to be based on analysis and principle.

A conviction that the mixed economy was failing underlay Benn's advocacy both of socialist economic policies and his explanation of the Conservative Government's interventionism. The parliamentary battles with Peter Walker — who became Secretary of State for Trade and Industry in 1972 — characterised the uncertainties of the period and the sharp differences of opinion that existed about the state of the economy. Heath and Walker believed that Britain was on the threshold of an economic miracle and talked about "the problems of success". The conventional view was that, in 1972, after the miners' strike, Heath had returned to consensus policies, obtained trade union cooperation, and the economy boomed; while the Labour Party, encouraged by Benn, indulged in damaging and extremist socialist speculation. Benn, on the other hand, maintained that "the economy's growth is not soundly based". In opposition, he had become aware of the long-term decline in investment and the erosion of Britain's manufacturing base. In a Commons debate on 12 December 1972 about the failure to secure an adequate level of industrial investment in the United Kingdom, he warned that Britain was enjoying an inflationary and transitory prosperity.

Who was right? The index of industrial production rose from 100.3 to 110.7 during 1972–73, the economy grew at an annual rate of over 5% and unemployment fell from 967,000 in the first quarter of 1972 to 510,000 two years later; but these statistics do not tell the whole truth. It was an inflationary spending spree rather than an export-led, investment-orientated boom, with a rate of inflation of over 10% in 1973, despite controls over prices and incomes. Investment in plant and machinery rose from £3658m in 1970 to only £3840 in 1973 at 1970 prices, and this represented a decline to 6% of GDP; while OECD surveys showed that other industrialised countries were reinvesting a significantly higher proportion of their national income. Output in the key sectors of the economy remained depressed, and though general engineering orders and stock levels rose encouragingly in 1973, there was a slump in machine tool and shipbuilding orders.

The debate about the economy is central to explaining why, by 1974, Benn had come to advocate, and the Labour Party to adopt, a socialist programme. The period of opposition began in painful reflection on the 1964–70 Labour Government's failure to reinvigorate the British economy. The NEC Industrial Policy Subcommittee studied techniques of industrial intervention, Labour's experience, and analysed the results. The Department of Economic Affairs had admitted in its 1969 report that "what happens in industry is not under the control of the government" and that industrial restructuring had failed to raise the rate of investment. Though a review of regional policy in 1970 had concluded that discretionary grants and industrial development certificates had influenced the location of industry, new evidence from leading UK companies indicated that investment grants and the regional employment premium had neither significantly affected investment decisions nor succeeded in creating self-sustaining economic growth in the development regions.

The quest for an explanation and a solution to Britain's economic problems led to renewed interest in socialist theory. Ideas which had long been confined to the extreme Left were now openly debated within the Labour Party. The philosophy of historical materialism, the nature of the class struggle and class consciousness, the contradictions and coming crisis of capitalism and the possibilities of revolutionary change in a democracy became part of the intellectual framework for policy-making. The chief controversy concerned the relationship between investment and profits, and whether the slump in investment was due to a collapse of profits. In the classical Marxist model, the pursuit of profit under the capitalist mode of production led inexorably to monopoly capitalism. Investment and the rate of profit would fall because total profits would decline as a proportion of total accumulated capital. The marginal efficiency of capital would subsequently fall, and these developments would culminate apocalyptically in under-consumption, unemployment and an absolute collapse of profits. The economists Glynn and Sutcliffe redefined this traditional model, arguing that as a result of pressures from workers for higher wages and intensified international competition, "British capitalism has suffered such a dramatic decline in profitability that it is now literally fighting for survival."[14]

Stuart Holland offered a different analysis, emphasising that the continuing concentration of economic power had led to super profits and the emergence of a meso-economic sector: "The main reason for the crisis has not been so much the misapplication of techniques of demand management as their erosion by a new mode of production which has divorced macro-policy from micro-structure." A meso-economic sector, consisting of giant corporations, could manipulate prices and profits so as to internalise and control the market mechanism. Holland found a positive correlation between inflation and monopoly, and he saw the growth of the multinational companies as exemplifying this process. He argued that it was undermining national economic sovereignty and explained why Government efforts to regulate the economy had become increasingly ineffective.[15]

As a former industrial minister, Benn was a major contributor to these discussions, arguing that the public sector must fill the investment gap and that an effective industrial policy required the coordination of government, company and trade union policy. Yet his evolution toward a fully socialist economic analysis was gradual and rooted in a democratic vision. He believed that the primary purpose of public ownership was to extend democracy into industry and to make it publicly accountable. In June 1971 he described the historical perspective of his democratic socialism to the NEC in a paper entitled, "Towards a Socialist Economic Policy. "

The long and bitter battle centering round industrial relations legislation over the last few years, has always been seen in narrow terms, as if it only involved the handling of industrial disputes. But what has been happening is of much greater political significance than that. The first industrial revolution created modern capitalism and made capital much stronger than labour. The second industrial revolution created modern management, systems — many of them international — and separated management from capital whilst reinforcing the power of management against Labour. But the third and current industrial revolution has now begun to tilt the power much more sharply back to labour and to separate management still further from capital. The growth of labour power in an interdependent and hence vulnerable and fragile system has alarmed capital, which is seeking to consolidate its own power by legislation directed at checking the growing power of labour.

Legislation of this kind, attempting to stem a historic trend will not work; and management may be the first to see and to identify more with labour on this issue than with capital. What is required, therefore, is a means of institutionalising the new power of labour so as to make management accountable to labour as well as to capital . . . I am suggesting that directors of public companies should not take up their appointments in law until those appointments have been ratified by a ballot of workers in that firm . . . [16]

The Paper also proposed that workers control the distribution of profits and the level of wages, stressing the positive contribution that industrial democracy could make to incomes policy, industrial relations and investment. Benn argued for a dramatic extension of public ownership on grounds of accountability where advanced or declining industries dependent upon Government support and the state had an obligation to channel and monitor public investment. Thus he felt that "with the amount of public money in shipbuilding, the case for public ownership is, in my judgement, unanswerable." The paper recommended that investment grants take the form of a state equity participation and that the Government be able to waive its right to dividends to encourage the location of industry in the regions: "Without additional public expenditure, public ownership and supervision would expand until the commanding heights of the economy were in public ownership."

The Labour Party Annual Conference also made plain that it considered revisionism had failed and wanted a return to socialist policies. In 1969 Conference passed resolutions calling for new public enterprise and industrial democracy; while an uncompromising motion by Eric Heffer to nationalise "the commanding heights" of the economy in 1970 was defeated, but obtained 1.7m votes. In 1971, Conference called for the public ownership of the aircraft and shipbuilding industries, and in 1972 of the banks and insurance companies.

The surge of activity which swept through the Labour Party after 1970 was only explicable in terms of the depth of the internal crisis which had just occurred. For Benn, the years between 1970–74 were productive ones. The changes he had seen in society as a whole during the late 'sixties were now engulfing the Labour movement, manifesting themselves in demands for greater democracy and socialism, as well as in specific policy commitments. Though the public gaze focussed on the parliamentary arena, the centre of action often lay beyond it, on the National Executive and its subcommittees where he and many others worked on the reappraisal of Labour policies; and the preparation of its *Programme for Britain* in the constituency Labour Parties and at Annual Conference. The *Programme for Britain* did not represent the thinking of the Left, but of the mainstream of the Labour movement; and at any one time there were over fifty committees, working parties or study groups and nearly a thousand people involved in its preparation. To look at the complex, collective process of policy-making in the Labour movement is also to understand that Benn's development as a socialist was in part due to this collective process of education and exchange of experience.

Benn's contribution to Labour's programme was mainly confined to industrial policy, where as chairman of the NEC's Industrial Policy Subcommittee in 1972–73 and as a member of the joint Labour Party-CSEU committees on the nationalisation of the aircraft and ship-building industries, he played a central role in the formulation of a coherent socialist strategy. However, he was also chairman of the NEC's Information Committee, and a member of its powerful Home Policy Committee which drafted the programme, as well as its Human Rights, Science and Education and Transport Subcommittees. Benn was determined that the next Labour Government would be able to control the economy, and he set out to translate this socialist economic analysis into policy with an ambitious plan for research. The programme of work for 1972–73 aimed to prepare Green Papers on the state holding company, industrial democracy and the reform of company law. It envisaged studies of economic planning, the machinery of government, competition, mergers and monopolies policy; price controls and food subsidies; a national labour board; the aircraft, construction, machine tools, pharmaceuticals and ship-building industries. By the end of 1973, most of this had been achieved.

Labour's Green Paper, *The National Enterprise Board*, published in April 1973, heralded a new approach to public ownership. Though Labour was committed to nationalise certain industries — such as aircraft and shipbuilding — on their merits, it had rejected wholesale nationalisation in favour of competitive, selective public enterprise. There was a deeper understanding of how market forces in a mixed economy operated and how the state could intervene to stimulate economic growth by interacting with the market using the price mechanism to raise the rate of investment. The NEB would acquire some twenty to twenty-five of the top one hundred companies — controlling approximately one-sixth of turnover, one-fifth of profits and one-quarter of employment in manufacturing industry —, operate on a commercial basis and be self-financing after the issue of an initial long-term public debt. The NEB would be the Government's chief instrument of economic planning through its strategic leadership, and exercise leverage over the private sector. Its objectives would include investment promotion, the creation and protection of employment, particularly in the regions, the promotion of industrial democracy and worker cooperatives, import substitution and the restructuring of industry. The NEB would be the nerve centre of a national network of written planning agreements embracing all other large companies. Partially inspired by economic planning in Western European countries — the IRI in Italy and the programme contracts in France — , the proposed system was conceived as an alternative to old style nationalisation and was designed to coordinate investment and production with national economic policy, as well as to ensure that the private sector followed the public interest. Planning agreements would operate by obtaining regular information from companies, on a confidential and tripartite basis with the trade unions concerned, in order to identify national objectives and channel selective government financial assistance.

Benn's role as chairman of the subcommittee preparing the Paper was to resolve controversies and define objectives — not a simple task given the wide differences of opinion that existed over the whole range of industrial issues, especially in relation to competition, the role of monopolies and the extent of public ownership.

But many commentators doubted whether Labour could effectively control the economy by limited public ownership and planning agreements. In particular the importance of the top hundred companies and their influence upon the market appears to have been over-estimated. Benn was certainly aware of the dilemmas of any socialist policy and for this reason was determined that the next Labour Government should enter power with the instruments needed to implement its programme. His Paper, "Industrial Power and Industrial Policy" concentrated on governmental machinery, proposing a central policy unit to support the Prime Minister, external ministerial advisers and an Industrial Power Bill to consolidate all the arbitrary powers taken by the Conservatives, and to strengthen parliamentary accountability.

By the end of 1973, Benn had drafted an Industry Bill in readiness for a change of Government; but the crucial decisions about Labour's programme were taken on the Home Policy Committee, when it met on 23 March 1973 to determine Labour's policy on public ownership. Callaghan, Healey and Wilson still considered it industrially irrelevant and electorally suicidal. Exasperated, Benn insisted that the Labour Party "could not go through 1964–70 all over again" and in a spontaneous outburst, reminded them that Labour existed "to bring about a fundamental and irreversible shift in the balance of power and wealth in favour of working people and their families". After a bitter and prolonged struggle, the NEC on 31 May eventually endorsed the proposal to nationalise twenty-five companies by only seven votes to six.

The importance of Labour's industrial policy was magnified by the weakness of its economic strategy which, as set out in "Economic Strategy, Growth and Unemployment" by the NEC in 1971, consisted of rising public expenditure, price controls and food subsidies in exchange for voluntary wage restraint, and was unlikely to control inflation. On the Industrial Policy Subcommittee, Benn admitted to the lack of any coherent incomes policy and that in practice Labour could only ever hope to influence the climate in which wage settlements were reached. However, as a socialist, he argued that without directed investment, Labour would not be able to overcome the inflationary pressures and achieve export-led growth. In this connection the NEC's rejection of the demands to nationalise the financial institutions had far-reaching consequences. It imposed severe restrictions on a Labour Government's financial ability to extend public ownership, which was to create the resources for Labour's ambitious social programme. Nevertheless, Benn reiterated that "the language of priorities was the religion of socialism", and that the Labour Government would allocate the resources available on the basis of need rather than of supply and demand.

On 8 June, Labour published its *Programme for Britain, 1973* — a culmination of three years' work which marked a return to Labour's original socialist inspiration, redefined for the 1970s. "Labour's aim is no less than a new social order. The people must determine the nation's destiny and only by economic liberation can they have the collective social strength to decide that destiny." Labour's objective was to democratise and socialise Britain, and the theme of equality permeated the programme. In addition to commitments on industrial policy and public ownership, it proposed the municipalisation of all development land, a voluntary incomes policy that helped low-paid workers, child benefits in place of family allowances, high pensions, the taxation of private wealth, complete comprehensivisation of public education and the abolition of direct grant grammar schools.

Such were the broad outlines of Labour's first genuinely socialist programme since 1945, which predictably was described in the press as anti-democratic and concerned exclusively with nationalisation. Benn correctly anticipated the onslaught from the media, but felt that Labour would do better to propagate than conceal its socialism. On 6 June he took the opportunity to attack some of the prevalent myths about the Labour Party at a conference organised by *The Financial Times* and *Investors' Chronicle*, on the future of the City as a financial centre.

> There is a debate — but no crisis. . . . We are proud of the fact that unlike the Conservative Party, our policy is not handed down from above but is decided at every level by democratic decision. . . . We believe that in putting forward our policies we are speaking for the majority of the British people and when they hear us argue for them they will recognise the authentic statement of their case — exactly as they did in 1945.[17]

On 1st October 1973, over a thousand delegates assembled in Blackpool to debate Labour's *Programme for Britain*. In *The Times* Benn identified the redistribution of economic power as the central theme of the Conference. Its relevance lay in the fact that "the framework of consensus policies within which successive governments have, since the war, sought to win public support has broken down." He hoped the Conference would catch the public imagination, emphasising that Labour's public ownership policies were conceived in a democratic spirit. "From now on there must be the fullest consultation with the workers in the firms that are to be acquired and we must be guided by what they themselves want."

The 1973 Labour Party Conference marked a high point in the influence of the Left within the Labour movement and was unprecedented in its unanimity. Conference passed far-reaching socialist resolutions on public ownership, industrial democracy, housing and land, social services and welfare and education. Differences of opinion and perspective were debated and clarified in a comradely and democratic spirit. Hugh Scanlon explained that the AUEW was opposed to Stage III because the prices and incomes policy was "just one more subtle continuation of the age-old policy of bashing the workers and attacking their unions". If the Labour Party and the TUC had rejected Scanlon's opposition to incomes policy, he accepted defeat in good grace because he had articulated the dilemma of Labour's position. As Denis Healey put it: "I think the way the TUC has handled a very difficult situation in the last twelve months has robbed Heath for good of his secret weapon 'The Unions against the people'," and he predicted that the Government's prices and incomes policy was doomed to failure because other policies were inflationary. There was a massive budget deficit, the money supply was out of control, and the pound was depreciating rapidly.

In the press, Healey's speech on economic policy was reported as a cry to soak the rich, whereas in fact he was emphasising that Labour's programme meant higher taxes; and was pleading for realism about costs, for idealism and not envy. The press suggested that the NEC was deeply divided, though the record showed that there was no real argument about public ownership or division about the direction in which Labour was going — only differences about the speed at which it travelled. At the pre-Conference meeting to determine the NEC's attitude to the motions for debate, Benn had argued that the commitment to nationalise twenty-five companies was crucial because it symbolised Labour's determination to carry out its policy on public ownership and would commit the leadership to doing so. If Wilson succeeded in persuading the NEC to oppose the motion on the grounds that a Labour Government would need flexibility of action, he failed to win agreement to a joint meeting with the Shadow Cabinet, which the NEC knew was generally opposed to public ownership.

On Tuesday, Conference reassembled to debate public ownership. After the results of the NEC elections had been announced — in which Benn was once more elected second in the constituency section — Harold Wilson delivered a speech which was a masterpiece of ambiguity, ostensibly in favour of public ownership and listing fourteen areas where Labour would extend it, but rejecting the argument for twenty-five companies. From the Left, Brighton-Kemptown urged the next Labour Government to nationalise twenty-five companies and approximately 250 major monopolies together with the land, banks, finance houses, insurance companies and building societies with minimum compensation on the basis of proven need. It fell to Benn to oppose the Brighton motion on behalf of the NEC and he told its movers that they had confused strategy with tactics:

> Now in all this the mention of twenty-five companies has played an interesting part. In choosing those figures we were seeking to give some numerical significance to a better known phrase "the commanding heights of the economy" long accepted as the party's objectives in its extension of public ownership . . . The violence of the attacks upon our public ownership plans and on us for defending them launched by big business and by the media confirm our judgement that these plans are a serious threat, as they are intended to be, to the unaccountable power they wield and the unacceptable privileges that they defend with that power . . . Our policy on public ownership is based upon a serious analysis of the developing power structure in our society: fewer, larger companies, many of them multinational, growing larger and more powerful, and we know . . . that if we do not own or control them they will own and control us, and that it is the challenge that we face. It is not just a matter of efficiency . . . of investment . . . of regional policy. It is a matter of political power . . . If we

are only concerned to win votes we shall never mobilise the strength we need
to implement the policy . . . We shall not change the power structure in our
society solely by conference resolutions, by Cabinet decisions or by
parliamentary legislation. . . . We are saying at this conference that the
crisis that we inherit when we come to power will be the occasion for
fundamental change and not the excuse for postponing it . . . [18]

Benn succeeded in persuading Conference to reject the Brighton
motion which had gone so far beyond NEC policy. The virtual
unanimity and sense of assurance of this Conference distinguished it
from recent ones. It reflected the resolution, if temporary, of the issues
which had divided the Labour movement since 1970 — state
intervention, the EEC, and the role of the trade unions in the economy.
Benn's analysis of these issues made democracy a cornerstone for them
all, and it was on the strength of this analysis that he emerged among
the many Conference voices as a figure of considerable stature.

No single issue more divided the Labour Party than the Common
Market and no single figure was more identified with the campaign for
a referendum on British membership than Benn. The question in the
1970s of Common Market entry both increased the influence and
strengthened the position of the Left. The subject raised strong
emotions, polarising opinion along non-party lines. As a politician who
had changed his position on British membership, Benn's motives were
inevitably questioned. He himself made "no apology, in the course of
having thought about this issue, for having changed the emphasis of
my view at different stages".[19] The consistent theme underlying Benn's
contradictory statements, was his concern with the meaning of
sovereignty, and it was from this preoccupation that the changes in his
views stemmed. His early opposition to the Common Market can be
traced back to the time of its formation in the 'fifties when, as a radical
and internationalist, Benn feared that the Treaty of Rome's laissez-
faire philosophy would curtail national sovereignty over areas of
economic policy and planning. He also argued that its ideology was a
bulwark against socialism in the West that would institutionalise the
Cold War. It was on these grounds that he opposed Harold
Macmillan's application in 1961. In addition, Benn considered that
membership would harm Britain's world influence and its trading
relations with developing countries. But by 1967, when Harold Wilson
made Britain's second application, he had reached the opposite
conclusion — that the technological and trade benefits of a large
grouping would in fact increase "practical" sovereignty, thus making
membership advantageous, provided that the constitution could be
changed from within. He told a German audience in 1968:

The political opposition to our membership will be ineffective because the
nationalistic arguments upon which it is based are becoming increasingly
irrelevant . . . Technology imposes on us all its inexorable logic of scale . . .

The full benefits of an integrated European technology can only be obtained when Britain is a full member of the EEC.[20]

Until 1971, Benn still believed that British membership of the EEC would prove beneficial; and if the technological determinism underlying his support contradicted the democratic nature of his opposition, he was nevertheless one of the first to realise that a decision of this magnitude had to have national consent and support. As he explored the implications of British membership and the democratic nature of national sovereignty, he came to realise that membership would involve a practical loss of self-government which overrode any technological benefits. It was at this point that he came to conclude that membership would not be in Britain's interest.

Benn was the first person to advocate a referendum on British membership. Following the Llandudno speech in May 1968, which set out the democratic arguments in favour of referenda, he raised the matter in Cabinet in October 1969, but it was dismissed out of hand. A year later, on 14 November 1970, he wrote an open letter to his constituents starting a national campaign for a referendum on the Common Market. Benn's letter stressed the political nature of the decision, denied that a referendum would be unconstitutional and that people were either not sufficiently intelligent or well-informed to take such a decision. Finally, a referendum on the Common Market would not necessarily create a precedent for referenda on every other issue, from hanging to immigration, because the case for each would have to be argued on its merits, and in practice would be confined to decisions of a permanent or irreversible nature.

We may be able to estimate the initial cost of going in, but we cannot possibly estimate with any accuracy either the long-term advantage of entry, or the long-term cost of not entering . . . It is a major political decision we have to make, and it must be seen as such . . . Successive British Governments have so far been singularly quiet on the idea of political union . . . But this really is to fudge the issue. It is inconceiveable that Britain with its strong Parliamentary tradition would allow a bureaucratic commission in Brussels to reach central decisions about economic policy without being subject to broad democratic control by an elected assembly. . . . The key question at this moment is how we are to decide whether we now want to join . . . It is an irreversible decision which would transfer certain sovereign power . . . It is for these reasons that we have got to consider the use of a unique mechanism to help us reach a unique decision . . .

The case for a referendum on the question of Britain's entry is, in my opinion, immensely powerful if not overwhelming. If people are not to participate in this decision, no one will ever take participation seriously again.

Those of us who feel that, given the right terms, the arguments for entry are strong should be the first to want to see that decision shared . . . The whole history of British democracy has been about *how you take decisions.*

If the Common Market question is decided without consulting the people, it will really split the country and both parties . . . It would be a very curious thing to try to take Britain into a new political unity with a huge potential for the future by a process that implied that the British public were unfit to see its historic importance for themselves.[21]

Benn's letter created considerable public interest and was reproduced by the *Observer* in full. But the Labour leadership accused him of introducing irrelevant factors, new uncertainty and damaging the prospects for Britain's negotiations, as well as Labour's unity. When he proposed a referendum in the Shadow Cabinet in December and on the NEC in March 1971, he could find no seconder. Only Jim Callaghan recognised the tactical advantages and was reported to have said: "Tony has launched a rubber dinghy into which we may all one day have to climb." Undeterred, Benn introduced a European Communities Referendum Bill in May to try and obtain public support. "I don't think you can ever launch anything unless there is a real case for it. I never believed in the capacity to persuade the people at the top unless you mobilised support from the rank and file and therefore I used to fight at all levels. It is part of my general belief that politics is about movement from outside the system into the system."

Behind its formal pro-market policy, the Labour Party was deeply divided on Britain's membership, and on 24 May the NEC decided in favour of a special Party Conference to resolve Labour's position. The breakthrough in negotiations during May helped concentrate minds on the importance of the decision, and increased awareness that a referendum offered a way out of Labour's internal difficulties. On 24 May Benn wrote to all constituency parties urging them to submit resolutions demanding a referendum and on the NEC argued for the acceptance of the special Conference's decision. Though accused of trying to frustrate British entry into the EEC, he did not view the referendum in that light. On 2 July the Bristol South East constituency party launched its own campaign to persuade Labour to adopt the referendum as its official policy. Benn told them:

I can see really significant long-term opportunities for ordinary people in Britain and in the Six, if we could persuade the British people to vote for entry and then work together to change and reshape the EEC from the inside to convert it progressively into a democratic socialist community. . . .
It is part of a deeply held personal conviction that modern democracy cannot survive unless it shares much more power with the people.[22]

On 17 July, the special Conference at Central Hall Westminster failed to solve Labour's problems, rejecting in the presence of international observers from 67 countries, the motion opposing entry on the terms negotiated and calling for a general election by the narrow margin of 3,185,000 votes to 2,624,000. After a full day of debate and powerful speeches by Wilson and Callaghan, who successfully lobbied the trade unions, the Conference overwhelmingly endorsed a motion for the NEC to compose a definitive resolution for decision at the October Conference. Benn's failure to address the Conference was noticeable, but in fact, he had not been chosen to speak as a member of the NEC.

On 22 July, the House of Commons debated the Government's White Paper on the terms of entry. In voting against them, Benn did not comment on the terms themselves, but because Labour's endorsement would have undermined the campaign and case for a referendum. "It would be the end of democratic politics as we know it in Britain if the Labour Party embraced an aristocratic view of its function, believed itself to be cleverer, wiser and more knowledgeable than those it was here to serve. I profoundly believe that. Indeed, I believe that this is the whole heart of the argument now going on inside the Labour Party."

Labour succeeded in forcing Heath to postpone the decision in order to allow a national debate on the common market. Promising "a great battle which would be fought up and down the country with public demonstrations and debates", Benn campaigned throughout the summer for a referendum. At the 1971 Labour Party Annual Conference in Brighton, Brian Stanley of the Post Office Engineering Union, supported by the TGWU executive, introduced a resolution demanding a referendum which was only defeated by 3,082,000 votes to 2,005,000; while the NEC statement of 28 July, opposing entry on the terms negotiated and calling for a general election, reflected the mood of the Party and was carried by 5,073,000 votes to 1,032,000, while a resolution opposing entry on principle was defeated by 3,082,000 votes to 2,005,000.

The Great Debate initiated by Heath in July culminated in an historic five-day debate in the House of Commons which endorsed entry by a majority of 112 on 28 October. Once again Benn affirmed that the people must decide, arguing that only they could ratify such a loss of sovereignty. On 7 November he addressed the Young Socialists rally in Trafalgar Square and criticised the sixty-nine Labour MPs who had rebelled against a three line whip, supported entry and had, thus, in his judgement, voted against the sovereignty of the people: "They have no moral right as individuals to form a temporary coalition, never tested at the polls, to give the people's power of self-government away to anyone." These remarks were unfortunate, in that they enabled his opponents to accuse him of totalitarian double-speak, of advocating the dictatorship of the people and denying basic freedoms to the representatives. But in reality two opposing concepts of delegative and representative democracy were at issue.

The campaign for a referendum reached its climax during the first half of 1972 while the European Communities Bill was going through Parliament. More and more, as the legislation progressed, Benn felt that the loss of sovereignty would involve a loss of self-government.

"Key areas of economic and financial policy are removed from the control of Parliament and the electorate." Labour fiercely contested the Bill on the floor of the House, as well as in committee, and the Government several times came close to defeat. On one occasion, after a long night of debate, the chairman of the committee charged Benn with obstruction.

As late as 15 March 1972, Benn was in a minority of four on the NEC in favour of a referendum; but several factors coalesced in March to alter the political balance. President Pompidou's announcement on 16 March of a French referendum on Britain's entry transformed the situation. At the next meeting of the NEC on 22 March, Benn argued that the growing demands for a British referendum were — now that Denmark, Ireland and Norway had agreed to hold their own — irresistible. A national opinion poll in *The Daily Mail* showed 78% to be in favour. After long and heated debate, the NEC endorsed a referendum by thirteen votes to eleven, with Wilson, Jenkins and Callaghan absent.

When the Shadow Cabinet met on 29 March, Wilson and Short appeared to have changed their minds, and — with Healey and Ross absent — a referendum was accepted by eight votes to six. For Benn it was a moment of triumph. But it had earned him the enduring enmity of the marketeers who saw in it a personal vendetta against the social democrats. Around this time, Benn had used his chairman's casting vote to secure the election of Ron Hayward, an anti-marketeer, as General-Secretary of the Party. Jenkins, Thomson, Lever and Owen resigned from their front-bench positions. "This constant shifting of ground I cannot accept," Jenkins bitterly commented. The marketeers, who were on the whole social democrats, had numerous European contacts and took their campaign abroad. The President of the EEC Commission, Dr Mansholt, a veteran Dutch socialist, "ashamed to see my socialist friends adopt such a negative attitude", attacked Labour's "stupidity". Benn was shocked by the rift the issue had caused and endeavoured to heal the wounds. In an exchange of letters with Mansholt he denied that Labour's attitude was one of narrow-minded nationalism and explained why Labour was opposing British membership and demanding a referendum. "Democracy means that people are given the chance to decide what is right or wrong for their country. . . . First the present terms were unfair and unfavourable; and second that on a matter of such importance the people should be consulted." He attempted to defuse the situation on 23 April by admitting to the guild of British Newspaper Editors that he had damaged the referendum campaign and provoked fears "by talking about a referendum rather than a straight vote through the ballot box". A referendum would promote responsibility rather than revolution and without it entry into the Common Market would lack moral authority, release dangerous tensions, encouraging extremism, and undermining public confidence in Parliament:

> We are being repeatedly told by our leaders that the public are, at best, irresponsible and ignorant, and, at worst, ungovernable and tending towards anarchy. The attitude of people generally towards those with political authority is that they are at best remote and unimaginative, and at worst, dictatorial and dishonest. Anyone who reads the press will find ample evidence of this analysis. This is not just an argument about Left and Right. It is an argument between Government and Governed.[23]

On 18 April, Benn spoke in support of Neil Marten and Enoch Powell's Conservative amendment for a consultative referendum. Once more, he was accused of hypocrisy in denying Parliament's right to decide; but in a powerful justification of popular sovereignty, exposed the anti-democratic nature of his opponents' arguments. "Freedom starts here," declared Jeremy Thorpe.

> Now we have it (replied Benn). Freedom began before the House of Commons was set up. Freedom was forced on the House by people outside it. Freedom is defended by the ballot box and not by the division lobby. The arguments against the referendum are the very same arguments as have been used against every extension of the people's rights for 140 years. I believe they will be ashamed at their blindness in failing to see that what they opposed in the name of parliamentary democracy was the floodtide of popular consent without which parliamentary democracy cannot survive.

Despite Benn's great "dialectical skill and vigour", which the Conservative MP, Sir Derek Walker Smith, felt forced to concede, the amendment was defeated. Thus on 13 July 1972, the European Communities Bill became law by 301 votes to 284. British entry, concluded Howe, had been "duly negotiated, duly provided for in this Bill, and duly examined and debated". "And the public duly ignored," interrupted Benn, adding that only a referendum "breathes life into the idea of full-hearted consent". He felt it was essential for Labour to boycott all EEC institutions in order to demonstrate its determination on renegotiation. At a Tribune Group meeting on 3 September, he demanded that there be either a general election or a referendum before 1 January 1973 and that Labour not attend the European Parliament or serve on the Westminster EEC Committee. "Non-cooperation is essential if we are to keep faith with millions of our fellow countrymen . . . if any future renegotiation is to have any chance of success . . . if we are to preserve public faith in parliamentary government."

In Tiverton on 23 September Benn explained why a loss of sovereignty would mean a loss of self-government:

> We shall have money taken from us by taxation by people we cannot remove for purposes we do not control. We shall be subject to laws, enforceable in the courts, that have been made by officials we did not elect and cannot hold to account . . . For all these reasons it is absolutely essential that

the Common Market issue should be decided democratically, at Conference. . . . . If the Conference decides to vote against entry in principle, that decision must be accepted by the movement.[24]

Enraged by these remarks, Wilson persuaded the NEC not to oppose entry on principle; but on 30 September it resolved by seventeen votes to ten that "we shall not regard the treaty obligations as binding upon us". The 1972 Conference endorsed a policy of renegotiation and referendum by 4,662,000 votes to 1,543,000, though the motion opposing entry on principle was only defeated by 128,000 votes. Benn told the Conference in his closing address as chairman : "The whole EEC argument was about democracy. It is about the right of people to decide things for themselves." In his view the boilermakers' resolution to boycott EEC institutions "did more than any other single thing to convince the EEC that Labour was in earnest about renegotiation in 1974". By the time of the 1973 Conference, Labour's approach to renegotiation had become clear. As he told the Foreign Press Association on 17 September 1973: "The only way in which a British voter can safeguard his rights of self-determination on the Common Market question will be by voting Labour. A Labour Government will seek to renegotiate the terms on a basis that will entirely safeguard our national interest."

The referendum campaign was one aspect of a much wider campaign which Benn fought during these years for the extension of democracy in all areas of public life and, particularly, within the Labour Party. Freed from the shackles of Government office, he was able to speak his mind about the questions which had preoccupied him while he had been a minister, and to use his influence as vice-chairman and chairman of the Labour Party between 1970–72. The realisation that democracy would never truly function until all power had been made accountable, focussed Benn's mind on the importance of open government. On the NEC, he argued for the introduction of external political advisers to ministers by the next Labour administration.

> The question of secrecy in government has now at last become a major political issue. For too long ministers and civil servants have justified the cloak of secrecy with which they have surrounded themselves by reference to some supposedly unchallengeable assertion that the national interest requires it. . . . There is a growing public recognition that democracy itself cannot function unless the people are allowed to know a great deal more about what goes on inside Government, even to the point of knowing when Ministers disagree on important issues coming up for decision. . . . The problem is essentially one of isolation rather than of sabotage or obstruction by the civil service.[25]

In a subsequent memorandum to the Home Policy Committee on the working methods of the next Labour Government, Benn advocated a greater openness and identified four problems: the secrecy of government, the lack of external communications between ministers and movement, the absence of internal communications between ministers due to the control by the Cabinet Office over papers, and finally, the political isolation of ministers. Benn's solution lay in a liberalised official secrets act, restricted so as to cover only defence, key economic policies and short-term political strategy; a system of paid ministerial advisers with access to papers, appointed and removable by Parliament, but without executive powers and bound by the confidentiality of their information. Such a system, he maintained, would mean "open government with proper safeguards. ... The main effect would be to open up new and important lines of communication within Government."

Benn considered open access to the mass media integral to any democratic society and open government because of the control exerted over the dissemination of information and opinion. As he told a symposium on broadcasting policy at Manchester University:

> The whole political process in a democracy rests on the maintenance of a delicate fabric of communication within society which reveals the common interest that exists, identifies conflict where it arises and painfully builds the consent which leads people to accept the policies that emerge as these conflicts are resolved by upholding the ground rules of the system. The political relevance of the media demands that broadcasters be accountable. ... What is required therefore is some way of developing a new framework to democratise this power without falling into the trap of state control or confusing commercial competition and free enterprise control with the free expression of different views on the air.[26]

In *The Sunday Times,* he also wrote an article entitled "Liberating the Lobby", criticising the narrow specialisation of journalism and the mutually advantageous, incestuous relationship between "politicians and the small select group of correspondents who write about them ... (and) tend to concentrate their attention too much on to the parliamentary arena to the exclusion of some of the new realities of modern politics which lie outside". The press campaign against the trade unions convinced Benn that unaccountable and undemocratic journalism would side with capital against labour. At the May Day demonstration in Queen's Square, Glasgow in 1971, he called for trade union right of access to television and radio time "to speak directly to its members without having everything they say edited away by self-appointed pundits and producers. It is an astonishing thing that working men and women do not yet have the means to speak to their fellows through the mass media." Benn's speech provoked a storm of criticism; but Harlech television took up the challenge by inviting the Bristol TGWU to make a documentary about themselves. The programme, *My Brother's Keeper,* about the life and work of a shop steward, was widely acclaimed and generally considered the precursor of the Open Door television series.

Benn's aim was to make Labour more effective within a more democratic system of government. Above all, he campaigned for the democratisation of the Labour Party, and in *Labour Weekly*, on 15 October 1971, he published "The Thoughts of Chairman Benn" which set out a populist programme to make Labour an instrument of change and to

> ... educate a new generation to see the necessity for a real change in the power structure. If we are... to revitalise British democracy, we must prove it by revitalising party democracy. ... Looking back over the last few years, the instincts of Conference have often been shown to be surer than the most measured judgement of the parliamentary leadership on many key issues. [27]

Benn's Fabian lecture on 3 November 1971, "The Labour Party and Democratic Politics", explained why he felt internal party democracy to be so important and wanted to stimulate an open debate about Labour's future. The lecture put the case for the party system as an instrument of the popular will, as against the aristocratic view of Parliament's divine right to govern. It examined the need for collective self-reliance, the importance of welding disconnected popular pressure groups into the mainstream of the Labour movement, the close relationship between party democracy and the pace of social change, and the way the Labour Party itself operated:

> If we look ahead and project existing trends ten years forward, we can already identify new social problems emerging that can only be solved by adopting a different philosophy of democratic socialism from the one that has inspired past consensus politics ... Unless we can tackle this problem of democratising power directly we shall find it harder and harder to win parliamentary majorities for socialist policies to create a fairer society ... We shall never change society unless we start to do it ourselves by directly challenging ... unaccountable power. Democratic change starts with a struggle at the bottom and ends with a peaceful parliamentary victory at the top. That is what I call Popular Democracy. This is not an appeal for violent revolution or even systematic and sustained civil disobedience. ... It is an appeal for the strategy of change from below to make the parliamentary system serve the people. ... The problem of achieving greater party democracy is now the central internal problem facing the movement ... and ... an essential preliminary to the process of getting those policies right, and seeing that they are really carried through ... [28]

As chairman of the Labour Party, Benn endeavoured to put these principles into practice at every level. In his own Bristol constituency, he made a conscious effort to contact and inform his electors: his correspondence in a single year, between April 1972 and March 1973, totalling 5011 letters. "I don't radicalise them — they radicalise me," he remarked. His determination to reconnect the parliamentary system with the grassroots, prompted a local group of Labour people to compile an index of community action. On its publication on 9 November 1973, it was described as "the most comprehensive list of community or voluntary organisations ever compiled for any city in Britain". Benn regarded it as primarily a means of communication which individuals, planners, social workers and pressure groups could use, and commented: "Community politics is not something that can be appropriated by a single political party, claiming to speak for all these groups. They must speak for themselves and political parties must be ready to listen to what they have to say."

Within the Labour Party, Benn wanted to "see to it that as many people as possible are able to join in this policy-making". If he failed to persuade the NEC to grant consultative status to progressively inclined pressure groups, the "Participation '72" campaign, of which he was the keenest supporter, involved over 10,000 party members in the discussion of policy directly.

At the national level Benn found that real democracy was even more difficult to attain. Though the Information and Research Departments published an unprecedented number of policy documents, the NEC itself resisted the move towards openness. After a prolonged campaign, his proposal to publish the minutes of NEC meetings and the names of those who voted for or against any resolution was eventually defeated by eleven votes to nine on 27 June 1973.

The prospects for party democracy rested most of all on the role of Labour Party Conference itself and on the constitutional right to determine policy. Benn considered conference resolutions a vital link in the process whereby popular pressure was converted into parliamentary action: if party policy was to work, it had to emerge through long public debate and be settled by Conference. As chairman of the 1972 Conference, he resolved to see that the collective will of the movement would be accurately expressed. The 1972 Labour Party Conference at Blackpool was the culmination of everything for which Benn had striven over the previous two years. However, his speech at Tiverton, on 23 September, demanding that Conference resolutions must be accepted by the movement, had been distorted by the press who described it as an attack upon the parliamentary leadership. In his opening address as chairman, Benn emphasised: "Conference never had and never would want to dictate to a Labour Government, but they do expect Labour Governments to take conference decisions seriously and not deliberately reverse or ignore them." He was determined to make the Conference a democratic success.

> I tried to interpret the role of chairman, not as the strong-arm man of the Executive, railroading NEC policy through, but as a servant of the delegates as a whole, treating them with respect and consciously helping them to arrive at the decisions they wanted to reach. ... I tried to treat the delegates with the respect due to a body of men and women who bring

together a wide experience of life, a high sense of personal responsibility, long service to the movement and deep convictions. . . . No chairman can fail to be deeply impressed by this Parliament of Labour, which is the only forum where working people . . . can actually reach real decisions.[29]

Attention focussed, however, on the way Benn managed the Conference. The press ridiculed the confusion caused by his innovations — such as the use of request-to-speak cards. In particular they criticised the second vote on a resolution supporting the Clay Cross Councillors' defiance of the Housing Finance Act, which Benn had ordered because Conference "did not understand the meaning of the NEC's reservation", as was proved by the overwhelming rejection which followed. The criticism was undoubtedly politically motivated. *The Times,* and other papers, launched their own campaign to promote a Democratic Labour Party led by Dick Taverne — unpopular with his own constituency party in Lincoln — who timed his resignation to coincide with Benn's closing speech. These pressures, a fierce loyalty to the Labour movement, and wounded pride, drove Benn to react emotionally and make a stinging attack on Taverne, the television companies and the editor of *The Times* in his closing address.

> We are for the first time in the history of British politics fighting a political party invented by the press of this country . . . as if they were designing some soap, detergent or beer. . . . I sometimes wish the trade unionists who work in the mass media, those who are writers and broadcasters and secretaries and printers and the lift operators of Thomson House would remember that they too are members of our working-class movement and have a responsibility to see that what is said about us is true. . . . We have in our history . . . taken on kings, we have taken on landowners, we have taken on factory owners, and now in this impending by-election, make no mistake, we are taking on the mass media in the campaign that is just about to begin.[30]

The Press, predictably enough, chose to concentrate on Benn's controversial closing speech, presenting it as a direct attack upon its freedom. They thus forced Wilson to issue a statement disowning Benn's remarks, in which he made it clear that the Labour Party was "totally opposed in all circumstances to the use of industrial action for the purpose of impeding the printing or dissemination of news, or the expression of views". And Benn was placed in a position in which he had to issue his own denial. But beyond the ephemera of press headlines, it was clear, as Benn had observed in his closing speech, that the Labour movement wanted more democracy, socialism and unity.

The polarisation of British politics in the early 'seventies did more than anything else to reunite the Labour Party with the trade union movement. The Conservatives undoubtedly saw the trade unions as the chief obstacle to the success of capitalism in Britain, and Heath was determined to reduce their power. "I have always made it plain that we are not going to have legal control of wages and prices; and I said

that we are going to carry through the reform of industrial relations."
The Industrial Relations Act dominated the 1970–71 parliamentary
session and reflected the widespread belief that Britain was crippled by
strikes. The Government aimed to eliminate unofficial strikes by
making them illegal and collective wage agreements legally binding.
The legislation would reduce the power of the trade unions by
outlawing the closed shop and sympathy strikes, and it sought to
regulate their activities.

No other measure could have done more to set labour against
capital, damage industrial relations and reignite the class war. At the
same time, its stormy passage through Parliament laid bare the
internal bitterness and divisions of the Labour movement. For the
most part, the ex-Cabinet secretly supported the Bill which set out to
achieve everything they had wanted to do in *In Place of Strife*. While
going through the motions of opposing the Bill, they hoped that the
trade unions would register once it had been enacted, and they refused
to commit the Labour Party to its repeal. The trade unions still bitterly
resented *In Place of Strife,* Labour's prices and incomes policy, and
remained deeply hostile to the Labour leadership. The TUC decided
to seek its own salvation, holding mass rallies at Trafalgar Square on
1 January and the Albert Hall on 12 January, organising a series of
one-day regional strikes and at their special conference on 18 March
1971, they adopted a policy of non-registration.

For Benn, Barbara Castle and many others, Labour's opposition to
the Industrial Relations Act was an education in the realities of trade
unionism. For Eric Heffer, singing the "Red Flag" late at night in the
House of Commons to obstruct its progress, constituted direct action
not romanticism, and he noted the change in Benn's thinking. "He
could not believe that the Government was alienating the trade unions
and their members. Today, of course, the same ex-Cabinet Minister
realises just how wrong the Government were. He at least is prepared
to admit his mistakes. Others are not."[31] The parliamentary struggle
over the Industrial Relations Act made Benn realise that the trade
unions were not defending their vested interests but the legitimate
interests of working people in their collective struggle against capital.
However imperfect, he came to see that the unions were democratic
organisations and that the fragile authority of their leaders rested on
their members' confidence. Benn was deeply disturbed by the
separation of the Labour Party from the unions; but when he
approached the TUC in November 1970 to discuss the possibility of a
joint fighting fund against the Industrial Relations Bill, he was
rebuffed. However, during the first half of 1971, he held several
meetings with the executive of the Bristol Transport and General
Workers Union.

At the first meeting, they said the Labour Government had completely
betrayed them and that what they needed was a trade union party. At the

second, they again considered this proposition and the alternative of working through the Labour Party in Parliament; and at the third, they agreed to set up a political action committee to play a more active role within the Labour Party.[32]

From these meetings developed Benn's close working relationship with the trade union movement and his determination to recreate a grand coalition of Labour. He had long seen the problem of industrial relations as one of industrial democracy and recent developments, particularly the UCS work-in and the corporate plan devised by the Bristol Aircraft Corporation workers, had convinced him that self-management or complete workers' control was the only practicable solution to the historic conflict of capital and labour. Industrial democracy was the central theme of Benn's efforts to bring about a rapprochement of the political and industrial wings of the Labour movement. At the AUEW Conference on 27 June 1971, he urged:

... the trade union movement ... to develop a conscious long-term policy of negotiating itself into a position of real power in industry. ... We must therefore, begin our talks with the trade union movement on future policy on a new basis. ... Unemployment is the right point of entry for joint policy-making within the Labour movement. In this way we can re-examine together the management of the economy and consider how to solve the problem of inflation. ... I am talking about democracy and democracy means that people ultimately control their managers. ... A firm managed by consent would not find any of its problems solved by magic. It would still have to attract investment by getting a return on its capital. ... It would still need the best management ... but with this one difference. They would be workers, as workers, for the other workers and not for the shareholders alone. ... One of the most powerful arguments for adopting the policies that I am discussing is exactly that responsibility would be placed upon workers in industry who already have massive power. ... The only way to get responsibility is to give responsibility, and that means legislating for industrial democracy, self-management, workers' control. ... A major change in the balance of power over management in favour of workers and against the exclusive rights of shareholders.[33]

In working towards a joint programme with the trade union movement Benn urged the Labour Party to see that the purpose of public ownership was industrial democracy. As he told the Public Enterprise Group:

Socialists have always seen common ownership as a major instrument for changing our society ... Nationalisation does not of itself, shift the balance of power in society, (or) democratise industry ... If nationalised industries were seen to be democratically run ... we could take a massive step towards democratic socialism.[34]

The turning point for Labour Party-trade union relations occurred in the summer of 1972, when following its defeat by the miners in February, the Conservative Government tried to implement the

Industrial Relations Act. The imposition of a 60 day cooling-off period and secret ballot on the railwaymen in June only hardened opinion and led to a strike, thus showing the act to be both divisive and ineffective. The NIRC fined the TGWU £55,000 because their members had blacked containerised goods at the London Docks and for contempt of court. On appeal, however, the High Court ruled that a union could not be held responsible collectively for the actions of its individual members. In July, TGWU dockers picketed a coldstore employing non-union labour, which led to the imprisonment of five dockers in Pentonville. A wave of protest swept the country. Three days later the TUC General Council called for a General Strike, unanimously supported by the NEC, and the men were released following the intervention of the official solicitor.

Enraged, Benn issued a statement on the eve of the Tolpuddle Martyrs rally in Dorchester, comparing the plight of the imprisoned dockers to the spirit of the six Dorset men who were transported to Australia in 1834 for attempting to form a trade union:

Millions of people in Britain . . . will in their hearts respect men who would rather go to jail than betray what they believe to be their duty to their fellow workers. For centuries Britain's democratic liberties have been won and upheld with the help of men and women who stood up for their beliefs and took the consequences. The right to worship freely, to organise trade unions, to vote, for men and women in Britain, were all won against powerful people who sought to maintain their privileges by stirring public fears about anarchy whenever anyone challenged those privileges . . . (but) in the end, each man is answerable to his own conviction as to what is right and wrong. If conscience lands him in jail, the laws that keep him there also imprison a part of all our freedoms. . . . The law which has put these men in prison is an evil law, drawn up by a Government which hates the trade unions. . . . We must all now rally to defend . . . the real bedrock of consent on which all our democratic institutions ultimately rest.[35]

Benn felt "deep disgust at the abuse which has been heaped upon the dockers in the present crisis". He told the Bristol dockers, "no other group of workers in Britain has been so violently attacked and insulted and misrepresented as you have been. The press, television and radio have for many years tried to make dockers the scapegoat for the difficulties facing our economy." These statements provoked some bitter attacks on Benn, most of them implying that "his respect for the law is only exceeded for those who break it". However, Hugh Cudlipp did offer him the centre pages of *The Daily Mirror* of 3 August to put the dockers' case. Benn wrote an article which argued that the dockers were neither anarchists nor revolutionaries, but simply workers defending the right to work. This resulted in over 1100 letters to the paper supporting his view by eight to one.

Benn was aware that his support for lawbreakers would be construed as an attack upon the rule of law, and in the Shadow Cabinet he urged

Labour to clarify its attitude to law and order:

> (The) concept of law-breaking in pursuit of conscience rests on our belief
> that our prime duty is to each other . . . No man should tell another man to
> break the law to by-pass Parliament. . . . But the person who is punished for
> breaking an unjust law, may if he is sincere and his cause wins public
> sympathy, create a public demand to have the unjust law changed through
> Parliament. . . . This is the first and most fundamental principle. It has a
> deep moral significance. Our religious and political liberties rest upon it. . .
> The second principle was that those with power must be accountable to the
> people and not the other way round. . . . The third principle is . . . that our
> national sovereignty belongs to the people. We only lend that sovereignty to
> our representatives to use for five years at a time. Any Government or MP
> pretending to give away these sovereign powers . . . is acting un-
> constitutionally. Laws that pretend to take away these powers permanently
> have no moral authority.[36]

Benn felt that the Pentonville five episode had re-politicised the trade
union movement. In January 1972 the NEC, PLP and TUC decided
to form a tripartite liaison committee "to discuss policies in the field of
industrial relations and the management of the economy". Wilson,
Lever and Houghton insisted that Labour would only agree to repeal
the Industrial Relations Act if the TUC agreed to voluntary wage
restraint which, they argued, was necessary for Labour's electoral
credibility. Out of these meetings grew the collective understanding
that a voluntary incomes policy would only work on the basis of
fairness, social justice and effective price controls. However, the joint
statement following the arrest of the Pentonville Five did commit the
next Labour Government to repeal the Industrial Relations Act, and
to establish the right to belong to a trade union in law. In addition, the
Committee undertook work on a programme to promote the
widespread development of industrial democracy.

The fact that the Labour Party-TUC Liaison Committee was
represented in the press as evidence of trade union domination, was
proof, in Benn's judgement, of consistent hostility and the need for a
labour alliance. On 5 September 1972, he addressed the TUC Annual
Conference as the NEC's fraternal delegate representing the Labour
Party. He made unity with the unions his message.

> You have allowed yourselves to be presented to the public as if you and the
> General Council actively favoured the Conservative philosophy of personal
> acquisitiveness. The fact that the trade union movement came into being to
> fight for social justice as well as higher wages has just not got across. The
> trade union movement must seek its political objectives as an integral part
> of an organised, democratic Labour Party in Parliament with a socialist
> programme. The Labour MPs we put in power must abide by majority
> decisions reached through its own democratic procedures and never forget
> those who put them there. The unions and the Party must shape policy
> together at every level.[37]

The publication of the Labour Party-TUC Liaison Committee's second joint statement, "Economic Policy and the Cost of Living", on 28 February 1973, cemented the alliance, making a social contract between the parliamentary leadership and the trade union movement the cornerstone of Labour's economic strategy. By the time of the 1973 Annual Conference, Benn felt that Labour had transformed itself from a demoralised, disillusioned and divided party into a movement confident and united on a socialist programme. At the same time, the Conservative Government also paradoxically believed that its policies were on the verge of success. Benn warned that their confidence was ill-founded: "The problem is basically political. The Government have not made up their minds whether they wish to establish a working relationship with the trade unions... yet it is upon the question of industrial relations that a great deal of the confidence and hence the prospect for higher investment must come."

The Government's problems began on Saturday, 6 October 1973, when Egypt invaded Israel to revenge its 1967 defeat. Only a day after the Labour Party Conference had ended, the crisis had started which would culminate in the downfall of the Conservative Government at the general election of 28 February 1974. By January 1974, oil prices had quadrupled to US $11.85 a barrel. The immediate effect on the British economy was to increase imports by approximately £2,500m a year and the cost of living by 2%. It was an inflationary hammer-blow which overnight rendered the Conservative economic strategy of expansion, combined with price and income controls, totally irrelevant. Nevertheless, the Government had gone ahead with the publication of Stage III of its counter-inflation programme on 8 October. Under the proposals, wages would be permitted to rise by the greater of £2.25 per week, or 7% over the following year, with 40p for every one per cent that the retail-price index rose above 7%. There were also special provisions for those who worked unsocial hours, specifically designed to make incomes policy acceptable to the coalminers.

With an inflation rate of around 15% widely predicted for 1974, the Government's prices and incomes policy was manifestly unsustainable — both economically and politically. Its pursuit would inevitably embroil it in direct conflict with the unions and the public. This was compounded by the fact that the oil crisis engendered "a sense of doom, as though a great tragedy were about to be acted out", as Robert Carr put it. Lord Armstrong, the chief architect of the incomes policy, was struck in retrospect by the inability to react to a changed situation. He concluded that Stage III should have been withdrawn, even though it would have been politically damaging in the short-term. Yet, at the time, he was obsessed above all by apocalyptical nightmares of ungovernability, the end of parliamentary democracy and hyper-inflation.

The economic situation was confused and demanded flexibility, because no one knew what the final price of oil might be or was able to quantify its inflationary impact. However, Heath's determination to make Stage III work made flexibility impossible, while the Government's strongly-held belief that a peaceful solution and an economic miracle both lay within their grasp, only enhanced the tragedy. It was a story of intransigence and indecision, misunderstanding and misjudgement; and as Fay and Young wrote: "Men became symbols of good and evil and readily appeared to be acting out the roles their opponents' mythology had assigned them."[38]

Stage III had been specifically tailored to suit the coalminers, and after a secret meeting on 16 July with Joe Gormley in the garden of No. 10 Downing Street, Heath believed that the miners would accept their special treatment. Gormley, however, had little reason to indicate that he could obtain a majority on the NUM executive. The miners were in a militant mood at their 1973 conference, passing a resolution for a 50% increase in their basic wage, while Mick McGahey called for direct action. "It is not negotiation in Downing Street, but it is agitation in the streets of this country that is required." The oil crisis had made the miners doubly aware of their political power, and on 12 September the NUM submitted their claim, rejecting the Coal Board's 16.6% offer on 10 October — the maximum permissible under Stage III. Both Derek Ezra, the NCB chairman, and Maurice Macmillan considered the Government's early intervention a grave tactical error because it undermined the process of negotiation and turned the oil crisis into an energy crisis. On 12 November the miners began an overtime ban which led to a 40% reduction in supplies to power stations. The following day, the Government proclaimed a state of emergency. Petrol coupons were issued in anticipation of rationing and legislation announced to enable the Secretary of State to take direct control of all fuels.

For Benn, the oil crisis was a moment of truth. During the debate on the Queen's Speech, he prophesied that "the policies that we advocate cannot be long delayed". The crisis was exposing the underlying weakness of the economy and in his view only socialist measures could tackle these problems on a basis of democratic consent. He welcomed the Fuel and Electricity Supply Bill as a measure which created the powers a Labour Government would want to control the acquisition, production, supply and use of petroleum, electricity and all other fuels. At a conference about the development of Britain's off-shore oil, he explained why Labour advocated a planned energy policy and planned investment. "Never again can we go back to the illusion that market forces will somehow allocate fuels rationally. . . . It is difficult to understand . . . the sheer magnitude of the task of industrial transformation and renewal that the United Kingdom will have to undertake . . . "

In *The Times*, he analysed why new policies were needed, connecting Britain's deepening crisis of confidence with the failure of traditional consensus policies to stimulate investment.

There is . . . growing agreement . . . (that) industrial investment in the private sector has been consistently lower than everyone . . . has known to be necessary if Britain was to remain a major industrial power. . . . Growing Government intervention within the market economy has not produced this investment . . . in industry we have had continuing trench warfare. Those who champion these discontents in Parliament . . . are now pilloried as inciters of the discontent they now articulate. This is the dead end of democratic politics. . . . Our real hope lies in our capacity to preserve and extend democratic self-government.[39]

Meanwhile the confrontation between the Government and the miners was moving swiftly towards its traumatic climax. All attempts to break the deadlock only worsened the conflict and hardened attitudes. The opposition was anxious to be conciliatory and responsible, and on 23 November Harold Wilson urged the Government to examine Mick McGahey's suggestion that extra pay was possible under Stage III for "waiting and washing" time. The effect of this was to deny Heath a way out of the impasse without loss of face — McGahey believed that Wilson deliberately "blew it" in order to exploit the Government's difficulties. On 28 November the Prime Minister invited the entire twenty-seven man executive of the NUM to Downing Street in a dramatic but empty gesture. Heath's plea that the executive ballot their members on the existing offer was psychologically disastrous because the miners realised the strength of their position. Lawrence Daly aggressively promised to bring down the Government, and the usual 14–13 moderate majority became a minority of seven as twenty members of the NUM executive rejected a ballot.

The crisis deepened on 13 December when Heath imposed a three-day working week in order to conserve dwindling fuel supplies. Benn's role in the three-day week and in the Government's eventual downfall was to sow the seeds of doubt in the public's mind about "the necessity of these dramatic measures" and to question Heath's motives in calling a General Election. From the start, he felt that "the Government have decided to use the counter-inflation act as an instrument of psychological warfare against the NUM". The suspicion of a sinister conspiracy drove him to an exchange of letters with Heath disputing the official figures about coal and oil supplies and demanding full disclosures of the facts about the true level of fuel stocks. But the Government refused. Benn next acted to organise Labour Party Monitoring and Information Services to collect the relevant facts, and on 31 December he issued a statement marking the start of Labour's full scale campaign against the three-day week. Questionnaires were sent to all affiliated trade unions and CLPs about the effects of the three-day week and the level of fuel supplies. The replies were used as a basis for formulating Labour Party policy and interrogating ministers.

The responses also indicated a wide-spread bitterness about the three-day week which confirmed Benn's original suspicions. In justifying the State of Emergency, the Government had set a minimum seven million tons of coal as a threshold, but stocks had fallen below this level in sixteen weeks over the previous four years. In addition, oil supplies had been fully restored and there was no evidence to suggest that the ASLEF work to rule had caused delays in transporting coal from railway depots to power stations. Though twelve million tons of coal were in fact available for the power stations in early January, the situation proved to be more a moral than a statistical victory for Benn. On the basis of Francis Cripps' projection of demand, a three-day week would have been necessary by mid-January.

The day after Parliament resumed, Benn deployed these findings in a debate on the three-day week, which he condemned as unworkable and an attack upon democracy and working people.

The Prime Minister's attempt to justify the three-day week was not concerned, as one would expect were it a genuine proposal, with husbanding the nation's fuel resources and protecting the people at a moment of shortage. It was an act of mobilisation for a long war against the miners. The Government have suppressed the oil figures . . . have ordered public authorities set up by Parliament not to answer questions put to them . . . which is a complete denial of the duty of a public authority to tell the public how it is discharging its statutory responsibility . . . The Government have themselves directly violated Stage III by announcing . . . substantial increases in coal and electricity prices which were not provided for in the Pay and Prices Code. Ministers have said. . . . that Stage III has the force of law. Stage III never had the force of law. It was an advisory document to the Pay Board. And it was for the Pay Board to consider it. . . . The Prime Minister is moving to 1984 ten years ahead of schedule, and he is doing so with a nightmare of centralised control, under the control not of the Left but of the Right. . . . Tight wage control by law will not work and by consent will never be achieved . . . unless there is a major social reform to make our society fairer and more equal. . . . The trade union . . . has to operate by consent . . . and . . . no one thinks that he will get 100% acceptance of anything in a voluntary society. . . . I do not believe for a moment that the problems confronting this country are insoluble within the framework of the parliamentary system. . . . The paradox is . . . that . . . today moderate people want radical change. . . . They want more democracy and not less democracy. They want a sharing of power and an enfranchisement of the community. . . . We cannot expect responsibility unless as a House we are prepared to share power. We cannot expect social justice unless as a House we legislate to dispense justice. We cannot save democracy unless we practice democracy.[40]

Benn felt that Britain had reached the end of an era. As the crisis deepened, he became conscious of the revolutionising effect it was having upon his own politics and those of the public. On 27 January he declared:

> The Conservative version of national unity rests upon the creation of an illusion that the rich are kind, and that if only working people would be restrained we could all raise our living standards together in an unending bonanza of capitalist growth fuelled by some necessary "inequalities" to provide the profits, mainly needed for investment. . . . That is the master illusion of British politics . . . The Conservative Party and their allies, including the mass media, are prepared to sacrifice even free enterprise itself in order to preserve the pattern of power and wealth that corresponds with their class interests. This is why they are moving towards an industrial system with some features drawn from the corporate state . . . Working people are becoming aware of . . . class privilege and class deprivation, the consequences of Mr. Heath's counter-inflation policy which is deliberately designed to bring about a substantial redistribution of wealth and income in favour of capital at the expense of Labour. . . . When historians come to write about this period of British history, Mr. Heath will certainly be credited with having awakened people, who had never thought about class before, to what class means and how it relates to their own experience.[41]

The effect of the three-day week and of Benn's attack upon it was to radicalise public opinion and frighten the Government into seeing a General Election as the only alternative to ignominious surrender. Yet most people, including the Labour leadership, did not share Benn's faith in the democratic instincts of the people and believed that the Conservatives would win a General Election. The fear of a right-wing triumph explains why Len Murray made Heath an offer on behalf of the TUC he could not refuse — a promise that the TUC would agree to carry out Stage III if the miners settled outside it. As Murray recalled: "Heath had us where he wanted us. We were in his hands and he could not lose. If he had taken the offer, and it had failed to work and other unions had broken through, he would have been home and dry with all his anti-union policies, the Industrial Relations Act and incomes policy. If it had worked, it would have been his great political triumph, showing he could bring the unions to heel."

But Heath rejected the offer. There was mounting pressure from within the Conservative Party upon him not to capitulate but to call an election. Moreover, the TUC were not aware of the magnitude of the miners' claim. This was compounded by the fact that there were too many uncertainties in the TUC solution and the Government felt it might be a trap. Confrontation had poisoned the atmosphere of politics and warped judgements. The damaging uncertainty continued until 7 February, when Heath finally announced the General Election in a broadcast to the nation.

The Labour Party's manifesto, *Let us Work Together: Labour's Way Out of the Crisis*, explained why the Conservatives were to lose. "The Government called this election in panic. They are unable to govern, and dare not tell the people the truth." In early January, the NEC and Shadow Cabinet had drafted the manifesto which fully reflected the socialist policies set out in the 1973 programme. Beyond achieving this, Benn was to play no part in the national campaign, but stayed in Bristol where he was fighting for political survival. The redrawing of the constituency boundaries had made Bristol South East a highly marginal seat. Yet he refused to accept the offer of another safer constituency: "I'm not a carpetbagger. My roots are here," he declared. His election in Bristol meant much more to him than his own political survival. It would be a test of the two party system at a time when it was being threatened by an unprecedented Liberal revival; and it would challenge Benn's conviction that moderate people wanted radical change. Once again his capacity to depersonalise his own predicament and see it in terms of wider issues gave him renewed confidence and strength. Though he realistically admitted his chances of victory as "fifty-fifty", he denied that his socialism was an obstacle. "The extremists in the colonies all ended up having tea with the queen, Nehru, Nkrumah. Extremist is the first compliment the Establishment pays you, before it recognises you are right. We are the last of the colonies and the Establishment is trying to stop us breaking away. But we won't be stopped."

Bristol South East was a microcosm of urban England in the 1970s and unusually representative in its social character. The proliferation of candidates was symptomatic of the increasing fragmentation of British party politics. There was a National Front candidate and a Democratic Labour candidate — largely due to the personal feud between Taverne and Benn —, while the Liberals hoped to win votes from the Conservatives who concentrated on the threatened nationalisation of the aircraft industry and the docks, as well as on the abolition of direct grant grammar schools. However, Benn was undeterred: "I am confident that the people will see the dangers that lie ahead if the present Government is re-elected and will look to us." He fought a low-key, traditional campaign of factory-gate and work meetings, canvassing at homes, in shopping centres and bus queues to establish direct contact with the electors and "to intensify the intention to vote". He obtained messages of support, including one from Roy Jenkins, to help convince the electorate that he was not an extremist. At meetings he conveyed the fundamentals of socialism in moderate and reasoned language; but his election address of 28 February fully expressed the democratic nature of his socialist vision: "I am fighting this election as a crusade for a fairer, more equal and more democratic Britain in which we rediscover our own identity and try to reestablish our basic freedoms." His election at Bristol South was more than a personal victory — an 8000 Labour majority in a highly marginal seat. He had proved that a socialist government could be elected by democratic means.

How far, though, did the national situation bear out his views? The course of events since October 1973 had seen the end of the old consensus, but this itself would create enormous problems for a socialist government. In a political atmosphere of hostility and suspicion it would be difficult to obtain acceptance for radical socialist measures. For Benn personally, the General Election had proved that the parliamentary system was working. Yet the results showed that Labour had not won — only that the Conservatives had lost. In the stalemate, Labour 307 seats, Conservatives 296, the electorate had not voted for socialist reforms, but for moderation and no particular solution — as the six million Liberal votes indicated. Labour lacked the mandate it had enjoyed in 1945. The question remained whether Benn could succeed in making this crisis the occasion for fundamental change, and not the excuse for postponing it.

VIII
1974-1975
SOCIALISM IN ONE COUNTRY

... The crisis that we inherit when we come to power will be the occasion for fundamental change and not the excuse for postponing it.
TONY BENN

Chaos reigned in Whitehall on 1 March 1974 when it became clear that the results of the General Election would not resolve the crisis paralysing Britain. Though the Conservatives had lost, Heath did not resign until negotiations with the Liberals had failed. On 4 March the Shadow Cabinet rejected the idea of a coalition and the following day Harold Wilson formed a minority Government, his third administration, in which Denis Healey became Chancellor of the Exchequer, Jim Callaghan Foreign Secretary, Roy Jenkins Home Secretary, Michael Foot, the Deputy Leader, Secretary of State for Employment; Tony Benn, Secretary of State for Industry as well as Minister of Posts and Telecommunications. The Establishment thought a revolution had occurred. No one appreciated its demoralisation more than Benn who, in a *Tribune* article, maintained that a socialist programme would command the confidence of the people.

Elation was short-lived: the fifteen months between the General Election of 28 February and the Referendum on Britain's membership of the Common Market on 5 June 1975 would prove to be some of the most difficult and turbulent in recent political history. The breakdown of the post-war consensus forced people to consider alternative policies. International events paralleled the domestic crisis with sudden changes of government in France, Germany and the United States, following the death of Pompidou and the resignations of Brandt and Nixon. In Britain, the Liberal revival, the renaissance of nationalism in Scotland and Wales, marked a temporary end to the two-party system, creating a political vacuum that enhanced the influence of the Labour Party as distinct from its parliamentary leadership — despite its precarious majority. The ensuing struggle for the control of the Labour Government dominated the entire period and took place against a background of economic crisis.

As one of the most articulate advocates of democratic socialism,

Benn was thrust into the centre of controversy. He was closely
identified with the issues that most divided and preoccupied Britain
during the period. Should the Labour Government implement its
socialist programme? Should Britain remain in the EEC? The
passionate and uncompromising language in which Benn expressed his
vision of a democratic society undoubtedly frightened, indeed
shocked, the Establishment. But this alone does not explain the
transformation of his public image at this time into that of national
bogeyman; the man the Tories and the media loved to hate. The
reasons for what was tantamount to a victimisation of Benn are rooted
in the political instability of the times, the polarisation of opinion and
the fears of ungovernability — which were themselves the
consequences of the underlying economic crisis. In the demonology of
the right, Benn became the incarnation of evil. The metamorphosis of
Viscount Stansgate into Count Dracula was vividly depicted as a
vampire sucking the lifeblood of free enterprise.

However, Benn's portrayal by the media as the enemy of
parliamentary democracy and a free press, as the arch-advocate of
nationalisation and central economic planning on a *dirigiste* Eastern
European model, bore little relation to reality. Rather, it reflected the
internal struggle for the control of the Labour Government; and the
civil service and Treasury's opposition to socialist policies. It was the
latter which coined the word "Bennery" to denigrate Benn's ideas.
The causes of Benn's public transformation into an "enemy of the
people" were at root psychological — as Paul Johnson explained in
"The Strange Case of the Anti-Benns":

> We are, by and large, idle, self-indulgent, pleasure-caring and lacking in
> public spirit. We are cynical about the state of our country, and cynical
> about the possible remedies . . . Above all, we do not want to change . . . The
> truth is, Mr. Benn aims to rob us of our illusions, and we resent it. He knocks
> at the door, and warns us that things cannot go on as they have. He nags. He
> questions everything. He produces new ideas (not all of them good ones, to
> be sure). He challenges the old relationships between the classes. He shows a
> rational contempt for established institutions. He is a great sweeper of
> cobwebs and opener of windows — a constitutional fresh-air fiend.
> Wherever he goes he is followed by icy draughts, and the unwelcome whiff
> of carbolic soap. We like the old dirt and disorder; how easy then to dismiss
> him as an eccentric, a crank, a tinkerer — indeed a public menace!
> Yet we know in our hearts . . . that Mr. Benn is probably right. Change,
> however uncongenial, is certainly coming. The old Britain has no future. It
> is a decaying Ruritania, full of bright uniforms and unpaid tailor's bills.
> You cannot live off history or eat nostalgia. Mr. Benn arouses enormous
> resentment because he tells us such plain truths. If we could dismiss his
> message as false, we would find him much less offensive. So we ignore logic
> and reason, and take refuge in abuse. If only Mr. Benn could be destroyed as
> a political symbol then perhaps our troubles would go away with him! This

is an ominous, even pitiful reaction of a great nation. The strange case of Mr. Benn, in fact indicates the seriousness of the British disease.[1]

Behind the psychological reality lay the economic one. The Labour Government took power at a time of accelerating inflation, mounting unemployment and a world economic crisis unparalleled since the 1930s. In Britain the rate of inflation rose from 10.7% in 1973 to 17.2% in 1974 and reached 24.6% in 1975, while sterling declined from $2.32 $2.02 or 13% over 1974–75. The balance of payments deteriorated from a deficit of £923m in 1973 to £3565m in 1974 on the current account. Between early 1974 and mid-1975 unemployment rose from just over a half million to nearly one million, and private sector capital investment fell from £6164m in 1973 to £5795m in 1975. Government action had played a part in fuelling inflation. Sudden reversals in monetary and, to a lesser extent, public expenditure policy by Barber and Healey, together with high interest rates, caused a severe cash crisis and a record number of bankruptcies and liquidations. Yet, however great Government responsibility, the economic crisis had exposed the long-term weakness of British industry. A visible trade deficit of £5195m in 1974 was indicative of increasing import penetration, and this disturbing trend was reflected in a 7% annual decline in manufacturing employment over 1970–74 with an average loss of 120,000 jobs a year. If commentators mostly agreed that a low rate of investment was the chief cause of Britain's economic decline, opinion was divided as to why this had occurred.

The chief controversy concerned the interrelationship of investment and profits. Some economists and socialists argued that profits had collapsed in the face of intensified international competition, the monopoly power of organised labour, inflation and taxation. Others denied the existence of any profit crisis; and there was a good deal of empirical evidence to suggest that profit margins on sales, as opposed to the return on capital employed, had only declined by 3% since the 1950s, that prices tended to rise with costs, though the short-term behaviour of profits was cyclical. The effects of inflation were widely disputed; but it was evident that it had created liquidity problems, and there was a strong argument that the increased working capital required to maintain the existing level of economic activity had reduced profit margins. On the other hand, profits after tax had risen because of investment incentives to offset inflation, in the form of accelerated capital allowances and stock appreciation relief. The role of profits in the economy was certainly a politically sensitive issue and the idea that profits had collapsed was more a reflection of fear and propaganda than of fact. Nevertheless, both Marxist and liberal economists agreed that companies only invested where there was the prospect of profit, and it was therefore likely that the long-term decline of profits in relation to capital, together with high inflation and interest rates, would be a powerful disincentive to investment.[2]

Benn argued that capitalism was in deep crisis for political reasons and urged a realistic appraisal of the situation. He drew attention to:

> ... the risk of rising unemployment general liquidity difficulties and profits squeeze that industry at large will experience following the three day week, accentuated by the heavier tax burdens on industry and the pressures of inflation. ... The industrial crisis now facing Britain is far deeper than is generally appreciated. ... A realistic evaluation of the working of Britain's economy is long overdue. For too long myth and propaganda have directed our understanding of how it works. ... We should agree on the extent of the industrial crisis.[3]

In Benn's view, years of low investment had re-enforced low profits, taking Britain into a spiral of decline that would end in de-industrialisation. As a socialist, he believed that the profit motive itself lay at the root of the problem: in the long run it was economically irrational and self-defeating, since it was divorced from production and wealth creation. The pursuit of profit had led to the excessive concentration of economic power, while the supremacy of financial considerations in decision-making discouraged investment in manufacturing industry where profits tended to be relatively low because of the high cost of labour and technology and the depressed state of the economy. The market mechanism had therefore failed and was now sharpening the struggle between capital and labour, manifesting itself in inflation, and even threatening the fabric of democracy itself.

Benn's strategy was shaped by his analysis of Britain's economic problems and the political situation as he saw it. Above all, it was vital that the Government retain the support of working people by cementing the social contract between the Labour Party and the trade union movement. All hope of confronting inflation and maintaining full employment depended on the implementation of their joint programme. Fragile though the social contract was in practice, Benn's conception of it was more revolutionary than either the Labour leadership or the TUC held, in that it involved a major extension of industrial democracy. "The social contract . . . is a commitment to socialist reform . . . Working people are not prepared, quite rightly, to make sacrifices in support of a system in which they have lost confidence . . . and, therefore, the process of social and industrial transformation is intimately connected with the prospects of our success in dealing with inflation."

But the situation was inimical to socialist reform: neither the Prime Minister nor his senior colleagues believed in Labour's industrial programme. In Cabinet, the Left (consisting of Benn, Castle, Foot, Shore and John Silkin) were in a small minority. Determined to limit Benn's influence, Wilson appointed Harold Lever, industrial policy adviser, as Chancellor of the Duchy of Lancaster, and divided the Department of Trade and Industry into two, creating a new department for Prices and Consumer Protection. He also transferred responsibility for broadcasting to the Home Office, in this way effectively isolating Benn from the media. Benn rapidly fathomed Wilson's intentions and, when told to go to Millbank Tower to take over Christopher Chataway's job of administering the 1972 Industry Act without overall responsibility for industrial policy, he immediately installed himself in Victoria Street during the post-election confusion. Here the Permanent Secretary is reported to have greeted him: "I presume, Secretary of State, that you do not intend to implement the industrial strategy in Labour's programme."[4]

Despite such formidable opposition, Benn enjoyed considerable support in many quarters. The weekly dinners of the Left ministers, with husbands and wives, which began on 23 April, helped develop a common approach in Cabinet on economic strategy. The Parliamentary Labour Party gave strong backing, and the Tribune Group now totalled eighty MPs. Two of Benn's ministers, Eric Heffer and Michael Meacher, were "both committed politically to the manifesto". Benn's advisers, Francis Cripps on economic and Frances Morrell on political matters, had a two-fold role: to develop external lines of communication with the Labour Movement, and internally to counter the influence of the civil service, as well as to argue for socialist policies from within the Government.

Government intervention in industry was one of the central issues of British politics during 1974–75. Most of Benn's time was spent in dealing with situations of industrial collapse rather than in carrying out Labour's manifesto. However, his close identification with its policies for public ownership, planning agreements and industrial democracy created the misleading impression that the Labour Government and Benn in particular sought to bring the entire economy under state control.

The first crisis Benn faced was an attempt by his civil servants to cancel Concorde. As he recalled:

> I think that there is no doubt whatever that they reckoned whichever Government was elected, either Tory or Labour, the cancellation would follow immediately: the Tories having got us into Europe wouldn't care anymore and the Labour Party with Denis Healey as Chancellor would be bound to want to kill it. So I took it to colleagues and I said: "Well, if the case is as bad as this, the figures are as bad as this, let's publish them. Then at any rate there will be some public understanding of the reasons for the cancellation!" They agreed to that, but when my officials discovered that I intended to publish them, they got into a great panic because they were afraid that the figures wouldn't stand up to examination. It was one of the strongest cases for open government.[5]

On 18 March, Benn revealed that Concorde had cost £1100m to develop, insisting tht "the public were entitled to know the figures . . .

It is accepted that in publishing the figures, there has to be anxiety, but in parallel with this will be opportunity for public discussion." There appeared to be little hope of saving Concorde, and as a Bristol MP with its production situated near his constituency, Benn realised that his support would be interpreted as politically motivated. On 1 April he announced a full public review of the project and was not afraid of encouraging the workers to make their case. They demonstrated in Downing Street on 23 May while the Cabinet were meeting to discuss Concorde's fate.

The actual review produced a much more balanced decision than would otherwise have occurred, and to that extent vindicated Benn's theory of open government. Though Concorde was not a commercial success, the report concluded that the only valid comparison was between cancellation and operating costs. Its recommendation of limited production of sixteen aircraft delighted Benn who had all along suspected an attempt at industrial and political sabotage that would do little to solve Britain's public expenditure problems. And after Wilson had met Giscard in June, Benn announced that Concorde would not be abandoned: "There has never been, in any major technical decision taken in this country, such an atmosphere of openness before the final decision came to be taken."

If the energy crisis had implications for the commercial viability of Concorde, the world recession it precipitated and the increasing price of energy had a far more direct and serious effect upon the steel industry, hastening the closures envisaged in its £4.5b modernisation scheme while making its plans for expansion wholly unrealistic. The British Steel Corporation's (BSC) decision to make 20,000 workers redundant — equivalent to nearly 10% of its work force — in areas of high unemployment had already caused great anxiety, and Labour was pledged to review the closures. On 18 March, Benn announced that closures would be suspended until the completion of a review by Lord Beswick. His intervention was predictably attacked as an act of political interference damaging to the steel industry. But the situation was not as straightforward as Benn's critics imagined. Far from ignoring economic realities, Benn agreed that modernisation, high productivity and the elimination of over-manning were vital to BSC's future; but he argued that this could only be done by consent: workers must be consulted. Furthermore, the boom of 1973 had exposed shortages of capacity, creating a black market in imported steel that had been aggravated by the three-day week from which production in coal-fired furnaces was still recovering. At the time, it was not clear how long the recession would last, and the suspension of the closures was consistent with the Government's strategy of maintaining employment and output.

Beswick reported that he was "immensely impressed by the positive and constructive attitude of management, trade unions and indeed workers at all levels". Steelworkers formed local action committees which he had to consult through local authorities, because they lacked official trade union status. He found "a valuable heritage of a skilled and loyal workforce and potential for development that must, if at all possible, be utilised". Beswick finally recommended the postponement of 13,500 redundancies in England and Wales where steel mills were currently profitable, and he envisaged a reduction in redundancies from 7000 to 2000 in Scotland through new investment, the postponement and reversal of closures. His objective was to minimise unemployment in a way that was consistent with BSC's long-term strategy — to synchronise closures with new investment. The report accepted the rapid end of unprofitable plants, such as Ebbw Vale in South Wales, but it emphasised "the role of BSC in creating new job opportunities" as "an important development in public ownership".

The Beswick review did not solve the closures dispute, and the affair came to a climax in a much publicised conflict between Benn and the BSC's chairman, Sir Monty Finniston, during April and May 1975. The economy had meanwhile deteriorated and the two sides were even further apart. Benn, who had ordered BSC in December to make "the collapse of the Jessell empire . . . an opportunity for extending public ownership" by taking over its specialist steel subsidiary, Johnson, Firth and Brown, publicly stated that "the safeguarding of jobs is the primary objective". Finniston demanded all 20,000 redundancies, but after the failure of a tripartite meeting with the trade unions on 5 May declared that he could do with 50,000 redundancies. On 14 May the steelworkers demonstrated in London to protest against Finniston's statement, though they finally reached agreement with BSC for savings of £100m a year with no redundancies.

Benn was violently attacked for preserving unviable jobs and for irresponsibility in addressing the steelworkers' rally in Westminster, but he remained defiant:

> The day that Ministers are afraid of meeting their own constituents, Parliament will perish or die. . . . My sole concern in this matter was that the board of BSC should discuss fully with the trade unions concerned the problems caused by a down-turn in the steel industry . . . for at no stage did I do more than seek to ensure that a nationalised industry chairman had good working relationships with his own employees . . . It is a good thing that the community interest, like the interest of the trade unions concerned, should be reflected in tripartite meetings.[6]

In assessing the Beswick review, it could be argued that Benn's insistence on basic industrial democracy created the climate for orderly change and did much to prevent industrial action and political dislocation. If the outcome was not in BSC's best commercial interests, it was important to distinguish profitability from benefits to the balance of payments and the general level of demand.[7]

British Steel's troubles were a reflection of the depressed state of the economy, which during 1974–75, seemed to be suffering industrial collapse. Benn was determined that short-term cyclical difficulties should not destroy otherwise viable companies, and that the crisis should be used to tackle the long-term weakness of British industry which it had exposed. Throughout the period, he operated under the Conservatives' 1972 Industry Act, assisted by its Industrial Development Advisory Board which recorded that "the greatest part of the Board's deliberations concerned assistance to help companies in acute liquidity difficulties", and complained that "too many cases are brought to the DOI only when the immediacy of the requirement for additional finance is such that no reasonable appraisal of the facts or prospects of future viability can be properly considered".[8]

The IDAB to which Benn appointed George Doughty of the AUEW and John Hughes of Ruskin College, Oxford, was chaired by Robert Clark of the Merchant Bank, Hill Samuel, and largely consisted of accountants and industrialists. It disputed many of Benn's decisions to support companies, and Benn maintained that its criteria of strict commercial viability were no longer tenable: "It would be quite wrong to subcontract decisions to the Advisory Board. . . . I think that Ministers must retain power to take a broader . . . longer-term view." In May he published details of public support for the private sector, which showed that the Conservative Government had given £3705m in assistance to industry between 1970–74 and that it was subsidising one-quarter of total manufacturing investment. He concluded that there was no disagreement on the principle of government intervention.

The rescue operations Benn mounted nevertheless aroused enormous controversy and he himself was accused of incompetence and of encouraging industrial anarchy and inefficiency. Yet, behind the wall of propaganda, lay the fact that relatively small amounts of money saved a large number of companies which subsequently prospered. During 1974–74, £213m was disbursed in regional development grants, while Benn authorised £2.5m in loans and £5.5m in grants under section seven of the 1972 Industry Act, and £10.58m in loans and £41.95m in grants and equity under section eight. The majority of cases involved bank overdraft guarantees when the burden of interest payments and the reluctance of the banks to allow credit to keep up with inflation threatened many companies with receivership. Thus £.35m for the hosiery firm Bear Brand Ltd and £2m for Fodens Ltd, the truck manufacturers, in the form of loans was enough to prevent collapse. But some attempts at rescue did fail, where firms were either intrinsically unviable or where the process of under-capitalisation and decline had gone too far to be reversed. Thus £2.5m could not save Triang toys of Merthyr Tydfill.

Benn found that he was invariably accused of exploiting temporary difficulties to extend public ownership for political ends. But the assessment of any company's viability is necessarily in part a matter of subjective judgement. He regarded public ownership as preferable to unnecessary closure which undermined confidence and destroyed productive capacity. If he insisted on a tripartite solution between government, management and the workers, it was because he aimed to make public support effective, foster a spirit of cooperation and extend industrial democracy, rather than impose state control. The collapse of the electronics group, Ferranti Ltd, for example, in August 1974 during a severe liquidity crisis, illustrated the choice between public ownership or liquidation. Benn did not hesitate to give bank guarantees of £6m and stopped the closure of its troubled transformer division. Meetings were held to work out the Company's long-term strategy: Benn felt that the tripartite meeting on 10 March 1975 was an historic occasion, because the management sided with the representatives of the 16,500 workers in support of public ownership against the owners — who were chiefly concerned with the value of their own shareholdings.

Ferranti was an example of successful government intervention; but the problems of other firms were frequently more intractable. In September, Britain's largest machine tool manufacturer, Alfred Herbert Ltd, got into difficulties and the IDAB recommended resurrection through receivership. A delegation of shop stewards had informed Benn of the situation as early as May, but he rejected rationalisation on the grounds that public investment and internal reorganisation were a better method of surviving recession. The Government announced bank guarantees of £5m, and following a tripartite agreement, put up £25m in 1975 in return for a 50% shareholding and the appointment of a non-executive trade union director. The results were not spectacular, but 5500 jobs were secured; and since most people agreed that Britain could not afford to allow its machine tool industry to disappear, there was in the circumstances little alternative to public ownership.[9]

Benn regarded public ownership as a means of protecting the national interest, but he always insisted that "firms cannot be nationalised without the workers wanting it". Though he intervened to fight the takeover of Britain's leading scientific instruments manufacturers, George Kent Ltd, by the Swiss multinational Brown Boveri, the majority of employees in the event supported it; while those at Cambridge Instruments opted for a takeover by GEC, with a continuing public equity of 25% in exchange for £1.75m in grants and £3.25m in loans. By contrast, the sports car makers, Aston Martin Lagonda, preferred a private capital reconstruction to any form of public ownership, and the workers themselves rejected Benn's offer to support a cooperative.

The largest rescue operation, and the most serious potential collapse Benn faced as Secretary of State, occurred in the motor vehicle industry. On 15 November, Lord Stokes told him that British Leyland was about to fold, having lost £24m in the year to the end of September 1974. Benn reacted by announcing government-backed bank guarantees of £50m on 18 December, after he had asked Sir Don Ryder to make "an overall assessment of BLMC's present situation and future prospects . . . because of the company's position in the economy as a leading exporter and its importance to employment".

Ryder reported in April 1975 that a massive investment of £1.5b would be required in order to save British Leyland and that nationalisation was inevitable because only the Government would be prepared to put up the necessary finance. The report was far-ranging and remarkable in that it recognised the contribution industrial democracy would make to labour relations and productivity. Benn saw the review as an embryonic planning agreement.

> The Government have made a conscious decision to reverse the long period of decline in investment which has brought British Leyland into its present position . . . and has decided to express more positively our confidence in the people who ultimately produce our wealth. . . . What I fear . . . is that when the upturn comes in world trade, we shall have so demobilised our manufacturing industry that we shall not be able to take advantage of it.

On 21 May, Benn introduced a Bill to nationalise British Leyland:

> . . . without Government and public funds, properly matched by investment, accountability and a sharing in the profits, it does not seem at present under any Government we can get the investment we need . . . We must do this by democratic discussion, for the consultative arrangements . . . lie at the heart of the prospects of the success of this enterprise.[10]

The most spectacular collapse of 1974 was the crash of Court Line on 15 August, which left 50,000 people stranded abroad and deprived a further 100,000 of their summer holidays. The episode embroiled Benn in a major political storm over his own role in the affair, since just a few weeks earlier on 26 June he had nationalised Court Line's shipbuilding interests and expressed confidence "that this should stabilise the situation . . . including the holidays booked for this summer". Court Line's collapse was a saga of financial mis-management. In 1973, the Company lost £3.5m and had borrowings of £23m, having acquired Horizon Tours to fill its empty aircraft. The Government only learned of its difficulties on 19 June 1974 when the Company informed the DOI that it would not be able to carry out its shipyard modernisation programme, though it had been offered £9m if it could put up £3m for its Pallion shipyard. Within five days, the two sides had agreed to the sale of Court Shipbuilders for £16m as a means of preventing an imminent catastrophe; but questions were inevitably asked about Benn's motives. However, the Department of Trade's independent inspectors considered £16m a fair price and did "not accept any suggestion that the Government made this acquisition . . . because of their nationalisation policy". In evidence to the inspectors, Benn denied that there "was a stratagem to acquire this company . . . It was a bona fide exercise of statutory powers." As minister responsible for shipbuilding, Benn's chief concern was to secure Court Shipbuilders' £133m orders and a further £48m under negotiation, which he argued anything less than 100% public ownership could not have achieved. "The dominant consideration in my mind," he recalled "was to safeguard the employment of nearly 9,000 people employed in the assisted areas by Court Shipbuilders."

Subsequent controversy centred on Benn's statement in Parliament, which, it was claimed, misled the public by raising hopes about Court Line's prospects. The Inspectors concluded: "We are of the opinion that . . . all the reference to holidays and holiday-makers are to be criticised for going too far by way of assurance . . . without sounding any note of caution or reserve. . . . (But) there is no question of the statement being in any way untrue or reckless."

The Government agreed to a holding statement because, as Benn put it, the alternative scenario was one of unnecessary collapse. Certainly, the events that followed did not warrant an expression of confidence, but it had been impossible to predict this outcome. Court Line's end had not been in sight until the beginning of August, and as late as 12 July the investigating accountants had reported that the short-term cash flow "appears to indicate that . . . there should be sufficient cash funds available for trading operations to continue". Court Line's difficulties had placed Benn in an impossible position, and if he was legitimately criticised, many more would have suffered had the Government not intervened in Court Line. It became obvious too that "no minister can guarantee the operations of a commercial company", and following the inspectors' praise for his handling of the affair in such adverse circumstances, Parliament acquitted Benn.[11]

The traumatic experience of Court Line and of other rescue operations, as well as the threat of an impending economic crisis, re-enforced Benn's determination to pursue a socialist course. With most of the Cabinet as well as the CBI and private industry hostile to the extension of socialist industrial policies, Benn was forced to fight in public, though he recognised that "there is no chance of success without a long period of public explanation. . . . We cannot hope to win support for it until we have described it and set it against a background of public understanding of Britain's longstanding industrial difficulties."

The aircraft industry was profitable, but it was overwhelmingly dependent on the Government for financial support, as well as for its main market; and it was of vital national interest in terms of employment and its contribution to the balance of payments. In advocating public ownership, Benn did not envisage a bureaucratic, centralised and inefficient organisation, but a decentralised and democratic structure with "the greatest possible commercial freedom consistent with public accountability". As the consultative document noted: "The Government attaches great importance to increasing the democratic participation of workers in decision making at all levels of industry." Nevertheless, nationalisation crystallised opposition: the battle over the aircraft industry was extremely bitter, taking place against a background of uncertainty. The rise in oil prices, the energy crisis, the Concorde and defence reviews, undermined confidence. Benn himself may well have aggravated matters by serving on the joint Labour Party-CSEU working party on the industry while a minister, by encouraging the Lucas aerospace workers in their plans for a democratic corporate strategy, and by openly debating "the scope, method or timing" which remained unsettled until January 1975. The row over the HS 146 with Sir Arnold Hall, chairman of Hawker Siddley, vividly illustrated the economic and political considerations at issue. In July, Hall informed the Government that he intended to cancel the HS 146 because the market no longer existed; but Benn suspected that nationalisation was the real reason. Both were probably right, in that only a nationalised industry could afford to take a long-term view; whereas Hawker Siddley would do nothing to reduce its valuation for the purposes of nationalisation by incurring development expenditure beforehand. The HS 146 was put on ice, but its eventual success — with prospective sales of 400 aircraft at an estimated value of £1.6b by 1979 — did much to support Benn's view. "At a time of great uncertainty, public ownership may well be the best way of building confidence in an industry that would otherwise find itself caught up by short-term calculations of profitability that might not relate to the country's long-term future as an engineering nation."

The case for the nationalisation of the shipbuilding industry was even stronger, though the inclusion of ship repairing was much criticised. Production had remained stagnant while the world market had grown, and after years of decline and £155m of government assistance, many firms had either collapsed or come into public ownership. Benn admitted that it would "not of itself solve the many problems of the shipbuilding industry", but argued that there was no alternative other than extinction in a world slump. On the positive side, he claimed that public investment and industrial democracy would remove restrictive practices, raise productivity, bring economies of scale, enable Britain to win a larger share of the world market and restore profitability. "It is clear that much of the industry will be unable to compete effectively in the world market unless there are changes in management methods and working practices which will allow the more efficient use of its resources and unless there is substantial further investment and modernisation, the funds for which are unlikely to be available from private sources."[12] The political implications were few, and on coming to the Department of Industry, Benn presented the joint Labour Party-CSEU proposals, which enjoyed the overwhelming support of the Labour movement, as the basis for legislation. On 31 July, he announced the plans for nationalisation: "Looking back on the history of this important industry with so many skills tied up in it, it is a great tragedy that public ownership did not take place a quarter of a century ago."

The aircraft and shipbuilding industries were in fact nationalised after Benn had left the DOI. During his time, he faced the difficult challenge of establishing the planned National Enterprise Board and Planning Agreement System (NEB and PAS). In April 1974, he set up a working party within the Department under Eric Heffer to prepare a Green Paper on industrial policy. Its meetings were largely concerned with theory and progress was slow. Labour members argued that these instruments of micro-intervention were indispensible to effective economic planning and the achievement of the macro-objectives, such as full employment, balance of payments equilibrium and high investment. The civil service, on the other hand, deployed almost exclusively legal arguments to obstruct the proposals, questioning whether an act enabling the NEB to acquire any company was constitutional, whether planning agreements could be contractually binding if the objectives were not necessarily workable or were beyond a company's control.

Benn knew that the proposals would meet with fierce opposition and that he would have to work fast to preempt the Establishment. Concentrating on consultations, he kept out of discussions and mobilised the trade union movement in support. On 17 May, the CBI expressed its unease over Labour's proposals for compulsory public ownership and planning agreements, and Wilson was furious when he learned that an important policy initiative had occurred without Cabinet approval. Healey reassured the CBI, and the Treasury claimed that British could not afford more public ownership on the grounds that it was inflationary. With most of the Cabinet hostile, Benn was forced to fight in public, and in May published a paper he had prepared for the Labour Party-TUC Liaison Committee, "A Note on the Current Work of the Department of Industry". The document rehearsed the socialist analysis of Britain's economic crisis, defined the role of the NEB, and in uncompromising language stated that the objective of planning agreements was "to secure the conformity of leading companies with national economic priorities in return for supporting requested industrial developments". The paper also envisaged a new tripartite relationship with industry and full disclosure of information to government and trade unions to facilitate their full participation in open policy-making.

TONY BENN

Benn's paper caused a great public stir. Such a naked declaration of aims seemed counter-productive. *The Times* noted that it provoked "bitter comments from senior politicians" and that "strenuous efforts are now being made to limit the damaging effect of these public ownership proposals". The CBI was appalled; the right-wing Aims of Industry launched a £100,000 anti-nationalisation campaign; rumours began to spread that Benn had lost the confidence of industry; and Wilson announced that he would "take charge", replacing Ted Short as Chairman of the Cabinet's Industrial Development Committee.

The draft Green Paper which Benn presented to Cabinet after Whitsun was explicitly socialist and led to heated arguments, from which he returned feeling utterly drained and exhausted. The draft proposed a £1000m a year for the NEB, compulsory planning agreements with category one firms and and disclosure of information, and the power to appoint an official trustee where companies failed to act in the public interest. But these ideas were never discussed on their merits, only in terms of immediate political advantage and in the context of enormous external pressure from industry to abandon the policy. Wilson and Lever wanted the NEB reduced to the status of a state merchant bank, along the lines of the IRC; while Jenkins favoured a holding company and Shirley Williams feared "a major extension of unrestricted state power. I would myself not wish to see that, any more than I would wish to see any further concentration of private power in our society." Wilson, who proclaimed himself the "guardian of the manifesto", was intensely annoyed when Benn quoted back at him his own radical speech on public ownership to the 1973 Labour Party Conference.

Wilson used every tactic to impose his own ideas, insisting to the Cabinet that the Government should publish a White instead of a Green Paper, on the grounds that further argument and uncertainty would damage Labour's election prospects. Thus, on 15 August, Benn published *The Regeneration of British Industry* as a White Paper. Wilson had suggested the title and had himself written in the introduction that "we need both efficient publicly-owned industries, and a vigorous, alert, responsible and profitable private sector", in order to stress Labour's commitment to the mixed economy. Yet Wilson remained hostile: "As I had feared, it proved to be a sloppy and half-baked document, polemical, indeed menacing in tone, redolent more of an NEC Home Policy Committee document than a command Paper."[13] Political arguments had prevailed over economic sense, in that according to the Paper, the NEB would only receive £1000m in total, insufficient to extend public ownership or increase investment significantly. Planning agreements would be voluntary, because they could not be "an agreement in the sense of a civil contract enforceable by law"; and the concept of an official trustee was abandoned on

208

similar grounds, though powers to demand information would be retained.

Wilson was frightened that Benn would dissent and instructed him to present the Paper as Government policy, leaving Harold Lever to conciliate: "What you lose in leverage, you will gain in receptivity." "I shall of course present it in the most conciliatory way possible," Benn replied, "as a Cabinet document, and if asked about Labour Party or TUC policy will make the distinction absolutely clear." At the press conference on publication, Benn maintained the White Paper "does correspond very closely to the proposals we put forward in the manifesto". It aimed to extend "public ownership into profitable manufacturing industry" and promote "large-scale sustained investment" through the NEB, which he saw as "encouraging real industrial democracy". He described the proposals as "a programme for industrial reform and reconstruction which most people in Britain know to be long overdue . . . (with) two very practical objectives . . . First, British industry now needs a sustained re-equipment programme. . . . Second, Britain must find a constructive way out of the trench warfare between government, management and working people."

Behind the conflict in Cabinet over industrial policy lay the fear that nationalisation could lose Labour the election. Indeed, all the Government's actions during this period were dictated by the need to get re-elected. Yet the strategy was ambiguous. Wilson wanted to project Labour as "the Party of cooperation", at the same time as maintaining the Government's political credibility with the Labour movement — through the Trades Union and Labour Relations Act, which repealed the Industrial Relations Act, and an aggressive start to the renegotiation of Britain's Common Market terms. The same defects were apparent in the management of the economy: the Government's strategy was to borrow and spend Britain's way through the world recession, sustaining output and employment. No one wanted deflation, and even Healey, advised by the Cambridge Economic Policy Group, contemplated selective import controls. Lever argued that deflation would destroy productive capacity and Crosland held public expenditure sacrosanct as an instrument of economic management and social progress. The actual measures, however, did more to exacerbate unemployment and inflation than to cure them. Healey's first socialist budget took £1100m out of the economy, aggravating industry's cash flow problems by increasing national insurance contributions, corporation tax and VAT on a selective basis. His second package in July did more to increase consumption than output by lowering the general rate of VAT to 8%, increasing regional employment premium and relaxing dividend controls. Thus, the prospects for moderating the rate of inflation through food subsidies, price controls and voluntary wage restraint were negligible.

Benn relentlessly denied that this approach would strengthen the economy, arguing that it would create mass unemployment, depress profits and increase the public sector borrowing requirement, while failing to reduce inflation. He told the Cabinet that new solutions were required now that capitalism was in crisis and urged it "to reindustrialise Britain by direct methods . . . raising production by industrial democracy". Above all, he argued that Labour would only get re-elected if it pursued socialist policies, since these alone would succeed. It was this difference in analysis which explained his conflicts with Labour's parliamentary leadership and their attempts to discredit him.

In a memorandum to the NEC on Party strategy in May 1974, Benn urged:

> A systematic and sustained campaign of public education . . . The main electoral danger now facing the Party derives from the unreality of the present situation . . . Apart from highly political comments in the context of the Labour Conference and the General Election, very few people really know what the programme says or what the argument is all about . . .
> Though these public consultations will necessarily stir controversy, they are bound to shift the ground of argument in our favour.[14]

The Conservative Party was working to project itself in the political vacuum as the guardian of national unity and Labour as the Party of extremism. At a time of illicit counter-revolutionary activity — with the emergence of private armies organised by Colonel Stirling and General Walker, to which over 200,000 people were affiliated — Benn warned against the forces which would create coalition. He told Durham miners in July that these aimed to suspend the democratic process by creating a one-party state: "This new coalition Party forming at Westminster would like to see us adopt the policies tried in the 1930s which led to such terrible suffering."

The conviction that the Government could only retain its credibility by keeping faith with its own people explains why Benn continued to work, while a Cabinet Minister within the Labour Party, both on policy-making and for the implementation of the manifesto. He strove to consolidate the social contract at all levels — on the Labour Party-TUC Liaison Committee, on the NEC, as Chairman of the Home Policy Committee and its working party on the media, as a member of its group on company law reform and on the joint committee with the CSEU on the aircraft industry. Such astonishing activity was perhaps counter-productive since it created the misleading impression of a left-wing plot to take over the Labour Party. Benn's efforts to involve the trade unions, in addressing conferences or at the Department of Industry, were considered even more sinister. His officials were alarmed by his instruction to invite the relevant shop stewards and trade unionists to all meetings; just as they were appalled by the large red trade union banner that hung in his office. Perhaps he romanticised the onward march of the people somewhat; but the banner was a reflection of his convictions and expressed his feeling that solidarity was more important to him than political expedience.

Benn's behaviour frequently brought him into conflict with the Prime Minister. At the monthly NEC meetings, he would "remind the Government of party policy in the area of public ownership", and these occasions invariably strained relations between the two. Incidents which were relatively insignificant to the public assumed enormous importance in political circles and were indicative of the extent to which ideology had permeated party politics. The trade union stamp row in April — when Benn proposed a commemorative TUC issue as "a great British institution" on the 50th anniversary of the General Strike; and still more, the Chile armaments episode in May, aroused great passions. The re-equiping of aircraft and warships for the Pinochet regime offended many consciences. Eric Heffer was very nearly dismissed for speaking out against it in Parliament. For Benn, it was "the first real test of a Labour Government vis-à-vis its clear commitments to the Party . . . and the Government changed its policy under pressure".

The right to speak and write freely preoccupied Benn, and he published his views widely on the political role of ministers. The moral and democratic arguments he advanced raised the question of what collective Cabinet responsibility meant. "Our right to speak and write freely is not a privilege but a constitutional duty deriving from our representative function as Members of Parliament. . . . I shall therefore continue to assist the Government and the Party by exercising basic rights of conscience and free political expression."[15] Harold Wilson interpreted all expressions of opinion as a challenge to his own authority, and he manipulated the principle of collective Cabinet responsibility to stifle discussion and prevent real collective Cabinet decision-making. It was strange that Benn's cancellation of an estimated £500m arms contracts with South Africa in April should have escaped criticism, while his support for an NEC resolution on 30 October censuring the Government over naval exercises with South Africa, off Simonstown, should have precipitated the first of many threats from Wilson to accept collective Cabinet responsibility or resign. After attempting to argue "an important distinction between the broad exercise of a minister's political role and official ministerial acts or statements," Benn capitulated to this ultimatum and on 6 November 1974 agreed to abide by it. He did not, however, retract his views and the affair continued to reverberate throughout the Labour Party. Ron Hayward called on the NEC to clarify the constitutional position; and Benn's constitutency condemned Wilson's interference in Party democracy, demanding an explanation of Benn's views on all important matters of principle and policy in future, as well as endorsing his stand. Benn stated:

I do not accept that ministers, by virtue of their appointment, can or should be any less responsible to the Party than any other elected representatives whether an MP, councillor or party officer. Our success must depend on maintaining the closest relations of trust and confidence between the Government and the Party. . . . Ministers are still themselves; they are Trade Union and Labour members, as well as being Ministers, and their accountability is to their constituencies, to the people, to the Labour Party and to the movement as well as to the Government.[16]

On 18 September, Wilson announced that an election would take place on 10 October, emphasising that the social contract lay at the heart of Labour's manifesto, *Britain will Win with Labour*. In the national campaign itself, Benn played little direct part. He deliberately avoided all publicity and concentrated on Labour's message of protecting working people from the economic crisis in his own marginal constituency. "A central objective of Government policy during our period of office has been to save jobs, to keep factories open and to keep production going in the immediate crisis." The result in Bristol South East showed, at any rate, that socialism might be possible by democratic means — though Benn's position as Cabinet Minister undoubtedly gave him some advantage over his rivals.

The full results of the October 1974 General Election gave Labour no such mandate. Labour won 319 seats and an overall majority of only three, excluding the speaker, against the Conservatives' 276, Liberals thirteen and combined nationalist parties' twenty-six members. Having clashed with Wilson, Benn was relieved to be reappointed Secretary of State for Industry, but he was amused to discover that the Department had prepared three briefs: for the incoming Conservative and Labour ministers, and for himself. He surmised that Wilson aimed to isolate him, calculating that he would do less damage to the renegotiation of the Common Market terms within the Government than outside it. Wilson's overriding objective throughout 1974-75 was to keep Britain in Europe, but until the issue was settled the Left remained ascendant. Benn knew that 1975 would be a year of decision both on Europe and the economy. During the coming months of struggle for the control and direction of the Labour Government, he would become Wilson's chief antagonist.

Which way would Labour turn? The Queen's speech foreshadowed a socialist legislative programme that Benn argued was democratic in spirit, relevant and in the national interest. "At the heart of our proposals lies not the vast apparatus of bureaucracy but the simple measure of disclosure." A jubilant Labour Party Conference, at the end of November, sensed that its hour had come, and Benn captured their optimism. As the economy deteriorated during 1975, so debate sharpened. The trade unions, increasingly worried about unemployment, supported Benn's plans for public investment and ownership. The Government's strategy was coming under increasing pressure; and in Cabinet, Benn discussed the implications of a severe recession in world trade, a continued balance of payments deficit of £4b and a budget deficit of £9b, with an inflation rate over 20% culminating in the exhaustion of borrowing powers, the flight of capital and a sterling crisis. He saw several courses of action: a return to incomes policy, a monetarist solution to inflation, or a siege economy with central planning. But a stark choice gradually emerged between deflation and protection.

Benn began to develop the idea of no-redundancy as a viable policy in response to the worsening industrial situation he faced during 1974; and in January 1975 presented an alternative strategy within the Government. The deflationary approach would defend sterling, improve the balance of payments and lower inflation through tax increases, reductions in public expenditure and incomes policy; but it would mean a significant fall in real wages, a deep and long-term slump, unemployment and the withdrawal of support from the Government by the TUC and the Labour movement. Benn's alternative was for Britain to produce its way out of the crisis on the axiom that what is good for working people is good for the country and the economy. The aim would be to preserve employment and industrial capacity, while the balance of payments improved more slowly. It would entail Government subsidies to industry, selective import controls, the rationing and allocation of certain key imported raw materials, the direction of the investment resources of the banks, insurance companies and through the NEB into industry, and a managed, downward float of sterling to maintain competitiveness. The policy would mean a slower reduction in the rate of inflation; it would strain international relations, and it might not be compatible with continued membership of the EEC.

The Cabinet regarded Benn's alternative strategy as politically unacceptable; but the economics merited serious consideration, and they could only be understood from an industrial perspective. "The need to work upwards from the points of production" derived from the view that Britain's "economic crisis is a crisis of manufacturing industry". In *A Ten Year Industrial Strategy for Britain,* Benn and his advisers argued that manufacturing industry was "trapped in a spiral of decline, and after thirty years of low investment is contracting under its own momentum". Redundancy, therefore, did not mean redeployment and exposure to international competition would not necessarily bring prosperity and enable British industry to re-equip.

Throughout the spring and summer of 1975, Benn campaigned for a temporary Transitional Employment Subsidy to help firms in difficulty, while long-term viable alternatives were worked out, and for the direction of institutional funds through the NEB to raise the annual level of investment to £6b, a rate equivalent to that of other industralised countries which would enable Britain to catch up.

During 1975, Benn was deeply involved in the implementation of Labour's industrial programme. On 17 March, he announced plans for the nationalisation of aircraft and shipbuilding, and on 30 April introduced legislation paving the way for the most significant extension of public ownership since the 1940's but with much less acrimony. The ferocity of the Opposition towards the Industry Bill was undiminished, however, even though the NEB was strictly accountable to Parliament, its powers of acquisition were non-compulsory and limited and its resources of £700m restricted to a maximum of £1000m.[17] Benn's rhetoric and public campaign for the Industry Bill were partly responsible for this resistance in that he presented the Bill as a programme for "far reaching democratic socialist reforms affecting the relations between the community, management and workers and . . . designed to deal direct with the problems of manufacturing industry that lie at the root of Britain's present industrial and economic weakness". His objectives were threefold: to reverse Britain's present decline by more investment; to reflect the national and regional interests in decisions. "The third objective is to extend industrial democracy in those firms to make them more accountable and (thus) help to bring about the shift in the balance of power towards working people which we see as a prime necessity if our underlying problems are to be overcome."[18]

Industry was especially enraged by the provisions for the compulsory disclosure of information to trade unions, and came to see the Industry Bill as a charter for workers' control. "Those who invest their lives in industry are entitled to know much more about the prospects for the firms in which they work", Benn affirmed, while pointing out that provision existed for "arbitration where the release of sensitive commercial information is at issue between the firm and the workers".

The growth of interest in industrial democracy ran parallel to Britain's economic crisis and manifested itself in workers' demands for self-management. Following the UCS work-in, 102 distinct occupations occurred between July 1971 and February 1974. A new awareness of the right to work was the primary cause and it soon led to proposals for workers' cooperatives which Benn was among the first to recognise. "What is happening in British industry today can best be understood as the beginnings of a struggle for the industrial franchise", he told the Bristol WEA; and his final speech as Secretary of State for Industry avidly expressed his inner conviction: "a great wind of change [is] blowing through British industry. I do no believe that it can be captured and frozen in a single manifesto statement or clause in an Act of Parliament. In general what is happening is that people who invest their lives in industry expect to have as much control as those who invest their money."[19]

No minister was more committed to the cause of workers' cooperatives than Benn, and nothing he did aroused such antipathy. Accused of squandering public money for political ends, he complained that "it was proper for the Government to make over hundreds of millions of pounds to private industry, apparently, but to decline to support a workers' cooperative were such a thing shown to be effective".The level of controversy bore no relation to the relatively small amounts involved — £10.161m in all, out of a total of over £800m distributed to industry in 1974-75 — but the cooperatives challenged the existing pattern of ownership and control. They raised a number of major questions as to whether industry could be run democratically, about the efficiency of public investment and about the inter-relationship of capitalism, competition and profits.

The Institute for Workers' Control, an organisation which spanned the entire socialist spectrum from cooperators to Marxists, gave Benn a platform to campaign for industrial democracy and provided a forum for debate. His address at an IWC meeting, at the Labour Party Conference in November 1974, received wide publicity. As he told the IWC: "The time has come for the Labour Party and movement to intensify its discussion about industrial democracy, to see it as one of the key components in the social contract for bringing Britain through the present crisis." Contrasting the proposals of management with the demands of workers, in order to distinguish genuine industrial democracy or workers' self-management from participation, he declared that there could be no single model or blue print. Indeed, Marx had urged socialists "to combine and generalise the spontaneous movements of the working classes, but not to dictate or impose any doctrinaire system whatsoever". However, he was convinced that the conditions for such development existed because the dependence of private industry upon public money and the divergent interests of capital meant that "the old distinctions between the responsibilities of management and . . . of workers no longer make sense."

Socialists were either divided or sceptical about whether workers' cooperatives could succeed. Many felt that "you cannot build islands of socialism in a sea of capitalism", echoing the Webbs' pessimism: "All such associations of producers that start as alternatives to the capitalist system either fail or cease to be democracies of producers." Benn argued that profits and competition between independent cooperatives were compatible with socialism and could enhance efficiency and innovation, as well as protecting political freedom and the interests of consumers, provided the capitalist framework was abolished. Indeed, his support for the cooperatives could not be separated from his assistance to industry generally and his view that they would only flourish with public investment protected from "capitalist" market forces. He recognised that a revolution in attitudes, with a fundamental reform of company law, was required, but he was realistic about the prospects and admitted: "I do not think that we are about to be transformed into a nation of cooperatives."

The motorcycle cooperative at Meriden was an important test-case and was the product of an eighteen month struggle by the workers against closure. The Conservative Government had encouraged rationalisation putting up £4.8m conditional upon Meriden's closure. But when the parent company, Norton-Villiers Triumph, announced in September 1973 that Meriden would close in order to concentrate production at Small Heath, all 1750 workers occupied the factory and began a work-in, continuing the business against every obstacle. Jack Jones brought the dispute to Benn's attention in March 1974, and a feasibility study was prepared which concluded that a cooperative could break even with sales of 24,000 motorcycles a year and 890 employees. Benn regarded contraction in an expanding market as folly. Following the oil crisis, the demand for motorcycles was increasing, particularly in the United States. Having secured Cabinet support, he announced an offer of £4.95m on 29 July, made up of £4.2m in loans and £.75m in grants, declaring: "It is in the national interest that this innovation should be tried." The chief obstacle was not the opposition of the IDAB, which considered the scheme unviable, but the attitude of the other Norton-Villiers-Triumph workers who feared that direct competition would damage their own position. On 8 November, Benn made a dramatic and unprecedented appeal at a stormy meeting of Small Heath workers and persuaded them to support the cooperative, which came into being on 10 March 1975 with Geoffrey Robinson, managing director of Jaguar cars, as its chairman. Benn felt that its birth was "a great turning-point in British industry. Its success would begin a new chapter in the history of industrial relations in this country." Meriden proved that industrial democracy could work. True, it failed commercially; but this failure was more a reflection of under-capitalisation, its inability to finance mass production, and it's lack of control over marketing, done by NVT, than of the unmarketability of its goods. Its continued existence depended on the support of a Government that valued production more than profit.

The experience of the Kirkby Manufacturing and Engineering Cooperative near Liverpool was less encouraging. It provided "sobering lessons for all those people who hoped that worker cooperatives would demonstrate an early route to industrial socialism". The history of Kirkby was that of post-war British capitalism, of expansion succeeded by frequent changes of ownership, management and product, ending in collapse. The radiator factory which had six owners since 1960 and produced Fisher-Bendix washing machines, before production was transferred to Spain, was the scene of a famous occupation in 1971. When a receiver was appointed in June 1974, the 1200 workers forced him to re-employ them. The two trade union convenors approached Benn, who suggested a cooperative solution; and on 6 September he visited Kirkby to express his "deep personal commitment . . . You have earned the right to find a new structure for the factory," he told them. After extensive but inconclusive investigations by Inbucon, the management consultants, which suggested that Kirkby might provide viable employment for 590 workers, Benn announced assistance of £3.9m in loans on 1 November. It was "an experiment in industrial organisation of great potential significance", and he explained that the Government had been greatly influenced by the high level of unemployment around Liverpool, as well as by "the resolution and determination of the workers concerned, who . . . have demonstrated their readiness to take responsibility for their own affairs and so see to it that the cooperative is a success". The IDAB, which was intensely hostile, publicly regretted that so large a sum should be advanced on a project which held out little prospect of providing long-term employment. In Parliament, Benn was much criticised; and in one sense the IDAB was right in fearing that the temptation would be to go on putting in more money. KME was badly under-capitalised, demand for its products poor, and it was unable either to develop or to exploit new products or use its unused capacity. Consequently, KME proved to be a commercial disaster, and without massive public investment it could not have succeeded. More disturbing was the cooperative's failure to develop a new non-hierarchical structure, and the old management structure which was implemented did not work well.[20]

KME managed to survive for four years; the *Scottish Daily News* folded after only six months. On 12 January 1974, Beaverbrook newspapers had announced the closure of the *Scottish Daily Express*, along with 2000 redundancies. But the solidarity of the journalists and printers was such that an action committee was formed within three days to oppose the decision. Allister Mackie, its moving spirit, recalled that "like so many cooperatives in the past, it was conceived in a womb of expectancy and despair and in an economic climate that had already forced the closure of a newspaper". Starting only with enthusiasm and local support, the cooperative managed to raise £.25m, organising feasibility studies which concluded the newspaper could be viable on the basis of a circulation of 240,000, 40% advertising content and 600 employees. Benn felt that the closure was barbaric and managed to obtain Government agreement to a loan of £1.75m, but was forced to accept conditions that eventually brought about the paper's demise. Right up to the last moment, the cooperators were short of capital, and it was at this late stage that Robert Maxwell, the publisher, intervened. Uncommitted to the Cooperative as such, he was nevertheless in a position to dictate terms.

The failure of the worker cooperatives greatly saddened Benn; but it did not mean that they were inherently unviable. Others, such as Scott Bader, had flourished and had proved more durable than private enterprise. But the general public concluded from the failure of the cooperatives in question that cooperatives as such were unviable and questioned Benn's judgement. Yet the fate of the cooperatives was in many respects inevitable. Born in the slump of 1975 and out of struggles with management, they were all severely under-capitalised. They could only have succeeded in a climate of prosperity. Benn did not regret supporting them, for they had stemmed from workers' initiatives. Meriden, moreover, demonstrated that industrial democracy could work in practice: "The hardship they have suffered has brought out qualities of character which we know are present in our society . . . Only when we have enough confidence in ourselves and each other to believe that we can solve our problems will things begin to change and the cooperatives reflect that spirit."

Benn had to surmount enormous obstacles to support the cooperatives. The hostility of his officials became apparent in January 1975 when his permanent secretary, Sir Anthony Part, warned that such assistance might be beyond the legitimate realm of policy and that as chief accounting officer, he would have to disassociate himself and report Benn to the Public Accounts Committee. When the Prime Minister demanded an explanation, Benn was able to demonstrate that he had in fact taken account of all the representations and had made amendments to them. He pointed out that if lack of viability were grounds for an accounting officer minute, it was strange that there had never been one on Concorde or Rolls Royce. He concluded that the real reason was that people objected to money being given to workers but not to industrialists. The ensuing leak enquiry was an example of Wilson's psychological warfare against Benn; and as on other occasions Benn was able to show that he had not been responsible for such leaks. However the campaign against Benn continued and reached its climax in moves to isolate him and remove him during the referendum campaign.

No other person had done more to bring about the referendum on the Common Market than Benn. During the campaign itself he dominated it singlehanded by speaking with an intellectual force and moral authority that overshadowed figures like Edward Heath, Roy Jenkins and Enoch Powell, and making the headlines day after day. Believing passionately in "the profound attachment of the British people to democratic ideas", he saw it as a moment of historic freedom. "I have always seen the democratic process as a healing process . . . I feel personally more strongly about this issue than any other issue in my life. But I'm also utterly committed to accepting the verdict of the British people."

"Benn factor now dominant issue in campaign", wrote *The Daily Telegraph,* and *The Times* explained why: He "has been the leader of the debate . . . whatever the result . . . his is a significant achievement. He was the author of the referendum itself and for most of the time he has managed to make his arguments the central arguments in the debate."[21] Benn's involvement in so many of the controversies preceding and surrounding the referendum — such as the postponement of the BSC closures, the nationalisation of British Leyland and the Ferranti affair — was a further factor in making him the dominant personality of the campaign. The violence of the personal attacks upon him, however, was only explicable in terms of the Labour Party's own internal power struggle waged in a context of 25% inflation, strikes and speculation against sterling, which gave the impression that Britain was speeding towards an economic precipice. As commentators put it: "drifting slowly towards a condition of ungovernability . . . sleep-walking into a social revolution".[22]

By this time it was clear to Benn that Britain's membership of the EEC was a supreme constitutional issue and that the theoretical loss of legal sovereignty would lead inexorably to the practical erosion of control over domestic policy and the transfer of effective power to an unelected bureaucracy in Brussels. His socialist analysis of the effects of EEC membership, his rejection of the power of market forces, were based on the same concern for national interest and democratic principles: people should be able to regulate their own economy and environment.

Benn's convictions brought him into frequent conflict with Wilson and his pro-market colleagues who sought to stifle all debate on renegotiation. In June 1974 he tried but failed to put amendments into Callaghan's speech to the Council of EEC Ministers, when the Prime Minister ruled these out of order. His subsequent sponsorship of, as well as election to, chairman of the NEC Monitoring Committee on Renegotiation plus his abstention on legislation while remaining in the Cabinet, provoked great indignation among colleagues. Yet he was not destructive, only anxious for real negotiations. Once the General Election was over, knowing that renegotiation would proceed very rapidly, he began to plan his campaign. Wilson had silenced him by prohibiting all discussion until renegotiation was complete, excluding him from the Cabinet's European Strategy Committee so that he could only influence the outcome of the European Questions Committee.

Benn knew that he would have to fight hard for the right to dissent and on 27 November demanded a discussion of the problem in a joint letter with Michael Foot and Peter Shore to the Prime Minister. "Ministers will have very deep convictions that cannot be shelved or set aside by the normal process of Cabinet decision-making. . . . The only solution might be to reach some understanding on the basis of 'agreement to differ' on this single issue and for a limited period."[23] On 12 December the Cabinet briefly discussed the issue; but Wilson's minute of 24 December promising a full debate in the new year though imposing collective silence until renegotiation was over, did not reach Benn until the beginning of January by which time he had published a new year message to his constituents on "The Loss of Self-Government". The letter was an appeal "to discuss the issues openly, calmly and seriously" and Benn considered it "a very significant démarche at a critical moment" because it widely publicised the Government's internal disagreements over the Common Market. Wilson was furious and after a very tense exchange with Downing Street, the Cabinet agreed to differ on 20 January.

Benn welcomed the Government's eventual decision in February to hold a referendum as an important extension of democracy; but he warned his constituents that there would be "a tremendous campaign launched . . . to persuade the British people that they have no alternative but to remain in the Common Market. This is simply not true. The problems of Britain will have to be solved by the British people whether we are in or out of the Common Market."[24]

The Dublin Summit completed the process of renegotiation, and on 18 March 1975 the Cabinet voted seventeen to six to accept the new terms, which consisted of a commitment to review the inequity of the budgetary system and concessions on New Zealand dairy foods and Caribbean sugar. But there were no reforms of the Common Agriculture Policy or constitutional safeguards against loss of sovereignty. Within hours Benn had issued a statement rejecting the terms:

> I believe the recommendation made today is wrong for Britain and contains a tragic error of judgement. The new terms that have been renegotiated do not meet the clear objectives which we set ourselves and pledged we would achieve in our manifesto last year. It must be clearly understood that membership of the Common Market, even on these new terms, is fundamentally incompatible with the maintenance of parliamentary democracy in Britain and our capacity to safeguard our vital national interest.[25]

The following day, the six dissenting ministers — Barbara Castle, Michael Foot, Judith Hart, Peter Shore, John Silkin and Benn — issued a joint declaration against the Market. Benn had drafted this and it formed the basis of an Early Day Motion that collected the signatures of 140 MPs.

The majority of Labour MP' were opposed to the terms — with 145 voting against and 33 abstaining —, but the House of Commons accepted them by 398 to 172 votes on 9 April. Wilson had issued guidelines on 7 April to limit the freedom of debate, forbidding ministers to speak against Government policy in Parliament or indulge in personal attacks. Consequently Eric Heffer was dismissed for speaking against the EEC during the debate.

The contrast between the "Yes" and "No" campaigns could hardly have been greater. The two umbrella organisations, Britain in Europe

(BIE) and the National Referendum Campaign (NRC) spent £1,481,583 and £133,630 respectively. BIE, which represented the Federalist European Movement and the Labour Committee for Europe, was efficient, well-organised and enjoyed the support of the Establishment, the press, the business community and was strong at local level. The NRC, which represented Get Britain Out, Douglas Jay's All Party Common Market Safeguards Committee and numerous small fringe groups, was a ramshackle coordinating body staffed by trade unionists and had few public figures. The dissenting ministers were supported by their advisers, Francis Cripps, Frances Morrell and Jack Straw, who acted as a secretariat. Benn himself did not belong to the NRC but concentrated upon mobilising the Labour Party behind the No campaign. The Scottish Labour Party and the NEC had rejected the renegotiation by twenty votes to one, but agreed not to campaign against the Government's recommendation. Throughout April, Benn worked for an overwhelming vote of opposition at the Special Party Conference on 26 April, sensing that "the instinct of the movement had already asserted itself. . . . The whole history of the movement points so clearly to the right course that the British people will respond." On 20 April the dissenting ministers issued "a strategy for withdrawal", and on the 24th Benn urged the Labour Party to oppose the Government. "It is now clear that the whole campaign for British withdrawal from the Common Market has got to be led and organised by the British Labour movement."

Despite Benn's appeal to journalists to print what was said, these activities led to a national campaign to dismiss him. He realised that the press reflected "the economic interests which find the Common Market attractive" and he predicted that they would seek "to make this campaign a campaign about personalities and about the Labour Party". The conflict with Shirley Williams at the NEDC — when Benn accused her of advocating coalition-type Conservative economic policies —; the speech in which Sir Keith Joseph compared Benn to Dracula; and the president of the CBI, Lord Watkinson's attack on Benn in the House of Lords, received wide coverage and caused Wilson to brief the press once more that he would take charge of industrial policy. On 11 May, Wilson hinted that he would remove Benn, comparing him to "an Old Testament prophet, without a beard who talks about the New Jerusalem he looks forward to at some future time; but the policy is decided quite clearly by the Cabinet. After 6 June there will be one Cabinet and one Cabinet view."[26] The personal attacks on Benn multiplied, with wounding speeches by Heath and David Steel. Heath stated that "before you could say Viscount Stansgate, he would be leading us into his vision of the promised land, not flowing with milk and honey but swamped with ration books and state directives". Steel criticised "upper class, public school and Oxford educated sons of the peerage, who seek to exploit mass grievances as the only means of obtaining political power for themselves; power which their own ability or record would deny them".[27]

Jack Jones, Clive Jenkins and the PLP condemned the witchhunt, and Benn's restraint was on the whole remarkable. Only once did he stoop to the tactics of his opponents, and even then only in reference to unfulfilled Conservative pledges on investment and trade in the Common Market. As he put it, "Heath has a deep contempt for Britain, the British people and for parliamentary democracy." Bitterness, indignation and wounded pride were understandable; but in Benn they expressed themselves in the language of socialism, with all the intensity of class-war feeling that the referendum had engendered. During the Ferranti debate, he asserted that "the passion for redundancies indicates a hatred of working people", and he denounced "the rank hypocrisy" of the Conservative Party "united in their opposition to the workers". At Bristol University, he felt that the two to one majority in favour of EEC membership "may tell us something about the social origins of university students".

Nevertheless, Benn endeavoured to raise the level of debate by making unemployment a key issue in the campaign. In *The Times* he drew a connection between the issue of national sovereignty and the socialist analysis of Britain's economic crisis:

> The treaty contains no commitment to maintain full employment in any member country . . . (People) are required to accept major limitations on their freedom . . . Unemployment has been a sharp and temporary reaction to the oil crisis, recession, redundancy and closure is establishing itself as a worsening trend . . . Industrial contraction in Britain would be the normal and necessary price to be paid for the creation of an integrated and prosperous West European economic system leading to a full political federation.[28]

At a press conference on 18 May, Benn claimed that "we have lost half a million jobs as a result of our trade deficit with the Six. Three years of EEC membership has been an industrial disaster for Britain. Our widening trade gap leads inexorably to accelerating loss of jobs and the Commission has the power to forbid us to act to halt this trend."[29] The statement caused panic in the pro-market camp. It attacked their argument at its strongest point and identified people's worst fears. It ignited the debate, producing the bitterest exchanges of the whole campaign. The Establishment's response was to close ranks and dismiss Benn's claim as "a classic mixture of doubtful logic and raging fantasy", "an absolute lie and a disgrace".[30] Denis Healey too accused Benn of "escaping from real life and retreating into cocoons of myth and fantasy," but he was right to criticise Benn's apparent tendency to make the Common Market the scapegoat for Britain's problems and to observe that there was no necessary correlation between the balance of payments and unemployment. It would have been necessary to look at changes in the volume of exports and the size of the deficit in relation to the total value of EEC-UK trade, as well as to undertake empirical studies of individual sectors, before such a conclusion could be drawn.

Yet no one tried to refute Benn's arguments seriously, and on 26 May he returned to the issue with evidence of a deteriorating trend in the balance of payments with the EEC, concluding that "as a nation we cannot afford to stay in the Common Market". The unemployment issue typified the campaign, in that it attracted more attention to Benn than to the arguments themselves. "Never in recent years has one Cabinet Minister gone for another in such language," declared *The Daily Express*. Roy Jenkins commented without explanation, "I find it increasingly difficult to take Mr Benn seriously as an economic minister," and when Michael Meacher suggested that the export of capital had caused a further 200,000 loss of jobs, Wilson said that he "believed the opposite to be the truth", claiming that an inflow of American investment had created jobs. Meanwhile, the press dwelt on Benn's impending fate and headlines described "The Debunking of Tony Benn", predicting "Time to Say Goodbye to Wedgie" and "Wedgie — His Days are Numbered".[31]

Yet at the very end of the campaign, the real issue of sovereignty began to come alive. It had needed Giscard to call for a two-tier community and the EEC commission to criticise the Anglo-Soviet Trade Agreement. "I have never seen the Establishment so frightened," Benn said in Coventry. "The anti-market meetings have been enormous, far bigger and more enthusiastic than any political meetings any of us have ever attended in our lives. . . . I meet warmth and goodwill as I move around the country. I am almost protected and it is rather moving." Wilson allowed ministers to confront each other in public during the last few days of the campaign, and on 2 June Benn took part in a televised debate with Roy Jenkins that summarised the arguments with exceptional lucidity. For Jenkins sovereignty was a practical issue that meant power and glory: "How we can best control our destiny and exercise influence in the world." But to Benn its surrender meant the loss of democracy and deindustrialisation: "Cut the umbilical cord that links the lawmakers with the people and you destroy the stability of this country."

On 5 June the British people voted to stay in the EEC by a majority of nearly two to one. On the doorstep of his home Benn accepted the popular verdict with good grace: "I have just been in receipt of a very big message from the British people. I read it loud and clear . . . By an overwhelming majority the British people have voted to stay in, and I am sure everyone would want to accept that. That has been the principle of all of us who have advocated the referendum."[32]

The people had voted against change. Opinion polls suggested that the Common Market remained unpopular and that the electorate would have opposed entry had they had the opportunity to do so in the first place. The constitutional crisis had been resolved, but the issue was not settled in the long-term, though it was thought to be then, because none could claim that either a law or a referendum could bind future Parliaments or generations. A whole range of issues, on economic and monetary union, on enlargement, federation, industrial intervention and protection had yet to be resolved and would dominate the 1980s.

The referendum was a turning point, "the most exhilerating event in British politics since the war", which transformed the political situation and was in effect a second general election, enormously increasing the power of the Labour Government vis-à-vis the Labour Party. Speculation began immediately about Benn's future; but Ron Hayward warned, "Sack Benn at your peril", and Jack Jones spoke up in defence, "Any move of Mr Benn away from the Secretaryship of Industry, and I think I can speak for the TUC, would be a grave affront to the Trade Union movement. It is vital if we are to maintain a degree of industrial unity that he stays where he is."[33] On 9 June, Wilson summoned him out of a meeting of the Home Policy committee, after parliamentary question time, and without explanation asked him to go to the Department of Energy, giving him until the evening to decide, Benn recorded in his diary: "This was the first ever broadcast of a House of Commons debate and my last appearance as Secretary of State for Industry." He held out for a little, while Michael Foot acted as mediator, but support failed to materialise, chiefly because the referendum had destroyed the morale of the parliamentary Left. Later consulting his constituency party, he decided against a dramatic gesture of resignation: principle would then be obscured by personal ambition and humiliation. Benn preferred influence to isolation and felt he had remained true to the traditions of the Labour movement by fighting loyally within the Government rather than attacking it from without. So, the following day, he accepted Wilson's offer and went to the Department of Energy, while Eric Varley went to Industry.

Though Benn's fifteen months in the Department of Industry had not been the occasion for fundamental change, a great deal had been achieved. He had established the NEB, taken the aircraft and ship-building industries into public ownership, rescued many companies from collapse, and he could consider the referendum, in part, a personal achievement. The speed had been breathtaking and everything had been accomplished despite the combined opposition of the Prime Minister, the majority of the Cabinet, the CBI and the civil service. When he reflected on the causes of the failure to bring about substantial change, he saw the lack of political momentum on the Left as prominent. At the critical moment, the trade unions had expressed their loyalty to the Government, fearing more than unemployment, the collapse of the Labour Government and a defeat on the scale of

1931 during an inflationary crisis. But Benn too had played some part in his own downfall by taking on so many in such unfavourable conditions. Paradoxically, the methods of open government had alienated more than conciliated, and the experiences of 1974–75 left Benn a changed man. The gravity of the economic crisis had strengthened his belief in the relevance of socialist policies; yet, his experience had revealed the harsh realities of political power. Given the system, one could not proceed at breakneck speed; while mass popular support was not necessarily enough to bring about substantial reforms. The character assassination he had endured left scars. But the traumas of the period would finally have a positive effect, identifying him still more closely with the mainstream of parliamentary socialism.

TONY BENN

IX
1975–1979
DISSENTING MINISTER

Give me the liberty to know, to utter and to argue freely according to conscience, above all liberties.
JOHN MILTON

Tony Benn felt like Malenkov exiled to a power station in Siberia after the move to the Department of Energy. "It was an absolutely major political reverse. The Department of Industry was glad to get rid of me; the Department of Energy didn't want to have me. Their general view was one of resentment and from the point of view of the Party and the country, it was a position of disgrace, or intended to be."[1] His initial temptation to resign — overcome at the bidding of his constituency Party — was to be followed by several more. As a dissenting minister who advocated policies different from those the Government was pursuing, his position was a difficult and often humiliating one. He was forced to compromise his convictions, while his ability to influence or openly oppose policy was severely restricted by his collective responsibility as a Cabinet Minister. Critics on the right argued that the only honourable course of action open to him was resignation. With the Left, his situation was even trickier. Should demonstrations of dissent yield no perceptible result, disillusion with his abilities and mistrust would follow. Meanwhile the press, particularly Russell Lewis in the *Daily Mail* and Terry Lancaster in the *Daily Mirror* started a long slow process of character assassination. Benn's vacillations of conscience were represented as cynical opportunism, and he was described as a grotesque figure, diseased by hatred and ambition.

The role of a dissenting minister was thus a taxing one and Benn did not relish it. Indeed, he regarded it as a position to be endured rather than envied. He felt like a caged lion, or a lion in a den of Daniels — as his wife, Caroline would have put it — unable to speak his mind publicly and in profound disagreement with the direction of Government policy. The moral pressures, often inapparent to the general public, were immense and forced Benn time and again to question the integrity of his actions. Only the sense that to resign would be to betray the people he represented kept him in office until the end.

At the Department of Energy Benn struggled to put into practice the open government he championed and to re-establish the credibility of workmanlike socialism by implementing — in the face of powerful opposition — Labour's programme of public control over North Sea oil and the multinational oil companies. As a Cabinet Minister his chief concern was to maintain the unity of the Labour movement and dialogue between Government and Party. The course he steered was perilous and he recognised that he was walking a tightrope: one slip would mean political destruction. Cabinet colleagues were bitterly hostile towards his conduct on the NEC and as chairman of its Home Policy Committee; while the stands he took over matters of principle and party policy led to frequent and much publicised prime-ministerial threats of dismissal.

The continuing controversy surrounding Benn's position in the Government was ultimately only explicable in the context of the widening gulf between Government, Party and trade unions during 1975–79. For most Party members, the experience of government in these years was one of successive defeats: a progressive abandonment of everything that Labour stood for, culminating in an unprecedented confrontation between Government and trade unions in the winter of 1978–79. Throughout these years Benn was acutely aware that a pronounced intellectual shift to the Right had occurred. Monetarists and laissez-faire economists had gained the initiative over the Left. He was disturbed that the failure of social democracy should be equated with that of socialism in the public's mind. He saw that Wilson's ambition of making Labour the natural party of Government had ended in its identification with the status quo. Between 1975–79 Labour propped up the old order and papered over the cracks with the TUC by means of a compromise: incomes policy and the maintenance of public expenditure, which cured neither inflation nor un-employment. Devolution in Scotland and Wales dominated the parliamentary sessions of 1976–78 and in the absence of an overall majority, resulted in coalition style government. The swing to the Right in the country manifested itself in a number of ways: the exodus of senior politicians and public figures from the Labour Party (including George Brown, Reg Prentice, Lord Chalfont, Richard Marsh and Paul Johnson); the growing unpopularity of trade union power; and the emergence of the National Front and of racialism as an issue.

The return to stability which outwardly characterised the period was illusory and thinly veiled the weakness of the economy. The strategy of concealing unemployment and controlling inflation by means of incomes, monetary and public expenditure policies was internally inconsistent and damaging to the economy. It encouraged consumption at the expense of investment and production; high interest rates to attract funds to finance the public sector borrowing requirement made it difficult for the private sector to raise capital, discouraged investment and borrowing. The story of Labour's economic strategy during these years was thus one of stagnation rather than recovery. The favourable impact of North Sea oil upon the balance of payments masked a deterioration of £1.5b by 1978 on the trade deficit in manufactured goods. This revealed worsening import penetration and uncompetitiveness as sterling rose in value on the strength of its oil. For working people the prospects were poor, with the total unemployed rising from under one million in June 1975 to 1.6m two years later, only falling to 1.4m when Labour left office in May 1979, while earnings declined marginally in real terms over the period.[2]

The reversals in Labour's economic policy dated back to the referendum and the sterling crisis in June and July of 1975. Just before the referendum Benn's senior civil servants had informed him that the crisis would occur and he suspected the Treasury of engineering the crisis in order to impose its own policy. At the beginning of July the Cabinet discussed the possibility of an incomes policy against a background of unrelenting speculation. The solution that Harold Wilson announced on 11 July in "The Attack on Inflation" was a minor moral victory for Benn and those who had opposed deflation. A universal entitlement and limit to £6 a week on wage increases during 1975-76, with none for those earning over £8500 a year, protected the lower paid, was egalitarian, voluntary and acceptable to the trade union movement. It was perhaps more generous than market forces would have provided and was as such cosmetic, designed chiefly to satisfy international opinion.

At the end of September the Labour Party Conference in Blackpool — after a passionate appeal for loyalty from Michael Foot — overwhelmingly endorsed incomes policy. Though the Conference recognised that inflation was a grave threat to democracy and the economy, it refused to sacrifice Labour's commitment to full employment, public ownership and investment. The NEC statements adopted by Conference, "Labour and Industry" and "Jobs and Prices", warned that: "If we fail to meet our industrial objectives our whole programme of economic and social reform will be dangerously undermined." The documents envisaged strict price control and the direction of company profits into approved investment projects in order to cement the social contract with the trade union movement and the incomes policy it had accepted. Introducing these policy statements to Conference, Benn was sceptical about the outcome of the Government's stabilisation programme: "The £6 limit . . . can only buy us time . . . We were not elected to nurse an unjust and inefficient system through yet another crisis. . . . We are not just here to manage capitalism but to change society and to define its finer values."[3]

Benn's efforts to sway Conference centered on the pamphlet, *Labour and the Slump,* he wrote during the summer of 1975. It summarised the democratic socialist analysis of Britain's industrial weakness:

> One reason why British capitalism is faltering and especially why it has failed to invest lies in the growth of democracy. . . . The slump in Britain cannot be resolved on the basis of the present distribution of power and wealth. . . . (People) reject as immoral the degree of inequality and the exercise of unaccountable power which traditional economics require to produce investment. . . . The Labour movement was founded to reform our society. . . . To realise its historic purpose (it had) to sustain the Government while remaining free to criticise its record, thus preventing the alienation of the people from the party.[4]

Labour's reversal of economic strategy was soon accompanied by the abandonment of its industrial policy, a spectacle which Benn had to endure in silence. On 24 July the Department of Industry refused to give additional support for the Meriden Motorcycle Cooperative. Subsequent announcements of assistance to help modernise private industry anticipated the meeting at Chequers on 5 November which Benn attended. Here the TUC agreed to the burial of Labour's industrial policy and its replacement by an industrial strategy identical to the one the civil service had presented him with in October 1974.

It was soon evident, following the establishment of sector working parties after the Chequers' meeting that limited financial support would not be able to stimulate the re-equipment of manufacturing industry or cope with the problems of contraction and decline. In December, Chrysler announced its withdrawal from the UK and was only persuaded to stay after Wilson offered £162.5m, despite protestations from Benn that only public ownership could solve Chrysler's difficulties.

Though policy had changed, Benn found that conflicts with the Prime Minister and certain Cabinet colleagues were as numerous and bitter as before. In November with some support from Peter Shore and others, he renewed his demands for import controls about which there was still official discussion. In February 1976 he opposed projected public expenditure cuts of £3b during 1977-78 and lost his parliamentary private secretary, Joe Ashton, whom Wilson dismissed on 11 March after he had courageously voted against the cuts. Benn felt strongly about this betrayal. At the meeting of the NEDC in early March he accused Shirley Williams of coalition politics when she suggested that the opposition be invited to attend the meeting. Meanwhile his relations with Wilson sunk to an all time low. On 8 March, after Benn had briefed the press on decisions taken by the NEC Home Policy Committee, Wilson ordered him to desist and accused him of initiating a study of the honours system which Wilson argued was his personal responsibility in contradiction to Government policy. Wilson once again claimed that collective Cabinet responsibility prohibited ministers from speaking publicly in a non-ministerial capacity. Though Benn had said nothing to the press about the honours system, the coincidence was prophetic. When Wilson resigned on 16 March he made one of the most controversial honours lists in history, selecting mainly personal friends, and brought the whole system once more into disrepute.

The leadership election provided an occasion when members of the Government were in theory free to speak openly. Benn was determined to take full advantage of this now rare opportunity. On 17 March he decided to contest the leadership. He declared that he was "standing for one reason and one reason only: to put forward policies in which I believe". His announcement was greeted with derision and disbelief. Friends saw it as a dangerous gamble and enemies readily predicted disaster. Benn himself held out no hopes for victory. He was more interested in launching a campaign for a change in economic policy, for open government and for a bigger role for MPs. *A New Course for Labour* put his case for democratic socialism and by fighting on issues rather than personalities broke new ground. At the heart of Benn's argument lay the proposition that capitalism was unable to restore full employment because companies demanded high profits before they were willing or able to invest. At this time such a course required either low wages or high productivity with consequent unemployment which in turn depressed the economy and rendered recovery impossible: "Given the nature of the crisis, the only possible leadership for the people of Britain at this moment lies in an active socialist programme."[5]

Benn confounded the sceptics by winning thirty-seven votes in the leadership ballot, ahead of both Denis Healey and Tony Crosland. "There was undoubtedly a build up of support during the week, I think it was for the policy", he commented, and then immediately gave his support to Michael Foot in the second ballot. Nevertheless, Foot bitterly resented his having divided the Left — though no one believed Foot could ever have won. *The Times* noted: "Benn did the right thing. He said: "I don't agree with the policy of the Cabinet.""

On 5 April the PLP elected James Callaghan leader of the Labour Party by a comfortable majority. Most people saw him as a caretaker and were sceptical about the Government's chances of survival. It was difficult to recognise Callaghan's imprint, for the new administration was very like the old. There was some rearrangement at the top, with Crosland in the unexpected role of Foreign Secretary from whom Peter Shore took over at Environment, while Michael Foot became Deputy Prime Minister as well as Lord President of the Council. There were only two casualties, Barbara Castle and Edward Short; and three new faces, Albert Booth at Employment, Edmund Dell at Trade and David

Ennals at Health and Social Security. Callaghan himself was the personification of labourism stripped of its ideological armour and socialist sophistication, an astute machine politician who knew how to manage the trade unions, as well as being a highly respected and popular figure in the Labour movement.

If privately he would have preferred to go to the Department of Employment Benn hoped for a new beginning when Callaghan asked him to continue as Secretary of State for Energy. His personal relations with Callaghan were far more cordial than they had ever been with Wilson, even though he had always voted for Mikardo against Callaghan as chairman of the Home Policy Committee. The two reached an informal understanding that the Government and the Party would agree to differ, the Government consulting the NEC and PLP on matters of policy, while the NEC would in return be able to approach ministers directly when it had misgivings — instead of passing critical resolutions. For a while Benn thought that the arrangement could work. His change in fortune was illustrated by his reappointment to the main economic strategy committee of the Cabinet, his reassumption of responsibility for oil policy from Harold Lever and the reinstatement of Joe Ashton as his PPS.

Benn was now able to begin to make an impression on Britain's energy policy. He aimed to fulfill Labour's objective in its 1973 programme and 1974 manifestos for an integrated national fuel policy. Though the DOE lacked gladiatorial glamour, it provided him with an opportunity to demonstrate the practicality of planning and socialism in the public sector in an undramatic and workmanlike manner. His first months had been taken up in mastering the complexities of the Department and establishing the contours of policy making. The chief issues which would now preoccupy him over the next three years concerned government regulation of the development of the North Sea; whether Britain should embark upon a massive long-term programme to develop coal or nuclear power in anticipation of the post-oil era; and whether the short-term profitability of the electricity generating industry should dictate the balance of fuels and the nature of their pricing structure. These issues, however, were not the ones which his officials considered the legitimate concern of the Department of Energy, whose role they saw as a passive one of ensuring that the laws of competition, demand and supply operated to provide energy at the most economic prices.

Thus even in his own Department Benn emerged as a dissenting minister. His efforts to stimulate a debate about policy choices with one-day mass meetings of the entire Department were a conspicuous failure. As he recalled: "The Department of Energy, the old Ministry of Power, had always taken the view that energy policy was non-political and that there was nothing to discuss. Opening the whole thing up and changing the whole policy there and getting towards a national fuel policy which was my intention took a great deal of time."[6]

Benn argued that the ideology of the Department bore little relation to reality and that the political aspects of energy could not be denied. Though Britain was rich in energy resources, availability and price remained a vital national interest because energy was the lifeblood of a modern industrial society. Producers wielded enormous power. Oil companies and state authorities exerted monopolistic influence since energy was a basic industry for which demand was highly inelastic. Thus forces of competition did not operate properly. The inherent difficulty in matching demand with supply was no argument for a return to market forces, which Benn warned would be to invite uncontrollable inflation and industrial paralysis, as the experience of 1973–74 had shown. He saw many strong practical arguments in favour of public sector planning: the long time leads in developing new sources of energy, the massive scale of the investment required and the need to maintain a stable market for mining machinery and power plant industries. But the most vital one was political. The conflicting interests of the state authorities and oil companies could only be harmonised and reconciled, their responsibility to the community discharged at national level.

Energy policy had taken on a new significance since the oil crisis of 1973–74. Conflict of public and private interests was sharpest in the oil industry, where the discovery of possibly 3200 million tons in the North Sea promised to make Britain self-sufficient for a generation. Benn's appointment as Secretary of State for Energy corresponded with the beginning of the oil era: on 11 June 1975, the Argyll field had come on stream. On the 18th Benn was present to welcome the first oil ashore at the Isle of Grain. The rapid build up of investment in the North Sea dated from the Conservative Government decision in 1971 to license 282 blocks on the UK continental shelf. The speed at which the North Sea was being developed was generally much criticised because of the feast and famine it created for British industry. But in fairness, Britain would otherwise not have been self-sufficient until the mid 1980s. Nevertheless the pace was too great for the struggling British offshore supply industry which, despite the 3% interest relief scheme subsidy, secured only 43% of the market for equipment in 1975 and required a stable flow of orders if it was to flourish. Continental and especially US companies, now dominated the North Sea, while the tax regime of only 12.5% royalties actually encouraged foreign companies to invest and repatriate profits.

Labour's oil policy aimed to remedy these defects. The Government's White Paper of June 1974 had defined the objectives as "to secure a fairer share of profits for the nation and to maximise the gain to the balance of payments". Early in 1975 Eric Varley had introduced two measures to give them effect: an Oil Taxation Bill, imposing a Petroleum Revenue Tax at 45% upon North Sea oil profits; and a more general Petroleum and Submarine Pipelines Bill, with new powers "to control the pace of depletion, pipelines, exploration and development and to protect the environment". Furthermore the White Paper had proposed the establishment of a British National Oil Corporation (BNOC), and to reach participation agreements with oil companies on the basis of a 51% public equity in the North Sea. By giving BNOC the right to buy and sell back oil in exchange for certain undertakings — such as the guarantee of a full and fair opportunity to UK suppliers — the policy would "enable the Government to exercise participation rights, to play an active role in future development, exploration and exploitation of offshore oil and to engage in the refinery and distribution of oil".[7]

The oil companies were bitterly hostile to the proposals, claiming that they caused uncertainty, undermined confidence and deterred investment. Benn's task was to carry through the legislation he had inherited and make the policy work. He introduced a guillotine motion against fierce opposition on 29 July 1975. The measure in his eyes was not an ideological one but "a major piece of legislation designed to develop and defend a basic British interest". Indeed most of the criticisms of Labour's oil policy were unfounded and Benn emphasised that the controls over production were designed to achieve an optimum depletion rate of Britain's oil reserves, as well as to regulate the export and refining of oil in the national interest. He also pointed out that the Varley assurances of December 1974 had effectively safeguarded the oil companies' interests. The Petroleum Revenue Tax was equally generous in its allowance of 175% investment expenditure and a healthy return on capital; but it was open to criticism for disallowing the interest payable on the loan capital raised to finance the development of the North Sea, which discouraged the exploitation of marginal fields. However BNOC in part existed to develop those very fields which the oil companies found unprofitable. Despite this, the oil companies stubbornly pursued a course of non-cooperation, waging an unrelenting war of propaganda.

On becoming Secretary of State for Energy, Benn had been appalled to discover that the public participation policy had been a charade, that the Government had relented in the face of opposition and Harold Lever had intended merely to sell back the oil unconditionally to the producing companies. The BNOC came into being on 1 January 1976 with Lord Kearton as chairman. He urged the Cabinet to strengthen the Company by putting BP under public control, after Burmah Oil's difficulties had increased the Government holding from 51% to 68%. Kearton, whom Benn regarded as a great industrialist, patriot and public servant, also contended that BNOC could only stimulate the private sector if it was an operator in the field; that it would fail if it was only marginal. This proposal was never examined on its merits, but simply dismissed as politically unacceptable by the Cabinet and the Department. BP was totally opposed, though it did eventually concede to a participation agreement: a breakthrough achieved during night-long negotiations on 27–28 June, when ministerial will power and sweltering heat triumphed over long resistance. The agreement with BP was a decisive victory which led to the establishment of much greater public control over the oil industry and improved the prospects for an integrated fuel policy.

Benn realised that North Sea oil was only a short-term solution to the energy problem and looking ahead he could see that Britain's long-term strength lay in its vast, untapped reserves of coal. These amounted to an estimated 140 billion tons, forty-five billion of which were thought to be recoverable and sufficient for 300 years at current rates of consumption. Such a cheap source of energy would bestow enormous economic benefits. Thus, from the start Benn sought to identify himself closely with the coal industry. On 13 June 1975 he went to Barnsley to express solidarity with the miners after a fatal pit accident had occurred there. On 7 July he told the NUM at its annual conference in Scarborough that he felt "deeply proud to serve" them, and that "coal is the main source of Britain's economic strength". He undertook "to defend the industry and speak for those who work in it"; encouraged the miners to produce their own plans for "democratic self-management", promising "to take a sympathetic interest". "Energy policy will be discussed openly and fully with all the unions", he said. The relevance of industrial democracy to planning could be judged from the success of the Tripartite Plan for Coal in creating an unprecedented consensus on the objectives of the industry and a real unity of purpose about its future. The Plan aimed to raise annual production from 128m tons in 1975 to 135m tons by 1985 and 170m tons by the year 2000, creating 42m tons of new capacity and investing £1400m. In return the miners undertook to increase productivity by 30%.

Just as he thought problems of the coal industry could only be resolved democratically, so Benn believed that the balance of fuels should be determined by democratic planning rather than by market forces. On 10 February 1976 he brought together management representatives of the coal and electricity generating industries at a tripartite meeting with the trade unions in an attempt to equate the planned increase in coal production with the CEGB's own assessment of electricity costs and demand. It was to this grand design of economic synthesis that he now turned his mind and to "the key role of Government in developing an integrated energy policy." [8] The outlines first began to emerge on a white drawing board in his office at the Department of Energy on which he summarised the relationships between consumers, producers and suppliers; between trade unions,

Government, Parliament and international organisations.

The conviction that planning could only work by consultation and consent led Benn to convene a National Energy Conference on 22 June as a first step in this direction. It was "a most interesting experiment in opening up and extending public debate on the energy issues and options confronting us as a nation", and was endorsed by the Prime Minister in his opening address: "It is right to publish the facts, to discuss the choices, to listen to the views of those concerned and to seek and to win agreement for the long-term strategy".[9] The public relations risks of such an occasion were considerable with over 400 senior delegates from 120 organisations taking part in a discussion on the entire range of energy issues from the forecasting of supply and demand, investment and pricing decisions to environmental protection. Sceptics like Enoch Powell considered the idea "pernicious" and ill-conceived", while Lord Ryder compared the proceedings to the Mad Hatter's Tea Party. In fairness there was little that could be achieved in a single day, but the conference did succeed in its original purpose of clarifying the disagreements, specifically over gas pricing policy and the scope of Britain's nuclear programme. More important, it generated the momentum to work towards the goal of an integrated energy policy.

The purpose and will which characterised Benn's approach to energy policy was conspicuously absent from the direction of the Government's affairs as a whole. The progress achieved appeared all the more remarkable in a context of economic uncertainty and speculation about the Government's survival. Official strategy was to avoid deflation and hope for a recovery in world trade, maintaining the competiveness of industry by the devaluation of sterling. Benn was sceptical and predicted that the stabilisation programme would fail because of its limited nature and that consequently working people would be called upon to make further sacrifices. In April he opposed the February public expenditure cuts on the NEC and renewed the demand in Cabinet for an alternative strategy arguing that the weakness of industry required direct Government action on imports and investment.

The economy offered a prospect of almost unrelieved gloom. Inflation had fallen from a rate of 24.2% in 1975 to 15.6% in 1976, but its underlying cause, the imbalance of demand and production, remained. Throughout 1976 the balance of payments deteriorated and the Government's own deficit was expected to exceed 1975's record of £10.5b. The symptoms of stagnation were clearly visible, with wages declining in real terms by 2.4%, investment by 4.6%, while the ranks of the unemployed swelled by 300,000 to 1,473,000, despite assistance of £325m under the industrial strategy and £200m in Temporary Employment Subsidy and under the Job Creation Scheme. Measures taken to stimulate the economy, such as the reduction in the

MLR from 12% to 9% and VAT in the higher rates from 25% to 12.5% in Denis Healey's neutral April budget had little effect. For the first time in history sterling fell below US $2 in value on 5 March and then nosedived to $1.71. In the face of an international crisis of confidence, Labour's response was to close ranks, the TUC agreeing on 5 May to an incomes policy of 5% or £2.50 for a further year which a special conference subsequently endorsed on 16 June. This expression of discipline and solidarity undoubtedly helped the Government obtain a six months $5.3b standby credit on 7 June from the IMF but its support was conditional upon further reductions in public expenditure. Only Benn and Lever protested against the damaging implications for industry, upon its liquidity and lack of employment, when Healey announced cuts of £1b and a £1b rise in employers' national insurance contributions on 22 July.[10]

No one believed that the solution was anything more than temporary and it was against this background that the Labour movement lived through a long hot spring, summer and autumn of argument, agonising over the Government's direction and divergence from the will of the Party. Throughout these months and indeed the entire period between 1975–1979 Benn sustained an unrelenting campaign at committee, ministerial and public meetings, travelling throughout the length and breadth of the country to persuade the Labour movement not to accept a deflationary solution. His political office at the Department of Energy, acted as a discussion centre in constant session and the continuing debate ebbed and flowed as daily decisions had to be taken. It was there that meetings with journalists and trade unionists took place, speeches were written and papers prepared by his advisers Francis Cripps and Frances Morrell, who enabled him to mount vigorous opposition to current policies from within the Government.

In successive public speeches Benn broadened and strengthened the arguments for socialism. On 15 May he examined its moral foundations in a lecture at Burford Church on "The Levellers and the English Democratic Tradition". The speech not only situated socialist principles within the context of English history, but gave a clear indication of the nature of Benn's own socialism. Labour was "the inheritor of a strong and ancient tradition of action and analysis" which went back to the Levellers and Diggers of the 17th century. Labour's vision of an egalitarian democracy sprang more from Christian teaching and values than from the historical vision of Marx, while the connection between political and religious liberty was a chief source of its strength. The moral force of the Bible, in preaching God-given conscience, had kindled in the hearts and minds of the 17th century dissenters demands for a wider sharing of power.

Looking back on these ideas . . . from the standpoint of the present and knowing that they grew out of the minds and experience of working people, few of whom enjoyed the formal education available today, it is impossible not to experience again the intense excitement and the controversy that these demands must have created when they were first formulated. . . . The human spirit and the ideas which it gives birth to do not die but live on to refresh those who follow. . . . For politics is really about education and not about propaganda, about ideas and values and not only about Acts of Parliament, political institutions and ministerial office.[11]

In the broadest terms, Benn was more of a Christian Socialist than a Marxist. Yet he felt compelled to defend the Marxists in the Labour Party whom he saw were increasingly becoming victims of a right-wing reaction, dissenters from within. The appointment in September 1976 of Andy Bevan, a militant former chairman of the Young Socialists, as the Party's first national youth officer sparked off an explosion of hysteria about Trotskyist infiltration into the Labour Party. Benn argued that Trotskyite Marxists should be allowed to belong to the Labour Party provided they accepted its commitment to parliamentary democracy. He was deeply disturbed by the undemocratic manner in which a Conference decision appointing a youth officer could be overturned; by the threat to intellectual freedom and civil liberties this contained. He considered these attacks as part of a calculated campaign to turn the debate on important policy decisions into a witch-hunt in order to divert attention from the Government's difficulties.

As a member of the Bristol South East Labour Party, Benn knew Andy Bevan personally to be a committed socialist and a democrat. He felt that Bevan's stirring speeches had deeply impressed the local Labour Party "as the authentic voice of a political faith they have not heard advocated with such moral force since their youth". The continuing attacks upon Bevan finally drove him to reassert Labour's tradition of undogmatic tolerance in a paper he prepared for the NEC about Marxism and the Labour Party. Here he sought to legitimise Marxism as "one of the main sources of inspiration" of the Labour movement as recognised by Attlee and Bevan, by demonstrating that Labour leaders such as Morrison, Laski and Crosland had been Marxists while also being committed democrats. Social Democrats like Willy Brandt and Olaf Palme had also acknowledged their debt to Marxism whose roots they saw lay deeply embedded in "Western European humanism". So strongly did Benn feel about the Bevan case that he published his paper in the national press when the NEC refused to circulate it. The crucial meeting of 15 December saw common sense prevail. Bevan's appointment was upheld, with the NEC conceding an inquiry into entryism and "the militant tendency" under Reg Underhill, the National Agent whose "Reds List" report had triggered off the pressure for an inquiry. The result of the inquiry revealed, as Benn had suspected, that the allegations of subversion could not be proved; but it did recommend ways in which party democracy could be safeguarded.

Benn was anxious to break out of the confines of the stale arguments which equated socialism with nationalisation and to revitalise the debate about their meaning and necessity. The Conservative motion on 19 May 1976 attacking Labour's plans for public ownership as interfering with the laws of the market and individual liberty, presented such an opportunity. "The truth is that their analysis of how the British economy should work does not conform to the experience of our people." Indeed, successive Conservative administrations had been forced to take firms into public ownership where the national interest was at stake. What differentiated the Conservative and Labour approaches to public ownership was the gulf in moral attitudes. Benn told Michael Heseltine that laissez-faire, the Tory vision, was essentially mechanistic, narrow and selfish:

> I believe that if the honourable gentleman had lived when Christ turned the money changers out of the temple, he would have moved a censure motion that Christ was damaging the viability of the temple. .... The Labour Party had won the last two elections on an open programme of public ownership. .... If people are to tighten their belts to earn a surplus, then they have the right to a say in how that surplus is to be spent.[12]

Thus the moral argument for equality was also intimately connected with the case for public ownership and industrial democracy, both of which, he emphasised were "absolutely compatible with the earning of a surplus".

On 7 July Benn explored this wider notion of public ownership in the Herbert Morrison memorial lecture at the LSE on "The Labour Movement and the Public Sector — a Reassessment". Praising Morrison's towering achievement of nationalising and reequiping Britain's basic industries and their contribution to Britain's post-war recovery, he emphasised Morrison's socialism, and belief that limited nationalisation combined with a welfare state could not resolve the contradictions of capitalism: "The paradox is that Morrison, the avowed planner, created nationalised industries whose status enshrined them as competitive monopolies which as time went by were required more and more to act on strictly commercial lines." Benn called for a re-examination of the relationships between nationalised industries and society because "the ideal of socialist planning which inspired him (Morrison) was lacking in the structures he created, and Benn put forward a new set of objectives: a challenge of socialisation in place of nationalisation, encouraging the area of industrial democracy "within the exercise of real public accountability" so as "to transform them into expressions of our socialist-purpose".[13]

The desire to redefine Labour's own objectives, its socialism, sprang from the same democratic source. During the summer recess of 1976 Benn embarked upon a commentary on the Party's constitution. In the uncompleted and unpublished manuscript, he criticised the obsessive fear of Labour's commitment to nationalisation and drew attention to the democratic nature of Clause IV which set out the Labour Party objectives including cooperation with the trade union movement, internationalism and the determination of policy by the Party Conference, "the hinge that joins the people to the Party". The latter did not imply the dictatorship of the Party "but it is intended to mean and must mean that Labour leaders must accept their obligations to carry out policies decided by the rank and file". Benn regarded Labour's constitution as "a commitment to democratic change through Parliament" and its proposals for public ownership as framed in that spirit. Unlike Gaitskell who had striven to eradicate socialism from Labour's constitution, he reasserted its "growing relevance". People were now looking to public ownership because they recognised that "the ideas of laissez faire and free enterprise propounded by Adam Smith have never achieved what was claimed for them", and that monopolistic industrial power had "repealed the laws of supply and demand". For these reasons he believed that industrial democracy, implicit in Clause IV's commitment to "the best obtainable means of popular administration" was "clearly the next step we must take if the existing public sector is not to develop into a corporatist nightmare". In the private sector too he saw "no valid reason why investors' money should lay claim to the prerogatives of capital against those who invest their lives."[14]

Benn's determination to reach as wide an audience as possible to influence the outcome of the struggle within the Labour Party expressed itself in intense activity on the NEC and its subcommittees. As chairman of the Home Policy Committee he was more closely involved than anyone in the preparation of Labour's *Programme for Britain, 1976,* but he also recognised that the prospect of defeat was real. The meeting of the Labour Party-TUC Liaison Committee in July confirmed his worst fears. The Statement it issued, "The Next Three Years : The Problems and Priorities", was, like many Labour Party documents, one of ambiguity, ostensibly endorsing a socialist industrial policy while complacently praising "the progress which the Labour Government has already made in dealing with our economic problems" and rationalising the reductions in Government expenditure: "We must have a far greater emphasis on the needs of manufacturing industry. That is why the Government has decided to level-off public expenditure."

Labour's programme was by contrast a comprehensive and radical statement of policy. Unlike 1973 it contained a fully costed social programme amounting to £5000m set in the context of a strategy for socialist planning, designed to tackle the slump and restore full employment. The programme envisaged the public ownership of the leading banks and insurance companies as well as its extension into construction and pharmaceuticals. A new Industry Bill with sweeping powers for rapid intervention provoked understandable hostility on the part of industry. The NEC's statement on the nationalisation of the financial institutions, for example, merited careful examination but was so controversial that the proposals had to be abandoned. It perceptively analysed the problem of low investment but failed to realise that its cause was lack of demand rather than supply. Consequently nationalisation would make little difference to the level of investment and the real choice lay between the planned and the free market economy.

At the Party Conference in Blackpool at the end of September, Benn introduced Labour's programme on behalf of the NEC. Conference endorsed it overwhelmingly by 5,833,000 to 122,000 votes together with the statement on banking and insurance by 3,314,000 to 526,000 votes. "The task of the party is to analyse the situation which confronts us, to think ahead, to prepare detailed proposals and to press for their implementation," he told the delegates. Turning to energy policy he admitted that there were "genuine uncertainties" and "long time leads", but this was why "we reject the idea of centralised dictation or of market forces as a guide to fuel policy". Instead Labour's approach "represents the first serious attempt . . . to hammer out new objectives and a new planning framework for the nation's energy resources". The Conference took its policymaking role seriously and passed a number of important resolutions, criticising the Government's management of the economy and reviewing the method for the election of the Party leader.

Yet there was an air of unreality about the Conference. In the background loomed renewed international speculation, as sterling fell in value from $1.77 on 1 September to $1.64 by the 29th. The mood of the delegates was unhappy: the 1976 Conference had marked the beginning of the alienation of the trade union movement from the Left, when Ian Mikardo accused the unions of conceding so much over incomes policy in return for so little. Jim Callaghan's blunt speech — largely written by Peter Jay for international consumption — was disastrously miscalculated. It appeared to repudiate everything Labour stood for. Callaghan defended the role of profits as an incentive and as the source of investment. He lectured delegates on the impossibility of restoring full employment by Keynesian social democratic means, of reflating the economy by public expenditure. There were emotional scenes when Denis Healey — off to an IMF meeting in Manila — turned back at Heathrow and arrived in Blackpool. "I come from the battlefront," he told delegates, appealing for solidarity in a stormy speech which was much interrupted, but which the media presented as a great success.

The truth was that the Government was living off rapidly dwindling reserves of borrowed money and time. On 29 September Healey applied to the IMF for further support and though he raised the minimum lending rate to 15%, sterling continued its decline, touching $1.55 on 25 October. The Treasury was reported to have thought that "the pound would go down the drain". For Healey it was a baptism of fire. And Callaghan who had lived through the experience before as Chancellor of the Exchequer in 1967 sadly commented that "all these little measures seem to be swept away". In the opinion of the political journalists Fay and Young, "The sterling crisis of 1976 was the definitive event in the life of the Labour administration." As one senior Treasury official recalled: "We faced the collapse of the currency, the collapse of the Government and the collapse of the Labour Party."

Would the Government survive? Callaghan appealed for international support from Helmut Schmidt and Henry Kissinger, sending Harold Lever on a mission to Washington. There, Lever used the threat of a takeover by Tony Benn to frighten the White House. The US Government believed sterling's weakness to be the "greatest single threat to the stability of the Western world", fearing that its collapse would precipitate a world slump on the scale of the 1930s. On 1 November the IMF team investigating Britain's finances booked in at Brookes Hotel under assumed names, but the secrecy only served to dramatise and heighten the sense of crisis. Healey first revealed the brutality of their diagnosis and prescription — consisting of an immediate £4b reduction in PSBR — to the Cabinet on 23 November. The Left — comprising Benn, Booth, Foot, Orme, Shore and Silkin — and the Right — consisting of Crosland, Ennals, Hattersley, Lever, Rodgers and Williams — expressed their total opposition to terms which they considered would cause a deep recession. They questioned the Treasury estimate of a £10.5b PSBR for 1976-77, that subsequently proved to be £9.1b. Callaghan who agreed with the IMF that excessive public expenditure was the chief cause of Britain's difficulties nevertheless acceded to Benn's demand for a full discussion of the alternative strategy, which took place on 2 December.

According to Fay and Young, "Benn was pulverised . . . the weakness of his argument for import controls, direction of investment and the siege economy exposed." Perhaps a more balanced judgement would be that the arguments for and against import controls remained hypothetical and unproven. Benn's alternative strategy was more likely to bring a faster improvement in the balance of payments and employment by reflating the economy behind a protective wall; but it was alleged that it would provoke a further international crisis of confidence in sterling which no form of exchange control could prevent. Ultimately the historic problem of funding the sterling balances could only be resolved by international agreement. However, the political consequences had still to be faced and Benn pointed out that the severity of the measures might destroy the social contract and bring down the Government. In a powerful and emotional appeal, he made the call for a fresh start with a plain recognition that the strategy since March 1974 had failed. The conditions for IMF support, he argued, would only be acceptable if combined with a bold socialist strategy and the IMF would capitulate to British demands rather than let its economy collapse.

In the detailed Cabinet discussions between 6–9 December, Benn strove to minimise the extent of the cuts and their impact on the social services. He circulated the minutes of the 1931 Ramsay MacDonald cabinet, whose cuts in public expenditure, especially unemployment benefit, "represented the negation of everything that Labour stood for". The actual measures which Denis Healey announced on 15 December represented a considerable political and moral victory. His letter of intent to the IMF left social services untouched in reductions of only £2.5b in the borrowing requirement over 1977–79, with a target PSBR of £7–8m and a 13% growth in the money supply over 1977–78. In exchange the Government obtained a $1.5b seven-year loan and a guaranteed "safety net" to finance the repayment of sterling balances.

The consequences of this crisis were far-reaching. It heralded a return of confidence in sterling which soon recovered to over $1.70 and it established Jim Callaghan as authoritative leader. In many ways it completed the process of stabilisation begun in June 1975; but it also marked the end of social democracy as a philosophy for managing the economy — a fact symbolised by Crosland's death in February. The events changed the face of the Labour Government. The tensions contributed to the resignation of Reg Prentice from the Labour Party in December and the departure of Roy Jenkins to Brussels. Callaghan's re-shuffle of September 1976 had already strengthened the right and the non-ideological centre which he represented, while Labour's lack of an overall majority re-enforced a resurgence of coalition politics — illustrated by Hailsham and Macmillan's call for a national Government to which Callaghan's style of leadership was eminently suited.

Economically the effects of the IMF measures proved to be as great as Benn and others had predicted. During 1977 the number of unemployed rose by 300,000 to 1.4m, living standards fell 2.7% in real terms, while inflation only fell marginally to 15.8%. In response to the classic deflationary strategy, interest rates fell from 15% to 5% between October 1976–77, while the balance of payments deficit on the current account declined from £1137m in 1976 to £298m in 1977[16]

The implications for energy policy were not encouraging, but Benn stubbornly resisted all attempts to cut back investment. 1977 was the first year North Sea oil made a significant contribution to the economy, benefiting the balance of payments by approximately £2b in savings on oil imports and accounting for much of the improvement in investment and production, as well as explaining to a great extent the return of confidence. It was evident that Labour's policy of public control had not deterred the oil companies and despite their criticisms of insufficient exploration, the depletion policy helped increase the U.K. content of the offshore supply industry to 57% in 1976 and employment to 100,000, while the blowout at Ekofisk Bravo in April vividly illustrated the need for public supervision. The fifth round of licenses, which Benn announced on 9 February, was conditional upon participation agreements but the response to the 71 blocks on offer was more enthusiastic than the fourth round and 44 were awarded to 51 applicants. Production rose from 12m tons in 1976 to 38m tons, representing over a third of Britain's total requirements, after four more fields had come on stream. BNOC had had a positive effect in the rapid build up, contributing to the finance of exploration and development. It was now a fully fledged oil company and by the end of 1977 had concluded participation agreements with 42 different companies and was a significant investor in several fields. In November Benn sought to formalise the scope of participation agreements but his attempts to transform them into planning agreements by involving the trade unions informally, met with total opposition from the oil companies and failed.[17]

The future of the coal industry was more directly threatened by the slow-down in the economy. Production actually fell from 124m tons to 122m tons; morale declined with productivity and the National Coal Board had difficulty in achieving the profitability it required to finance its massive investment programme. The recession in the steel industry, in addition, had reduced the demand for coking coal from 22m to 15m tons. Yet in the public sector Benn was able to deal with these problems on a democratic basis and in February 1977 reconvened the tripartite group to reconsider the "Plan for Coal" or "Coal for the Future", reviewing the prospects to the year 2000. It reaffirmed the commitments on productivity, re-estimated the cost of the NCB's investment plans upward to £3.7b and resolved to finance it in the short-term by borrowing, setting a target for 75% self-financing in the long-term. In Parliament Benn introduced further legislation to promote expansion rather than contraction of the coal industry, demonstrating that Britain paid lower coal subsidies than any other EEC country. The benefits of public sector planning would be seen most of all in the transition from oil to coal in electricity generation, supported by the coal burn scheme which saved an estimated £60m in oil imports, £50m in interest and stockholding charges at a cost of only £12m in subsidies to marginal coal fields.[18]

The strength of coal and oil both partly caused and was overshadowed by speculation about the future of Britain's nuclear programme. The re-emergence of nuclear power as a major political issue reflected the uncertainty about the world's economic prospects, a new awareness that energy was indispensible to modern industrial societies and of the interconnections between nuclear and political power. Benn was personally in favour of the development of nuclear power, as a solution to the long-term energy problem — provided it occurred within a framework of parliamentary accountability, political control and proper safeguards. He also intuitively recognised the political dimensions of nuclear power, the strength of vested interests which greatly complicated the decision he faced concerning which reactor system Britain should adopt and to what extent it should become dependent on nuclear energy.

As Minister of Technology with responsibility for the industry, he had encouraged the reprocessing and export of nuclear fuels, and on becoming Secretary of State for Energy, he visited Japan and discussed British nuclear exports. But the discovery of a radioactive leak at British Nuclear Fuel's re-processing plant at Windscale in Cumbria on 10 October 1976 suddenly made nuclear power a major political issue. Later, in 1979 it became known that a second leak involving hundreds of gallons of toxic waste, lying some ten feet beneath the surface, had put the £900m expansion plan of Windscale in doubt again.

Benn sympathised with the fears of the public and the Friends of the Earth, insisting that their criticisms "must be faced and cannot be dismissed as the work of cranks and subversives". Yet he was as much disturbed by the secrecy he encountered as by the accident itself and maintained that the public had a right to know the facts. "The more candid one is with the media in such matters, the better the balance of reporting one will get."[19] He had agreed to the arming of the Atomic Energy Association's constabulary to prevent terrorist attacks, acknowledging that "nuclear technology has considerable implications for democracy". And following the Windscale leak, he demanded a full report on all incidents. Lord Justice Parker who conducted a full inquiry into reprocessing at Windscale, eventually reported on 26 January — after the longest public inquiry in British history — recommending Windscale's expansion. Thus on 6 March, Peter Shore announced a special development order which Parliament ratified by 224 votes to 80 on 15 May 1978. The reaction of the ecologists was hostile: they felt their arguments had not been properly represented. Yet the Parker enquiry following as it did Sir Brian Flowers' Royal Commission on Environmental Pollution was at least an attempt at open government — even if the actual Windscale decision was perhaps a wrong one.

Benn made the question of nuclear safety paramount in the choice of Britain's thermal reactor system, insisting that a rational decision could only be reached through open discussion: "The full scale development of nuclear power, including the fast breeder reactor, is neither self-evidently inevitable nor self-evidently wrong (but) the decision must be a political one, otherwise we are abnegating our responsibilities to the experts." Therefore, there must be "a proper public debate before a decision is reached on the fast breeder".[20]

The enormous pressures Benn faced in resolving these issues were of an order that he had never previously experienced. As he recalled: "In all my political life I have never known such a well-organised scientific, industrial and technical lobby as the nuclear power lobby." The battle over the choice of Britain's nuclear reactor system exposed the naked self-interest that lay behind the economic arguments deployed by the proponents of the various systems. In 1973 Sir Arnold Weinstock, managing director of GEC, supported by Lord Aldington, chairman of the National Nuclear Corporation, for which GEC had the management contract, and Sir Arthur Hawkins, the new chairman of the CEGB, all said they wanted to order eighteen Pressure Water Reactor (PWR) power stations by 1983. The Select Committee on Science and Technology however was not impressed in part because the cost would amount to £10.8b at current prices. Moreover the Government's chief scientist, Sir Alan Cottrell, had grave doubts about the PWR's safety because of the loss of coolant that could occur. Eric Varley accepted these criticisms and in July 1974 authorised the construction of two Steam Generating Heavy Water Reactors (SGHWR), instead of the Advanced Gas Cooled Reactor (AGR) — both of which had been developed by the AEA — because the problems met in construction had dramatically escalated the cost of the latter and delayed commissioning. Yet after the oil crisis had turned the boom into a slump, Sir Arthur Hawkins was soon claiming that the CEGB did not require any more nuclear power stations at all.

On becoming Secretary of State for Energy, Benn was immediately inundated with demands for the PWR, intensified by the AEA's recommendation to abandon the SGHWR which had not turned out to be an economic or technical proposition. In addition, there was pressure to develop a fast breeder reactor at a cost of £1–2b, counteracted by the growing moral opposition to nuclear power following the Windscale accident. Benn considered a nuclear capability integral to a balanced energy policy since "all the forecasts point to the need for one" and he revived the idea of "atoms for peace". He regarded fear as the product of ignorance and secrecy and asked the Select Committee and the National Nuclear Inspectorate to review the economics as well as the safety of the systems on offer. In December 1976 the Select Committee came out in favour of the AGR — which by then was proving its operational efficiency — but in June 1977, the Inspectorate concluded that safety was not an obstacle to the adoption of the PWR.

The clarification of the facts, which Benn had sought, only increased the struggle between opposing groups. The fast breeder reactor would take twenty-five years to generate enough nuclear fuel for an additional reactor; and on grounds of cost, it was agreed to postpone its development. The PWR emerged as slightly more efficient and less expensive without additional safety provisions, but the purchase of its US technology would damage the balance of payments and Britain's own power plant industry. Benn declared his support for the AGR. He was accused of economic illiteracy, strongly opposed by his own permanent secretary, Sir Jack Rampton who briefed other ministers to support the PWR; by the head of the Government's think tank, Sir Kenneth Berrill, who relied upon the narrowest of commercial arguments and was perhaps even influenced by the Shah of Iran's offer to buy into the British Nuclear Industry and then to order PWRs if they were built in Britain. But Benn won the Cabinet battle and on 25 January 1978 announced the order of two AGRs together with further research and an option on the PWR. He claimed that "it was not an arid technical decision. . . . The importation of reactors from abroad, without regard to our domestic industry would be absolutely fatal to this country's long-term interests.[21]

In the light of the PWR accident that occurred at Harrisburg, on Three Mile Island, Pennsylvania, USA in March 1979, Benn's caution proved wise, but the decision to order nuclear reactors at all remained open to question. The CEGB faced a situation of chronic over-capacity and its chairman was already clashing with Benn over the order of a further coal-fired power station. In Parliament Benn was attacked for subsidising inefficiency yet again. But his real motive for ordering the new coal-fired power station, Drax B, at this time was the crisis in the power plant industry — which Benn judged was too serious to risk making Drax B conditional upon its reorganisation as the think tank had recommended. In publishing his correspondence with the CEGB chairman, Sir Arthur Hawkins, he demonstrated that the dispute was not about the viability of Drax B itself, but about timing.

The profitability of the largely coal-fired electricity generating industry was not in question. The real problems lay in forecasting demand, caused by the lack of coordination between the Electricity Council and the regional supply boards. The Plowden Report of January 1976 had recommended that the CEGB and the Electricity Council merge into a single centralised authority because "the existing structure (did) not provide the focus necessary to give a central sense of direction to the electricity industry". Benn rejected this classic bureaucratic solution and after prolonged consultations announced agreement on a reorganisation in July 1977 which brought "greater coherence in policy and planning (as well as) the accountability of local boards to local communities". Though the proposals never became law because of combined Conservative and Liberal opposition in Parliament, they nevertheless represented a genuine attempt to organise the public sector along democratic and socialist lines.

247

One of the problems confronting Benn's energy policy was perhaps not so much the choice between different ways of generating electricity but the choice between electricity and other sources. The British Gas Corporation was beginning to develop North Sea Gas in the Brent and Frigg fields and its commercial success posed an economic threat to electricity as a more competitive source of power. The controversy over the pricing of gas clearly illustrated the arguments about planning and free competition. In April 1977, BGC was forced to raise its charges by 10% to help reduce the Government's borrowing requirement and consequently it generated "excess" profits. In the short-term gas offered the advantage of cheap fuel; but the case for planning was that price should reflect ultimate scarcity and secure the long-term stability of both price and supply.

The development of alternative energy sources such as solar or combined heat and energy excited Benn's imagination as a route to future self-sufficiency. He actively promoted conservation and research, encouraging public debate about an alternative long-term strategy that emphasised benign and renewable resources. The conservation programme, which concentrated on pricing policy, a national "save it" publicity campaign, building and housing insulation, cost less than £200m between 1974–79, was labour intensive and saved an estimated £2.5b a year, representing "probably the biggest single return on investment". The research programme was equally diverse and aimed at producing between 10m and 39m tons of coal equivalent energy by the year 2000.[22]

By 1978 the prospect of "an integrated and coordinated energy policy evolved by discussion and enjoying public consent" lay within Benn's grasp. The open government he initiated at the Energy Conference in June 1976 had resulted in a twenty-four member Energy Commission, reflecting the interests of producers, consumers, environmentalists, trade unionists and Government. During its four meetings, it made public and resolved many contentious issues. All its papers and proceedings were published and Benn commented: "I regard that as the most significant development that has occurred . . . It means I am no longer confined to the advice of officials, but am exposed to the advice of others . . . and it has opened up the debate about political choices."[23] Yet the difficulties he encountered in preparing the consultative Green Paper on Energy Policy — which he presented to Parliament in February 1978 — were indicative of the inherent problems of planning. His Department had "worked consistently to promote an open public discussion on energy issues, to make widely available all relevant information and to draw into the process of energy policy formulation all those who have something to contribute to it". He had come to the conclusion that only a flexible strategy was possible and that the Government's role was "to prevent short-term fluctuations from changing the long-term prospects of the industry". The Green Paper rested on a solid basis of fact and analysis and defined "the function of energy policy as to intervene in the national interest".[24] It assessed Britain's resources in a world context, offering a synthesis of a balanced four-fuel economy.

In Benn's view energy planning had to be international in scope if it was to be truly effective. As President of the EEC Energy Council during the first half of 1977, he worked diligently for genuine cooperation founded upon common interest; "as a constructive member of the Council, but defending the national interest". "We want a successful community policy for energy," he declared, but warned that harmonisation had to be voluntary and could not be imposed. As President, Benn aimed to bring about greater realism and stronger ministerial control, giving evidence to the Energy and Research Committees of the European Assembly, and setting energy policy in an informal, open and world context. The year began with a tour of the European capitals "to discover the objectives of member states", followed by visits to the United States, Soviet Union, Saudi Arabia and Norway to cement relations with OPEC and the IEA.

Benn's pragmatic approach resulted in solid if unspectacular progress based upon a common programme of work. By the end of June, agreement had been reached on a number of energy issues including coal, oil and nuclear policy, as well as conservation. However, none had been reached over the proposed minimum selling price for oil — which could do much to Britain's confidence and stimulate investment — while the disputes over refinery policy revealed the underlying divergence of national interests. When the EEC Commission unsuccessfully attempted to reduce refining in Britain to help deal with the over-capacity in other member countries, Benn assured Parliament: "There is no question of the Community controlling EEC energy resources (or) HMG encouraging refinery closures." The EEC's strategy was to decrease the level of oil imports to a half of total requirements by encouraging the exploitation of coal and nuclear power. Faced with declining coal production, the energy ministers resolved to monitor all imports, to continue the coal subsidy, and allocated £327m for the conversion of oil fired power stations. Loans for the construction of nuclear power stations were also made available through Euratom.

Benn could look back at this record with "some satisfaction" in the knowledge that "there are no public relations successes in energy policy; no short cuts". He took with him three main impressions: first, "the need for international . . . consultations . . . to fill the vacuum in international institutions which is remarkable considering the energy interdependence of nations"; secondly, the complexity of policy making in this field; and finally, an "increasing awareness of the overriding need for coal, energy conservation and nuclear power if we are to fuel our economies". He concluded: "My only regret is the failure to persuade my community colleagues to open part of the Council's discussions to representatives of the press and European Assembly."[25]

1977 also marked the re-emergence of the Common Market as a political issue following the Government's agreement to direct elections for a European Assembly. At the Department of Energy Benn increasingly felt "that the handling of energy policy in the Community requires some important changes if it is to be acceptable to us". In July 1978 he detailed the conflicts over a whole range of energy issues in a speech on "External Pressure on British Energy Policy". The EEC Commissioner, Guido Brunner, had claimed authority over refinery policy and disputed BNOC's requirement to land oil in Britain. The competition commissioner, Mr. Vouel, had questioned the legality of the interest relief grant scheme for the offshore oil industry and BGC's monopoly on gas supply. By March 1979 Benn was attacking the "creeping competence" of the EEC Commission, emphasising the importance for Britain "to retain control over its own resources . . . EEC energy policy must be firmly based on national policy."

While Benn acknowledged that the referendum had resolved the question of British membership of the Common Market, his experience of government had confirmed his original fears. In particular, the Common Agricultural Policy had made Britain the largest net contributor to the Community budget. During his presidency of the Energy Council, he had seen real differences of interest emerging between Britain and the EEC and had come to the conclusion that Britain could no longer continue to work constructively within the EEC while ignoring its longer term economic and political implications.

In both 1976 and 1977 Benn addressed the Labour Common Market Safeguards Committee on the anniversary of the Referendum, and argued that events had proved his predictions correct because the Common Agricultural Policy was increasingly oppressive and Britain's balance of trade with the EEC continued to deteriorate:

> Earlier expectations of more jobs being created as a result of our membership have not materialised . . . Given that this is so, I feel that in retrospect we were right to raise these issues . . . during the period leading up to the Referendum . . . Although our views were the object of ridicule by a large section of the press, the business and political establishment, I believe that history will treat us more kindly.[26]

Benn's opposition to further European integration proved a growing source of conflict and tension between himself and Callaghan, especially his revival of the question of withdrawal is reviewing Britain's membership. He particularly opposed British membership of the European Monetary System (EMS) which he regarded as politically motivated and not in Britain's best interests. The Labour Party too was sceptical and at the Annual Conference passed an anti-

EEC resolution by 4,846,000 votes to 1,639,000 votes, demanding a reduction in the powers of the EEC commission and opposing monetary union. The EMS, which Leo Tindemanns, the Belgian Prime Minister and Roy Jenkins, President of the EEC Commission, had widely canvassed, aimed at creating a zone of currency stability in Western Europe as a prerequisite for the expansion of world trade and the integration of the EEC's divergent member economies. The EMS was thus a political initiative about European unity and at Bremen on 6 July, 1978 the leaders of the nine agreed to a $50b fund to limit the fluctuations of each currency to a $2\frac{3}{4}\%$ band, allowing devaluation only by common agreement. Negotiations began on 27 July with the aim of agreement by 5 December at the Brussels summit; and the Declaration was cemented at a meeting between Giscard and Schmidt at Aachen on 15 September. However practical difficulties and conflicts of interest soon emerged at the meeting of Finance Ministers on 18 September, when Germany supported the parity grid system, and Britain came out in favour of the basket system of currencies that made the stronger currencies support the weaker ones.

Benn argued that deflation and a loss of sovereignty over economic policy would be the price for monetary stability and he mobilised the NEC into opposing the EMS in the draft Queen's Speech which it had controversially prepared. Callaghan was furious, and a tense exchange followed with threats of dismissal. Yet many economists and the Expenditure Committee supported Benn, concluding that the EMS would mean major changes in economic policy. On 13 November the Government had to tell its European partners that the EMS would prove unworkable without a significant transfer of resources to weaker currencies; but that it would support the EEC's initiative and try to alter the scheme. The UK compromise involving wider bands of 6% within which currencies would be allowed to fluctuate was no more than a version of the failed European snake, and Britain did not succeed in persuading the other weaker members like Ireland and Italy to support it.

The Green Paper, published on 24 November, was positive about the EMS but non-committal. It recognised that currency stability could lead to a virtuous circle of lower costs and higher exports and that devaluation was not a solution to a lack of competitiveness. But it noted that the weakness of the economy could lead to deflation if Britain were in the EMS. At this juncture Benn intensified his opposition, drafting a resolution for the NEC which asserted that the EMS "would mean a major move towards a federal Europe" and would "inflict long-term damage upon the employment, growth and living standards of the British people". He demanded that the Government "publish immediately all EMS working papers prepared for Ministers". The NEC call to boycott the EMS could not be ignored. On 29 November Healey retreated in the House of

Commons and the Cabinet decided the following day to approach the summit with caution at which Britain decided to stay out.

The Government's commitment to an European Assembly was an even greater test of its loyalty to the Common Market. In Cabinet Benn remarked that it would ignite the long fuse to revolution by creating a dual sovereignty. After voting against direct elections in the summer of 1978, Callaghan told him either to resign or abstain. The legislation had in fact as much to do with the Government's survival as with its European commitments and was the price David Steel demanded for the Lib-Lab pact on 23 March, 1977. The Government had just been defeated on the Devolution Bill the previous day and the ensuing motion of No Confidence made the pact essential. The arrangement with the Liberals pushed Benn to the brink of resignation because he felt it abhorrent that the power of making governments should be thus transferred from the people to the intrigue-and-smoke-filled rooms of Westminster. He argued that the Government could instead retain its integrity by constructing a majority on each measure — and he underlined that they would lose nothing by this since he felt confident that the Liberals did not want to provoke an early election. Despite his arguments, Benn did not resign. Instead he committed himself to intensive work from within the administration to establish a "Lab-Lab pact" — between the Labour Government and the Labour party in order to maintain the unity of the Labour movement.

But the Lib-Lab pact was a turning point for both Benn and the Labour Government. He felt increasingly isolated. In the summer of 1977 Callaghan threatened to remove him from the Cabinet Committee dealing with the sale of BP shares because of his opposition to ritual sacrifice of the public sector to the IMF. On 29 March Healey had introduced a further budget linking reductions in income tax with incomes policy — another condition of the Lib-Lab pact — and wage increases under Stage III would be limited to 10% despite the TUC's declared opposition. At this juncture Benn was outflanked in Cabinet over incomes policy, forced to deal with the power workers under intense pressure and to recommend a productivity scheme which the coalminers only reluctantly accepted.

After these various set backs he was determined that Labour should start to prepare for the future and the next General Election. He thus did all he could to dissociate himself from the Government by concentrating on party work. The 1977 annual conference document presented by the NEC as a basis for the party's campaign, called for a planned economy and was supplemented by statements proposing the abolition of the House of Lords, the reform of the EEC, and the public control of multinational companies. Outwardly, the Annual Conference at Brighton in October was a subdued affair, but the NEC documents and the TUC-Labour Party Liaison Committee statement

"The next three years and into the eighties", re-emphasised the egalitarian and socialist nature of the social contract and commanded overwhelming support, as did a resolution demanding the reselection of MPs by constituency parties between elections. Benn's speech on economic policy was an honest and unflamboyant assessment of the Government's record, attributing the racialism, discontent and other social tensions of the times to unemployment. He reminded Conference:

> The Labour Cabinet has fought off the most sustained international attack upon our currency and our living standards we have seen since 1931. The Government has had to win through without a parliamentary majority to sustain it . . . How do we answer the Chancellor's dilemma? If he reflates to bring down unemployment, the balance of payments goes into deficit, investors lose confidence and our financial security is imperilled; but if he holds down public spending to create financial security then production falls, jobs are lost, investment ceases and unemployment rises even higher. This is the as yet unsolved problem of Labour Governments. But in a paragraph it also contains the socialist case for structural change.[27]

At the Conference Benn used the debate about Britain's use of North Sea oil revenues as an opportunity to renew the argument for the alternative economic strategy and for socialist planning. He demanded that the revenues that flowed from North Sea oil should be invested in industry, describing the North Sea as "our greatest hope and our greatest challenge . . . There is not a single oil producer in the world that has not now set itself that objective . . . Therefore energy is now not a peripheral but a central issue in the economy." In July Callaghan had asked him to prepare a paper outlining the options for using the benefits of North Sea oil in conjunction with Healey who displayed very little interest. Though the civil service gave little assistance, Benn took the matter seriously. The Paper which he submitted to Cabinet, the NEC and the Liaison Committee estimated that by 1985 North Sea oil would raise the national income by £5b, government revenue by £3.5b and improve the balance of payments by £7.8b. It identified six main alternative uses: overseas investment, repayment of international debts, reductions in taxation and investment in manufacturing industry, in energy or in the public services and social infrastructure.

In examining these choices Benn emphasised that the direct benefits were relatively "modest" and that "the economic strategy which accompanies the oil revenues will be as important as the revenues themselves". Any policy should aim to restore full employment, raise the scope of economic growth and reduce inflation and this meant the sustained expansion of production and demand. Judged by these criteria the abolition of exchange controls and the reduction of taxation would lessen the upward pressures on the value of sterling and of wage inflation, but they would not necessarily expand production and employment in Britain. Investment in the social services would create employment while Britain would need to invest significantly in energy after the early 1980's and "the reconstruction of industry cannot be left entirely to market forces but must be stimulated by investment of public funds."

But the Cabinet had no intention of taking up the challenge that Benn had offered them and the White Paper which the Government eventually published in March 1978 *The Challenge of North Sea Oil*, was a testament to its political bankruptcy, little more than a public relations exercise which sought to dampen the hopes it had aroused.

Benn may nevertheless have strengthened the Government's resolve to control the exploitation of North Sea oil. Though production in 1978 amounted to over half Britain's requirements, technological difficulties had slowed down its build-up and the Government found that it entered a probable election year without the advantages it had hoped. Revenues would be lower than anticipated and on 2 August Joel Barnett, prodded by Benn over a long period, announced changes in Petroleum Revenue Tax, raising its rate to 60% but still maintaining a healthy return on capital. "The public share of these profits can and should be increased without endangering the exploitation of the less well placed fields." More and more Benn thought that the Government would be unable to meet its objectives on investment, production and refining without a further major reform of its relationship with the oil companies. At the Labour Party Conference in October he warned that "in time the multinational oil companies will have to move from being concessionaires to being contractors". Within the Government he renewed his campaign for the nationalisation of BP so that the state could directly and significantly influence the development of the UK Continental Shelf. Though these proposals aroused enormous antagonism, the pace of development did not slacken, and on 20 November Benn announced that 94 companies had applied for 46 blocks and that the Government had awarded 42 licences in the 6th round, including a number in which BNOC was operator in the less profitable North and South Western approaches of the British Isles.

Benn had won a new credibility for workmanlike socialism and as Labour entered an expected election year, he strove to broaden its appeal. He helped persuade radicals like Peter Hain to join the Labour Party; actively supported the anti-Nazi league and drew attention to the links between human rights and the ideals of economic and social justice for which Labour stood. In particular he felt a growing "need for a clearer understanding of how parliamentary democracy really works. Modern British Government and politics are in fact run collectively through a huge network of interlocking committees, consultation and conferences." In February he prepared an annual report for his constituency, detailing the way in which as minister and MP he had actually spent his time over the previous year. The report gave a picture of extraordinary activity and showed the extent to which Benn was attached to the grass roots of the Labour movement. In addition to ministerial work, he had made over 300 public speeches and attended over 250 Labour Party meetings during 1977. As he noted: "Travel and meetings also provide a great deal of information and experience which is of real value in keeping in touch with what is going on and formulating future policy." He emphasised that the concept of accountability had "the most profound effect in shaping our system of government. . . . Everyone should use to the full the influence they have. . . . Our democratic structure is rich with possibilities for effective political action and it is important that people should understand how it works so that they can use them." In Bristol he found the level of political debate to be "uniformly high and well-informed. The Minute Books of the Party over the years show the consistently principled stand taken on matters of contemporary concern which often anticipated the views later adopted by the party conference and leadership."[28]

Political democracy alone, Benn felt, could preserve human dignity in an anonymous industrial society and at Imperial College on 15 June he re-examined the political implications of scientific progress in a lecture on "Industry and Democracy". Throughout history science had been a source of enlightenment and a liberator of mankind but gradually it became closely associated through technology with the development of capitalism and was now the nerve centre of the power structure. As an industrial minister between 1964–78 Benn had often felt more the servant than the master of technology. He saw that it had been manipulated to diminish rather than enlarge freedom. Just as industrialisation had led to democracy, so he now appealed for an understanding of the demands for the democratic control of technology such as nuclear power. "The values and power structure of any society determine the ends to which science is used." Thus he called for scientists to recover their historic, but revolutionary tradition of science as the servant of mankind and not the state.

Benn developed this theme more fully in a further lecture at the British Association for the Advancement of Science at Bath University on 8 September 1978. His emphasis was on the numerous practical ways in which science (and its servicing) was used as a justification and a method for controlling the spread of information. "My thesis is that secrecy is the great enemy of democracy and science, and the way to the advance of both lies in the wider spread of knowledge." The threat to democracy was real "but the demand for openness is a clear sign of democratic pressure" and the reforms Benn proposed involved a freedom of information act with popular access to the mass media and education; the scrutiny of Government by select committees; and the election of ministers.

On 30 October Benn took these arguments a stage further at the NEC demanding that "the security services should be accountable to Parliament and the people", and the election of the Cabinet. The uproar that greeted these proposals did not deter him:

> When the history of this period comes to be studied in greater depth, it may well be that Britain's worse problems will be seen to stem from too little democracy and not too much. . . . Modern democracy requires a revitalisation and a reformulation. . . . A socialist should never forget that he is in office in a representative capacity. . . . Perhaps the hardest thing for politicians to understand is that government no longer revolves entirely around Parliament.

He concluded with the observation that politicians looked to secrecy to protect their diminishing power.

The episode was a foretaste of the bitter struggle that would take place over the manifesto itself. Benn called for a comprehensive statement of Party policy and a long public campaign, while Callaghan wanted to write as much of the statement himself as late as possible and for the manifesto to be as short as possible. Benn urged: "Early in the New Year the Labour Party must start work in earnest on its next Election Manifesto", recalling that in 1945 Labour "won overwhelming support for policies which committed us to full employment by planning, public investment and public ownership; and to a greatly expanded welfare state". The continuing relevance of that socialist programme derived from the fact that

> Capitalism is still unjust and inefficient and still produces insecurity. . . . The economic crisis in the capitalistic world can only be solved by . . . socialist programmes. . . . (Therefore) 1978 must be a year for boldness in putting forward fundamental solutions to deal with fundamental weaknesses in our present economic system. . . . We must offer a real vision backed by "workmanlike plans", as Clement Attlee called them, to climb out of the recession. . . . The British people know in their hearts that the time for fundamental reform has come.

This confident assertion stemmed from the view that Labour would not win by hypocritically defending a bankrupt economic system:

> I am firmly convinced that our best if not our only hope of winning . . . the Election is if we are to campaign vigorously, openly and courageously for the implementation of policies . . . inspired by Democracy and Socialism . . . hammered out within the movement, in factories, in shops, offices or localities as well as the higher levels of the party and trade union movement.[29]

It was in this spirit that Benn discussed the manifesto during 1978, urging loyalty to the Government throughout. "All our achievements over the years have been gained by driving back the frontier of the market economy, by limiting unaccountable power and by enlarging the areas of human responsibility and self-management in industry and government."

Like many others Benn thought that the General Election would take place in October because the economy would then appear at its best. The rate of inflation had fallen to 8.2%, the balance of payments deficit had declined to £1175m on the visible account and wages had risen by under 14% contained by further reductions in direct taxation. Yet Benn knew that the recovery was only limited because the balance of payments and the level of import penetration remained disturbing. Unemployment had only fallen marginally to 1.4m; investment was still below its 1970 peak and half the modest 3% increase in output was attributable to North Sea oil. The Callaghan Government had become identified with the status quo, with stagnation and its chief strength was that it alone could work with the trade unions.

Benn argued for an autumn election but was not surprised when the Prime Minister announced on 7 September that there would be none. He knew Callaghan's instinct was not to call an unnecessary election as Attlee had done in 1951 and Wilson in 1970. Benn least of all wanted Labour to lose because he feared that a right-wing reaction was more likely than a left one in the Labour Party. Yet he predicted that the Government would end in confrontation with working people, after the TUC had overwhelmingly rejected the 5% incomes policy on 4 September. In Cabinet he contended that such a restrictive incomes policy would be deflationary, that its rigid application would lead to industrial unrest. He was incensed when Callaghan refused to circulate his own paper questioning the wisdom of incomes policy.

The Labour Party Conference at Blackpool in October ominously rejected the 5% incomes policy by 4,077,000 votes to 194,000 and the Government's economic strategy by 3,626,000 to 2,806,000 votes, after Benn had warned against complacency and self-satisfaction infecting the movement: "Manufacturing industry is and will remain the foundation and strength of this country long after oil runs out," he warned.

If the oil crisis caused by the revolution in Iran during 1979 had shown the wisdom of Labour's policy of controlling the landing and distribution of North Sea oil, it also aggravated the industrial unrest which the Government's rigid incomes policy had provoked. The strike at Fords in November was the prelude to a long winter of discontent. When the Government acted to bring sanctions against the Company after its wage settlement, it was defeated in the House of Commons on 13 December by 285 to 279 votes. The way was now open for other groups of workers to press their claims and between December to February the lorry drivers and local government workers almost reduced the economy to paralysis. The confrontation between the Labour Government and its own supporters was the culmination of a process of progressive alienation which would lead both Benn and the Labour movement to see the power structure as the real obstacle to socialism. Benn and others successfully urged agreement with the trade union movement on the maintenance of essential services and the conduct of non-violent picketing. Following this dislocation, the effect of the Government's defeat in the referenda on Scottish and Welsh devolution on 1 March — when less than 40% of the electorate voted in favour — was to bring about the Government's rapid defeat in a motion of no confidence on 28 March by only a single vote: 311 to 310.

Against this background Benn's message of socialist cooperation inevitably sounded hollow. Throughout that winter, he had urged people not to lose sight of the need for reform, intervening in *The Times* dispute to recommend its public ownership by the BBC on the basis of journalists and printers' self-management. But argument now that the election was approaching, centred immediately on the contents of the manifesto. The NEC had produced its own draft version in December and forced Callaghan to agree to a series of joint meetings with the Cabinet during the winter. It demanded the abolition of the House of Lords, an annual wealth tax, compulsory planning agreements and the nationalisation of the construction industry, which Conference had asked for. The struggle culminated in a meeting from 7pm to 3am on the night of 2–3 April at which Callaghan in effect used the power of the Prime Minister to dictate the policy of the Party.

The manifesto which resulted — *The Labour Way is the Better Way* — and the campaign which Callaghan personally dominated were the final testimony to the Government's political bankruptcy, offering the electorate only more of the same, incomes policy and low living standards, stagnation and unemployment and little prospect of improvement. It was not surprising therefore that the electorate responded positively to the Conservative Party's radical message of low taxation, less public expenditure, a reformed welfare state and the limitation of trade union power. During the campaign Labour argued that the price of Conservative tax cuts would be drastic reductions in public expenditure and mass unemployment; but the claim that Labour was the only party that could work with the trade union movement now rang hollow and the prophecies of class war if a Conservative Government attacked trade union power never sounded convincing from a Party that had provoked the previous winter's industrial strikes. One thing was certain: Labour had not lost the General Election because of too much socialism.

X
THE NEW CONSENSUS

Man's capacity for evil makes democracy necessary. Man's capacity for good makes democracy possible.
REINHOLD NIEBUHR

Every modern society which aspires to democracy requires consensus about the values it holds and the way it is governed, needs institutions and policies that command general support if it is to flourish. Both Tony Benn's political development and the course of British history since 1945 have been shaped by the experience of the post-war consensus, its disintegration and the search for a new consensus.

Benn's political career seems at first glance to contain many paradoxes: a peer who renounced his title, rejected privilege and embraced socialism; a radical and internationalist in the 1950s who thereafter came to be identified with domestic economic and industrial issues; an advocate of the existing mixed economy and government collaboration with industry who, in the 1970s, became the proponent of public ownership and workers' control.

These apparent contradictions and shifts in direction in Benn's career have given rise to a sense of uncertainty about his character and have resulted in a "mythological Benn" — largely the creation of the media. The public image of Benn is that of a demonic, destructive figure, perhaps even a megalomaniac; a wealthy, unscrupulous aristocrat who has betrayed his class to indulge in Marxist fantasies. The portrait which emerges of a "red bogeyman" is hardly credible in human terms and is indicative of Benn's role as a champion of change in a troubled and divided society, rather than of his character and opinions. Underlying the Benn enigma is the simple fact that unlike most politicians, he has with age and experience moved increasingly towards the Left, towards a vision of an extended democracy based on popular consensus. The experience of power and responsibility of government office have not led him to the sort of reactionary, cynical opportunism the British media and public seem to expect in prominent politicians. Rather he has questioned his own and others' beliefs with a rigorous honesty, and has been prepared to develop his views in the light of experience.

A close examination of Benn's life reveals the continuities in his development to be more striking than the apparent contradictions. Though he grew up in the comfort and security of an upper middle class home, enjoyed a public school and Oxford education, was confirmed an Anglican and moved among the political Establishment, he never fully belonged to it. On the contrary, he was born into and brought up in a radical dissenting tradition which put freedom of conscience above the law and authority, held all people to be naturally free and equal and saw democratic self-government as the goal towards which humanity was striving. The dissenting tradition preached the interaction of faith and works, regarding experience as the greatest teacher of all. This dialectic of thought and action gave birth in Benn to a creative tension which drove him relentlessly to bridge the gulf between the ideals which he had inherited and the reality that surrounded him. The revolutionary nature of these convictions has had a profound influence on his outlook: the moral vision of dissent informs his notions of democracy and socialism. It underlies his belief in the accountability of power and makes him particularly sensitive to any attacks on democracy from Right or Left.

The radicalism for which Benn was known in the 1950s, as an anti-colonialist and defender of human rights, was similarly the product of respectable middle-class nonconformity and dissent. The radical view of British history as a progressive enlargement of liberty has provided an historical framework for Benn's democratic socialism and a world perspective that has shaped his attitude towards East-West relations, the Third World, defence and the Common Market.

People, however, are not born socialists: they become socialists. Perhaps the single most important event that made Benn receptive to socialist ideas was his struggle to renounce the peerage and remain a commoner. Embittering and formative, the experience opened his eyes to the continuing strength of the British Establishment; taught him how the British constitution worked and helped to maintain privilege. The episode crystallised his understanding of democracy, making him focus on domestic politics, and conscious of the need for an institutional and social revolution in Britain. It led him to embrace the hopes of a New Britain on which the Labour Government of 1964–70 was elected.

The policies of industrial modernisation with which Benn was associated during his time as Postmaster-General and then Minister of Technology were thus democratic and progressive in origin, though in execution, they were manifestly technocratic. The contradictions which emerged between the libertarian nature of Benn's politics and the reforms he implemented as a minister drove him in the late 'sixties to initiate public debate about the future and meaning of democracy in an advanced technological society. The Ministry of Technology made him reflect on the effects of technological change on individuals, society as a whole and the economy; and the challenge this posed for democracy. If the rhetoric he employed as a minister in championing the existing mixed economy was revisionist, Labour's interventionist policies were nevertheless an acknowledgement that laissez-faire capitalism was not producing the desired results.

Benn became increasingly aware during the 'seventies of the existence of a serious and long-term economic crisis. In analysing the causes of this crisis, he reached a destination which bears some resemblance to voluntarist Marxism. Perhaps the crucial difference between his position and orthodox Marxism is that Benn remains free of economic determinism, though he acknowledges that the class struggle is grounded in economic inequality. Rather he retains a faith in moral and popular determination. Events such as the collapse of Upper Clyde Shipbuilders — when workers combined to resist unemployment and temporarily took control of their own affairs — provided for him "an education in the real meaning of practical socialism which no books or teachers could have matched".[1] Ministerial experience taught him that technological progress was hastening the accumulation and concentration of financial and industrial power. The consequent division and specialisation of labour had simultaneously alienated people, shifted the balance of power from capital to labour by making them highly interdependent, and revolutionised popular expectations. In Benn's view, structural economic and social changes of this kind, combined with democratic pressures for rising living standards and improved social services, explained the gathering inflationary crisis which was resulting in under-investment, deindustrialisation and mass unemployment. In the 'seventies he came to realise that in the struggle between capital and labour and the class system lay the root of Britain's economic decline:

. . . It is now becoming clear that there are fundamental conflicts of interest between laissez-faire economics, industrial monopolies, free-trade, unions and the universal adult suffrage which cannot be reconciled without major changes in the structure of the economy.[2]

Yet Benn's socialism cannot be narrowed to an explanation of the failures of capitalism. Rather it is a belief in democracy taken to its logical conclusion:

(Socialism) has nothing whatever in common with the harsh, centralised, dictatorial and mechanistic images . . . presented by the . . . media. . . . (It) is open, libertarian, pluralistic, humane and democratic.[3]

Benn's democratic analysis of Britain's problems underlies his opposition to the Common Market on grounds of loss of sovereignty and self-government, as much as his commitment to the democratic control of the economy through public ownership, planning agreements and workers' self-management.

If Benn's development into a democratic socialist possesses a certain intellectual coherence and consistency, the direction in which he has travelled has in no sense been inevitable. The apparent contradictions of his political career can only be fully understood in the context of British political history since 1945 and the breakdown of the post-war consensus. For a generation the policies of Beveridge and Keynes brought increasing prosperity and social progress. Full employment in a free society was achieved by means of demand management and public expenditure, the political stability of the post-war era resting on an historic compromise between capital and labour. Both Conservative and Labour leaders accepted the nationalisation of essential public services, the basic and declining industries, on non-ideological grounds, within the framework of a mixed economy. The two political parties agreed to the establishment of a Welfare State and the provision of free, universal secondary education as set out in the 1944 Butler Education Act. They also endorsed a strategy of gradual decolonisation and the defence of Western Europe and its interests against Soviet expansionism.

Yet the post-war consensus contained the seeds of it own destruction. The prosperity of the "Butskellite" years was arguably in large measure due to the survival of captive, preferential colonial markets for British manufactured goods, the growth of world trade and the initial absence of serious international competition. These advantages concealed the fact that the objectives governments pursued in relation to economic growth, full employment, price stability, a strong currency and balance of payments were contradictory. If they expanded the economy through public expenditure, they invited inflation, balance of payments deficits and sterling crises. When they deflated to protect the exchange rate and balance of payments, stagnation and unemployment resulted. This has been the experience of all Governments since 1945. By 1960 the limitations and inflationary implications of this approach had become evident in a pattern of slow economic growth re-enforced by intensifying international competition and deflationary policies that dealt equally ineffectively with inflation.

During 1961-62 these contradictions culminated in a crisis of confidence, causing a major realignment of policy and a realisation that productivity and technology had become the two most important factors in determining the rate of economic growth. The revamped consensus that emerged by 1964 consisted of an aggressive competition policy, membership of the EEC, a devaluation strategy, interventionist industrial and regional policies, which were designed to stimulate exports and restructure industry. These were supported by incomes policy and trade union reform intended to make non-inflationary expansion possible at full employment, with higher productivity and fewer strikes. Yet apart from two ill-fated dashes for growth by Maudling in 1963–64 and Barber in 1972–73, the policies and years associated with the leadership of Heath and Wilson were characterised by almost unrelieved stagnation. For all the optimism about dynamic, purposive government, the actual policies were essentially negative in conception. Indirect government intervention had only a marginal impact; devaluation was generally considered self-defeating, while prices and incomes controls were used only as a short-term expedient, and were inevitably unworkable in an unplanned market economy.

The frustrations and failures of the years between 1964–74, the contrast between the optimism of the 'sixties and the pessimism of the 'seventies, and the traumatic nature of the experience of national decline explain why the Labour Party and Benn went back to first principles and their own political roots in search of a solution. Benn's socialism and advocacy of the "alternative strategy" was to that extent a pragmatic response to the prevailing economic circumstances, as well as a reflection of the climate of confrontation which prevailed during the early 'seventies.

The economic crisis which Labour inherited in 1974 was, by general agreement, the most serious since 1945 and an indictment of Government policies. Prices and the money supply were rising by over 20%; the public sector borrowing requirement was over £10b; and the deficit on the balance of payments was approaching £4b. Benn nevertheless felt confident because "the Labour Party's election manifesto contained policies worked out to open up a really new vision of industrial life that would have transformed the situation in a decade".[4] However, the dilemma the Labour Government faced was that any attempt to reduce the rate of inflation and the PSBR could provoke a prolonged and serious slump, reducing tax revenues and worsening the PSBR still further; while reflation could precipitate hyperinflation and a collapse of the currency. The Labour Government of 1974–79 remained a prisoner of these contradictions and became a Conservative one in all but name, imposing incomes and monetary policies that eventually brought it down in the industrial unrest that these had engendered.

The General Election of 3 May 1979 was a watershed in British politics, bringing to power a radical Conservative Government on a laissez-faire and monetarist programme. Labour had suffered its worst electoral defeat since 1959 and a slump in its popular and traditional working class support. The result clarified the choices facing Britain between laissez-faire conservatism, democratic socialism, as represented by Benn, and the failed "corporate state" type consensus policies of the Heath, Wilson and Callaghan Governments.

After the defeat of Labour, Benn returned to the back-benches. Because of the difficulties he had endured as a dissenting minister in the last Government, he had already decided before the election that he would not take on a Government post were Labour re-elected. Once in Opposition, he felt he could be most effective from the back-benches and thus preferred not to stand for the Shadow Cabinet. He now had time for reflection, for numerous meetings with the Labour movement, and he saw clearly that Labour's loss was a result of its failure to make the crisis of 1974–75 the occasion for fundamental change. He concluded that this had occurred because the Labour Party was undemocratic and consequently its leadership unrepresentative and lacking in popular support. In the face of pressure from the civil service, the EEC, the IMF, industry, the financial community and the press, the leadership had abandoned socialist policies and had as a result failed its supporters. Benn concluded that Britain's future as a democratic nation would largely depend on Labour's capacity to transform itself into an instrument of popular change. As he told a 1979 May Day rally in Birmingham:

> We must rebuild the Labour Party as a mass party with a mass membership based upon the constituencies and upon factory and office branches, working closely at every level with the trade unions on policy and organisation.[5]

Immediately after the election, Benn started a campaign for the "intensive, rapid and comprehensive reform" of the Labour Party. In June he demanded that the NEC determine the Labour Party's manifesto, arguing that this should be the responsibility of the Party nationally rather than of the parliamentary leadership alone. He also supported the demands for a mandatory re-selection procedure of Labour MPs as candidates before general elections in order to make the PLP more representative of and accountable to the rank and file. Though the majority of the PLP was inevitably hostile to proposals which diminished their independence, Benn emphasised that he wanted to make the PLP more influential by making any Labour Government and Opposition spokesmen subject to election by the PLP; by strengthening the role of the Party meeting as a forum for debate; and by involving back-bench MPs more closely in policy and parliamentary strategy. In a lecture setting out "The Case for a Constitutional Premiership" in July 1979, he warned:

> . . . The wide range of powers at present exercised by a British Prime Minister . . . are now so great as to encroach upon the legitimate rights of the electorate, undermine the essential role of Parliament, usurp some of the functions of collective Cabinet decision-making, and neutralise much of the influence deriving from the internal democracy of the Party.[6]

He argued that the growing centralisation of power should be reversed by stripping the Prime Minister and Party leader of many powers over the control of information, the conduct of Government business, appointments and patronage, as well as by the direct election of the leader from a new tripartite electoral college representing MPs, constituency parties and the trade unions in equal proportions. Benn hoped that such a reform would form the basis of a reconstituted Party.

Benn's campaign for internal Party democracy was inevitably interpreted as a naked bid for power and the leadership of a Labour Party which had been taken over by a left-wing dominated NEC. Nevertheless, he strove to defuse the situation, pointing out that the trade unions, which were allegedly anti-left-wing, in fact controlled the election of 18 of the 29 members of the NEC, and the militant constituency parties, only six; while the reforms he was proposing in the election and powers of the leadership meant that the identity of the leader would cease to be so relevant. A power struggle for the control of the Commission of Inquiry into the election of the Party leader and the Labour Party's organisation could not be avoided, following the Party Conference in October 1979, which endorsed the reselection of MPs as candidates and the control of the manifesto. But Benn was determined that the real issues should not be obscured and that the debate be conducted in a comradely and constructive spirit. Thus he condemned the campaign which equated militancy in the Labour Party with Trotskyite subversion, as an attempt to distract attention from and prevent the Party's reform. In a statement of unequivocal support for parliamentary democracy, he argued that no firm evidence of subversion had been produced.

Though the Labour Party remains divided about its own future, the argument about its internal organisation is not a narrow, ideological feud, but a debate about the nature of democracy itself whose outcome will have profound consequences for the policies of future Labour Governments. Benn regards parliamentary democracy as primarily a two-way channel of communication between leaders and the people; a mutual educative process rather than merely a system of government. In Opposition, he has devoted himself to reconnecting the leadership with the grass roots of the Labour movement. During 1979 alone, he addressed 215 meetings. He used his new found freedom as a back-bench MP to broaden the range of issues discussed and give leadership to the Left, arguing the renewed relevance of democratic and libertarian principles internally and in international affairs. He condemned the political exploitation of human rights by the Right, warned against a return to the Cold War and a new arms race, insisting that detente constituted the only basis for lasting world peace: "We should reject all mechanistic projections that suggest an inescapable fate for humanity, ending in a nuclear

Armageddon."[7]

At the same time, Benn has been increasingly identified with the anti-nuclear lobby, opposing the development of civil nuclear power — though he remains convinced that a nuclear component will be necessary until alternative and renewable energy sources are available. The potential dangers to democracy posed by international nuclear proliferation; pressures from the nuclear power industry more interested in economic gain than in public safety; and the adoption of a large scale PWR reactor programme following the Three Mile Island accident have all made him highly conscious of the grave dangers of nuclear power and the political threat it poses.

During 1979–80 Benn has also worked to reunite the Labour movement, urging solidarity between the Labour Party and the trade union movement in defence of working peoples' interests. Despite what some see as the problematic nature of the political relationship between the Labour Party and the trade unions, he regards this alliance as Labour's greatest strength. Thus he has opposed the Conservative Government's anti-inflationary strategy of high interest rates, increased indirect taxation, combined with reductions in public expenditure as destructive and divisive, criticising the "economics of the madhouse":

> How can anyone explain the logic of an economic system which permits human need to co-exist with unemployed people, able and anxious to meet it, whilst unused financial resources are diverted into speculation that does not add one penny to our real wealth?[8]

Benn's final objective in Opposition has been to unite the Labour movement behind a democratic socialist programme. His views about the issues of the 1980s are shaped by his understanding that the contradictions and crisis of capitalism can only be resolved by democratic socialism. On the central questions of economic policy, he and the majority in the Labour Party support the alternative strategy as a solution to Britain's problems. The strategy entails the redefinition of the mixed economy and the reindustrialisation of Britain by direct means, using temporary import controls, directed public investment and increased public expenditure to reflate the economy and re-equip industry. It envisages the public ownership of twenty-five leading companies and planning agreements with another seventy-five of the top hundred firms. The NEB is seen as an instrument for the creation of new public and cooperative enterprise, the restructuring of declining industries and the rescue of basically viable firms which have nevertheless collapsed.

The demand for import controls stems from an analysis that sees intensifying international competition and the growing concentration of multinational industrial power as impoverishing Britain and many other countries. In Benn's view the imbalance of trade between rich, poor and oil-producing countries is the underlying cause of the world economic depression. The balance of payments deficits of the developing and of many industrialised countries have limited the scope to increase imports and caused the stagnation of world trade, while the surpluses of wealthy countries have fuelled inflation and destabilised the international monetary system. Thus Benn does not see import controls in unilateral or narrowly nationalistic terms, but in the context of an international redistribution of wealth in favour of developing countries; of the planning of international trade balances and of a new economic order.

In the present inflationary crisis, Benn argues that import controls are the means by which production can be raised and full employment restored. Thus import controls cannot be divorced from the wider concept of protection, particularly that of industry and employment. Benn regards this as a prime obligation of any government and sees public investment as a form of such protection. He is less concerned with nationalisation than with channelling investment capital into manufacturing industry on the basis of full public accountability and in so doing, helping to democratise the economy. In the final analysis, he believes that Britain's economic problems are political in origin; that industrial democracy is a prerequisite for their solution: "We have got to make the leap from the world of market forces towards more democratic decisions about resources and a greater respect for human values."[9] As Benn sees it the benefits of industrial democracy are not limited to the economic sphere. The very process of running one's own working life can release a new positive energy in people which in the long term will affect all aspects of existence.

Thus Benn envisages a new relationship between capital and labour, moving from a situation where capital hires labour to one where labour hires capital. Though he recognises that the complexity of modern society precludes any blueprint for industrial democracy, he considers full workers' control and workers' cooperatives as the most likely models. In addition he believes that planning agreements, as a means of directing investment, will, by expanding the sphere of collective bargaining, stimulate the democratisation of the trade unions.

The intensity of Benn's democratic vision also helps explain his hostility to the Common Market and his reasons for demanding the return of full law-making powers to a democratically elected British Parliament. The socialist policies he advocates would mean a major reform of the Common Market with its current close identification with laissez-faire capitalism. However, he is confident that its member nations will come to accept the protection of industry just as they did of agriculture.

To what extent could these policies — supported by, and indeed, arrived at, with the help of the Labour movement — represent a solution to Britain's problems and form the basis of a new consensus?

In assessing the relevance of Benn's democratic socialism, it is useful to consider the alternative solutions, specifically the corporatism of the Heath, Wilson and Callaghan years and the monetarist laissez-faire capitalism of the Thatcher Government. Corporatism in Britain has come to mean the joint regulation of the economy by government, industry, and trade unions on the basis of temporary incomes policies, assistance to industry, and the maintenance of public expenditure in order to conceal unemployment. The experience of the last fifteen years suggests that a further attempt is unlikely to succeed, and that the causes of failure bode ill for any laissez-faire solution.

Monetarism is also an essentially negative instrument for managing the economy and deals ineffectively with inflation because the factors influencing the level of, and balance between, demand and supply are more complex than is admitted by the simple relationship between the quantity of money and the supply of goods or services. The Conservative Government's apparent objective of squeezing inflation out of the economy by competition and monetary policies, may, in addition, permanently destroy productive capacity because of the underlying weakness of industry. The inherent disequilibrium of the economy stems from the monopoly character of capital and labour, which means that inflationary tendencies will increase as the discipline of competition diminishes. It is therefore unlikely that a laissez-faire policy will succeed and a resurrected capitalism arise phoenix-like from the ashes.

Benn himself is convinced that Labour's "alternative strategy is an invitation for a new consensus without which no modern industrial society can work". In assessing its capacity to revitalise the British economy, it is perhaps best to examine the issues which the alternative strategy raises, rather than to pronounce judgement on what is still an untried policy. The democratic reforms Benn advocates so strongly in government, industry and the media, do not in themselves constitute a solution to Britain's problems of inflation, industrial unrest and economic stagnation, but equally, they are not, as his critics suggest, a charter for anarchy. Indeed, they may point the way to a consensus more actively engaged in by the mass of people. The opponents of industrial democracy fear that workers' control will mean management by committee, inefficiency, low productivity and industrial rigidity. On the other hand, its proponents claim that the responsibility conferred by self-management will revolutionise trade unions and labour attitudes, offering the prospect of improved industrial relations and management by consent, stability in prices and incomes, as well as greater investment and productivity.

Labour's industrial policy and programme of expanded public ownership with planning agreements as an alternative to public ownership is a form of indirect state intervention. It rests on the use of the market mechanism and the interaction of public with private industry to stimulate economic growth. Such an assumption remains unproved; while the varying objectives of the NEB, for example, as an instrument of price control may be contradictory and deter investment by the private sector. Labour's hopes for regenerating British industry may, however, come to depend more on the direction of the funds of the financial institutions and of North Sea oil tax revenues into the manufacturing sector of the economy through its proposed planning agreements system. The role envisaged for planning agreements is an all-embracing one, and the complexity and size of the companies concerned, as well as the changing nature of external factors, may reduce their effectiveness. But despite the inherent problems of planning at a micro-economic level in a market economy, planning agreements would provide a mechanism for effectively chanelling investment funds into industry, on a more flexible and systematic basis than has hitherto occurred, and a way of coordinating industrial policy with the Government's overall economic strategy.

Benn claims that protectionism can restore full employment. If this is the case, then the criticisms about the protection of inefficiency diminish because the pressure on resources at full employment will necessitate high productivity. He believes that the dangers of international retaliation against import controls are exaggerated and stresses that Britain would negotiate an agreement with the EEC, GATT and IMF on the nature and extent of protection. On the other hand, the alternative strategy may undermine Labour's attempts to harness the market mechanism to industrial policy, because the effect of import controls is to weaken the forces of competition. Moreover, reflation by means of public expenditure, investment and borrowing implies a continuation of high inflation and interest rates which are likely to discourage capital investment still further because, in a market economy, the reaction of industry will depend on the *relative* profitability of industry.

In the final analysis the case for public intervention rests on the argument that the private sector is either unable and/or unwilling to invest in industry. Underlying this view is the conclusion that market forces will not necessarily stimulate investment because the profit motive is ultimately self-defeating, and as a measure neither of efficiency nor wealth creation should not therefore be used as the criterion for allocating all resources. Nevertheless, the possible political implications of Labour's democratic planning have to be recognised, in that the pressure to preserve employment may in fact lead to economically disadvantageous decisions. Moreover, the political nature of any choice about the allocation of public funds raises the central political dilemma of *who* plans and in *whose* interests.

Benn is not immediately associated with the conventional idea of consensus politics as a bi-partisan agreement within a two-party system. Indeed, he has consistently attacked it because he believes that consensus politics of this type have led to the personalisation and trivialisation of political life by preventing any real debate about alternatives and choices. In his view, the consensus policies of the post-war era have increasingly become the creation of a ruling élite and have rested on the existing and unjust distribution of wealth and power.

Yet, as a democratic socialist, Benn accepts that any political party must win a decisive electoral victory and consent for its policies, if it is to command the necessary authority to carry through major reforms by democratic and parliamentary means. The consensus for which Benn is striving, and the only one he is prepared to entertain, is a genuinely democratic and socialist one. Indeed, his belief in parliamentary democracy, itself, springs from his belief in Parliament as an instrument of the popular will. He is acutely aware of the fragile nature of the consent that binds the people to their rulers. He is above all a realist, simultaneously conscious of the threats to democracy as well as its potentiality.

Benn realises that the task of creating a new consensus and re-uniting a divided society is a formidable one. He recognises the difficulty of bringing together the Left, the problematic role of the trade unions stemming from the conflict of capital and labour. He is equally conscious of the threat from the authoritarian Right, who fundamentally believe capitalism and extended democracy to be incompatible — though they speak of individual liberty.

At the same time he remains convinced that the demands of ordinary people, including the middle classes, for economic security and social justice will necessitate the peaceful, socialist transformation of society. Experience has taught him that it takes a long time, at least a decade, to change public attitudes — as the Common Market referendum showed — and his tenacity of purpose is a source of his strength. He believes that Labour's 1974 manifesto will lead to the reforms which can constitute the basis of a new consensus; just as its 1935 programme was the basis of the reforms of 1945 and the ensuing post-war consensus. Thus Benn emerges as both a revolutionary and a reformer; a revolutionary in the intensity of his commitment to democracy and socialism in Britain; a reformer in his commitment to a procedure of change which begins with pressure from the people reflected through parliamentary democracy and

THE NEW CONSENSUS

finally securing public consent. Benn's optimism is combined with a
realistic awareness of the difficulties intrinsic to the struggle for a
more broadly-based democracy in times when, if not cynicism, then
disillusionment seems to be a predominant feature of political life. It
is this combination which gives his vision a tragic edge.

Perhaps Benn's uniqueness among politicians is that he believes
that the purpose of winning power is to give it away. He feels politics
to be primarily about the nature of society and only secondly about
government:

> For politics is really about education and not about propaganda. It is
> about teaching more than management. It is about ideas and values and
> not only about Acts of Parliament, political institutions and ministerial
> office.[10]

And so it will always be. Future generations will come to appreciate
that Benn was no extremist, but a person who dedicated his life to
and fought hard for democracy and defended it when it was under
attack. They will see him as a fearless politician, unafraid to change his
own views and to criticise others'.

The test of Benn's new consensus lies in the viability of socialist
economic policies and their compatibility with democracy. Benn's
ability to convince the Labour Party and the electorate will be the
vindication of the concept of democracy he holds. Only time will tell
whether he will become one of the architects of a new order; whether
democratic socialism or authoritarian conservatism will form the
basis of Britain's future.

But whether we agree or disagree with Tony Benn, history will
judge him as a man who gave politics a good name.

NOTES

I. *The Inheritance of Dissent*

1 A.G. Gardiner, *John Benn and the Progressive Movement*, Ernest Benn, London, 1925. p.31.

2 *John Benn and the Progressive Movement.* p.vi.

3 P. Thompson, *Socialists, Liberals and Labour. The Struggle for London 1885 - 1914*, Routledge & Kegan Paul, London 1967. p. 105.

4 *John Benn and the Progressive Movement.* p.464.

5 *The Dictionary of National Biography 1951 - 1960*, Oxford University Press, 1971.

6 A.N.W. Benn, "A Radical in Politics," *The Times*, 7th May, 1977.

7 W.W. Benn, *In The Side Shows*, Hodder & Stoughton, London, 1919. pp73-4 and pp.66-8.

8 Philip Snowdon (Lord), *Autobiography*, Nicholson & Watson, London, 1934.

9 W.W. Benn, *Election Address*, Dudley Constituency, General Election 1935.

10 Hansard Vol. 682 Col. 941, 24 October 1963. Interview with author.

11 "The Levellers and the English Democratic Tradition," speech at Burford Church, 15 May, 1976.

12 Speech at the Oxford Union Society, 4 March, 1943.

13 "The Labour Party in Power: The Government's Domestic Policy," speech at the Oxford Union Society, 1947.

14 K. Harris, *Travelling Tongues*, John Murray, London, 1945. p.200.

NOTES

II *Benn and the Radical Tradition*

1 Selection Conference Speech, 1 November, 1950.

2 Interview with author.

3 Hansard Vol. 531 Cols. 941 — 950, 30 July, 1954.

4 Hansard Vol. 550 Cols. 1296 — 1300, 21 March, 1956.

5 D.J. Goldsworthy, *Colonial Affairs in British Politics 1945 - 59.* D. Phil Thesis, Oxford 1968.

6 Patricia Rushton, *Colonial Affairs in British Politics 1945 - 59.*

7 *The Listener,* Vol. 69, No. 1778, 25 April, 1963.

8 Hansard Vol. 574 Cols. 880 — 889, 29 July, 1957.

9 *The Spectator,* Vol. 199 No. 6736, 2 August, 1957.

10 Labour Party Conference Annual Report, 1959.

11 Labour Party Conference Annual Report, 1960.

III *The Persistent Commoner*

1 Personal Bills Committee Report, 28 February, 1955.

2 Minutes of the Personal Bills Committee, 18 February, 1955.

3 *The Privy Council as a Second Chamber,* Fabian Tract 305, January, 1957.

4 *Ibid.*

5 The above quotations and those in the following paragraph are taken from the "Report from the Committee of Privileges", 14 March, 1961.

6 *Keesing's Contemporary Archives,* 13 — 20 May, 1961.

7 *Ibid.*

8 *The Bristol Campaigner,* 20 April, 1961.

9 "Tribute to Bristol", *Tribune* Vol. 27 No. 31, 23 August, 1963.

10 Letter from Hugh Gaitskell, 27 April, 1961.

11 Letter from Professor Arnold Toynbee, 26 March, 1961.

12 Letter from Richard Clements, 24 April, 1961.

13 *Keesing's Contemporary Archives,* 13 — 20 May, 1961.

14 *Ibid.*

15 Election Agent's Report, 29 May, 1961.

16 *Keesing's Contemporary Archives*, 13 — 20 May, 1961.

17 *Ibid.*

18 Speech at the Bar for 8 May, 1961.

19 *Keesing's Contemporary Archives*, 26 August — 2 September, 1961.

20 *Ibid.*

21 *Keesing's Contemporary Archives*, 17 — 24 August, 1963.

22 Interview with author.

23 H. Macmillan, *At the End of the Day*, Macmillan, London, 1973, pp 508–509.

24 Hansard, Vol. 682 Cols. 936—942, 24 October, 1963.

25 Tony Benn, *Arguments for Socialism*, Jonathan Cape, London, 1979, pp 15-16.

IV *The New Britain*

1 *The Guardian*, February and 10th April, 1964.

2 *The Guardian*, 3 January, 1964.

3 Election Agent's Report, 29 May, 1961.

4 "Re-Integrating the Left", Nuffield Political Seminar, 27 November, 1961.

5 Labour Party Annual Conference Report, 1961.

6 The actual visible trade deficit for 1964 turned out to be £500 million and the deficit on the current account £356 million.
   The Labour Government's economic record: 1964-78. Edited by Wilfred Beckerman, Duckworth, London 1972.

7 Post Office Recollections, Private Note, 15 January, 1970.

8 *The Sunday Times*, 20 February, 1966.

9 *The Sunday Times*, 20 February, 1966.

10 The National Giro Results:

Year	Income £m	Profit/(loss) £m	Year	Income £m	Profit/(loss) £m
68/9	1.5	(1.7)	73/4	19.1	(5.1)
69/70	5.3	(6.0)	74/5	24.6	0.1
70/71	7.2	(6.0)	75/6	36.4	0.8
71/2	8.6	(7.8)	76/7	46.8	2.1
72/3	12.8	(7.1)	77/8	60.4	2.8

Source: The Department of Industry.

NOTES

11 Post Office Results

Postal Services	1964-5 £m	1965-6 £m	1966-7 £m
Turnover	273.6	318.8	340.6
Profit/(loss)	(19.6)	0.9	6.6
Return on capital employed	-24.6%	7.7%	13.2%
Capital expenditure	13.6	16.2	24.0
Telecommunications			
Turnover	372.9	404.0	441.8
Profit/(loss)	39.7	39.3	37.8
Return on capital employed	8.6%	8.2%	7.7%
Capital expenditure	173.9	193.5	242.0

Source: Annual Report and Accounts.

12 Hansard Vol. 710, 14 April, 1965 and Vol. 702 Cols. 184-191.

13 Sources: Economic Trends.

The Labour Governments Economic record: 1964-70
The joint declaration of intent in September, 1965 on productivity, prices and incomes did not prevent incomes from rising at the annual rate of 9.5 per cent during the first four months of 1966. The potential for economic growth had been greatly overestimated, as M.C. Kennedy noted:

"The Plan's choice of an overall income in GDP of 25 per cent from 1964-70 appears to have been made without any attempt to relate the growth of output to the growth of productive resources." (*U.K. Economy,* Third Edition, Ed. A.R. Prest, Weidenfeld and Nicholson, London, 1970).

V *Mintech*

1 H. Wilson, *The Labour Government 1964-70,* Weidenfeld & Nicholson and Michael Joseph, London, 1971. p.318.

2 *The Ministry of Technology,* 1970 (Unpublished).

3 Interview with author.

4 Rootes Motors Financial Results:

Year	1964 £m	1965 £m	1966 £m	1967 £m
Profit/(loss) year to 31st July	1.8	(2.1)	(3.6)	(10.5)

Source: Annual Report and Accounts.

5 Hansard Vol. 742 Cols. 1773-1788 9 March, 1967.

6 R. Lewis, *Tony Benn: A Critical Biography,* Associated Business Press, London 1978.

7 J. McGill, *Crisis on The Clyde: The Story of UCS,* Davis-Poynter, London 1973.

8 *Ibid.*

9 Hansard Vol. 750 Cols. 1138-1150, 13 July, 1967.

11   "The Government's Policy for Technology", lecture at Imperial College, London, 17 October, 1967.

12   The hidden reflation was reflected by the following:

	1965 £m	1966 £m	1967 £m
Consumer expenditure	22,685	24,238	25,357
Public expenditure	14,137	15,317	17,520
Money supply (M3 at year end)	12,750	13,200	14,510

Source: Economic Trends

13   Labour Party Conference Annual Report, 1968.

14   Hansard Vol. 757 Cols. 1571–1592, 1 February, 1968.

15   Hansard Vol. 757 Cols. 1571–1592, 1 February, 1968.

16   Hansard Vol. 765 Col. 2188, 30 May, 1968.

17   Hansard Vol. 791 Cols. 1130—1196, 10 March, 1970.

18   Memorandum to Sir William (Lord) Armstrong, April, 1970.

19   The symtoms of industrial decline were already apparent:

	1964	1965	1966	1967	1968	1969	1970
Rate of profit:							
on investment : pre-tax %	13.7	12.8	11.3	11.7	11.6	11.1	9.7
post-tax %	7.1	7.8	4.9	6.1	5.2	4.7	4.1
on output %	21.2	20.2	17.6	18.1	16.8	14.2	12.1
Employment:							
market sector millions			21.3	20.8	20.5	20.5	20.3
non-market sector millions			4.1	4.2	4.3	4.4	4.5
Unemployment millions			0.4	0.6	0.6	0.6	0.6
Investment in Plant and Machinery £m		3011	3219	3365	3366	3469	

Source: R.W. Bacon and W. Eltis, *Britain's Economic Problem: Too Few Producers*, First Edition, Macmillan, London, 1976.

20   "Mintech 1970—75", 18 March, 1970.

VI *The New Politics*

1   Progress Report and Mid-term Manifesto, 22 May, 1968.

2   Labour Party Annual Conference Report, 1968.

3   Marx Engels Works Capital, I, 159, Lawrence & Wishart, London, 1970.

4   "From Parliamentary to Popular Democracy", Speech at Welsh Council of Labour Conference, Llandudno, 25 May, 1968.

5   *Ibid.*

6 "Broadcasting in a Participating Democracy", Hanham Labour Party, 18 October, 1968.

7 *Daily Telegraph,* 20 October, 1968.

8 *The Times,* 19 October, 1968.

9 "Technology and The Quality of Life", Lecture at the Manchester Technology Association, 25 February, 1970.

10 "Labour and the New Politics", Speech to the Young Fabians, 5 November, 1968.

11 "Labour and the New Politics", Speech to the Young Fabians, 5 November, 1968.

12 "Mergers and Takeovers", Interview, July, 1969.

13 "Industrial Democracy", Speech at Industrial Society Lunch, 27 November, 1968.

14 "Industrial Relations", Speech at Southern Regional Labour Party Conference, 19 April, 1969.

15 "Campaign Strategy", NEC paper, 9 August, 1969.

16 "Enoch Powell and Racialism", Speech to Students for Labour Victory, Central Hall, Westminster, 3 June, 1970.

17 *The New Politics. A Socialist Reconnaissance,* Fabian Tract 402, September 1970.

VII *Chairman Benn*

1 Interview with author.

2 Hansard Vol. 810 Cols. 354—371, 26 January, 1971.

3 Interview with author.

4 Hansard Vol. 819 Cols. 242—256, 15 June, 1971.

5 Upper Clyde Shipbuilders (Public Ownership) Bill, Hansard Vol. 819 Col. 1174, 22 June, 1971.

6 The Advisory Group consisted of Sir Alexander Glen of Clarksons, Lord Robens, A. Forbes McDonald of Distillers and D. Macdonald of Hill Samuel.

7 Hansard Vol. 822 Cols. 1084—1095, 2 August, 1971.

8 Hansard Vol. 816 Cols. 721—730, 29 April, 1971.
The underlying weakness of the economy and the inflationary consequences of the Government's reflation during 1972—3 can be seen as folows:

		1970	1971	1972	1973	Notes
Gross Domestic Product (expenditure)		100.0	102.6	104.3	111.1	(i)
Index of Production		100.0	100.3	102.5	110.0	(i)
Employment: market sector	m	20.3	19.8	19.7	20.0	(ii)

non-market sector	m	4.5	4.6	4.7	4.9	(ii)
Unemployment	m	0.6	0.8	0.9	0.6	(ii)
Investment in plant and machinery	£m	3,658	3,600	3,432	3,840	(iii)
Incomes % increase		12.1	11.3	13.0	13.4	(iv)
Prices % increase		6.4	9.4	7.1	9.2	(iv)
Public sector borrowing requirement	£m	0.0	1.4	2.0	4.2	(v)
Balance of Payments: visible balance	£m	− 25	+280	−702	−2,353	(v)
current account	£m	+695	+1,058	+105	−922	(v)

Notes
(i)   Source: Economic Trends, at 1970 market prices.
(ii) Source: *Britain's Economic Problem: Too Few Producers*
(iii) Source: Economic Trends, at 1970 market prices.
(iv) Source: Economic Trends.
(v)   Source: Economic Trends, at current prices.

Comment
The Index for Industrial Production concealed the relative stagnation of the engineering sectors and decline of shipbuilding as well as mining during the period.
    The statistics mentioned in the text for the public sector borrowing requirement differ slightly from those above because they reflect provisional estimates.
(Source: *British Economic Policy 1970-74* : Two Views, Hobart Paperback No. 7, Institute for Economic Affairs).

9 Hansard Vol. 827 Cols. 1755-1767, 10 December, 1971, and Vol. 825 Cols. 937—948, 9 November, 1971.

10 Law and Order: Democracy and Moral Responsibility, Paper for Shadow Cabinet, 31 October, 1972.

11 Hansard Vol. 849 Col. 1064, 29 January, 1973, and Vol. 852 Col. 929, 12 March, 1973.

12 Hansard Vol. 849 Cols. 1052—1064, 29 January, 1973.

13 Hansard Vol. 860 Cols. 1266—1276, 23 July, 1973.

14 A. Glyn and R.B. Sutcliffe, *British Capitalism, Workers and the Profits Squeeze,* Penguin Books, London 1972.

15 See: S. Holland, *The Socialist Challenge,* Quartet Books, London, 1975.

16 NEC Papers, June 1971.

17 Speech at the Conference of "The Future of the City of London", 6 June, 1973.

18 Labour Party Annual Conference Report, 1973.

19 Hansard Vol. 823 Cols. 1751—1764, 27 October, 1971.

20 "Technology and Politics", Speech to German Institute for Foreign Affairs, Bonn, 20 February, 1968.

21 "The Common Market — The Case for a Referendum", Letter to the constituents of Bristol South East, 14 November, 1970.

22 "Labour and the Common Market", Speech at a public meeting in Bristol, 2 July, 1971.

23 "The Case for Reform", Speech to the Guild of Bristol Newspaper Editors, 23 April, 1971.

24 "Conference and the Market" Speech at Tiverton County Rally, 23 September, 1973.

25 "The Civil Service and Political Advisers", *The Times,* 11 July, 1973.

26 "A Voice for the People", Paper given at the Fourth Manchester University Symposium on Broadcasting Policy, 11 February, 1972.

27 *Labour Weekly,* No. 3, 15 October, 1971.

28 "The Labour Party and Democratic Politics", Fabian Lecture, 3 November, 1971.

29 "Conference Democracy", *Tribune* Vol. 37 No. 3, 19 January, 1973.

30 Labour Party Annual Conference Report, 1972.

31 E.S. Heffer, *The Class Struggle in Parliament: a Socialist view of industrial relations,* Victor Gollancz, London 1973. p.52.

32 Interview with author.

33 "Rethinking Industrial Policy", Speech at Annual Delegate Meeting at the AUEW, Foundry Section, Morecombe, 27 May, 1971.

34 Speech to the Public Enterprise Group, Metropole Hotel, Brighton, 5 October, 1971.

35 "Dockers in Jail", Statement, 22 July, 1972.

36 "Law and Order: Democracy and Moral Responsibility", Paper for Shadow Cabinet, 31 October, 1972.

37 Fraternal Greetings from the Chairman of the Labour Party to the Trade Union Congress at Brighton, 5 September, 1972.

38 "The Fall of Heath", *The Sunday Times,* 22 February, 29 February and 7 March, 1976 as well as for the above and following quotations about the Three Day Week.

39 *The Times,* 7 December, 1973.

40 Hansard Vol. 867 Cols. 298—309, 10 January, 1974.

41 "Challenging the Class Structure", Speech at Conference sponsored by the London Co-operative Party Education and Political Committees and the London Federation of Trade Councils, 27 February, 1974.

VIII *Socialism in One Country*

1   *Daily Telegraph,* 4 January, 1975. At the time Paul Johnson was still a member of the Labour Party.

2   Sources: Economic Trends and Cambridge Economic Policy Group for decline in employment in manufacturing industry and import penetration.
    Evidence of the seriousness of the inflationary crisis is as follows:

		1973	1974	1975
Index of industrial production		110.6	106.9	101.7
Unemployment — million		0.6	0.6	0.9
Private sector fixed investmen	£m	6,164	6,103	5,795
Public sector borrowing requirement		4,182	6,382	10,502

Source: Economic Trends

For a discussion of the profits crisis controversy see:
"The United Kingdom profits crisis : myth or reality?" M.A. King, *Economic Journal* Vol. 85, March 1975.

"Short-run variation in company profits" W. Coutts
Economic Policy Review No. 4 University of Cambridge, Department of Applied Economics, March 1978.
"Stock appreciation and the crisis of British Industry further considered" W.A.H. Godley & A. Wood *Economic Policy Review* No. 1 February 1975, University of Cambridge, Department of Applied Economics.

3   "The Department of Industry's Current Work," Memorandum to P.M. 29 April, 1974. "Trade and Industry" Vol. 19 No. 1, 4 April 1975. "Overhauling the Mixed Economy" speech to Nottinghamshire miners, 8 June, 1974. Hansard Vol. 880 Cols. 714—727, 4 November, 1974.

4   T. Forester, "How Labour's Industrial Strategy got the chop", *New Society* Vol. 45 No. 822, 6 July, 1975.

5   Interview with author.

6   Hansard Vol. 892 Cols. 1002, 19 May, 1975, and Vol. 893 Cols. 5—8, 9 June, 1975.

7   BSC's losses appear to be also due to the burden of interest payments caused by BSC's expansion plan as well as the fall in demand and production: information from BSC Annual Reports:

Year ended 31 March		1974	1975	1976	1977	1978	1980
Pre-tax profits/(loss) before interest	£m	56	89	(246)	(83)	(442)	
Interest payments (mainly Govt. loans)	£m	53	67	108	167	197	
Employees	'000	233	220	228	210	197	
U.K. Crude Steel production m.tons		22.3	19.8	22.3	20.4	20.3	42.0*

Source: Economic Trends, Annual Report and Accounts
* BSC Plan

8   1972 Industry Act Annual Report for the year to 31 March, 1975.

9   Information regarding assistance to industry is based on the 1972 Industry Act Annual Report for the year to 31 March, 1975.

The subsequent results of Ferranti and Alfred Herbert indicated that both companies were commercially viable while Fodens and Kearney Trecker, Marwin were more marginal cases:

	Ferranti Ltd.			Herbert Ltd.		
			Pre-tax			Pre-tax
Year	Sales	Exports	Profit/loss	Sales	Exports	Profit/loss
	£m	£m	£m	£m	£m	£m
1975	86.3	21.4	0.5	49.7	12.4	(13.4)
1976	108.5	27.4	4.1	49.4	11.6	0.7
1977	125.4	22.1	4.5	54.3	12.8	0.6

	Fodens Ltd.				Kearney Trecker, Marwin Ltd.	
	Sales	Pre-tax Profit/(loss)	Interest		Sales	Pre-tax Profit/(loss)
	£m	£m	£m		£m	£m
1974	22.6	0.2	0.4	1973	5.2	(2.8)
1975	28.3	0.9	0.8	1974	9.9	(1.6)
1976	28.6	(1.0)	1.2	1975	13.0	0.1
1977	47.1	1.7	1.3	1976	10.4	0.2
1978	52.8	2.8	0.8	1977	12.5	0.9

Sources: Extel Company Information Service
        The Department of Industry

10   Hansard Vol. 892 Cols. 1419—1434, 21 May, 1975. The Rider Report "British Leyland: the next decade", concluded that "profits were wholly inadequate and insufficient to maintain the business on a viable basis . . . A massive programme to modernise plant and machinery at British Leyland must . . . be put in hand immediately".

11   Source: Court Line Limited, Department of Trade Report.
    The company's legal adviser, Michael Sayers of Norton Rose, considered that an expression of confidence might be reckless:
    "It must be clearly understood that pending the availability of the Price Waterhouse report, Court Line is in no position to guarantee that the price would necessarily enable the Aviation and Leisure Division to continue throughout the 1974 summer season."
    In the event half of the £16m was owed by Court Line to Court Shipbuilders because of intercompany borrowings, while the reporting accountants, Price Waterhouse, noted that cash flow projections had not been prepared and that therefore a "critical aspect of the present exercise is still incomplete".

12   Sources: British Aerospace for estimates of HS146 sales; the Booz — Allen Report for information relating to state assistance to the shipbuilding industry.

13   H. Wilson, *Final Term: the Labour Government 1974-1976*, Weidenfeld & Nicholson and Michael Joseph 1979. p.33.

14   "Party Strategy", NEC Campaign Committee, 15 May, 1974.

15   "The Control of Ministers", Draft of letter to P.M., September, 1974.

16   Letter to Herbert Rogers, Bristol South East Labour Party.

17   By 1979 these limits had been increased to £3000m and £4000m respectively reflecting the NEB's increasing role as a rescue vehicle. The main difference between the proposed legislation and the White Paper, *The Regeneration of British Industry,* was that the disclosure requirements would not form part of the proposed voluntary planning agreements system.

18   Hansard Vol. 886 Cols. 935—946, 17 February, 1975.

19   Hansard Vol. 893 Cols. 21, 9 June, 1975.

20   The financial results of the two cooperatives were as follows:

Synova Motors Limited (Meriden)	Sales	(Loss)
	£m	£m
56 weeks to 31st March, 1976	3.97	(1.03)
78 weeks to 30 September, 1977	11.26	(1.63)
Kirkby Manufacturing and Engineering Co. Ltd.		
15 months to 2 April, 1976	6.46	(1.52)
year to 1st April, 1977	7.11	(0.38)

Source: The Department of Industry.

21   *Daily Telegraph,* 20 May, 1975; *The Times,* 5 June, 1975.

22   David Butler and Uwe Kitzinger, *The 1975 Referendum,* Macmillan, London, 1976. p.162.

23   Draft of letter to Prime Minister by Tony Benn, Michael Foot and Peter Shore.

24   Bristol South East Constituency, Stockwood Ward Newsletter, 24 February, 1975.

25   Statement on the Renegotiation, 18 March, 1975.

26   *The 1975 Referendum.* p.177.

27   *Ibid.* p.178.

28   *The Times,* 16 May, 1975.

29   National Referendum Campaign Press Conference, 18 May, 1975.

30   The Labour M.P. Robert Mellish and the Liberal M.P. Cyril Smith.

31   *Daily Mail,* 4 June, 1975.

32   *The 1975 Referendum.* p.273.

33   M. Hatfield, *The House the Left Built: Inside Labour Policy Making 1970-1975,* Victor Gollancz, London 1978.

IX *Dissenting Minister*

1   Interview with author.

2   The continued weakness of the economy during this period of stabilisation can
    be seen as follows:

		1975	1976	1977	1978
Gross domestic product (income)		100.0	103.2	105.0	108.1
Index of industrial production		100.0	101.4	102.8	103.6
Unemployment		0.93	1.27	1.38	1.38
Consumer expenditure	£b	63.2	62.9	62.8	66.3
Private fixed investment	£b	11.9	11.8	12.2	13.6
(both at 1975 market prices)					
Price inflation % rate		24.6	16.9	13.7	8.8
Public sector borrowing					
requirement	£b	10.5	7.9	4.5	5.9
Balance of payments:					
visible balance	£m	−3,236	−3,601	−1,744	−1,175
current account	£m	−1,843	−1,137	+298	+254

Sources: Economic Trends
    Cambridge Economic Policy Review No. 5 April 1979

Comment:
Much of the growth in national income, production and private sector investment
over the period was attributable to North Sea Oil. Without savings in oil imports
the balance of payments would also have been correspondingly worse.

3   Labour Party Conference Annual Report, 1975.

4   Text of letter to the Bristol South East Constituency Labour Party, September,
    1975. IWC Pamphlet No. 48.

5   *A New Course for Labour,* IWC Pamphlet No. 51.

6   Interview with author.

7   *United Kingdom Offshore Oil and Gas Policy,* Cmnd. 5696, 1974.

8   National Energy Conference, 22 June, 1976, transcript.

9   Prime Minister's Address to National Energy Conference, 22 June, 1976,
    transcript.

10 Source: Economic Trends.

11 "The Levellers and the English Democratic Tradition", Burford Church, Burford,
    Oxfordshire, 15 May, 1976.

12 Hansard Vol. 911 Cols. 1545—1556, 19 May, 1976.

13 "The Labour movement and the Public Sector — a Reassessment", Caxton Hall,
    Westminster, 7 July, 1976.

14 "The Labour Party", (Unpublished) first draft, August, 1976.

15 "The Day the £ nearly died" by Stephen Fay and Hugo Young. *The Sunday Times* 14, 21 and 28 May, 1978. The above and following quotations as well as this account of the 1976 sterling crisis are all taken from and based on Fay and Young's account.

16 Source: Economic Trends.
Cambridge Economic Policy Review.

17 Source: Development of the oil and gas resources of the United Kingdom *(The Brown Book)*, Department of Energy, 1979.
Capital expenditure was not deterred by Labour's taxation régime while the decline in exploratory drilling reflected its policy of more frequent and smaller licensing rounds in conformity with its strategy of slow depletion.

		1976	1977	1978
Production in tons		11.6	37.3	52.8
Development expenditure	£m	1522.9	1555.6	1731.8
Offshore exploration wells		58	67	37

Comments: total investment in oil and gas amounted to approximately £2.36b in 1978 equivalent to 22% of total UK industrial investment. At the end of 1978 estimated recoverable reserves amounted to 2,400m — 4,400m tons oil.

By the end of 1978 BNOC had concluded participation agreements with 62 companies under pre-fifth round licences. In general these gave it the right to buy up to 51% of the oil companies' share of production at market prices together with full membership of the operating committees for fields, pipelines and terminals. Under the fifth and sixth rounds it concluded equity agreements in seventy-seven licences contributing over 10% of total capital expenditure on the UK continental shelf in 1978.

BNOC Results:		1977	1978	1979
Sales	£m	27.8	431.8	3,244.9
Operating profit		4.8	10.9	136.3
Pre-tax profit/(loss)		(1.8)	2.1	15.4
Capital employed		557.0	262.7	968.5

Sources:
Development of the oil and gas resources of the United Kingdom 1979; Department of Energy.
The British National Oil Corporation annual report and accounts.

18 The National Coal Board finances grew in strength despite its large capital expenditure programme and large interest payments on borrowed capital. Subsidies were lower than any other EEC country.

	1975 £m	1976 £m	1977 £m	1978 £m
Sales	1589.6	1982.2	2426.6	2733.1
Trading profit	40.4	52.2	109.8	108.7
Interest payments	(36.2)	(51.8)	(78.0)	(87.0)
Profit after interest and tax	0.0	5.3	22.7	20.4
Capital expenditure	143.0	216.9	273.8	342.3

		1975	1976	1977	1978
Coal production	m tons	128.7	123.8	122.1	123.6
Coal burn in power stations m tons		74.6	77.8	79.9	80.6

Source: Annual Reports and Accounts.

In 1977 direct coal production subsidies in the European Coal and Steel Community were as follows:

	£m	£ per ton
Belgium	138	19.8
France	278	13.3
Federal Republic of Germany	247	2.8
United Kingdom	67	0.5

Source: ESCC

The CEGB was concerned about its current overcapacity and the schedules of its power station ordering programme. It was estimated that Drax B could increase coal production by 4.75m tons p.a. and save 2m tons p.a. of oil.

19 Hansard Vol. 923 Cols. 967—971, 13 December, 1976.

20 Hansard Vol. 925 Cols. 1253—1267, 8 February, 1977.

21 Hansard Vol. 942 Cols. 1391—1408, 25 January, 1978.
Both the Royal Commission on environmental pollution (Cmnd. 6618 September 1976) and the Government's White Paper *Nuclear Power and the Environment* (Cmnd. 6820, May 1977) insisted that safety considerations should overide economic factors in determining the choice of Britain's nuclear reactor. The Government's Chief Scientist, Sir Alan Cottrell, and many others took the view that the PWR would not be safe without considerable additional capital expenditure.
The National Nuclear Corporation's report "The choice of Thermal Reactor Systems" emphasised the AGR's larger generating capacity in comparing costs as well as its advantages to the balance of payments and the UK's nuclear industry:

		AGR	PWR	SGHWR
Generating capacity MW		1227	1095	1244
Capital costs	£m	515-597	421-502	580-698
Generating costs p/kwh		1.48-1.67	1.78-1.46	1.61-1.86
Imports:				
first station	£m	1.6	44	59
subsequent stations	£m	1.6	20	48

Source: Tables 9 and 11

22 Results of the CEGB

Year ended 31st December	1976	1977	1978
	£m	£m	£m
Turnover	2663.1	3094.6	3546.4
Operating profit	331.9	416.8	315.8
Interest	(273.1)	(286.3)	(297.1)
Net profit	58.8	129.8	18.7
Supplementary Depreciation	—	—	(108.8)
Capital Expenditure	462.0	534.0	501.0
Borrowing	226.0	37.0	70.0

Source: CEGB Annual Report and Accounts

Generating capacity MW	58,677	56,365
Maximum demand MW	41,353	42,110
Spare capacity %	30	25

Benn's proposed reorganisation of the electricity supply industry defined its social obligations, including the right of pensioners to heat and light which he had established in 1976 in the code of conduct on disconnection.

The British Gas Corporation's profitability reflected its efficiency and the Government's parity pricing policy treating all energy as a scarce commodity:

Year	1976 £m	1977 £m	1978 £m
Turnover	1565.6	1968.5	2568.1
Trading Profit	201.9	212.1	313.7
Interest	(171.6)	(180.5)	(133.4)
Profit after taxation	(25.1)	31.5	103.9
Supplementary depreciation		(102.6)	(145.2)
Return on capital employed %	1.1	1.3	8.2
Other interest capital Investment	347.0	244.0	201.0
Self financing ratio %	66	100	100

Source: B.G.C. Annual Report and Accounts

The potential of renewable energy sources was estimated as follows:

Approximate annual contribution:

	Millions of tons coal equivalent
Solar power	8
Wave	15
Wind	8
Tidal	4
	4
	39

Source: *Energy policy: A consultative document,* Cmnd. 7101, 13 February 1978.

23 Speech to Parliamentary Liaison Group for an Alternative Energy Strategy, 29 January, 1979.

24 *Energy Policy. A Consultative Document,* Cmnd. 7101, 13 February 1978.

25 *United Kingdom and Community Energy Policy.* A record of the UK Presidency of the Energy Council, Department of Energy 1977.

26 Labour Common Market Safeguards Committee, Waldorf Hotel, London, 2 June, 1977.

27 Labour Party Conference Annual Report, 1978.

28 Bristol South East Constituency. Annual Report, February, 1978.

29 Speech at the Annual Dinner of the Labour Economic Finance and Taxation Association, 12 December, 1977 including the previous quotation.

X *The New Consensus*

1 Tony Benn, *Arguments for Socialism,* Jonathan Cape, London 1979. p. 17.

2 *Ibid,* p. 143

3 *Ibid,* p. 17.

4 *Ibid,* p. 17.

NOTES

5 May Day Rally, Digbeth Civic Hall, Birmingham, 7 May 1979.

6 *The Case for a Constitutional Premiership,* IWC pamphlet, no. 67.

7 "Our future is in our own Hands," speech at Annual Luncheon of the Newspaper Press Fund, Glasgow, 22 January 1980.

8 *Ibid.*

9 *Arguments for Socialism,* p. 153.

10 "The Levellers and the English Democratic Tradition."

INDEX

Writers and Readers

The Writers and Readers Publishing Cooperative was formed in the autumn of 1974 as an independent, self-governing publisher.

We are a cooperative collectively owned and operated by its worker and writer members.

We are members of the industrial Common Ownership Movement (ICOM).

Our policy is to encourage writers to assume greater control over the production of their own books; and teachers, booksellers and readers generally to engage in a more active relationship with publisher and writer.

Our list is collectively selected by an editorial group which includes writers themselves. If you would like to be put on our mailing list and receive regular information about our books, please write to:

Writers and Readers Publishing Cooperative,
9-19 Rupert Street, London W1V 7FS
Tel: 01 437 8942   01 437 8917
VAT No. 231 041231